Labor Market Segmentation

Conference on Labor Market Segmentation

Labor Market Segmentation

Edited by
Richard C. Edwards
University of Massachusetts

Michael Reich
University of California

David M. Gordon
New School for Social Research

D.C. HEATH AND COMPANY
Lexington, Massachusetts   Toronto   London

Clothbound edition by Lexington Books

Library of Congress Cataloging in Publication Data

Conference on Labor Market Segmentation, Harvard University, 1973.
 Labor market segmentation.

 Includes index.
 1. Industrial sociology—United States—Congresses. 2. Women—Employ-
ment—United States—Congresses. 3. Industrial organization—United
States—Congresses. 4. Labor supply—United States—Congresses. I. Ed-
wards, Richard C. II. Reich, Michael. III. Gordon, David M. IV. Harvard
University. V. Title.
HD6957.U6C57   1973   331.1'0973   74-316
ISBN 0-669-93138-1

Published simultaneously in Canada.

Printed in the United States of America.

Paperbound International Standard Book Number: 0-669-95547-7

Clothbound International Standard Book Number: 0-669-93138-1

Library of Congress Catalog Card Number: 74-316

Contents

List of Figures and Tables

Preface

The essays found in the chapters of this book were presented at a conference on Labor Market Segmentation, held at Harvard University, March 16 to 17, 1973. The purpose of the conference was to bring together and encourage further development of research on the segmentation of labor processes and labor markets in the United States. In response to the considerable interest shown at and since the conference, we have prepared this volume to give the papers the widest possible circulation.

The conference itself was part of a larger research project on labor market segmentation conducted by us, with financial support from the Office of Manpower Research, U.S. Department of Labor. We are indebted to Howard Rosen, Director of the Office of Manpower Research, for his support, and we want particularly to express our gratitude to two of his colleagues, Sheridan Maitland and Herman Travis, for their assistance throughout the duration of our project.

A number of the papers presented at the conference and contained in this volume were written by members of our project as part of our research effort: the introductory essay and the chapters by Margery Davies, Richard Edwards, Francesca Maltese, and Katherine Stone. The views expressed in these chapters are of course the authors', and not necessarily those of the U.S. Department of Labor.

At the conference we also presented a long overview in a paper entitled *Labor Market Segmentation in American Capitalism*. In revising that paper for publication, we found that the historical and theoretical issues raised by our earlier work demanded further research and revision of our own paper. At the same time we three were dispersing to various universities around the country. Rather than delay further the dissemination of the other papers presented at the conference, we decided to publish this volume now with a short introduction in place of the longer paper. We intend the Introduction to indicate the basic structure of our larger argument. At various points, we have referred to other chapters in the book to suggest some of the available evidence that supports our assertions. (For those who notice such details, we have been rotating the order in which our names appear in our various joint essays to indicate the collective nature of our own labor process.)

Introduction

The essays found in the chapters of this book are each concerned with aspects of a major characteristic of twentieth-century U.S. capitalism: persistent and important *objective* divisions among American workers. The premise of the book is that these objective divisions have played a major role in forestalling the efforts of U.S. workers to build a unified anticapitalist working-class movement.

In this Introduction we sketch an argument that the redivision of labor in the period of monopoly capitalism has resulted not in a unified and homogeneous working class, as many had expected, but in segmentation of the labor process and of labor markets,[a] and therefore a divided working class.[b] These divisions in the American working class can best be understood by tracing their evolution through the course of development of American capitalism.

Our argument can be summarized in four major historical propositions:

(1) During the development of competitive capitalism in the nineteenth century, the creation and extension of a wage-labor system and wage-labor class were associated with a progressive homogenization of working conditions in the capitalist sector of the economy and a homogenization of labor markets. As production increasingly took the form of commodity production for profit, labor power itself increasingly became a commodity, and growing numbers of Americans sold their labor power in exchange for a wage or salary. The elimination of earlier precapitalist modes of production, the expansion of the competitive capitalist sector, and the evolution of factory production all pointed toward the homogenization of labor. The factory system eliminated many skilled crafts, creating large pools of operative jobs; mass production and greater mechanization forged standardized work requirements; larger establishments drew greater numbers of workers into common working environments. These developments laid the basis for the increasingly militant, class-conscious, anti-capitalist labor movement that appeared toward the end of the century.

(2) Between roughly 1890 and 1920 the American economy experienced a critical transition—from a more or less open, competitive, local-market-oriented, laissez-faire, entrepreneurial capitalism to a more or less closed, oligopolistic, national- and international-market-oriented capitalism dominated by giant corporate enterprises. This transition consisted of several components: First, the

---

[a]The *labor market* consists of those institutions which mediate, effect, or determine the purchase and sale of labor power; the *labor process* consists of the organization and conditioning of the activity of production itself, i.e., the consumption of labor power by the capitalist. Segmentation occurs when the labor market or labor process is divided into separate submarkets or subprocesses, or segments, distinguished by different characteristics, behavioral rules, and working conditions.

[b]For those who are not familiar with the evidence documenting the significance and persistence of these divisions, we conclude this introductory essay with a brief discussion of some of that evidence.

change from the entrepreneurial family firm, in which one or a few capitalists were dominant, to the corporation, with ownership of each individual firm more widely dispersed within the capitalist class and controlled at the top by financiers and other capitalists whose interests and perspective transcended the individual firms or industries. Second, the rise of substantial product market concentration. The transition cannot be summarized simplistically as a change from perfect competition to monopolistic competition, for both these elements were evident in both periods. However, the character of the competition that continued did change dramatically; it became a closed competition, a struggle among and exclusively dominated by reigning, established corporate giants. Third, the change from the simple enterprise, in which administrative functions were limited, to the large bureaucratic enterprise, in which many productive and administrative functions were internalized and vastly reorganized.

In this system of monopoly capitalism, the giant oligopolistic corporations that dominated the economy coexisted with a surviving peripheral competitive capitalist sector. The two sectors developed according to quite different laws of motion.

(3) A consequence of the dualistic industrial structure was a corollary dualism in labor markets. This dualism constituted a clear *reversal* of those forces which, during the nineteenth century, had led to increasingly common, or shared, work experiences. In particular, the large oligopolistic corporations instituted a new system of labor management that was bureaucratic in form and emphasized the differentiation of jobs, rather than their homogenization. Although proletarianization continued, jobs in the capitalist sector became increasingly dissimilar, and labor markets became increasingly segmented. While these markets reflect (are a natural corollary of) divisions in the labor process, they have also institutionalized those divisions and hence perpetuated them.

(4) The dualistic industrial and labor market structures have interacted with preexisting divisions by race and by sex to produce enduring divisions which are likewise rooted in objective economic structures. Segmentation of working conditions and of labor markets thus created the objective basis for the fragmented working-class politics of the twentieth century.

In what follows, we shall elaborate briefly our third and fourth propositions, beginning with the changes wrought by the transition to monopoly capitalism.

Monopoly Capitalism and the Redivision of Labor

The captains of the new monopoly capitalist era, released from short-run competitive pressures and in search of long-run stability, turned to the capture of strategic control over product and factor markets. Their new concerns were the creation and exploitation of monopolistic control, rather than the allocational calculus of short-run profit maximization.

The new needs of monopoly capitalism for control were threatened by the tremendous upsurge in labor conflict, already apparent as early as the 1870s, and reaching new levels of militancy around the turn of the century. As the work force became increasingly homogeneous and proletarian in character, the labor movement gained in strength and militancy. Large corporations were aware of the potentially revolutionary character of these movements. For example, John Commons notes that the employers' "mass offensive" on unions between 1903 and 1908 was more of an ideological crusade than a matter of specific demands. As James Weinstein has argued, the formation of the National Civic Federation (NCF), a group dominated by large "progressive" capitalists, was another explicit manifestation of the fundamental crises facing the capitalist class during this period.

To meet these threats, employers turned to strategies designed to divide and conquer the work force. The central thrust of the new strategies was to break down the increasingly unified worker interests that grew out of both the proletarianization of work and the concentration of workers in urban areas. As exhibited in several aspects of these large firms' operations, this effort aimed to divide the labor force into various segments so that the actual experiences of workers would be different and the basis of their common opposition to capitalists would be undermined.

The first element in the new strategy involved the internal relations of the firm. The tremendous growth in the size of monopoly capitalist work forces, along with the demise of craft-governed production, necessitated a change in the authority relations upon which control in the firm rested (Edwards, Chapter One). Efforts toward change in this area included Taylorism and Scientific Management, the establishment of personnel departments, experimentation with different organizational structures, the use of industrial psychologists, "human relations experts," and others to devise appropriate "motivating" incentives, and so forth. From this effort emerged the intensification of hierarchical control, particularly the "bureaucratic form" of modern corporations. In the steel industry, for example, a whole new system of stratified jobs was introduced shortly after the formation of U.S. Steel (Stone, Chapter Two). The effect of bureaucratization was to establish a rigidly graded hierarchy of jobs and power by which "top-down" authority could be exercised.

The restructuring of the internal relations of the firm exacerbated labor market segmentation through the creation of "internal labor markets." Job ladders were created, with definite "entry-level" jobs and patterns of promotion. Workers who were not employed in these "career" jobs—for example, those who were black or female, or who lacked the qualifications for particular entry-level jobs—were excluded from access to that entire job ladder. In response, unions often sought to gain freedom from the arbitrary discretionary power of supervisors by demanding a seniority criterion for promotion. In such cases, the union essentially took over some of the management of the internal labor process, agreeing to help allocate workers and discipline recalcitrants, obtaining in return some reduction in the arbitrary treatment of workers by management.

An important example of the effects of such policies can be seen in the evolution of employee benefits. Firms had initially attempted to raise the cost to workers of leaving individual companies (but not the cost of entering) by restricting certain benefits to continued employment in that company. Part of this strategy was "welfare capitalism" which emerged from the NCF in particular, and achieved most pronounced form in the advanced industries. At Ford, for example, education for the workers' children, credit, and other benefits were dependent on the workers' continued employment by the firm and therefore tied the worker more securely to the firm. For these workers, the loss of one's job meant a complete disruption in all aspects of the family's life. Likewise, seniority benefits were lost when workers switched companies. The net effect of these new policies was an intensification of barriers between structured and unstructured labor processes.

At the same time that firms were structuring their internal labor processes, they undertook similar efforts to divide the groups they faced in external markets. Employers quite consciously exploited race, ethnic, and sex antagonisms in order to undercut unionism and to break strikes. In numerous instances during the consolidation of monopoly capitalism, employers manipulated the mechanisms of labor supply in order to import blacks as strikebreakers, and racial hostility was stirred up to deflect class conflicts into race conflicts. For example, during the steel strike of 1919, some 30,000 to 40,000 blacks were imported as strikebreakers in a matter of a few weeks. Similarly, employers frequently transformed jobs into "female jobs" in order to render those jobs less susceptible to unionization.

Employers also consciously manipulated ethnic antagonisms to achieve segmentation. They often hired groups from rival nationalities in the same plant or in different plants. During labor unrest the companies sent spies and rumor mongers to each camp, stirring up fears, hatred, and antagonisms of other groups. The strategy was most successful when many immigrant groups spoke little English.

The manipulation of ethnic differences was, however, subject to two grave limitations as a tool in the strategy of "divide and conquer." First, increasing English literacy among immigrants allowed them to communicate more directly with each other; second, mass immigration ended in 1924. Corporations then looked to other segmentations of more lasting significance.

Employers also tried to weaken the union movement by favoring the conservative "business-oriented" craft unions against the newer "social-oriented" industrial unions. An ideology of corporate liberalism toward labor was articulated around the turn of the century in the NCF. Corporate liberalism recognized the potential gains of legitimizing some unions but not others; the NCF worked jointly with the craft-dominated American Federation of Labor to undermine the more militant industrial unions, the Socialist party, and the Industrial Workers of the World (IWW).

As the period progressed, employers also turned to a relatively new divisive means, the use of educational "credentials." For the first time, educational credentials were used to routinize skill requirements for jobs. Employers played an active role in molding educational institutions to serve these channeling functions. The new requirements helped maintain the somewhat artificial distinctions between factory workers and those in routinized office jobs and helped generate some strong divisions within the office between semiskilled white-collar workers and their more highly skilled office mates.

The rise of giant corporations and the emergence of a monopolistic core in the economy accentuated forces that stimulated and reinforced segmentation. As different firms and industries grew at different rates, a dichotomization of industrial structure developed. The larger, more capital-intensive firms were generally sheltered by barriers to entry; enjoyed technological, market power, and financial economies of scale; and generated higher rates of profit and growth than their smaller, labor-intensive competitive counterparts. However, it did not turn out that the monopolistic core firms were wholly to swallow up the competitive periphery firms.

Given their large capital investments, the large monopolistic corporations required stable market demand and stable planning horizons in order to ensure that their investments would not go unutilized. Where demand could be stabilized, large corporations developed concentrated market power. Where demand was cyclical, seasonal, or otherwise unstable, it was difficult for a monopolistic environment for production to develop. These industries (textiles and leather goods are prime examples) retained a generally competitive structure. Moreover, even in the concentrated industries, production of certain products was subcontracted or "exported" to small, more competitive and less capital-intensive firms on the industrial periphery.

Along with the dualism in the industrial structure, there developed a corresponding dualism of working environments, wages, and mobility patterns. Monopoly corporations, with more stable production and sales, developed job structures and internal relations reflecting that stability. For example, the bureaucratization of work rewarded and elicited stable work habits in employees. In peripheral firms, where product demand was unstable, jobs tended to be marked also by instability; therefore, workers in the secondary labor market experienced higher turnover rates. The result was the dichotomization of the urban labor market into "primary" and "secondary" sectors, as the dual labor market theory has proposed.

In addition, as the primary labor market has itself developed, a division has emerged between an "independent primary" and a "subordinate primary" segment. The independent primary sector includes many professional, managerial, and technical jobs, where professional standards tend to govern work

xvi

performance, and employees are often free of specific instruction and authority. Independent primary workers tend to acquire *general* skills through formal education, and to apply those skills to variable individual situations they encounter in their work. They tend to internalize the formal objectives of their organizations and often experience substantial job mobility.

The subordinate primary segment includes many semiskilled, primary sector blue-collar and white-collar jobs that generally involve routinized, repetitive tasks, specific supervision, and formalized work rules. Most subordinate primary workers acquire specific job skills on the job, rarely learning generalized skills. Given corporate rules and union provisions, blue-collar workers in particular are more likely to remain within a single firm or within a single industry. (See also Piore, Chapter 5, who refers to these segments as the upper and lower tiers of the primary market.)

Race and Sex and the Redivision of Labor

Our fourth proposition is that dualistic industrial and labor-market structures interacted with preexisting differences by race and sex to produce persistent objective differences along these dimensions.

During the period of transition to monopoly capitalism, blacks still remained largely in the rural South. As late as World War I the only industries to which blacks had gained access were those which had imported black workers for strikebreaking purposes. Blacks made greater inroads into manufacturing during World War I and the 1920s, with the demand caused by the war and then the closing of foreign immigration, but they were concentrated in the least skilled and least desirable jobs. In both the steel and auto industries, for example, the large employers began systematically to segregate blacks into unskilled manufacturing jobs as a way of dividing the work force and reinforcing structured divisions within the firm's job hierarchies.

The more recent patterns of economic life for blacks developed during and after World War II. Many blacks came north during the labor shortages of the war and the subsequent mechanization of agriculture, and found themselves in segregated and isolated urban ghettos. In that context, black employment began to be dominated increasingly by three kinds of jobs: (1) low-wage jobs in the secondary market, mainly in peripheral industries; (2) some jobs in the primary labor market, largely in the core industries into which blacks had already gained access before World War II; and (3) jobs in the rapidly expanding service sectors, most of them in the secondary labor market (Baron, Chapter 7).

The factors affecting patterns of female employment were different, though related. Although the first textile mills relied chiefly on female and child labor (women accounted for over half of the textile factory labor force in the 1840s), women workers never moved out of the clothing industries into any other manufacturing industries in significant numbers (Harris, Chapter 8). In 1870, 70 percent of non-farm-working women were domestic servants, and another 24 percent worked in textiles and apparel. Most of the working women were young and unmarried; as late as 1890 less than 2 percent of married white women were counted in the labor force.

During the period of transition to monopoly capitalism, 1890 to 1920, the exclusion of women from nonhome production began to break down further. The growth in demand for labor generally, the particular expansion of demand for office workers—an occupation experiencing feminization in this period—and the growth of demand for teachers provided positions which were filled by women (Davies, Chapter 11). On the other hand, the segregation of women in manufacturing continued, and their employment in that sector did not grow as rapidly. In part because of the protective legislation of the period, women continued to be excluded from the better-paying manufacturing jobs, particularly in the capital-goods sectors.

After 1920, the number of women workers increased even more rapidly than during the transitional period. After stagnating during the 1920s and 1930s, female labor force participation rates virtually doubled between 1940 and 1970, as married women with children entered the labor force in large numbers.

The patterns of female employment that emerged after 1920 reflected both the patterns already established during the transitional period and the continuing influence of segmentation within the labor process and labor markets. First, the continued dramatic expansion of clerical work and the channeling of women in the lower-level clerical occupations were a major development in this period. Second, the equally dramatic increase in the number of service jobs in the economy, particularly in health and education, also resulted in large increases in female employment. But again a sexual stratification emerged, so that the top of the occupational hierarchies in both schools and hospitals was dominated by men. Finally, employers in the secondary labor market in peripheral manufacturing industries, in retail trade, and in some services turned increasingly to female employees. These three categories—clerical occupations, health and educational occupations, and employment in peripheral manufacturing industries and retail trade—dominate female employment today.[c]

Empirical Evidence of Divisions

We conclude this introductory essay with a brief review of some of the empirical evidence documenting the significance and persistence of the divisions in the

[c]Relying on empirical definitions of peripheral industries and secondary labor markets, we have found that these three broad categories account for roughly 90 percent of all female employment (Gordon, in progress).

labor market and the labor force, along the dimensions that we have discussed above. Many of the empirical issues are themselves further developed in some of the essays presented later in this book. We begin by indicating some of the evidence for the dual labor market hypothesis, and then look at segmentation by race and by sex. [This evidence is further reviewed, sifted, and developed empirically in Gordon (in progress).]

Dual Labor Markets

Some early work by Bluestone (1971) and by Wachtel and Betsey (1973) indicated that industrial structure and other "demand side" variables had far greater explanatory power than educational attainment or other "supply side" variables in predicting earnings of individuals. Several recent studies have extended these results by dividing jobs into primary and secondary clusters and testing explicitly for barriers to mobility between labor market segments as hypothesized by the dual labor market hypothesis. For example, Gordon (1971), in his studies of the Detroit and New York ghetto labor markets, found that a "dual labor market factor" was the second most important factor in explaining the variance in the data. A ranking of jobs by their scores on this factor was bimodally distributed, permitting a separation of the jobs into primary and secondary clusters, with job characteristics corresponding roughly to the hypothesized characteristics in the two markets. Using longitudinal data, Andrisani (1973) found significant immobilities between primary and secondary segments for both black and white youths; a similar analysis and results are presented by Birnbaum, this volume. Rosenberg (1975), using cross-sectional data, also tested for existence of duality and obtained significant results indicating immobilities between sectors. The role of unions in labor market segmentation was investigated by Kahn (1975) in his comparison of the San Francisco and Los Angeles labor markets; he found that unions played an important role in determining whether particular jobs fell into the primary or secondary segment. These and other studies, such as Edwards (Chapter 1), lend considerable empirical support to the dual labor market theory.

Race

The ratio of black incomes to white incomes has remained roughly constant since World War II. Some improvements were registered during economic upswings, particularly in the long boom of the second half of the 1960s, but many of these gains were eliminated in economic downturns. As a result, careful attempts in the late 1960s to distinguish between cyclical and secular trends in racial income differentials found a very small secular improvement in the relative income of black families (Reich, 1973). Black-white income ratios have in fact declined in the recession of the early 1970s. Moreover, even those analysts who found the greatest gains for blacks (e.g., Freeman, 1973) observed that much of these statistical gains reflected a very real improvement in the relative position of a small black middle class, with much less improvement for the majority of blacks.

Equally important, many studies have discovered substantial racial differences in the operation of labor market mechanisms, in economic returns to schooling, and in access to job ladders. These include Parnes et al. (1970), who found greater occupational differences between whites and blacks in their current jobs than at the beginning of their careers, as well as Tucker (1970) and Alexander (1974), who found substantial racial differences in intrafirm tenure using longitudinal data.

Sex

While there is some small suggestion of relative improvement for blacks, the data suggest clearly that the relative economic position of women has worsened in recent decades. Since 1957 the median earnings of women relative to men has fallen from 63 to 58 percent. Among full-time, year-round workers, Goldberg (1971) found that the median income of women as a proportion of that of men fell between 1939 and 1964 in every major industrial group in which the number of women employed is significant.

As with blacks, one could not explain income inequalities between men and women by simple adjustments for unequal factor endowments. In detailed studies of hourly earnings in the 1960 Census data, for instance, Fuchs (1971) found that controls for color, schooling, age, city size, length of trip to work, marital status, and class of worker reduced the male-female differential by only 15 percent.

Even more clearly than in the case of blacks, women seemed to work in different labor markets. Occupational segregation was persistent. Zellner (1972) found that half of women workers were concentrated in only 21 of nearly 300 three-digit occupational categories; one-quarter of all women workers were crowded in only five of those cells. Controlling for general and specific job skill requirements, Stevenson (Chapter 9) found the same patterns of occupational segregation. Even with narrowly defined occupations, Blau (Chapter 10) found substantial evidence of segregation by sex among establishments. Despite the increases in female labor force participation rates during the twentieth century, these patterns of sex segregation have resisted change.

The chapters that follow analyze divisions in the labor process and divisions in labor markets. Edwards examines the internal structures of capitalist enterprises, contrasting the control mechanisms in the primary and secondary segments of the labor market. Stone (Chapter 2) looks at the evolution of the labor process in a particular industry—steel—tracing the redivision of labor that underlies the present hierarchy of jobs in the steel industry. Maltese (Chapter 3) examines the evolution of the labor process in another important case—the automobile industry—indicating the strategy followed by Henry Ford.

The remainder of the chapters are concerned primarily with divisions in labor markets. In Chapter 4 Wachtel relates the Marxian theory of class and class conflict to the evolution of stratification within the working class during the period of monopoly capitalism. Piore, by contrast, begins with the dual labor market hypothesis, and seeks on a conceptual level to expand and clarify that initial hypothesis (Chapter 5). Chapter 6 reports on Birnbaum's use of empirical tests to discern between the human capital and segmentation hypotheses. The next chapter, by Baron, is concerned with the role of racism and black and white nationalism in advanced capitalism, focusing on how one particular division in the labor market develops and eventually faces its own contradictions. Harris, in a historical essay (Chapter 8), examines the role played by sexual divisions in the labor market, including class divisions among women, and the role of ideology. Stevenson and Blau (in Chapters 9 and 10, respectively) each present the results of empirical analyses of labor market segmentation by sex; Stevenson examines the effects of the segregation of women into particular occupations on the low wages women receive in the labor market, while Blau finds that such sexual segregation is pervasive on a detailed occupational level, with different firms employing highly sexually homogeneous labor forces. Finally, Davies, in a historical study (Chapter 11) examines the factors that led to the feminization of clerical work, and goes beyond a simple supply-and-demand model of the clerical labor market.

Of course, this book by no means exhausts all the important research questions, nor does it incorporate all the major findings to date in this field. But, on the whole, we feel these chapters present major contributions to the questions raised by our general approach.

Bibliography

Alexander, Arthur, "Income, Experience, and the Structure of Internal Labor Markets," *Quarterly Journal of Economics*, February 1974.

Andrisani, Paul, "An Empirical Analysis of the Dual Labor Market Theory," Columbus: Ohio State University, Center for Human Resource Research, 1973.

Bluestone, Barry, "The Personal Earnings Distribution: Individual and Institutional Determinants," mimeo, Boston College, 1971.

Commons, John R., *History of Labor in the United States*, New York, 1935.

Freeman, Richard, "Changes in the Labor Market for Black Americans, 1948-1972," *Brookings Papers on Economic Activity*, No. 1, Summer 1973.

Fuchs, Victor, "Differences in Hourly Earnings between Men and Women," *Monthly Labor Review*, 94, 1971.

Goldberg, Marilyn, "The Economic Exploitation of Women," *Review of Radical Political Economics*, 1971.

Gordon, David M., "Class, Productivity, and the Ghetto: An Analysis of Labor Market Stratification," unpublished Ph.D. dissertation, Harvard University, 1971.

_____, "Class and Segmentation in the United States: An Empirical and Methodological Review," New School for Social Research, in progress.

Kahn, Lawrence, "Unions and Labor Market Segmentation," unpublished Ph.D. dissertation, University of California, Berkeley, 1975.

Parnes, Herbert, et al., *Career Thresholds*, U.S. Department of Labor Research Monograph No. 15, Washington, D.C.: U.S. Government Printing Office, 1970.

Reich, Michael, "Racial Discrimination and the White Income Distribution," unpublished Ph.D. dissertation, Harvard University, 1973.

Rosenberg, Samuel, "The Dual Labor Market: Its Existence and Consequences," unpublished Ph.D. dissertation, University of California, Berkeley, 1975.

Tucker, Donald, "Intra-Firm Earnings and Mobility of Whites and Nonwhites, 1962-66," The Urban Institute, Working Paper No. 113-36, August 1970.

Wachtel, Howard, and Betsey, Charles, "Employment at Low Wages," *Review of Economics and Statistics*, May 1973.

Weinstein, James, *The Corporate Ideal in the Liberal State*, Boston: Beacon Press, 1968.

Zellner, Harriet, "Discrimination against Women, Occupational Segregation, and the Relative Wage," *American Economic Review*, May 1972.

Part I:
The Labor Process

1

The Social Relations of Production in the Firm and Labor Market Structure

Richard C. Edwards

Inequality, poverty, unemployment, and discrimination are not new features of capitalist society. But the protests of the sixties forced Americans to recognize how pervasive and urgent these problems were. The problems seemed largely economic in nature, so attention naturally turned to analyses of the operation of economic institutions.

Economists studying labor markets responded by observing that differences in earnings and unemployment levels by race, sex, age, and social class were simply outcomes of labor market processes. Inasmuch as this was true, the differences must either reflect objective differences between advantaged and disadvantaged groups or imperfections in the market process itself. Yet the differences were not satisfactorily explained by group differences: for example, when equalized on all seemingly relevant dimensions (measures of "ability," training, educational attainment, labor force experience, industry, occupation, region, and so on), difference by race, sex, age, and social class remained.[1]

To account for the remaining income and unemployment differences among groups, economists proposed a variety of explanations reflecting market "imperfections": statistical discrimination, occupational crowding, the queue theory, employer or worker "distastes," segmented markets, and internal markets.[2] These theories have all been subjected to empirical testing, with both cross-sectional and some time series data, and while all have received some support, none can be said to have been demonstrated as clearly superior. Thus these theories exist in an empirical no-man's land, being neither decisively supported nor rejected.

A more serious objection to these theories is that, by focussing narrowly on labor market processes, they have remained largely taxonomic and descriptive. Whether or not they are adequate for classifying market behavior, they do not explain that behavior as part of the broader economic process. Specifically, these concepts were not grounded in an analysis of the development of capitalist production, and hence the analytical framework on which they are based is either *ad hoc*, deriving from anecdotal observations of what aspects of the firm's organization and operations seemed important, or ahistorical altogether.

In this paper I intend to articulate a more adequate theoretical basis for two

This paper has already appeared in *Politics and Society*. (Permission to reprint from publisher and author.)

of the theories, those emphasizing internal and segmented labor markets. The central theoretical assertion of the paper is that behavior observed in the labor market (the "sphere of circulation") reflects more fundamental processes in production itself (the "sphere of production").[3] To understand the labor market processes which "produce" group differences in incomes, unemployment, and mobility, then, we must investigate the institutional arrangements governing production—that is, the "social relations of production."[4]

This paper is divided into five sections. First, I define more precisely what is meant by "internal" markets. Second, I argue that internal markets were created as part of an effort to alter the social relations of production within large firms, and I then analyze the historical development of those relations. A firm is defined as the activities over which the capitalist enjoys legal hegemony, and the social relations of production *in the firm* take the specific form of a *system of control:* the sanctions, incentives, distribution of responsibility, and other apparatus by means of which power is exercised. In what follows, I distinguish between two essentially different systems of control: what I term "simple hierarchy," in which power is hierarchically distributed but more or less openly, arbitrarily, and personally exercised; and "bureaucratic control," in which the exercise of power is institutionalized and made impersonal.[5] Large ("monopoly capitalist") firms have moved beyond simple hierarchy and instituted bureaucratic control as a more sophisticated and subtle means of controlling their workforces. In doing so, they have created internal labor markets. Third, I explore what effect the imposition of bureaucratic control had on the particular qualities required of workers, arguing that workers who develop stable work habits get rewarded in bureaucratic enterprises.

In the last two sections, I consider the general relation between the social relations of production in firms and labor market structure. The basic logic of the argument can be stated as follows: The position of a firm in the monopoly capitalist system (i.e., whether the firm is small and competitive or large and monopolistic) largely determines the nature of control (i.e., simple hierarchy or bureaucratic control) within that firm, since with few exceptions only large and monopolistic firms have the stability and resources to institute bureaucratic control. From the system of control is obtained the "derived demand" for labor—not the quantity of labor demanded, but rather the conditions of work and therefore the qualities and characteristics required of workers. Bureaucratic control depends on internal markets and implies one set of labor requirements, those centered on stability and predictability. Simple hierarchy relies on external markets and fosters a different set of labor attributes, especially high turnover and instability in work habits. Firms organized bureaucratically operate through one set of labor markets, the primary markets, while those organized along lines of simple hierarchy operate through other markets, the secondary markets.[6] Thus differing systems of control underlie differences in labor markets, both in the nature and conditions of jobs available (labor demand), and in the attributes and response of workers offering labor power for sale (labor supply).

The argument demonstrates, I think, that the structure and operation of labor markets cannot be understood outside of a wider analysis of capitalist production. Moreover, that wider analysis "explains," in a way that pure market theories cannot, the outcome or result of the market process as a result of capitalist development.

1. Internal Markets and Big Enterprises

Internal labor markets exist in big firms.[7] As the monopoly capitalist firms have grown larger and become more powerful, they have consistently drawn more and more of their environments under their control—that is, each has "internalized" forces which potentially threatened its existence. Thus they were initially formed out of previously competing firms, as a means of bringing competition within their control. Big firms have vertically integrated their operations, to ensure proper supplies of raw materials. They have learned to stimulate and shape demand, to eliminate the vagaries of fickle consumer tastes. They have institutionalized the product research and development process, to minimize the risks of "outside" technical change and discovery. When possible, they have generated investment funds from retained earnings rather than depend on uncertain bank finance. And they have created internal labor markets.

The term "labor market" as used herein refers to those specific mechanisms and institutions through which the purchase and sale of labor power are arranged. Thus "internal labor markets" may be distinguished from the more general labor process or other day-by-day operations within the enterprise, since the former are specific, usually contrived mechanisms by which job vacancies are filled. For example, job bidding systems, regularized promotion procedures requiring periodic supervisors' evaluations, customs restricting job access to apprentices or assistants, and "management development" programs all constitute internal market mechanisms. The jobs filled through the operation of internal markets are restricted to the firm's existing workforce and thus, with regard to these jobs, internal markets determine the conditions on which the enterprise's workers can renegotiate the terms of their wage bargains.

Traditional views of labor markets focus on external markets—seeing a market in which competing (potential) employers face competing (potential) workers. But the pervasiveness of large corporations, with their internal markets, makes this view incomplete. The traditional view is only applicable when firms operate through the external market—as, for example, when they attempt to increase the size of their labor forces. But for allocation within a firm's job structure, the traditional theory has little to say.

The analysis of internal labor markets attempts to break open the "black box" of the neoclassical firm by viewing the social relations at the workplace in part as a system of labor exchange within the firm, regulating promotion, job placement, the setting of wage rates, and so forth. In some cases workers may have the right to "bid" for jobs when a vacancy occurs; the actual allocation in such cases is usually based on seniority.[8] More generally, firms establish promotion ladders. New workers are recruited from the "external" labor market only for the bottom-rung jobs, and all higher vacancies are filled "internally," from the labor pool of workers already employed by the firm. In this case, the worker's work record and recommendations from supervisors, as well as his or her formal training, skills, and seniority determine whether he or she gets the job or not.

The customs, rules, and procedures which govern job allocation within the firm must be relatively shielded from the influence of the wider external markets if they are to play an independent role in job allocation. Thus, for example, if a firm frequently recruits "outsiders" for jobs other than entry-level vacancies, then its workers are effectively in competition with workers in the wider external markets.[9]

Three features of monopoly capitalist corporations have increasingly made internal markets important. First, the growth of these firms' workforces has correspondingly increased the possibilities for filling jobs through internal mechanisms. In an industry where there are many small firms, most of the job allocations will necessarily occur between firms; assuming no increase in job turnover, workers will necessarily move less frequently among firms where there are but one or a few large firms.

Second, as large firms have turned to bureaucratic control, they have proliferated hierarchical inequalities and job categories, so that there are many more positions which are formally distinct. Jobs within each firm have become increasingly differentiated in terms of wages, status, responsibility, and power. Thus, for any given size of a firm's workforce, the possibility of job movement within the firm became much greater. Ignoring changes in the scale of production, an industry which is organized so that workers are in a more or less homogeneous job category must fill jobs when workers move between firms, but within a firm little job movement is possible; in an industry where each firm has many job categories, the worker has (potentially) available to him or her many different jobs within the firm.[10]

Third, the increasing stability exhibited in the operation of monopoly firms implied that they did relatively less cyclical adjustment in the size of their labor forces—stable demand and production implied a stable derived demand for labor. Stable employment was particularly true for that growing body of workers performing administrative, sales, legal, research and development, and other tasks not directly related to production. Hence, one of the impulses traditionally pushing firms to enter the labor market was weakened.

Internal labor markets, then, go hand in hand with big corporations. Big corporations exist to earn profits.[11] But to earn profits, the corporation must maintain its hegemony over its workforce. The organizational structure of the firm—the incentives, demarcated areas of responsibility, distribution of power, and so on—represent a system in large part contrived and consciously designed to perpetuate the capitalist's control over the firm's workforce. Since the operation of internal labor markets follows the firm's method of organizing its workers, the next problem is to understand its structure and development.

2. From Simple Hierarchy to Bureaucratic
Control in the Monopoly Capitalist Firm

Bureaucratic control had its roots in the dramatic economic transition which occurred in the United States between roughly 1890 and 1920. The American economy during this period changed from a more or less open, competitive, local-market-oriented, laissez-faire, small-business capitalism, to a more or less closed, oligopolistic, national- (and international-) oriented capitalism of giant corporate enterprises. For individual firms which succeeded in making the transition, and not all did, the transition meant a change from the entrepreneurial form, in which one or a few capitalists were dominant, to the corporation, for which ownership of each individual firm was more widely dispersed within the capitalist class, and which was controlled at the top by financiers and other capitalists whose interests and perspective transcended the particular firm or industry. The transition increased industrial concentration, though it cannot be adequately summarized as simply one of competition versus monopoly, since both of these elements existed in each period. But there was a vast change in the nature and role of the competition that remained: it became a closed competition, a struggle solely among already-established giants. And while all aspects of the change were not strictly confined to the 30-year period, the transition did reflect a rather rapid and comprehensive reorganization of industry. It was during this period that the system of monopoly capitalism which persists to the present was established.[12]

What is of particular relevance here is that the transition from competitive to monopoly capitalism created contradictions between the firm's traditional structure and organization and its new scale and economic status. It was out of this contradiction that emerged the present form of its internal relations. In particular, a series of changes in the scale and technique of production and in the economic position of large firms combined to undermine the prevailing system of control within the firm—that system of open, arbitrary, highly visible, direct command-rule by superiors over subordinates that I termed "simple hierarchy."

Simple hierarchy required personal supervision. But expansion implied increasing separation of those most motivated to supervise properly (the owners and high-level managers) from the actual production activities. The expansion of each (surviving) firm's production required ever-proliferating layers of intervening—and less reliable—supervisors. The top-echelon managers were further separated from contact by the type of expansion. Since expansion often occurred by merger of competing companies, the new giants tended to be multi-plant concerns: the scattered production facilities of the previously independent companies became linked, not through geographical proximity, but rather through the administrative and supervisory apparatus. "Headquarters," rather than being divided among separate offices adjoining the dispersed plants, was centralized in the financial districts, away from all plants.

Increasing industrial concentration forced firms to concentrate more carefully on long-range planning, market manipulation, advertising, and other aspects of the sales effort, as opposed to production itself. But the actual work activities of these increasingly important administrative and other non-production operations were more complex, subtle, and less standardized than production tasks. The new tasks tended to diminish the possibility of easy, unambiguous, and quickly available evaluation of a worker's performance; these new jobs came into conflict with "close supervision," the day-to-day relation through which the authority of simple hierarchy was effected.

Finally, the principal sanction in simple hierarchy—frequent threats of and often massive use of firings and layoffs—was undermined by the increasingly high cost of the response which it provoked. As unions during this period threatened to achieve more comprehensive (e.g., industrywide and cross-craft) organization, unionization and worker militancy among production workers increasingly meant that firing workers to maintain discipline resulted in long and costly strikes.

Thus capitalists found that for both the rapidly expanding white-collar staff and for the more organized blue-collar workers, they could no longer rely solely on mass dismissals and the "reserve army of the unemployed." While their power to fire recalcitrant workers remained the ultimate sanction on which their power was based, they needed alternative and more subtle control mechanisms.

These developments were most acutely felt in the emerging "core" firms of monopoly capitalism, which because of their vast size and rapid growth, found that control from the top through the mechanisms of simple hierarchy was most attenuated and difficult. On the other hand, it was precisely these firms which could benefit most from new internal structures. They had the resources to experiment with new organizational forms. They had sufficient power to withstand shortrun disruptions. They began from an entrenched, stable economic position which allowed them to experiment with new forms and then to institute and capture the benefits from the procedures they devised.

Increasingly after the turn of the century, capitalists became aware of the need for *systematically* and *consciously* designing the organizational structure to meet this requirement of institutionalized control. Frederick Taylor and his scientific management disciples spread one part of the gospel, that of time and motion studies and the technical details of "human engineering." Alfred Chandler (1962) describes the continual experimentation in organizational forms at the higher corporate levels which managers at General Motors, Standard Oil

(N.J.), du Pont, and Sears, Roebuck carried out. Industrial psychology and personnel management grew from tiny beginnings at the turn of the century to central features of big corporations within two or three decades. As David Montgomery (1973) notes, the Employment Managers Association, formed by 50 corporate officials in 1911, gathered 900 members at its 1918 convention. Corporations gave support to the establishment of business schools, and Harvard's, started in 1908, was soon followed by Princeton, Stanford, and elsewhere. F.B. Miller and M.A. Coghill (1961), in introducing their historical review of industrial psychology literature, noted that

Our findings led us to decide that the major facets of modern personnel administration . . . existed, at least in embryo, by [1923] . . . The fundamentals of personnel work were being practiced in representative firms, preached in five or six standard texts, and celebrated periodically in conventions of specialized practitioner associations.

The new system of control, devised both as part of the corporation's response to the general worker threat to capitalist hegemony and as a specific strategy to ameliorate the crisis of control in the firm, was bureaucratic control.[13] The defining feature of bureaucratic control was the institutionalization of hierarchical power. "Rule of law"—the firm's law—replaced "rule by supervisor command" both in the organization and direction of work tasks and in the exercise of the firm's power to enforce compliance. Work activities became defined and directed by a set of work criteria—the rules, procedures, and expectations governing particular jobs. Thus for the individual worker, his or her job tended to be defined more by formalized work criteria attached to the job (or more precisely, by the interpretation given to those criteria by his or her supervisor and higher levels of supervision) rather than by specific orders, directions, and whims of the supervisor. Moreover, it is against those criteria that the worker's performance came to be measured. Both written and unwritten requirements were included in the criteria, but the essential characteristic was that the worker was able to ascertain them and that they were highly stable. The firm no longer altered the worker's tasks and responsibilities by having the supervisor tell the worker to do something different; rather, it "created a new job" or "redefined the job." From these criteria derived the "customary law" notions of "equity" or "just cause" in firing, promotions, and job assignments.[14]

The top-echelon management retained their control over the enterprise through their ability to determine the rules, set the criteria, establish the structure, and enforce compliance. For the latter concern, enforcing compliance, bureaucratic organization again marked a departure from simple hierarchy. In simple hierarchy, power was vested in individuals and exercised arbitrarily according to their discretion, but with bureaucratic control power became institutionalized by vesting it in official positions or roles and permitting its exercise only according to prescribed rules, procedures, and expectations; rules governing the exercise of power were elements of the work criteria defining supervisor's jobs. Since there were formally established criteria for evaluating the exercise of power, it also was made accountable to top-down control.

The work activities could never be completely specified by job criteria in advance, and the "rule of law" could never completely replace the "rule by command" in an hierarchical enterprise. Some situations or problems always arose which had to be handled in an *ad hoc*, particularistic way, and so supervisors could never be content merely to evaluate and never instigate. The shift to bureaucratic control must therefore be seen as a shift towards *relatively* greater dependence on institutionalized power, and bureaucratic control came to exist alongside and was reinforced by elements of simple hierarchy. Bureaucratic control became, then, the predominant system of control, giving shape and logic to the firm's organization, although not completely eliminating elements of simple hierarchy.

The imposition of bureaucratic control in the monopoly firm had four specific consequences for the social relations of the firm:

a) The power relations of hierarchical authority were made invisible, submerged and embedded in the structure and organization of the firm rather than visible and openly manifest in personal, arbitrary power.

b) Bureaucratic control, because of its emphasis on *formal* structure and status distinctions, made it possible to differentiate jobs more finely. Organizational as well as technical (i.e., production) aspects of jobs defined their status. Each job appeared more unique and individualized by its particular position in the finely-graded hierarchical order, by the job criteria which specified work activities, and by distinct status, power, responsibilities, and so on. Elements of the social organization of the firm which differentiated between jobs were emphasized, while those which created commonality diminished.

c) The role of the supervisor was transformed from that of active instigator, director, and overseer of work activities to that of monitor and evaluator of the worker's performance—the superior now judged the subordinate's work according to the work criteria. Moreover, the supervisor's own work—his use of sanctions, for example—became subject to much greater evaluation and control from above.

d) The first two changes tended to erode the bases for common worker opposition. Increasingly, the individual worker came to face an impersonal and massive organization more or less alone. In general, the work environment became less conducive to unions and strike or other opposition activities. In those bureaucratized industries where unions remained, more and more the unions accepted the organization of work and directed their energies towards non-control issues (wages, fringe benefits, procedures for promotion, hiring, and firing). Even where unions turned their attention to the work activities themselves, their efforts were mainly defensive, directed towards making the job criteria more explicit and openly articulated; while this tended to undermine the authority of arbitrary foremen, it strengthened the legitimacy of the overall structure. As the common basis of work experience declined, so did the possibility for united worker action concerning control over work.

3. Bureaucratic Control and the Characteristics
Required of the Firm's Workforce

I now wish to turn to the particular requirements which the introduction of bureaucratic control imposed on a firm's workforce. The foregoing has argued that, as part of their drive to internalize risky elements in their environment, monopoly capitalist firms established internal labor markets to thwart the development of class consciousness and maintain their control over production; that jobs within these firms were organized along bureaucratic control lines; and that bureaucratic control involves formalized definitions ("work criteria") for directing work tasks, and institutionalized power to enforce compliance. If this description of the development of the internal structure of enterprises is correct, it suggests that the skills, attitudes, behavior, and other characteristics of workers which firms seek out and reward—that is, the requirements which workers face in their jobs—have changed as well. Specifically, we would expect behavior characteristics associated with bureaucratic control to have become essential.

What is relevant here is the increased importance of the work habits and types of behavior which are consonant with the form of control in the firm, not with the actual work tasks themselves. As the firm evolved, actual work tasks changed in response to the firm's productive needs, not as a consequence of bureaucratic control. Thus as IBM's business changed from providing card-tabulating machines to computer services, IBM hired electrical engineers. Mapping changes in the criteria content would demonstrate the changes in job skills required of the labor force.

What bureaucratic control changed was the worker traits required for the *manner* in which work tasks are done. These traits derive directly from the ways in which firms through bureaucratic control seek to elicit compliance from the worker. Three principal modes of compliance—that is, work habits or "behavior traits" which are "appropriate" responses to the enterprise's power and facilitate its control—can be distinguished:

a) The simplest way in which institutionalized power is used to direct work tasks is through the establishment of work rules. Correct work behavior is unambiguously defined as following the rules. The corresponding worker behavior trait which we would expect to be rewarded is *rules orientation*—an awareness of and sustained propensity to follow the rules.

b) A more sophisticated form of control involves encouraging workers to perform their tasks according to the spirit of the work criteria; correct work behavior in this sense implies performing tasks in a reliable, predictable, and dependable manner. Thus we might term the second mode of compliance *habits of predictability and dependability.*

c) The most sophisticated form of control grows out of incentives for the worker to identify himself or herself with the enterprise, incentives leading the worker to be "loyal," "committed," and thus self-directed or self-controlled. This level of compliance requires a behavior trait which might be termed the *internalization of the enterprise's goals and values.*

Evidence supporting these propositions comes from a study I recently completed of worker traits and organizational incentives.[15] The results were based on a sample of 455 adult workers in the Boston area who were employed in large bureaucratic enterprises. For each worker, I obtained measures of behavior traits reflecting the three modes of compliance outlined above. These behavior traits, then, were those characteristics which the theory outlined above would indicate were important in a system of bureaucratic control. To discover which workers were actually rewarded by the enterprise, I obtained two measures of organizational incentives: first, each worker's supervisor provided a rating of how well, in the supervisor's view, that worker performed his or her job; second, for 340 of the workers, I obtained their wages. Finally, in order to provide experimental control and ensure that the behavior measures were not simply surrogates for other, excluded variables, I collected data on IQ, educational attainment, family background, age, sex, and job history. The data were analyzed in a series of multiple regressions in which I attempted to "predict," on the basis of the behavior traits and other personal information, how well each worker would be rewarded by the enterprise. The hypothesis was that the behavior traits should be good predictors of attainment of the enterprise's rewards.

The results strikingly supported the hypothesis. The three behavior measures were used to predict separately supervisors' ratings and wage differentials. I first considered the statistical significance of the coefficients relating the behavior measures to the supervisors' ratings and wages, to determine how likely it was that the estimates were simply random results. The tests indicated that his probability was very low: for five of the six coefficients, these results would arise by chance no more than once every thousand times ($p < .001$); for the sixth, no more than twice every hundred times ($p < .02$).

Next, I included the other variables (IQ, sex, age, educational attainment, job history, and family background) to check whether the behavior traits were simply surrogates or "proxy" variables for other, excluded factors. But while some of these new variables—especially sex, age, and educational level—were, as expected, also important predictors, including them in the equation did not significantly undermine the effect of the behavior traits. Thus apparently it is the behavior traits themselves which are relevant.

I next considered the best estimate of how large an effect these behavior traits appeared to have. The behavior measures predicted supervisors' ratings extremely well (variance explained = 38%), indicating that these traits are probably the most significant single element in determining the supervisor's evaluation of the worker. These results are particularly strong when viewed in the light of other attempts to use personality measures to predict job performance; for example, of the hundreds of studies reviewed by E.E. Ghiselli (1966), only 4 achieved a higher explained variance. The behavior traits also had a relatively large impact on wage differentials. Approximately 20% of the differences in wages within each work group could be explained by the behavior traits.[16] Thus not only were the behavior traits statistically significant, their quantitative impact was also large.

In a separate analysis, I divided the sample into hierarchical levels (low-level jobs, middle-level jobs, etc.) in order to gain some insight into these behavior traits as *alternative* modes of control. Arbitrarily, four levels of roughly equal size were chosen, and the jobs divided accordingly. A strong pattern emerged from the exercise. Rules orientation was most important at the lowest-level jobs in the enterprise, such as entry-level operatives' jobs. Habits of dependability and predictability were important at the lower and middle levels, including all jobs such as maintenance, sales, and records-keeping jobs, which are not machine-paced. Internalization of the enterprise's goals and values was important at the higher levels of jobs, such as those involving some technical and professional skills or some supervisory responsibility. These results would suggest the further hypothesis that, in entry-level jobs, rules orientation is a significant criterion in the enterprise's decision whether to keep or fire workers, and that habits of dependability and predictability and internalization of the enterprise's values are important dimensions on which promotion is determined.

4. Worker Traits and Labor Market Structure: Internal Markets

While the imposition of bureaucratic control had an impact on the characteristics which monopoly capitalist firms sought and rewarded in their workers, its particular relevance for the operation of labor markets lay in the exaggerated importance which its structure and incentives imparted to *stability* characteristics in worker behavior.

All three modes of compliance can, in part, be interpreted as stability elements. The elimination of arbitrary, unpredictable, and random supervisory power and its replacement by more systematic, "rational," and institutionalized power made the firm's system of rewards and sanctions more conducive to attaining preditable behavior.[17] That is, it tended to elicit an acceptance of the firm's power as authority and reinforce a *stable orientation to that authority*, by which I mean having "appropriate" attitudes and behavior towards the enterprise's power structure and those delegated by the enterprise to exercise power. Simple hierarchy maximized the visibility of the power relations by making them personal: the authority of the foreman depended on the personal distance between him or her and his or her workers. These highly visible inequalities created resentments, provoking disputes and challenges to or sabotage of authority. External, personal, arbitrary control tended to engender unpredictable and frequent disruptions. The system, being more brutal and less subtle, often evoked worker responses which were similarly brutal and unstable. On the other hand, bureaucratic power was embedded in the organizational structure of the enterprise, and was more hidden from view because its nature was institutional rather than personal. Power could be exercised only in accord with established criteria and procedures. Bureaucratic rules allowed the supervisor to appear to detach his or her own feeling from his or her "responsibility" as supervisor. Established work criteria provided a substitute for the personal repetition of orders by the supervisor, so that the supervisor needed to intervene less often and power was seemingly less often appealed to. The existence of work criteria permitted supervisors several levels higher to evaluate both workers and their supervisors, so irregular or unpredictable behavior on the part of *supervisors* was minimized. Finally, bureaucratic rules made the use of punishment seem more legitimate by making them appear as "company policy"; moreover, the rules established a kind of "conspicuous bargaining point" such that a supervisor who simply chose to be less harsh than the rules, was judged "permissive" or lenient.[18] In these ways, then, bureaucratic control rationalized the enterprise's power by making its application more predictable and stable, and hence bureaucratic control evoked more stable and predictable behavior from workers; that is, bureaucratic control tended to legitimize the firm's exercise of power, and translate it into authority.

The worker characteristics which in the last section were found to be highly correlated with rewards in large enterprises also have an impact on the firm's desire to reward employment stability and tenure. Consider the problem the firm has when hiring a worker who is new to that firm. The employer cannot easily determine whether or not this worker has those behavior traits which employers find important in their workers. Despite millions of dollars and forty years of research, no psychological test exists which (a) can be given to new workers,[19] (b) predicts job success reasonably well (e.g., as well as my study reported in the previous section), and (c) is relatively inexpensive. So personnel managers use psychological tests that admittedly predict very little; they fall back on educational credentials as screening devices, on the (not unwarranted but imprecise) assumption that diligence at work depends on the same characteristics as success in schooling; they rely heavily on recommendations from previous employers and on the workers's work record, though it is usually difficult to evaluate the context of previous work experience. So *mainly*, the firm can only learn whether a worker has the appropriate traits through a long process of actual experience with the worker on the job, and to do so it must keep workers sufficiently long to make its assessment.[20]

Bureaucratic control fostered employment stability by creating career ladders and instituting rewards for tenure and seniority within the firm. Career ladders and explicit rules governing promotion were simply an extension of the bureaucratic method of organizing work by explicit rules and procedures. Promotion, as one reward, became integrated with the enterprise's system of sanctions and incentives and harnessed to its goals. That promotion and job tenure should become important in bureaucratic control is not surprising, since bureaucratic control was an explicit attempt to move away from harsh negative sanctions (frequent firings, quick and arbitrary foreman control) and towards positive incentives (promotion, some job security). Finally, it should be noted that a system rewarding seniority and employment stability for the enterprise's workers in general could only occur where the firm itself had a stable basis—that is, in the solidly entrenched monopoly capitalist firms.

Thus bureaucratic control increased the rewards to those workers who demonstrated stability, both in the everyday behavior at the job and in the length of time they stayed at a job. These are the characteristics which dominate the operation of internal labor markets. For an individual worker, mobility in the internal market depends upon the firm's assessment of his or her job performance and work behavior as revealed in that job. Stability in work performance, stable orientation to authority, and employment stability are central elements in this evaluation. This finding concerning the derived demand for labor is consistent with the large firm's consolidation of power and its attempt to achieve stability throughout its operations, and it issues directly from its imposition of bureaucratic control.

Internal job allocations, like the filling of jobs in the economy at large, do not all follow the common pattern outlined above. There are always exceptions. Not all internal jobs are filled through the market—as when, for example, workers are able to switch jobs through personal contacts or other particularistic factors. Some job allocations do not involve promotion, but rather are lateral movements, which may occur for reasons different from those outlined above. Criteria other than supervisors' recommendations may sometimes be primary— competitive exams for some jobs, seniority points, licenses, or union cards for others. Yet to the extent that a general pattern characterizes internal markets, it follows bureaucratic lines, involving graduated career steps through which the worker's progression depends upon obtaining positive recommendations and notice from superiors. For this, as I have shown, stability in work behavior is essential.

5. Worker Traits and Labor Market
Structure: Segmented Markets

A second way in which economists have proposed revising traditional notions of the operation of labor markets involves the concept of segmented markets. The idea of segmented markets grew out of studies of the poverty, unemployment, and oppressive job conditions of those persons working outside the normal white male career channels of middle-class America. To explain these workers' situation, the traditional notion of a more or less all-encompassing and homogeneous labor market has been replaced with an emphasis on multiple and differentiated markets, of which, for our purposes, the "dual" market distinction between "primary" and "secondary" markets is most relevant.[21] The primary market includes those workers, especially white males, who tend to have "careers"; i.e., who follow a logical progression from job to job, in which pay, responsibility, authority, and status increase with labor force experience. Internal markets thus form a part, indeed the largest part, of the primary market. The primary market also includes academics, professionals, and others who, although they follow logically progressive careers, nonetheless have relatively high mobility.

On the other hand, the secondary market is comprised of workers, especially women, blacks, teenagers, and the urban poor, who follow a much more random series of jobs and are generally denied opportunities for acquiring skills and for advancement.

The segmented markets are distinguished by separate systems of rules, different channels of information, and different skill and job behavior requirements. Little mobility between the primary and secondary markets is thought to exist. Segmented and internal markets are often seen to be related, since the dichotemization of the industrial structure, of which the rise of large corporations with their internal markets forms one part, is seen as one cause of segmented (external) markets.

Those who have formulated the dual market theory have consistently argued that the dichotemization which they propose differentiates between (external) markets servicing jobs which require or at least elicit essentially different types of behavior. The principal behavior differences between primary jobs (and workers) and secondary jobs (and workers) is taken to be stability: employers in the primary market expect, reward, and therefore elicit stability in work behavior, while those in the secondary market do not expect, may even discourage, and therefore fail to elicit stability. Thus Michael Piore (1970, p. 55) states, "the most important characteristic distinguishing jobs in the primary from the secondary sector appears to be the behavioral requirements which they impose on the work force, particularly that of employment stability."[22]

Once again, however, observations on the operations of labor markets by themselves reveal little. While the dual market theory may allow us to classify market behavior, it does not necessarily explain it. As in the case of internal markets, we must return to the sphere of production for an adequate explanation. In this final section, then I consider two points: first, I review the evidence and conclude that work stability is indeed a sensible criterion for the dual market division; and second, I attempt to anchor the differing behavior observed in the labor market to differing systems of control in the workplaces.

Dualism and Stability

What prevents secondary workers from getting primary jobs? Work skills, which receive considerable emphasis in most discussions of poverty and employment, do not appear a major barrier to primary employment. For example, most primary work skills, especially those in entry-level production jobs, appear to be learned on the job itself (Doeringer and Piore, p. 18). On the other hand, insofar as secondary workers are barred from primary jobs by a real qualification, that qualification is probably stable work habits; Piore (1970, p. 55) notes, for example, that it is generally secondary workers' inability or unwillingness to show up for work regularly and on time which prevents primary employment. Secondary employers are far more tolerant of lateness and absenteeism, and many secondary jobs are of such short duration that these do not matter.

Perhaps the strongest evidence concerning stability differences between

Table 1-1
Median Years on Current Job (January, 1968)

	White Males	Women	Non-White Males	Teenagers (16-19 Years)
Median Years on Job	5.0	2.4	3.3	0.5*
Median Years on Job, by Age Categories				
20-24 years	0.8	0.9	0.7	—
25-29 years	2.2	1.4	1.9	—
30-34 years	4.0	1.8	3.1	—
35-39 years	6.0	2.6	4.1	—
40-44 years	8.7	3.2	5.8	—
45-49 years	10.4	4.4	8.8	—
50-54 years	12.8	6.2	10.1	—
55-59 years	14.9	8.2	11.9	—
60-64 years	15.5	9.4	11.7	—

*Estimated.
Source: *Monthly Labor Review*, U.S. Bureau of Labor Statistics, September, 1969, p. 18, Table 1.

markets is that of turnover and job tenure differences. One job tenure test of dual market assertions can be made by comparing job tenure rates of those groups heavily represented in the primary market (essentially white males) with those in the secondary market (teenagers, black males, black females, all females over 25). Leaving aside the high turnover of all categories of teenagers, it is well documented that white males starting at age 25 have consistently longer job tenure than any of the other groups, and the absolute gap increases with age. This test suffers because demographically defined groups must be used as proxies for market-defined categories. A more direct test can be inferred from data reported by David Gordon (1971). Using a factor analysis of multiple occupational and industry characteristics, Gordon was able to divide two Urban Employment Survey job samples into primary and secondary sectors on the basis of job characteristics. If we accept this division as valid, then tenure differences between the two groups represent a more precise comparison of employment stability than is possible from comparing demographically defined proxy groups. Both first-job tenure and present-job tenure were significantly higher for primary than secondary workers. These data on job tenure, despite demonstrating significant differences between primary and secondary markets, nonetheless *understate* the actual differences and thus represent an overly stringent test.[23]

"Employment stability" should be defined as "number of years in a given job ladder" rather than "years in present job." Gordon's "dual market" factor loads on a series of variables relating to employment stability: weeks worked per year, whether or not the worker looked for work during the year, and several stability-related personal background variables (marital status, head of household, years in labor force, etc.). Unfortunately, none of the measures available for analysis exactly measures job stability—as, for example, "years employed by present employer" would. Nonetheless, the general test that Gordon proposes offers strong confirmation of the results obtained from looking simply at tenure differences among demographically-defined groups: stability characteristics reflect fundamental behavior difference between the two markets.

An alternative argument for employment instability as a characteristic of the secondary market derives from observations about the unemployment and

Table 1-2
Average Job Tenure by Dual Market Sector (In years)

	Primary White Males	Secondary White Males	Primary Black Males	Secondary Black Males
First-job tenure	5.71	3.48	5.18	2.69
Present job tenure	11.75	8.90	10.87	5.95

Source: David Gordon (1971), p. 385.

poverty of urban blacks. It is a well-established fact that blacks, and even more so blacks who are males, teenagers, or live in core-city areas, have substantially higher unemployment than their white counterparts. By themselves high unemployment rates need not call forth a dual labor market theory, but when the stability of employment (or the frequency of unemployment) is considered, market differences emerge. As Robert Hall (1970, p. 389) put it:

The central problem [of unemployment at 'full employment'] seems to be that some groups in the labor force have rates of unemployment that are far in excess of rates that would accord with the hypothesis that the unemployed are making a normal transition from one job to another. Some groups exhibit what seems to be pathological instability in holding jobs. Changing from one low-paying, unpleasant job to another, often several times a year, is the typical pattern of some workers.

While Hall is incorrect in ascribing the "pathology" to the workers rather than the system,[24] his description of the facts is doubtless correct. As evidence for his proposition, Hall cites two sorts of data. The first, aggregate data by sex-age groups showing the percentage distribution of unemployment by weeks, indicates that approximately 60% of those unemployed were unemployed for less than four weeks. That is, most of this "unemployment at full employment" is of very short duration. This aggregate impression is supported by a further survey of individuals one week after they reported that they were unemployed. Ignoring those who were out of work due to disability, health, or retirement reasons, nearly half of the remaining individuals were already back at work, a fact which supports the contention that the period of unemployment is relatively short. But short periods of unemployment can only be reconciled with high average rates of unemployment for these groups if there are relatively *many* of these short periods—i.e., if turnover is high.

Hall then turns to a second type of data which is somewhat more direct. Using unemployment figures by race and sex, he demonstrates that given a set of "reasonable" assumptions about the time required for normal job searching, black males, black females, and white females over 25—that is, groups heavily represented in the secondary market—have unemployment rates in excess of that expected from "frictional" (i.e., normal job-switching) causes. He concludes that the excess represents high turnover due to job instability, a finding he asserts is consistent with yet a third fact, namely, that wage-age profiles of the relevant groups indicate that there exists little or no advantage for those workers to continue at one job since their wages do not increase with seniority.

We find, then, that instability in work behavior pervades the secondary market. Although the statistical evidence is more fragmentary and less persuasive than in the case of primary markets, its direction is nonetheless clear. Employers offer little incentive to workers to stay at one job; workers respond by switching jobs frequently, as they suffer little or no reduction in their wage rate and at least achieve job variety. Job performance tends to be unstable, unreliable, and unpredictable; secondary workers demonstrate high absenteeism, are often not punctual, and typically work with little "discipline." Since they have little reason for long-run commitment to their jobs, these workers are rebellious towards the tyrannical power of their employers, but because of the high turnover, the worker resistance is usually individualistic rather than organized. Finally, job turnover is high, and consequently, "frictional" unemployment is also high. In all three areas, then, secondary workers compared to primary workers exhibit extreme instability.

Dualism in Production and Dualism in the Market

The instability which secondary workers manifest in their work behavior must be seen as the consequence of the organizational context of their jobs. Instability, I would assert, derives in large part from the social relations of production which characterize establishments employing secondary workers. In particular, secondary establishments tend to be characterized by "simple hierarchy" rather than "bureaucratic control," and the behavioral dimensions of secondary job and workers follow directly from simple hierarchy.

As Michael Piore (1970, p. 57) has observed, "reward and punishment in the [secondary] workplace are continually based upon personal relationships between worker and supervisor" and (p. 55) discipline is "harsh and often arbitrary." Since the power structure tends not to be formalized (at least in the sense that bureaucratic control is institutionalized), discipline and the exercise of power are harsh, personalized, and often arbitrary. Employers frequently resort to firings to discipline workers, as the reserve army of the unemployed stands as a ready replacement (and hence sanctioning agent) for secondary workers. Few job ladders exist, and as Hall's age-wage data demonstrate, few returns accrue to the secondary worker who remains at one job.

While the instability of secondary work behavior flows from the organizational context of secondary jobs, the question nonetheless remains as to why establishments hiring secondary workers should have failed to make the transition from simple hierarchy to bureaucratic control. Formulating the issue this way already is an advance over earlier discussions, which tended to see the secondary market as an aberration from the "normal" state of affairs. It is obvious, however, that it is the primary market which has been the new development, new, that is, with the rise of the monopoly capitalist system. The secondary market is simply the continuation of the employment practices of an earlier, more competitive capitalism.[25]

In seeking an explanation for the dualistic structure of labor markets, then, we are led to the question of why large firms were able to internalize certain labor market processes which were formerly beyond their control. But that, of course, is the essence of their position within monopoly capitalism: having stable markets, they also had a stable derived demand for labor; being entrenched and thus facing minimal threats to their survival, they had the resources to maintain an internal market for long-run considerations, whether or not it contributed to strict or short-run economic efficiency.

It would, of course, be incorrect to view the secondary market as exclusively the preserve of small firms. Since large firms often have the option of separating their operations, they can employ secondary workers in those aspects of their operations which are conducive to it: as for example, where there is unstable or unpredictable demand, or where operations are not disrupted by the instability of secondary work behavior. In these workplaces, the system of control more nearly resembles simple hierarchy than bureaucratic control, precisely for the reason that bureaucratic control involves the longer-run commitment to the labor force, provision of training and promotion opportunities, and other attributes which would undermine the advantage of operating in the secondary market.

6. Conclusion

The argument of this paper is that the social relations of the firm—particularly the "system of control"—underlie the structure and operation of labor markets. Differences between firms in the form of control imply differences in the characteristics which employers look for in workers, in how workers respond or are socialized in those jobs, and, finally, in what labor market opportunities are available to various workers.

Internal markets are a direct offspring of the consolidation of monopoly capitalist power and the consequent imposition of bureaucratic control in the large enterprise. Bureaucratic control, by design, implied an organizational structure for regulating labor allocation, pricing, and mobility, which greatly increased the need for an incentives to stability in worker behavior.

While the development of the primary market, especially internal markets, was linked to the rise of monopoly capitalism, the secondary market represents a continuation of the characteristics of a more competitive, small-business capitalism. In the secondary market, control is based on more open and arbitrary power, and the sanction of surplus labor tends to prevail. This system has none of the built-in stability features of primary jobs, and tends to produce both jobs and workers in which stability is neither rewarded nor particularly desired.

Thus, while it is true that it is impossible to explain employers' and workers' behavior in labor markets without a wider theory of capitalist development, it is also true that study of the labor market reveals much about the production process itself. That the social relations of production, embodying elements of power and control, are essential in explaining the market process should not be surprising, since the labor market is one arena, and an important arena, in which the conflicting interests of capitalists and workers meet. But the conflict between Capital and Labor is by no means confined to the market, nor is it confined to those issues—the price and quantity of labor—determined through the market process. Instead, the conflict extends as well to the "point of production" and to issues of control over work and the labor process. To understand these issues, one must look beyond simple market processes to the struggle between workers and capitalists in all its forms.

Notes

1. See, for example, Christopher Jencks, et al (1973).

2. For examples, see David Gordon (1972); Lester Thurow (1969); Barbara Bergmann (1971); Gary Becker (1957); and Kenneth Arrow (1971).

3. Since labor market behavior (turnover, differential wage rates, unemployment, etc.) is comprehensively measured and widely reported, while the internal operations of firms are largely shielded from view, this theoretical assertion has an important implication: labor market behavior can be used to elucidate not just the operation of labor markets but can aid the investigation of the process of capitalist production itself.

4. The other element in the analysis, given only cursory treatment below, is the development of the forces of production; for a recent good treatment of technical relations, see Harry Braverman (1974).

5. I here exclude consideration of proprietorships, family businesses, and other small concerns where power is concentrated in the person of the entrepreneur himself, and there is no hierarchy of employees with whom power is shared.

6. This statement, as I note below, needs to be qualified. Large firms organize some operations bureaucratically, others along lines of simple hierarchy. Those firms and/or workplaces organized bureaucratically recruit in the primary market; others in the secondary market.

7. "Large corporations," "big enterprises," and "monopoly capitalist corporations" are all used more or less interchangeably in this paper. They all refer to large, oligopolistic corporations which constitute the core of the monopoly capitalist system (see Gordon, Edwards, and Reich, forthcoming); the terms are *not* restricted to (though include) firms operating in single-seller markets.

8. See U.S. Bureau of Labor Statistics (1970).

9. Doeringer and Piore (1971), pp. 5-6.

10. As Katherine Stone (this volume) notes, U.S. Steel at one point had between 45,000 and 50,000 job titles. Its workforce numbered around 250,000.

11. While the question of whether profit-maximization or other goals moti-

vate individuals who own and/or control big corporations is complex, it is reasonably certain that (a) evidence on profit rates by enterprise size indicates no lessening of the profit drive in big firms (Howard Sherman, 1968); (b) institutions external to the firm, especially the stock and bond markets and financial investors (e.g., banks, insurance companies) enforce a profit discipline (Robert Solow, 1967); (c) the actual managerial incentives within the firm (Robert Larner, 1970) and the managerial ideology (Paul Baran and Paul Sweezy, 1966) reinforce these external mechanisms.

12. For a fuller discussion, see Gordon, Edwards, and Reich (forthcoming) and Richard Edwards (1975).

13. The concept and characteristics of "bureaucratic control" are explored more fully in Richard Edwards (1972). An (extremely conservative) estimate of the number of workers in bureaucratic workplaces may be derived as follows: at least 50% of the national workforce is employed in enterprises (private, public, non-profit) employing over 250 workers (Richard Edwards, 1972, Appendix IX); assuming that the proportion of white-collar to blue-collar workers is the same in large enterprises as the labor force at large—which is, according to Michael Reich (1972, p. 178), approximately one to one—and accepting that white-collar workers in large enterprises are all bureaucratically organized, we can infer that 25% of the workforce works in bureaucratic workplaces. This is a low estimate on three scores: (1) bureaucratic control is *not* confined to white-collar workers, and as white-collar work becomes proletarianized, blue-collar work becomes bureaucratized; see, for example, Alvin Gouldner (1954); (2) large corporations undoubtedly employ more than one white-collar worker for every blue-collar worker; and (3) some small enterprises are also bureaucratically organized. Apparently this designation applies to a major segment of the workforce.

14. See Peter Doeringer and Michael Piore (1971) for a lengthy discussion of the customary law aspects of workplace rules.

15. See Richard Edwards (1976).

16. Since the behavior traits were measured by the group peer rating technique, the resulting scores were ordinal within work groups, and cross-group comparisons were invalid. As a consequence, the behavior traits can be used to predict within-group wage differentials, not cross-group differentials. The within-group wage variance in this sample was exactly one-third of the total variance in wages, so the explained variance reported in the text amounts to roughly 6 to 7% of the overall wage variance. However, since supervisors' recommendations are the principal criterion for promotion (movement between groups), and the behavior traits are good predictors of supervisors' ratings, we have good cause to think that the 6-to-7% estimate seriously understates the true impact of behavior traits on overall wage differentials.

17. These characteristics are at the very core of control. As Michel Crozier (1967, p. 158) notes, the nature of control within an organization is quite

specific: "people have power over other people insofar as the latter's behavior is narrowly limited by rules whereas their own behavior is not . . . the predictability of one's behavior is the sure test of one's own inferiority."

18. See Alvin Gouldner (1954).

19. The instrument used in my study to measure behavior traits was the group peer rating technique. Since this device has quite high reliability and predicts job success quite well, the reader may wonder why employers would not use this same test. Indeed they would, if they could. But the peer rating depends on the actual experience that a work group has in working together; hence, it would *not* be possible to use it for new workers with whom no one in the firm has any experience. Moreover, the technique relies on gaining the workers' cooperation, which, I gratefully acknowledge, they gave to me but would not give to management.

20. Such a process would explain, for example, some initial results which indicate that workers in large firms continue to get wage increases beyond the time when they are still acquiring technical skills (Paul Ryan, in progress; Albert Rees and George Schultz, 1970; Bureau of Labor Statistics, 1970).

21. In what follows I consider only the dual labor market part of the segmentation theory.

22. Similar sentiments are expressed in other formulations; for example, in David Gordon (1972, p. 43), Bennet Harrison (1972, pp. 132-35); and Peter Doeringer et al. (1971).

23. If we accept for a moment that secondary markets have no or few job ladders, then low tenure rates for secondary workers would imply high between-firm movement, since workers by assumption cannot move within the firm. A relatively low tenure rate for secondary workers thus represents actual job instability; i.e., it is a "true" stability measure. For primary workers, however, there is the possibility of advancement within a job ladder. Such movement, while it would reduce present job tenure, is nonetheless eminently "stable" behavior from the employer's perspective. Assuming "present-job tenure" measures time in job title, "present-job tenure" understates actual job stability for primary workers and should be corrected by subtracting job changes within the job ladder. The appropriate comparison would be to "years employed by present employer." Thus the present-job tenure differences reported above are all the more significant. On the other hand, it is not clear to what extent there are age differences between the samples.

24. Secondary workers' behavior seems quite sensible given the opportunities they confront. Since there is little reward for stability in these jobs, they have no incentive to remain for long periods at one job. By switching, they lose little and at least gain some job variety and freedom from tyrannical bosses (see below); on the other hand, it is precisely these characteristics which prevent them from getting and keeping primary jobs.

25. David Montgomery explicitly links high turnover in industry, especially

among immigrants, to the early (circa 1910) attempts to develop time-and-motion studies.

Bibliography

Arrow, Kenneth, "Some Models of Racial Discrimination in the Labor Market," in Anthony Pascal, *The American Economy in Black and White*. Rand Corporation, Santa Monica, California, 1971.

Baran, Paul, and Sweezy, Paul, *Monopoly Capital*. Monthly Review Press, New York, 1966.

Becker, Gary, *The Economics of Discrimination*. University of Chicago Press, Chicago, 1957.

Bergmann, Barbara R, "The Effect on White Incomes of Discrimination in Employment," *Journal of Political Economy*. January-February, 1971.

Bowles, Samuel, and Gintis, Herbert, "IQ in the U.S. Class Structure," *Social Policy*. January-February, 1973.

Braverman, Harry, "Labor and Monopoly Capital," *Monthly Review*, 26:3, July-August, 1974.

Chandler, Alfred, *Strategy and Structure*. MIT Press, Cambridge, Massachusetts, 1962.

Coase, Ronald, "The Nature of the Firm," *Economica*, NS, No. 4, November, 1937.

Crozier, Michel, *The Bureaucratic Phenomenon*, University of Chicago Press, Chicago, 1964.

Doeringer, Peter, and Piore, Michael, *Internal Labor Markets and Manpower Analysis*, Lexington Books, Lexington, Massachusetts, 1971.

Doeringer, Peter, et al., *Urban Manpower Programs and Low-Income Labor Markets: A Critical Assessment*. Report to the U.S. Department of Labor, 1972.

Edwards, Richard C., *Alienation and Inequality: Capitalist Relations of Production in Bureaucratic Enterprises*. Unpublished Harvard Ph.D. thesis, Cambridge, Massachusetts, 1972.

_____ , "Stages in Corporate Stability and the Risks of Corporate Failure," *Journal of Economic History*, June 1975.

_____ , "Worker Traits and Organizational Incentives: What Makes a 'Good' Worker?" *Journal of Human Resources*, Winter 1976.

Galbraith, J.K., *The New Industrial State*. Houghton-Mifflin, Boston, 1967.

Gheselli, E.E. *The Validity of Occupational Aptitude Tests*. John Wiley, New York, 1966.

Gordon, David M., *Class, Productivity, and the Ghetto: A Study of Labor Market Stratification*. Unpublished Harvard Ph.D. thesis, Cambridge, Massachusetts, 1971.

Gordon, David M., *Theories of Poverty and Underemployment.* Lexington Books, Lexington, Massachusetts, 1972.

Gordon, David M., Edwards, Richard C., and Reich, Michael, "Labor Market Segmentation in American Capitalism," forthcoming.

Gouldner, Alvin, *Patterns of Industrial Bureaucracy.* The Free Press, Glencoe, Illinois, 1954.

Hall, Robert E., "Why Is the Unemployment Rate so High at Full Employment?" *Brookings Papers on Economic Activity*, No. 3, 1970.

Harrison, Bennett, *Education, Training and the Urban Ghetto.* Johns Hopkins Press, Baltimore, 1972.

Jencks, Christopher, et al., *Inequality.* Basic Books, New York, 1973.

Larner, Robert J., "The Effect of Management-Control on the Profits of Large Corporations," in Maurice Zeitlin, ed., *American Society, Inc.* Markham, Chicago, 1970.

Miller, F.B., and Coghill, M.A., *The Historical Sources of Personnel Work.* New York State School of Industrial and Labor Relations, Ithaca, N.Y., 1961.

Montgomery, David, "Immigrant Workers and Scientific Management." Paper prepared for the "Immigrants in Industry" Conference of the Eleutherian Mills Historical Society and the Balch Institute, November 2, 1973.

Piore, Michael, "On-the-Job Training in the Dual Labor Market," in Arnold Weber, et al., *Public-Private Manpower Policies.* Industrial Relations Research Association, Madison, Wisconsin, 1969.

_____ , "Manpower Policy," in S. Beer and R. Barringer, eds., *The State and the Poor.* Winthrop Publishing, Cambridge, Massachusetts, 1970.

Rees, Albert, and Schultz, George, *Workers and Wages in an Urban Labor Market.* University of Chicago Press, Chicago, 1970.

Reich, Michael, "The Evolution of the U.S. Labor Force," in Richard C. Edwards, Michael Reich, and Thomas E. Weisskopf, *The Capitalist System.* Prentice-Hall, Englewood Cliffs, New Jersey, 1972.

Ryan, Paul, *Seniority, Experience, and Skill-Learning in the Age-Wage Relationship.* Unpublished Harvard Ph.D. thesis, Cambridge, Massachusetts, in progress.

Sherman, Howard, *Profits in the U.S. Economy.* Cornell University Press, Ithaca, N.Y., 1968.

Solow, Robert, "The New Industrial State or Son of Affluence," *Public Interest*, No. 9, Fall, 1967.

Stone, Katherine, "The Origin of Job Structures in the Steel Industry," this volume.

Thurow, Lester, *Poverty and Discrimination.* The Brookings Institution, Washington, D.C., 1969.

U.S. Bureau of Labor Statistics, *Seniority in Promotion and Transfer Provisions.* Bulletin 1425-11, March, 1970.

2

The Origins of Job Structures in the Steel Industry

Katherine Stone

Introduction

Recently economists have taken a new look at the labor market, in an attempt to understand the concentration of unemployment and underemployment among specific groups. In doing so, they have rejected the neoclassical model of a free and open market allocating labor according to comparative marginal costs and distributing income according to respective marginal productivity. A new set of categories, such as "dual labor markets" and "internal labor markets," and a new set of concepts, such as "hierarchy" and "stratification," have been introduced to better explain the functioning of the labor market.

This chapter attempts to trace the development of labor market structures in one major industry, the steel industry.[a] The bulk of the chapter concentrates on the period between 1890 and 1920, for during that time the essentials of today's labor system took form. The intention is to show that by understanding how various structures came to be, we can better understand what perpetuates them and what might change them.

Part 1 of the chapter describes the labor system of the steel industry in the nineteenth century, in which skilled workers controlled the production process and made steel by using the employers' capital. This system came into conflict with the employers' need to expand production without giving the workers a substantial share of the proceeds. They therefore moved to break the workers' power over production and all the institutions that had been a part of it—the skilled workers' union, the contract system, the sliding scale for wages, and the apprenticeship-helper system. They were successful, and the prize they won was the power to introduce labor-saving technology, to control the production process, and to become the sole beneficiary of the innovations.

© 1974 by Katherine Stone.

This article has already appeared in the *Review of Radical Political Economics*. (Permission to reprint from publisher and author.) I want to give special thanks to Jeremy Brecher, who helped me sift through the evidence and piece together the ideas that went into this paper. Without his patience as an editor and his enthusiasm for the project, this paper would never have been possible.

[a]This chapter deals with certain selected aspects of the industry's labor relations. It is by no means intended to be a general survey. Specifically omitted is discussion of the role played by racial and ethnic divisions and the role played by company repression in dispersing discontent.

Part 2 shows how, under the impact of the new technology, the skilled craftsmen and the heavy laborers were both transformed into semiskilled machine operators.

Part 3 presents the efforts of the employers to create a new labor system that would institutionalize their control over production. It deals with the development of three specific institutions that were central to this process: wage incentive schemes, promotion hierarchies, and welfare programs. The employers' reasons for setting up each of these institutions are unraveled, to demonstrate that, far from being inevitable, the institutions were chosen from several alternatives in order to maximize the power of employers over workers. These institutions are the foundation for today's "internal labor market."

Part 4 describes the redivision of labor which employers engineered to perpetuate their power. The essence of the redivision was to take knowledge about production away from the skilled workers and to transfer it to the side of management. They accomplished this by devising new ways to train skilled workers, by reeducating their own foremen and by recruiting new types of managers. This redivision of labor created a status and pay hierarchy based on "mental skills," and is the basis of today's education fetishism.

Part 5 brings the analysis up to the present by describing the only major change in the labor system of the past 50 years, the organization of the United Steelworkers of America. It shows how little the presence of the union affected the institutions employers had set up earlier.

The following major themes, which are elaborated and generalized to other industries in the concluding Part 6, run through the entire paper:

1. Technology, by itself, did not create today's labor system. Technology merely defined the realm of possibilities.
2. The development of hierarchy in the labor force was not a response to the increased complexity of jobs, but rather a device to counter the increased simplicity and homogeneity of jobs.
3. The issues of how work shall be organized, how jobs shall be defined, and how workers shall be paid are points of conflict and class struggle between workers and employers. The structures that emerge can be understood in only those terms. Any explanation based on impersonal market forces or natural economic laws misses the actual historical development.
4. The division of labor of today that separates mental work from physical work is an artificial and unnecessary division, that only serves to maintain the power of employers over their workers.
5. The labor market structures that were developed in the early part of this century under the banner of "scientific management" have lasted, in refined forms, until today. No labor movement or reform group has yet developed successful means for overthrowing them and establishing a more rational system for getting work done.

**Part 1: The Breakdown of the
Traditional Labor System**

In 1908 John Fitch, an American journalist who had interviewed hundreds of steelworkers and steel officials, described the labor system in the steel industry of his day.

In every department of mill work, there is a more or less rigid line of promotion. Every man is in a training for the next position above . . . The course would vary in the different styles of mills, as the positions vary in number and character, but the operating principle is everywhere the same. In the open-hearth department the line of promotion runs through common labor, metal wheelers, stock handlers, cinder-pit man, second helper and first helper, to melter foreman. In this way, the companies develop and train their own men. They seldom hire a stranger for a position as roller or heater. Thus the working force is pyramided and is held together by the ambition of the men lower down; and even a serious break in the ranks adjusts itself all but automatically.[1]

Anyone familiar with industry today will recognize this arrangement immediately. It is precisely the type of internal labor market, with orderly promotion hierarchies and limited ports of entry, which economists have recently begun to analyze. When Fitch was writing, it was a new development for American industry. Only 20 years earlier, the steel industry had had a system for organizing production which appears very strange to us today.

Although steel had been produced in this country since colonial times, it was not until after the Civil War that the steel industry reached substantial size. In 1860, there were only 13 establishments producing steel, which employed a total of 748 workers to produce less than 12,000 net tons of steel a year.[2] After the Civil War, the industry began to expand rapidly, so that by 1890 there were 110 Bessemer converters and 167 open-hearth converters[3] producing 4.8 million net tons of steel per year.[4] This expansion is generally attributed to the protective tariff for steel imports, the increased use of steel for railroads, and changes in the technology of steel production.

The pivotal period for the U.S. steel industry was the years 1890 to 1910. During that period, steel replaced iron as the building block of industrial society, and the United States surpassed Great Britain as the world's prime steel producer. Also during the 1890s, Andrew Carnegie completed his vertically integrated empire, the Carnegie Corporation, and captured 25 percent of the nation's steel market. His activities led to a wave of corporate mergers which finally culminated in the creation, in 1901, of the world's first billion-dollar corporation, the U.S. Steel Corporation. U.S. Steel was built by the financier J.P. Morgan on the back of the Carnegie Corporation. At its inception, it controlled 80 percent of the United States' output of steel.

Table 2-1 summarizes the development of the steel industry in the nineteenth century.[5]

Table 2-1
The Development of the Steel Industry in the Nineteenth Century

	Pig Iron Production (million tons)	Steel Production (million net tons)
1860	0.9	n.a.
1870	1.9	n.a.
1880	4.3	1.4
1890	10.3	4.8
1900	15.4	11.4

Source: Hogan, William T., *Economic History of the Iron and Steel Industry in the United States* (Lexington, Mass.: Lexington Books, D.C. Heath and Co., 1971) Vol. 1, pp. 91-94.

In the nineteenth century, the steel industry, like the iron industry from which it grew, had a labor system in which the workers contracted with the steel companies to produce steel. In this labor system, there were two types of workers—"skilled" and "unskilled." Skilled workers did work that required training, experience, dexterity, and judgment; unskilled workers performed the heavy manual labor—lifting, pushing, carrying, hoisting, and wheeling raw materials from one operation to the next. The skilled workers were highly skilled industrial craftsmen who enjoyed high prestige in their communities. Steel was made by teams of skilled workers with unskilled helpers, who used the companies' equipment and raw materials.

The unskilled workers resembled what we call "workers" today. Some were hired directly by the steel companies, as they are today. The others were hired by the skilled workers, under what was known as the "contract system." Under the contract system, the skilled workers would hire helpers to do the heavy parts of the work, and pay the helpers out of their own paychecks. Helpers earned between one-sixth and one-half of the wages of skilled workers.

The contract system was never fully developed in the steel industry. Often the steel companies paid part of the helpers' wages or provided helpers themselves for certain skilled workers, so that a hybrid system was prevalent. For example, in one iron works in Pittsburgh in 1878, puddlers were paid $5 per ton, of which one-third went to pay their helper. Of the helper's pay 5 percent was also received from the company. In the same works, a heater was paid $.65 per ton and received one helper, paid by the company, with the option of hiring a second helper who would be paid by the heater himself. The number of unskilled workers who were hired and/or paid by the skilled workers was declining in the late nineteenth century.[6]

The skilled steel workers saw production as a cooperative endeavor, where labor and capital were equal partners. The partnership was reflected in the method of wage payment. Skilled workers were paid a certain sum for each ton of steel they produced. This sum, called the tonnage rate, was governed by the "sliding scale," which made the tonnage rate fluctuate with the market price of iron and steel, above a specified minimum rate below which wages could not fall. The sliding scale was introduced in the iron works of Pittsburgh as early as 1865, and in the 25 years that followed, it spread throughout the industry. The original agreement that established the system read as follows:

Memorandum of Agreement made this 13th day of February, 1865, between a committee of boilers and a committee from the iron manufacturers appointed to fix a scale of prices to be paid for boiling pig-iron, based on the manufacturers' card of prices.[7]

The sliding scale was actually an arrangement for sharing the profits between two partners in production, the skilled workers and the steel masters. It was based on the principle that the workers should share in the risks and the fruits of production, benefiting when prices were high and sacrificing when prices were low. John Jarrett, the president of the iron and steel workers union, referring to another aspect of this partnership, described the system as a:

kind of co-operation offered by the company, in which were certain conditions, the principal of which was that the men agreed to allow the company to retain the first four weeks wages in hand, and also twenty-five percent of all wages earned thereafter, the same to be paid to men at the end of the year, if the profits of the business would justify such payment.[8]

Andrew Carnegie, the largest steel employer of them all, concurred in this view of the sliding scale by saying, "It is the solution of the capital and labor problem because it really makes them partners—alike in prosperity and adversity."[9]

Another effect of the sliding scale was that by pegging tonnage rates directly to market prices, the role of the employer in wage determination was eliminated. Consider, for example, the following account, summarized by David Montgomery from the records of the Amalgamated Association of Iron, Steel and Tin Workers. [The Columbus Rolling Mill Company contracted to reheat and roll some railroad tracks in January, 1874. The union elected a committee of four to work with the plant superintendent to consult about the price the workmen would receive for the work. They agreed on a scale of $1.13 per ton, which the committee brought back to the union for approval.]

There followed an intriguing process. The members soon accepted the company offer, then turned to the major task of dividing the $1.13 among themselves. Each member stated his own price. When they were added up, the total was 3¾ cents higher than the company offer. By a careful revision of the figures, each runback buggyman was cut 2 cents, and the gang buggyman given an extra ¼ of a cent to settle the bill.

In the final reckoning, 19¼ cents went to the roller, 18 cents to the rougher up, 10 cents to the rougher down, 9 cents to the catcher, 8¼ cents to each of the four hookers, 5 cents each to the runout hooker and the two runback buggymen, and 13¾ cents to the gang buggyman, half of whose earnings were to be turned over to his non-union helper.[10]

The employers had relatively little control over the skilled workers' income. Nor could they use the wage as an incentive to ensure them a desired level of output. Employers could only contract for a job. The price was determined by the market, and the division of labor and the pace of work were decided by the workers themselves. Thus, the sliding scale and the contract system defined the relationship between capital and labor in the nineteenth century.

The skilled steel workers had a union, the Amalgamated Association of Iron, Steel and Tin Workers, which was the strongest union of its day. Formed in 1876 by a merger of the Heaters Union, the Roll Hands Union, and the Sons of Vulcan, by 1891, Amalgamated represented 25 percent of all steelworkers. Through their union, they were able to formalize their control over production. For example, at Carnegie's Homestead mill, a contract was won in 1889 that gave the skilled workers authority over every aspect of steel production there. A company historian described it this way:

Every department and sub-department had its workmen's 'committee', with a 'chairman' and full corps of officers . . . During the ensuing three years hardly a day passed that a 'committee" did not come forward with some demand or grievance. If a man with a desireable job died or left the works, his position could not be filled without the consent and approval of an Amalgamated committee . . . The method of apportioning the work, of regulating the turns, of altering the machinery, in short, every detail of working the great plant, was subject to the interference of some busybody representing the Amalgamated Association. Some of this meddling was specified under the agreement that had been signed by the Carnegies, but much of it was not; it was only in line with the general policy of the union . . . The heats of a turn were designated, as were the weights of the various charges constituting a heat. The product per worker was limited; the proportion of scrap that might be used in running a furnace was fixed; the quality of pig-iron was stated; the puddlers' use of brick and fire clay was forbidden, with exceptions; the labor of assistants was defined; the teaching of other workmen was prohibited, nor might one man lend his tools to another except as provided for.[11]

John Fitch confirmed this account of worker control at Homestead when he interviewed Homestead workers and managers in 1908. Fitch reported:

A prominent official of the Carnegie Steel Company told me that before the strike of 1892, when the union was firmly entrenched in Homestead, the men ran the mill and the foreman had little authority. There were innumerable vexations. Incompetent men had to be retained in the employ of the company, and changes for the improvement of the mill could not be made without the consent of the mill committees. I had opportunity to talk with a considerable number of men employed at Homestead before 1892, among them several prominent leaders of the strike. From these conversations I gathered little that would contradict the statement of the official, and much that would corroborate it.[12]

The cooperative relationship between the skilled steelworkers and the steel employers became strained in the 1880s. The market for steel products began to expand rapidly. Domestically, the railroads began to generate high levels of demand for steel, and internationally, the U.S. steel industry began to compete successfully with the British and the German steel industries for the world market. (In 1890, for the first time, U.S. steel exports surpassed those of Great Britain.) The effect of this massive increase in demand was to intensify competition in the U.S. industry. What had been a stable market structure was disrupted by the new markets opening up.

Firms competed for the new markets by trying to increase their output and cut their costs. To do that, they had to increase the productivity of their workers—but the labor system did not allow them to do that. For example, from 1880 on, the market price for iron and steel products was falling drastically, so that the price for bar iron was below the minimum specified in the union's sliding scale, *even though* the negotiated minimum rates were also declining. As Peter Doeringer says in his essay on the subject, "the negotiated minimum piece rates ... became the *de facto* standard rates for the organized sector of the industry during most of the period from 1880 to the end of the century."[13] This meant that employers were paying a higher percentage of their income out in wages than they would have if the sliding feature of the sliding scale were operative, or if they had had the power to reduce wages unilaterally in the face of declining prices.

At the same time that their labor costs as a percentage of revenue were rising, the labor system also prevented employers from increasing their productivity through reorganizing or mechanizing their operations. The workers controlled the plants and decided how the work was to be done. Employers had no way to speed up the workers, nor could they introduce new machinery that eliminated or redefined jobs.

In the past, employers had introduced new machinery, but not labor-saving machinery. The many innovations introduced between 1860 and 1890, of which the most notable was the Bessemer converter, increased the size and capacity of the furnaces and mills, but they generally did not replace workers with machines. Sir Lowthian Bill, a British innovator, who toured the U.S. steel industry in 1890, reported:

Usually a large make of any commodity is accomplished by a saving of labor, but it may be questioned whether in the case of the modern blast furnace this holds good. To a limited, but a very limited, extent some economy might be effected, but if an account were taken of the weight of material moved in connection with one of our Cleveland furnaces, and the number of men by whom it is handled, much cannot, at all events with us, be hoped for.[14]

However, in the late 1880s and 1890s, the steel companies needed more than just bigger machines and better methods of metallurgy. Bottlenecks were developing in production, so that they needed to mechanize their entire operations. For example, the problem with pig iron production—the first stage of steelmaking—was that with increased demand, the larger blast furnaces could produce pig iron faster than the workers could load them, so that the use of manual labor became a serious hindrance to expanding output. As one technical authority wrote in 1897:

The evolution of the blast furnace, especially the American blast furnace, during the last third of a century has indeed been radical, making the question of getting the material to the furnace and the product away from it promptly, cheaply and regularly—the problem once satisfactorily solved by the cart or sled, and wheelbarrow and manual labor—one of great difficulty and importance.[15]

The steel masters needed to replace workers with machines, which meant changing the methods of production. To do that, they needed to control production, unilaterally. The social relations of cooperation and partnership had to go if capitalist steel production was to progress. The steel companies understood this well, and decided to break the union. In 1892, Henry Clay Frick, chairman of the Carnegie Steel Company, wrote to Andrew Carnegie that "The mills have never been able to turn out the product they should owing to being held back by the Amalgamated men."[16]

The strongest lodge of the Amalgamated Association was at Carnegie's Homestead mill; it is no wonder that the battle between capital and labor shaped up there. In 1892, just before the contract with the Amalgamated was to expire, Carnegie transferred managing authority of the mill to Frick. Frick was already notorious for his brutal treatment of strikers in the Connellsville coke regions, and he wasted no time making his intentions known at Homestead. He ordered a fence built, 3 miles long and topped with barbed wire, around the entire Homestead Works; he had platforms for sentinels constructed and holes for rifles put in along the fence; and he had barracks built inside it to house strikebreakers. Thus fortified, Frick ordered 300 guards from the Pinkerton National Detective Agency, closed down the Works, laid off the entire work force, and announced they would henceforth operate nonunion. The famous Homestead Strike began as a lockout, with the explicit aim of breaking the union. Dozens of men were killed in the 4 months that followed, as the Homestead workers fought Pinkertons, scabs, the Sheriff, and the state militia. In the end, the intervention of the state and federal governments on the side of the Carnegie Corporation beat the strikers. The Works were reopened with strikebreakers, and Frick wrote to Carnegie, "Our victory is now complete and most gratifying. Do not think we will ever have any serious labor trouble again."[17]

The Homestead Strike was the turning point for the Amalgamated Association throughout the country. Other employers, newly invigorated by Frick's performance, took a hard line against the Union, and the morale of the members, their strongest local broken, was too low to fight back. Within 2 years of the Homestead defeat, the Amalgamated had lost 10,000 members. Lodge after lodge was lost in the following years, so that membership, having peaked at 25,000 in 1892, was down to 10,000 by 1898, and most of that was in the iron industry.[18] The union never recovered from these losses. The locals that remained were one by one destroyed by the U.S. Steel Corporation, so that by 1910 the steel industry was entirely nonunion.

With the power of the Amalgamated broken, steel employers were left to mechanize as much as they needed. The decade that followed the Homestead defeat brought unprecedented developments in every stage of steelmaking. The rate of innovation in steel has never been equaled. Electric trolleys, the pig casting machine, the Jones mixer, and mechanical ladle cars transformed the blast furnace. Electric traveling cranes in the Bessemer converter and the Wellman charger in the open hearth did away with almost all the manual aspects of steel production proper. And electric cars and rising-and-falling tables made the rolling mills a continuous operation.[19] These developments led the British Iron and Steel Institute to conclude after its visit in 1903 that

the [U.S.] steel industry had made considerable advances in the ten years ending with 1890. It is, however, mainly since that year that the steel manufacture has made its greatest strides in every direction, and it is wholly since that date that costs have been so far reduced as to enable the United States to compete with Great Britain and Germany in the leading markets of the world.[20]

Several visitors to the steel mills around the turn of the century described the new steelmaking processes introduced in the wake of the Homestead conflict. One British economist, Frank Poppelwell, was particularly amazed by the degree to which new innovations were labor-saving. He concluded:

Perhaps the greatest difference between English and American conditions in steel-works practice is the very conspicuous absence of labourers in the American mills. The large and growing employment of every kind of both propelling and directing machinery—electric-trolleys, rising and falling tables, live rollers, side-racks, shears, machine stamps, endless chain tables for charging on the cars, overhead travelling cranes—is responsible for this state of things. It is no exaggeration to say that in a mill rolling three thousand tons of rails a day, not a dozen men are to be seen on the mill floor.[21]

A group of British iron masters from the British Iron and Steel Institute also toured America in 1903, and they, too, were impressed to find in the blast furnaces that

the bulk of the heavy drudgery has been obviated by the use of machinery. There is no pig-lifting, no hand shovelling of stock, no hauling of charging barrows. All the tedious clay work around the hearth, the incessant changing of tuyeres, is done away with.[22]

They found that in the rolling mills

the appliances introduced have effected the best results in doing away with manual labor. A tongs or hook is not seen near any of the rail mills visited, and the whole operation is conducted from a platform, where levers connected with the various live rollers and lifting tables are collected together.[23]

And as far as the open-hearth operations were concerned, perhaps the most vivid description was left by J.H. Bridge, an American journalist who wrote a series of articles about the steel industry for *Everybody's Magazine:*

It is at Homestead that wonders are performed as amazing as those of the Arabian Nights. Here machines endowed with the strength of a hundred giants move obedient to a touch, opening furnace doors and lifting out of the glowing flames enormous slabs of white-hot steel, much as a child would pick up a match-box from the table. Two of these machines, appropriately named by the men "Leviathan and Behemoth," seemed gifted with intelligence. Each is attended by a little trolley-car that runs busily to and fro, its movements controlled by the more sluggish monster. This little attendant may be at one end of the long shed and the Leviathan at the other; but no sooner does it seem to see its giant master open a furnace door and put in his great hand for a fresh lump of hot steel, than it runs back like a terrier to its owner and arrives just as the huge fist is withdrawn with a glowing scab. This the Leviathan gently places on its attendant's back; and, to the admiration of all beholders, the little thing trots gayly off with it to the end of the building. Even then the wonder is not ended; for the little fellow gives a shake to his back, and the glittering mass, twice as big as a Saratoga trunk, slides onto a platform of rollers which carry it to the mill. And no human hand is seen in the operation.[24]

In this way, the steel masters succeeded in eliminating the bottlenecks in production by replacing workers with machines at every opportunity. This mechanization would not have been possible without the employers' victory over the workers at Homestead. Thus we can see how the prize in the class struggle was control over the production process and the distribution of the benefits of technology. As David Brody summarizes it:

In the two decades after 1890, the furnace worker's productivity tripled in exchange for an income rise of one-half; the steel workers output doubled in exchange for an income rise of one-fifth ... At bottom, the remarkable cost reduction of American steel manufacture rested on those figures.

The accomplishment was possible only with a labor force powerless to oppose the decisions of the steel men.[25]

The victory of the employers in 1892 allowed them to destroy the old labor system in the industry. They could then begin to create a new system, one that would reflect and help to perpetuate their ascendancy. Specifically, this meant that they had three separate tasks: to adapt the jobs to the new technology, to motivate workers to perform the new jobs efficiently, and to establish lasting control over the entire production process. The next three sections will deal with each one of these in turn.

Part 2: Effects of the New Technology
on Job Structure

Unlike earlier innovations in steelmaking, the mechanization of the 1890s transformed the tasks involved in steel production. The traditional skills of heating, roughing, catching, and rolling were built into the new machines. Machines also moved the raw materials and products through the plants. Thus the new process required neither the heavy laborers nor the highly skilled craftsmen of the past. Rather, they required workers to operate the machines, to feed them and tend them, to start them and stop them. A new class of workers was created to perform these tasks, a class of machines operators known by the label "semiskilled."

The new machine operators were described by the British Iron and Steel Institute after their visit in 1903 as men who

have to be attentive to guiding operations, and quick in manipulating levers and similarly easy work . . . the various operations are so much simplified that an experienced man is not required to conduct any part of the process.[26]

Similarly, the U.S. Department of Labor noted the rise of this new type of steelworker in its report of 1910:

The semiskilled among the production force consist for the most part of workmen who have been taught to perform relatively complex functions, such as the operation of cranes and other mechanical appliances, but who possess little or no general mechanical or metallurgical knowledge . . . This class has been developed largely within recent years along with the growth in the use of machinery and electrical power in the industry. The whole tendency of the industry is to greatly increase the proportion of the production force formed by this semiskilled class of workmen. They are displacing both the skilled and the unskilled workmen.[27]

The semiskilled workers were created by the downgrading of the skilled workers and the upgrading of the unskilled. These shifts proceeded throughout the 1890s and early 1900s, as more and more plants were mechanized. Although there are no hard data on these shifts in job categories,[b] they are reflected in the

---

[b]Usually time series data on percentage employed in the different categories are used to demonstrate the changing mix of skill requirements in the industry. For my purpose, however, such data are more misleading than helpful. In part, this is because there is no way to know how the Census Department or the individual steel companies are defining "skilled," "semiskilled," and "unskilled," so that comparisons between them are impossible. Also, the meaning of the categories changes over time. In 1890, "unskilled" work in the steel mills meant purely heavy manual labor. By 1910, "unskilled" work included simple machine operating jobs, as well as laborers. Similarly, "skilled" work in 1890 meant all workers who had a particular craft. By 1910, "skilled" workers were either maintenance

change in relative wage rates. Between 1890 and 1910, the hourly wages of the unskilled steelworkers rose by about 20 percent, while the daily earnings of the skilled workers fell by as much as 70 percent. Also after 1892, the wage differential between the various types of skilled workers narrowed substantially.[c] Thus, the British iron masters reported in 1903:

The tendency in the American steel industry is to reduce by every possible means the number of highly-skilled men employed and more and more to establish the general wage on the basis of common unskilled labour. This is not a new thing, but it becomes every year more accentuated as a result of the use of automatic appliances which unskilled labor is usually competent to control.[28]

One consequence of the diminished importance of the skilled workers once their power was broken was the dramatic decline in their earnings. The following table (Table 2-2) of wage rates for selected positions at the Homestead plant mill between 1892 and 1908 illustrates the fate of skilled workers throughout the industry.[29] Bear in mind that during this interval, their productivity was multiplying and wages throughout the nation were rising. Also, their workday was increased from 8 hours to 12 hours, so that the decline in daily earnings understates their reduction in real wages.

These reductions were part of the steel companies' policy of reducing the wage differentials between the classes of workers to make them more consistent with differentials in skill requirements for the different jobs. An official of one Pittsburgh steel company put it this way:

It is perfectly true that the tonnage rates, and in some instances the actual daily earnings of skilled laborers, have been largely decreased. The reason for this is, mainly, the tremendous increase in production, due to improved equipment,

---

men (mechanics, machinists, etc.) or workers holding supervisory-type functions, directing and coordinating the various men and machines.

The other reason that time series data are not germane is that even when data are available for particular job titles at different periods of time, there is no way to know that the job itself remained unchanged. The following passage from Fitch gives us one example of how job titles were changing during this period:

There were three men regularly employed at an open-hearth furnace—'first helper', 'second helper' and 'cinder-pit man.' The first helper was formerly called a 'melter', but now, with a different organization, a melter has charge of several furnaces. In an open-hearthplant there are usually a superintendent and an assistant superintendent in control, a foreman or boss melter in active charge of from three to five furnaces.

Thus, I have concluded that contemporary accounts are more valuable than statistical data to describe the changing content and categories of work in steel mills. Only in this way is it possible to go behind the statistical data and show the concrete content often masked in the abstract categories.

[c]Doeringer, "Piece Rate Wage Structures." Doeringer attributes this shift purely to commodity market forces. He argues that shifts in demand for different kinds of steel products narrowed the wage differentials between steel workers. He mentions the decline of the Amalgamated after Homestead and the skilled workers' subsequent inability to hold their own against the employers, but does not relate this to the change in wage differentials.

Table 2-2
Wages in Plate Mills, Homestead, 1889-1908

Position	Tonnage Rates			Daily Rates		
	1889-1892	1908	% decl.	1892	1907	% decl.
Roller	$14.00	$4.75	66.07	$11.84	$8.44	28.72
Heater	11.00	3.99	63.73	8.16	7.21	11.64
Heater's Helpers	7.50	2.09	72.13	5.80	4.09	29.48
Hooker	8.50	2.40	71.76	n.a.	n.a.	n.a.
Shearman	13.00	n.a.	n.a.	9.49	5.58	41.20

Source: Fitch, John, *The Steel Workers* (New York: Charities Publications Commerce, 1920), pp. 153, 156.

representing very large capital investment, enabling the men at lower rates to make equal, or even higher daily earnings.

He then added, somewhat more straightforwardedly:

At the same time the daily earnings of some of the most highly paid men have been systematically brought down to a level consistent with the pay of other workers, having in mind skill and training required and a good many other factors.[30]

The other side of the picture was the upgrading effect that the new technology had on the unskilled workers. Their wages were increased considerably during that same period. In part this was accomplished by a raise in the hourly rate for unskilled labor, from $.14 per hour in 1892 to $.175 per hour in 1910,[31] and in part it was the result of the steel companies putting more men on tonnage rates, enabling them to make higher daily earnings.[32]

Many unskilled workers were put in charge of expensive machines and made responsible for operating them at full capacity. (It turned out to be very easy to train unskilled workers for these jobs, as will be shown in Part 3, Section 2.) Fewer and fewer men were hired just to push wheelbarrows and load ingots, so that, as an official of the Pennsylvania Steel Company said, "While machinery may decrease the number of men, it demands a higher grade of workmen."[33]

Thus, the effect of the new technology was to level the work force and to create a new class of workers. Table 2-3 shows this process as a whole. The data is based on a survey of 28 steel plants, conducted by the U.S. Commissioner of Labor in 1913. The table reports earnings only of production workers, omitting the earnings of foremen, clerks, timekeepers, weighters, and chemists. As can be seen from the table,[34] the percentage of workers earning in the middle two categories went from 35 to 58 percent in the 10-year period.

The existence of the growing group of semiskilled workers created certain problems for the employers, which will be explored in Part 3.

Table 2-3
Percent of Employees Earning Each Classified Amount

Hourly Earnings	1900	1905	1910
Under 18 cents	65.0	64.3	41.8
18 and 25 cents	17.4	20.6	32.8
25 cents and over	17.6	15.1	25.4
70 cents and over	1.9	0.9	1.2

Part 3: Solving the Labor Problem

In Part 1 we saw how the market conditions in the industry led employers to destroy the skilled steelworkers' union in order to mechanize their operations. Employers therefore became the unilateral controllers of steel production. However, by doing that they created for themselves the problem of labor discipline. When the skilled workers had been partners in production, the problem of worker motivation did not arise. Skilled workers felt that they were working for themselves because they controlled the process of production. They set their own pace and work load without input from the bosses. In the 1890s, however, when the steel masters showed them who was boss, workers lost their stake in production, so that the problem of motivation arose. How hard workers worked became an issue of class struggle.

In Part 2 we saw how the effect of the new technology introduced in the 1890s was to narrow the skills differentials between the two grades of workers, producing a work force predominantly "semiskilled." This homogenization of the work force produced another new "problem" for the employers. That is, without the old skilled/unskilled dichotomy and the exclusiveness of the craft unions, the possibility was greater than ever that workers might as a class unite to oppose the employers. Frederick Winslow Taylor, the renowned management theorist who began his career as a foreman in a steel plant, warned employers of this danger in 1905:

When employers herd their men together in classes, pay all of each class the same wages, and offer none of them inducements to work harder or do better than the average, the only remedy for the men comes in combination; and frequently the only possible answer to encroachments on the part of their employers is a strike.[35]

Ultimately, however, both the problem of worker motivation and the problem of preventing unified opposition were the same problem. They both revolved around the question of controlling worker behavior. To do that, employers realized they had to control the workers' perceptions of their own self-interests. Employers had to create the illusion that the workers had a stake in production, even though this was no longer true. This problem was known as "the labor problem."

To solve the labor problem, employers developed strategies to break down the basis for a unity of interest among workers, and to convince them that, as individuals, their interests were identical with those of their company.

Out of these efforts, they developed new methods of wage payments and new advancement policies, which relied on stimulating individual ambition. These policies were designed to create psychological divisions among the workers, to make them perceive their interests as different from, indeed in conflict with, those of their coworkers. Employers also began to use paternalistic welfare policies in order to win the loyalty of their employees. The effect of all these new policies was to establish an internal labor market in the major steel companies, which has lasted, in its essentials, until today. This section will describe the new labor system that was created and the reasons why employers created it.

1. Development of Wage Incentive
Schemes

With the defeat of the Amalgamated Association, the entire complex traditional system of wage payments collapsed. The sliding scale of wages for paying skilled workers and the contract system for paying their helpers rapidly declined. Employers considered them a vestige of worker power and rooted them out of shop after shop. As the British Iron and Steel Institute noted in 1902,

Many owners of the works in the United States have set their faces so completely against the contract system that in the opinion of the most experienced authorities, the contractor, as hitherto established, is likely, before long, to entirely disappear.[36]

Thus, the employers had the opportunity to establish unilaterally a new system of wage payment. Initially, they began to pay the new semiskilled workers day wages, as they had paid the unskilled workers. Soon, however, they switched to the system of piecework, paying a fixed sum for each unit produced. The British visitors found, in 1902, "in most of the works and shops visited that piecework is very general in all operations that call for a considerable amount of skill, and, indeed, wherever the work is above the level of unskilled labor."[37]

The most obvious function of piecework was, of course, to increase output by making each worker drive himself or herself to work harder. Employers also contended that the system was in the workers' best interests because it allowed each one to raise his or her own wages.

However, the employers soon found that straight piecework gave the workers too much control over their wages. That is, when it succeeded in stimulating workers to increase their output, their wages soared above the going rate. Employers would then cut the piece rates to keep the wages in line. Once they did that, however, they had reduced the piece-rate system to simple speed-up—a way of getting more work for the same pay. Workers responded to the rate cuts by collectively slowing down their output, so that the system defeated itself, leaving employers back where they had started. An article in *Iron Age*, entitled "Wage Payment Systems: How to Secure the Maximum Efficiency of Labor," gives an interesting account of this process:

It is in the administration of the piecework system that manufacturers, sooner or later, make their great mistake and over-reach themselves, with the result that the system becomes a mockery and the evil conditions of the old day work system reappears. Regardless of the continually increasing cost of living, the manufacturers decide among themselves, for example, that $1.50 for 10 hours is enough for a woman and that $2.50 a day is enough for the ordinary workingman and a family. The piece work prices are then adjusted so that the normal day's output will just bring about these wages . . . Immediately throughout the entire shop the news of the cuts is whispered about . . . with the result that there is a general slowing down of all producers.[38]

Thus, employers began to experiment with modifications of the piece rate. They developed several new methods of payment at this time, known as "premium" or "bonus" plans. These differed from piecework only in that they gave the workers smaller increments in pay for each additional piece.

The Halsey premium plan, developed in 1891, served as a model for most of the others. It called for establishing a base time period for a job, and setting one rate for workers who completed the job in that period. If a worker could finish the job faster, then he or she received a bonus in addition to the standard rate. The bonus was figured so that only a part of the money saved by the worker's extra productivity went to him/her, with the rest going to the company. Different plans varied according to how the base time period and the base wage were set and how the more efficient workers' savings were divided between the worker and the company. *Iron Age* recommended one particular variation, called the half and half premium plan, in which the rule was "to pay the more efficient workman only one-half what he saves by speeding up." The article described one example where, under the plan,

for every extra $1 the man earned by his extra effort, the manufacturers would gain $7. Not a bad investment, this premium system. It betters the workingman's condition materially, and, best of all, improves his frame of mind.[39]

Frederick Winslow Taylor's differential piece rate is basically another variation of the Halsey premium plan. Under Taylor's system, the employer established two separate rates, a low day rate for the "average workman" and a high piece rate for the "first class workman," with the stipulation that only the fast and efficient workers were entitled to the higher rate. He suggests setting the high rate to give the worker about 60 percent increase in earnings, and for this, the employer would demand a 300 to 400 percent increase in output. Like the Halsey plan, it was simply the piece-rate system modified to give the worker diminishing returns for the extra effort.

In order for any of the output incentive plans to work, management had to be able to measure each worker's output separately. All the premium plans stressed the importance of treating each worker individually, but only Taylor gave them a method for doing so. His great contribution was systematic time study—giving employers a yardstick to measure an individual's productivity. The emphasis on individual productivity measures reinforced the fragmenting effect of the plans. As Taylor said about his experience implementing the system at the Bethlehem Steel Works,

Whenever it was practicable, each man's work was measured by itself . . . Only on a few occasions and then upon special permission . . . were more than two men allowed to work on gang work, dividing their earnings between them. Gang work almost invariably results in a falling off of earnings and consequent dissatisfaction.[40]

Output incentives were designed to increase individual worker output. Employers understood that to do that, they had to play upon individual worker's ambitions, which meant breaking down workers' collective identity. They gave each worker inducement to work harder, and also divided the workers into different groups, according to their output. They also increased the social distance between the "more efficient" and the "less efficient" workers.

Thus, output incentives served as a lever to prevent workers from taking collective action. As one manufacturer explained in 1928, he had originally adopted output incentives

To break up the flat rate for the various classes of workers. That is the surest preventative of strikes and discontent. When all are paid one rate, it is the simplest and almost inevitable thing for all to unite in the support of a common demand. When each worker is paid according to his record there is not the same community of interest. The good worker who is adequately paid does not consider himself aggrieved so willingly nor will he so freely jeopardize his standing by joining with the so-called 'Marginal Worker.' There are not likely to be union strikes where there is no union of interest.[41]

Taylor, too, boasted in 1895 that

There has never been a strike by men working under this system, although it has been applied at the Midvale Steel Works for the past ten years; and the steel business has proved during this period the most fruitful field for labor organization . . . I attribute a great part of this success in avoiding strikes to the high wages which the best men were able to earn with the differential rates, and to the pleasant feeling fostered by this system.[42]

An editorial in *Iron Age*, 1905, entitled "Union Restriction of Output," reveals much about employers' views of the incentive plans:

The premium plan, which has done for the machine shop, and on a smaller scale for the foundry, what the introduction of non-union men did at the Gamble mine—increasing wages and reducing the cost per ton—has been resisted by the molders' union, as it has been steadily opposed by the machinists' union. As ground for this opposition it is urged that the premium plan is only a modification of what the unions regard as the vicious piece price system, and that the union must prevent a greedy scramble for high wages by workmen who take no account of the pace they are setting for the less capable . . . [43]

This article tells us how conscious both the employers and the unions were about effects of the premium plan on the social relations inside the plant. Employers saw it as the equivalent of bringing in scabs to a union shop in its power to break up unity between the workers and advocated it for that reason. The unions opposed it, not because they misunderstood, but because they saw it in precisely the same way.

Quite explicitly, then, the aim of the premium plans was to break up any community of interest that might lead workers to slow their pace (what employers call "restriction of output") or unite in other ways to oppose management. They were a weapon in the psychological war that employers were waging against their workers, and were, at least for a while, quite successful. A survey of plant managers made in 1928 by the National Industrial Conference Board found that

There was little dissent from the opinion that the [premium plan] is effective in promoting industrial harmony. The responsibility for low earnings is placed squarely on the shoulders of the worker, leaving no room for complaint of favoritism or neglect on the part of management.[44]

Between 1900 and World War I, piecework and premium plans became more and more prevalent in the steel industry. Although there are no figures on the percentage of workers on incentive plans, as compared with percentage on day work, there is evidence that piecework and the premium system became the preferred methods of wage payment and were used whenever possible. The number of articles in *Iron Age* advising employers to use output incentives increased every year during this period, and they gave more and more examples of companies which had employed it successfully. By 1912, there were articles about the system almost every month in *Iron Age*, with titles like "A Sliding Scale Premium System" (March 14), "The Sphere of the Premium Plan" (April 25), "Success with Bonus Wage Systems" (July 4), "Productivity Betterment by Time Studies" (April 4), and "Adopting Piece Work and Premium Systems" (December 5).

Bethlehem Steel Company was one of the first major companies to adopt premium plans. Charles Schwab, president of the company, attributed his uncanny success in buying out bankrupt shipbuilding companies and turning them into profitable ventures to the introduction of premium plans. In one particularly dramatic case, he bought the bankrupt Fore River Shipbuilding Company in Quincy, Massachusetts, and claimed, with the bonus plan, to have revived the company so as to make a million dollars' profit from it in the first year![45]

Steelworkers opposed the new methods of payment, and the residual unions in the industry raised objections at every opportunity. In one instance, at Bethlehem Steel's South Bethlehem Works, opposition to the bonus system exploded into a major strike in February, 1910. Approximately 5,000 of the 7,000 workers there went out on strike spontaneously. The strike lasted several weeks, during which time one man was killed and many were injured. Strike demands were drawn up separately by each department or group of workers, and every single one called for uniform rates of pay *to be paid by the hour*, and time-and-a-half for overtime. Several added to that an explicit demand for the elimination of piecework and a return to the "day-work" system. A U.S. Senate investigation into the strike found that the " 'Time-Bonus' System in use was one of its major causes."[46]

However, worker opposition proved ineffective in preventing the use of output incentive schemes. Since 1892, the employers had held the upper hand in the industry, and they used it to perpetuate their power. The wage incentive schemes were aimed at doing just that.

2. New Promotion Policies and the Development of Job Ladders

As we saw in Part 2 of this chapter, the new technology diminished the skill requirements for virtually all the jobs involved in making steel, so that even the most difficult jobs could be learned quickly. The gulf separating the skilled workers from the unskilled workers became virtually meaningless. Charles

Schwab himself said in 1902 that he could "take a green hand—say a fairly intelligent agricultural labourer—and make a steel melter of him in six or eight weeks."[47] When we realize that the job of melter was the most highly skilled job in the open-hearth department, we can see how narrow the skill range in the industry really was. The employers knew this, and put their knowledge to good use during strikes. For example, during a strike at the Hyde Park Mill in 1901,

it was resolved that the works should be continued with green hands, aided by one or two skilled men who remained loyal. The five mills thus manned were started on the 3rd of August, and up to the date of my visit, near the end of October, they had not lost a single turn.[48]

Around the turn of the century, employers began to recognize the dangers inherent in the homogenization of the work force. They formulated this problem as worker discontent caused by "dead-end jobs." Meyer Bloomfield, an industrial manager who in 1918 wrote a textbook in factory management, summarized their discussion on this subject:

A good deal of literature has been published within the last dozen years in which scathing criticism is made of what has come to be known as "blind alley" or "dead-end" jobs. By these phrases is meant work of a character which leads to nothing in the way of further interest, opportunity, acquisition of skill, experience, or anything else which makes an appeal to normal human intelligence and ambition. The work itself is not under attack as much as the lack of incentive and appeal in the scheme of management.[49]

Boomfield says right off, then, that the problem of "dead-end" jobs need not be solved by changing the jobs themselves. The better solution is to change the arrangement of the jobs. To do this, he says,

a liberal system of promotion and transfer has therefore become one of the most familiar features of a modern personnel plan, and some of the most interesting achievements of management may be traced to the workings of such a system.[50]

Thus, the response of employers to the newly homogenized jobs was to create strictly demarcated job ladders, linking each job to one above and one below it in status and in pay, to make a chain along which workers could progress. The reason for this response was their view that

what makes men restless is the inability to move, or to get ahead. This fundamental law of human nature is forgotten frequently, and its neglect gives rise to situations that are never understood by the employer who looks upon a working force as something rigid.[51]

The establishment of a job ladder has two advantages, from the employers' point of view. First, it gave workers a sense of vertical mobility as they made their way up the ladder, and was an incentive to workers to work harder. Like the premium plan, the promise of advancement was used as a carrot to lure the men to produce more and more. As Charles Hook, the vice president of the American Rolling Mill Company, a major subsidiary of U.S. Steel, told the Third International Management Congress:

a few general policies govern the selection of all (our employees). One of the most important of these is the policy of promotion within the organization. This is done wherever possible and has several advantages; the most important of which is the stimulating effect upon the ambitions of workers throughout the organization.[52]

The other advantage of the job ladder arrangement was that it gave the employers more leverage with which to maintain discipline. The system pitted each worker against all the others in rivalry for advancement and undercut any feeling of unity which might develop among them. Instead of acting in concert with other workers, workers had to learn to curry favor with their supervisors, to play by their rules, in order to get ahead. As one steelworker described the effect this had on workers during the 1919 organizing campaign, "Naw, they won't join no union; they're all after every other feller's job."[53] This competition also meant that workers on different ladder rungs had different vested interests, and that those higher up had something to lose by offending their bosses or disrupting production.

As early as 1900, *Iron Age* was advising employers to fill production work vacancies from inside the firm. They advocated a policy of hiring only at the lowest job levels and filling higher jobs by promotion—what contemporary economists refer to as limiting the ports of entry. In one article, titled "Developing Employees," a columnist sharply criticizes a specific employer who

has very often failed to find the proper qualifications among his employees to promote any one of them to certain higher positions which had become vacant from various causes . . . At such times he usually hired outsiders to fill the positions and thus engendered dissatisfaction among his helpers.[54]

In the following years, the journal suggested that employers issue special employer certificates to their more faithful and efficient employees, which would serve as tickets to advancement when openings became available. By 1905, they concluded that

the plan is working so well that already employers' certificates are held in higher favor by the industrious, well-disposed workmen than a union card could ever be by such a man.[55]

Clearly, the employers' certificates were a gimmick to further the workers' sense of opportunity by holding out the promise of promotions even before there were jobs available. Thus, workers were made to compete with each other for the certificates, as well as for the better jobs. The certificates in themselves did not guarantee anything; they merely improved one's chances—so the "certified" loyal ones still had to compete.

The principle of internal promotion was expounded by Judge Gary, the president of the U.S. Steel Corporation, in his dealings with the subsidiaries. For example, in a speech to the presidents of the subsidiary companies in 1922, Gary said:

We should give careful thought to the question as to who could be selected to satisfactorily fill any unoccupied place; and like suggestions should be made to the heads of all departments. Positions should be filled by promotions from the ranks, and if in any locations there are none competent, this fact should be given attention and men trained accordingly. It is only necessary to make and urge the point. You will know what to do, if indeed any of you has not already well deliberated and acted upon it.[56]

Observers of the steel industry in the early years of this century saw the effects of these new policies on the structure of jobs. The British economist, Poppelwell, visited the American steel industry in 1902 and concluded that

the most characteristic feature of American industrial life and the most far-reaching in its effects is what may be shortly termed the mobility of labour ... Under a competitive system, a large degree of mobility, not only in the various grades of labour themselves, but also between the different grades, allows the best man to come rapidly to the top, and promotion is very much quicker in America than here.[57]

As we saw in Part 1 of this chapter, John Fitch, the American journalist who made a study of the steel industry in 1908, also found a rigid line of promotion within each department, and a work force that was "pyramided and ... held together by the ambition of the men lower down."[58]

On an aggregate level, the vertical mobility inside the steel industry can be traced through the rise of the various immigrant groups, all of whom entered the industry as common laborers. David Brody, in his book *Steel Workers in America*, gives the following data about one large Pittsburgh mill for the year 1910:[59]

| Years Service | Number of Immigrants Holding: | | |
	Unskilled Jobs	Semiskilled Jobs	Skilled Jobs
Under 2 years	314	56	0
2-5 years	544	243	17
5-10 years	475	441	79
Over 10 years	439	398	184

John Fitch also noted that one could chart mobility through the rise of the various groups of immigrants. In the open-hearth department, for example, he noted that the newly arrived Slav is put to work in the cinder pit; from here he is promoted to be second helper and then first helper. Practically all of the cinder-pit men now are Slavs, and a majority of the second helpers are Slavs, and it would seem to be only a question of time when the first helpers and even the melter foremen will be men of these races promoted from the lower positions.[60]

In this way, the steel companies opened up lines of promotion in the early years of the century by creating job ladders. Employers claimed that each rung of the ladder provided the necessary training for the job above it. But the skilled jobs in the steel industry had been virtually eliminated, and production jobs were becoming more homogeneous in their content. If, as Charles Schwab said, one could learn to be a melter in 6 weeks, then certainly the training required for most jobs was so minimal that no job ladder and only the minimum of job tenure were needed to acquire the necessary skills.

At that time, technological development made it possible to do away with distinctions between skilled and unskilled workers. Instead of following this trend, employers introduced divisions to avoid the consequences of a uniform and homogeneous work force. Therefore, the minutely graded job ladders that developed were a solution to the "labor problem," rather than a necessary input for production itself.

3. The Welfare Policies

The history of this period also sheds light on another important aspect of the steel industry's labor policies—the welfare programs. U.S. Steel's policy on welfare was formulated during the first few years of the corporation's life, and specific programs were established throughout the early years. These programs included a stock subscription plan for workers and a profit-sharing plan for executives; old-age pensions and accident insurance; a safety and sanitation campaign; and efforts to provide community housing, education, and recreation facilities. Indeed, they included most of the functions performed today by the so-called welfare state. The welfare policies were the most visible and best publicized part of the industry's labor policies. They were set up to serve the interests of the employers as a *class*, rather than as individual manufacturers.

The stock subscription plan, the first of the welfare measures, went into effect in 1903. It involved the sale of stock at reduced rates to corporation employees, paid for by monthly paycheck deductions. The plan provided the subscribers with a bonus, in addition to the regular dividends, of $5 for each of the first 5 years that the subscriber remained in the employ of the corporation and retained the stock, provided she or he showed "a proper interest in its welfare and progress." Also, the deserving subscribers received an extra bonus after owning the stock for 5 years.

The idea of the stock subscription plan was to give employees a share in the growth of the corporation. As such, it was a form of profit-sharing. However, the bonuses and the extra bonuses made the plan something more. They gave employees an incentive to stay with the corporation for 5 years, and to show "a proper interest" in its welfare. Although it did not specify what showing "a proper interest" involved, certainly joining a union or sabotaging production were not included. The plan was clearly designed to control workers' behavior. One of the workers interviewed by John Fitch saw it simply as ". . . a scheme to keep out unionism and prevent the men from protesting against bad conditions."[61]

The stock subscription plan set the tone for all the later insurance measures. They all contained clauses and subparagraphs stipulating how workers had to behave to be eligible for benefits. For example, the pension fund established in 1911, which was made up solely of corporation contributions, offered retirement benefits at age 60 for employees of 20 years' seniority, *except* "in case of misconduct on the part of the beneficiaries or for other cause sufficient in the judgement of the Board of Trustees."[62] Similarly, a Voluntary Accident Relief Plan was inaugurated in 1910 to pay workers' benefits in case of temporary disability, permanent disability, or death resulting from on-the-job injuries. The plan (which was soon superseded by state workmen's compensation laws) was the first of its kind in the United States, and for all its liberality, was also a device to ward off lawsuits in accident cases caused by company negligence. The plan said explicitly that "No relief will be paid to any employee or his family if suit is brought against the company," and "all employees of the company who accept and receive any of this relief will be required to sign a release to the company."[63]

Other aspects of the welfare program contained more subtle behavior modification devices, aimed at changing behavior indirectly, through changing the attitudes of employees. For example, the steel industry was notorious for its hazardous working conditions and the high accident rate that resulted. The corporation, as part of its welfare program, began a safety propaganda campaign in 1908. They hung safety posters around the plants, distributed safety handbills to all the workers, circulated safety bulletins, and showed safety films—all of which were designed to convince the workers that "workers are solely or partially responsible [for accidents] in ninety percent of the cases."[64] U.S. Steel maintained, and preached, this position despite conclusive statistical evidence published at the time which showed that plant and equipment design were the cause of most work accidents in the steel industry.[65] In other words, the point of the elaborate and highly praised safety campaign was to convince the workers that accidents were their own fault, and so to ward off any blame for the companies' unsafe production practices.

Another part of the corporation's welfare program was to encourage workers to build houses by giving them low-income loans for that purpose. Although the program benefited workers, the motives for the program were, at best, mixed.

An editorial in *Iron Age* in 1905 praised the corporation's housing program because

workmen will build homes of their own, which is most desireable as bearing upon permanency of employment and its influence against labor agitation, for the home-owning workman is less apt to be lead astray by the professional agitator than the man whose industrial life is a transient one.[66]

The corporation's welfare efforts in the communities of its employees were extensive and impressive. The corporation by 1924 built 28,000 dwellings, which it rented to its employees, and built entire towns around some of its subsidiaries. Gary, Indiana, for example, was built from scratch by the corporation, and was acclaimed at the time as a model of town planning techniques and modern social services. In these company towns, the corporation built water purification facilities and sewage sytems. They employed nurses to visit the families of their employees, instructing them in methods of hygiene, and they employed dentists to visit the children's schools and give them "toothbrush drills." They built emergency hospitals to serve their towns, charging special low rates to the families of workers. They helped build the public schools and often supplemented teachers' salaries in order to attract good teachers. They built libraries and club houses for the workers, at which they offered night courses in English, civics, arithmetic, and technical subjects. Every plant had its own glee club, band, or orchestra, with instruments provided by the company. Unoccupied company land was turned over to the workers for gardens, where with seed provided by the company, about a million dollars' worth of vegetables were produced each year. And for its employees' recreation, the corporation had built, by January 1, 1924, 175 playgrounds, 125 athletic fields, 112 tennis courts, 19 swimming pools, and 21 band stands.[67]

Such was the welfare program of the U.S. Steel Corporation. The question that remains is, why?

Most writers about the industry treat the welfare work either as a sincere expression of good intentions on the part of the steel management or as a public relations ploy. Friends of the corporation, such as Arundel Cotter, a personal acquaintance of Judge Gary, argue that the welfare work proved that labor and capital could progress together in harmony, providing better lives for the workers and higher profits for the corporation at the same time. He sums up his review of the welfare work by saying, "the organization of the U.S. Steel Corporation was the greatest step that has ever been made toward the highest form of socialism."[68] Critics of the corporation like John Garraty and Robert Weibe, both historians of the period, argue that the welfare work was designed to convince the public that the corporation was a "good trust," in order to avoid the furor of the trust-busting sentiment of the times, but that in fact they benefited very few workers.

A look at the origins of the welfare programs gives a more rounded view of the role they served. The welfare programs were designed by George Perkins, one of J.P. Morgan's top men. Perkins had originally attracted Morgan's attention when, as a vice president of New York Life Insurance Company, he had developed an extraordinary innovation in labor relations, the NYLIC club. The purpose of the scheme was to reduce employee turnover. Perkins set up the club for all employees who would promise never to work for another business. Members of the NYLIC club received monthly bonuses and a life-time pension after 20 years of service. According to Perkins' biographer,

"The idea of this plan," Perkins told the agents, "is to say to the solicitor . . . that if he will give up . . . any thought of going into any business, or into any other company, no matter what the inducements might be, and will accept . . . the New York Life Insurance Company for his Company, then we will do something for him that is . . . better than any other Company can do."[69]

The plan was enormously successful at reducing turnover, and it made Perkins' career. He went to work for Morgan, and he was put in charge of labor relations for all Morgan's concerns. He designed welfare policies for Morgan's railroads, the International Harvester Corporation and U.S. Steel, all with the same goal—to bind workers to the company for a long time.[70] Again, Perkins' biographer reports that the stock subscription plan at U.S. Steel

had certain special features intended to make the employees identify their personal interests with that of U.S. Steel. These features reflected clearly Perkins' experience in the life insurance business, and especially with the NYLIC organization. Just as he had worked to retain his agents on a permanent basis, Perkins was eager to avoid a labor turnover at every level.[71]

The welfare policies caused a bitter dispute within the corporation's executive board when they were first proposed. U.S. Steel's original executive board was made up of two groups—the Wall Street bankers who had organized the merger, and the presidents of the large steel companies who had been merged. On November 22, 1902, less than a year after the corporation was formed, the financiers on the board, Judge Elbert Gary and George Perkins, presented the stock subscription plan. The old-time steelmen on the board immediately opposed the plan and the paternalistic labor policy it represented. Their labor policy, so effective in the 1890s, was straightforward, out-and-out repression. Charles Schwab, president of the corporation, characterized their attitude by saying, "When a workman raises his head, beat it down." Thus a fight developed between the bankers and the steelmen over the labor policy of the new corporation—a fight which was ultimately settled by J.P. Morgan who threw his support to the bankers.[72] Schwab resigned as president of the corporation soon thereafter, and Gary was made chairman of the board of directors. With the victory of the financiers, the welfare programs were begun.

The welfare programs, then, were part of a broader strategy on the part of the finance capitalists to break down the interfirm mobility of workers. The reason for this was not simply that labor turnover was expensive—for indeed turnover was not particularly expensive in those days when there was little on-the-job training and none of the negotiated fringe benefits which make turnover costly today. The reason for reducing turnover was, as Perkins and other managers of the day noted, that changing jobs had an unsettling effect upon the workers. It tended to make them identify with other workers, and to see themselves as a class. All the major strikes of the nineteenth century had shown that steelworkers were quick to go out in sympathy with striking workers in other companies and industries. The welfare programs were supposed to combat this tendency, by giving workers both a psychological and an economic motive for remaining loyal to their employer.

The steel companies regarded their welfare work as their greatest contribution to domestic tranquility. They saw welfarism as the way to head off class struggle in society as a whole. For example, during the discussion of welfare work at the 1912 convention of Iron and Steel Institute, one of the directors of U.S. Steel, Percival Roberts, said:

We live in an age of discontent and great unrest. It is world-wide, not peculiar to this country at all. And I believe that no body of men is doing more to restore confidence today than those assembled here tonight. It is the one thing which we need today, eliminating all class distinctions, and restoring not only politically, but industrially, good fellowship; and I believe that the Iron and Steel industry is taking a leading position in that work.[73]

The U.S. Steel Corporation advertised its welfare work widely. Beginning in 1913, they began an "Iron and Steel Institute Monthly Bulletin" which did nothing but report on the welfare work of the different steel companies. Judge Gary and George Perkins gave many speeches about the welfare work, and encouraged other corporations to follow their example. They sought publicity for the programs in the business press and in the popular press. They did this because they saw the programs as more than a labor policy for U.S. Steel. They believed that if all companies followed their example, it would prove to be a solution to the "labor problem" nationally. Welfarism was their answer to the class politics represented by the Socialist Party, which was making great headway at the time. By increasing the ties between workers and their employer, they hoped to weaken the ties between workers and their class. (For a discussion on the class-conscious nature of the welfare work and the leading role played by U.S. Steel, see Weinstein, *The Corporate Ideal in the Liberal State* and Weibe, Robert, *Businessmen and Reform.*)

Perhaps the best statement of the strategy of the welfare policies was given by Judge Gary, who ended a meeting with the presidents of the U.S. Steel subsidiary companies in January, 1919, as saying:

Above everything else, as we have been talking this morning, satisfy your men if you can that your treatment is fair and reasonable and generous. Make the Steel Corporation a good place for them to work and live. Don't let the families go hungry or cold; give them playgrounds and parks and schools and churches, pure water to drink, and recreation, treating the whole thing as a business proposition, drawing the line so that you are just and generous and yet at the same time keeping your position and permitting others to keep theirs, retaining the control and management of your affairs, keeping the whole thing in your own hands.[74]

Part 4: The Redivision of Labor

While employers were developing new systems for managing their work forces, they also altered the definition of jobs and the division of labor between workers and management. They did this by revising the training mechanism for skilled workers, retraining the foremen, and changing their methods of recruiting managers. The result of these changes was to take knowledge about production away from the skilled workers, thus separating "physical work" from "mental work." This further consolidated the employers' unilateral control over production, for once all knowledge about production was placed on the side of management, there would be no way for workers to carry on production without them.

Frederick Winslow Taylor was one of the first theorists to discuss the importance of taking all mental skills away from the worker. In his book *Principles of Scientific Management* (1905), he gives a description of the division of knowledge in the recent past:

Now, in the best of the ordinary types of management, the managers recognize the fact that the 500 or 1000 workmen, included in the twenty or thirty trades, who are under them, possess this mass of traditional knowledge, a large part of which is not in the possession of the management. The management, of course, includes foremen and superintendents, who themselves have been in most cases first-class workers at their trades. And yet these foremen and superintendents know, better than anyone else, that their own knowledge and personal skill falls far short of the combined knowledge and dexterity of all the workmen under them.[75]

Taylor insists that employers must gain control over this knowledge, and take it away from the workers. In his manual *Shop Management*, he says quite simply, "All possible brain work should be removed from the shop and centered in the planning or laying-out department."[76]

Taylor suggested several techniques for accomplishing this. They were all based on the notion that work was a precise science, that there was "one best way" to do every task, and that the duty of the managers was to discover the best way and force all their workers to follow it. Taylorites used films of men working to break down each job into its component motions, and used stop watches to find out which was the "one best way" to do them. Taylor also insisted that all work should be programed in advance, and coordinated out of a "planning department." He gave elaborate details for how the planning department should function—using flowcharts to program the entire production process and direction cards to communicate with foremen and workers. These were called "routing" systems. One historian summarizes this aspect of scientific management thus:

One of the most important general principles of Taylor's system was that the man who did the work could not derive or fully understand its science. The result was a radical separation of thinking from doing. Those who understood were to plan the work and set the procedures; the workmen were simply to carry them into effect.[77]

Although most steel executives did not formulate the problem as clearly as Taylor, they did try to follow his advice. Around 1910, they began to develop "dispatching systems" to centralize their knowledge about production. These systems consisted of a series of charts showing the path of each piece of material as it progressed through the plant and how much time each operation took—enabling the supervisors to know exactly where each item was at any point in time. The purpose of these systems was to give the supervisors complete knowledge of the production process. Between 1910 and 1915, *Iron Age* carried innumerable articles about steel plants that had adopted dispatching systems.

At the same time that they systematized their own knowledge about production, the steel companies took that knowledge away from steelworkers. Previously, the skilled steelworkers, acting in teams, possessed all the skills and know-how necessary to make steel. They also had had authority over their own methods of work. Now employers moved to transfer that authority to the foremen and to transfer that knowledge to new strata of managers. This section will describe and document that process, in order to show that this redivision of labor was not a necessary outgrowth of the new technology, but rather an adaptation of employers to meet their own needs, as capitalists, to maintain discipline and control.

1. The New Skilled Workers

As we saw in Part 2, the mechanization of production largely eliminated the role of the traditional skilled worker. However, the steel industry still needed skilled workers. Machines required skilled mechanics to perform maintenance and repair work. Also, certain skills were needed for specialized production processes which had not yet been mechanized. However, these skilled workers were very different from the skilled workers of the nineteenth century, who collectively possessed all the skills necessary to produce steel. The new skilled workers had skills of a specific nature that enabled them to perform specific tasks, but did not have a general knowledge of the production process. This new class of skilled workers had to be created by the employers.

One would think that finding skilled men should have been no problem because of the huge numbers of skilled workers who were displaced and downgraded in the 1890s. However, by 1905, employers' associations began to complain about the shortage of skilled men. The reason for this paradox is that when the employers destroyed the unions and the old social relations, they destroyed at the same time the mechanism through which men had received their training.

Previously, the selection, training, and promotion of future skilled steelworkers had been controlled by the skilled craftsmen and their unions.[d] The constitution of the Amalgamated Association of Iron, Steel and Tin Workers had a clause that insisted that "all men are to have the privilege of hiring their own helpers without dictation from the management."[78] The men would then train their helpers in their trade. The union also regulated the helpers' advancement. For example, in 1881, it passed a resolution saying "Each puddler helper must help one year and be six months a member of the Association before he be allowed the privilege of boiling a heat."[79] After the union was destroyed, the skilled workers were no longer able to hire and train their own helpers.

Within a few years, employers, realizing that no new men were being trained, began to worry about their future supply of skilled workers. In 1905, *Iron Age* reported that

the imperative necessity of renewing the apprentice system on a general and comprehensive scale has become apparent to every employer who is dependent on the skilled mechanic (craftsman) for his working force.[80]

Statistics collected by the Department of Labor in 1910 show that the skilled workers were considerably older than the other workers, their median age being roughly 37 while that of semiskilled was 27 and that of unskilled workers was 26.[e] By the 1920s, the situation was critical. Associations of steel employers

---

[d]In other industries, a formal apprenticeship system provided the future skilled workers, and the attempts by employers to replace that system with a helper system was the source of much conflict between workers and employers in the 19th century. The importance of the distinction was that the apprenticeship system meant control by the skilled workers, and the helper system meant control by employers. In the steel industry, the helper system was controlled by the workers, so the distinction was not important.

[e]Calculated on the basis of table in *Labor Conditions*, p. 480. A more detailed age breakdown is:

Age	Skilled	Semiskilled	Unskilled
Under 30	29%	54%	52%
30-40	38	30	26
Over 40	33	16	22
Over 50	11	5	7

We would, of course, expect skilled workers to be somewhat older than the others, but we would hardly expect a variation of this extent.

decried the extinction of skilled workers at their conventions and in their publications. One contemporary economist, after a study of skilled workers in iron and steel foundries in Philadelphia, concluded

that there are proportionately too few men who are in their twenties and an exceptionally large number who are in their fifties and sixties . . . The number of complaints about the lack of apprentices voiced in all the publications has increased.[81]

During this period, employers began to develop a new type of skilled worker, one whose skills were highly specialized and limited in their scope. In 1912, *Iron Age* described the evolution of this class of workers:

That the supply of American mechanics is altogether too small is an old story. The apprentice system was permitted to die out and the relative supply of skilled men fell away rapidly. In the last ten years, a more or less organized effort has been made to increase the number and has met with considerable success. Nevertheless, the demand for this class of labor has increased so greatly that each year the proportion of trained men to the total number of mechanics which must be employed has become smaller.

The consequence has been that vast numbers of men have been trained for specialized work in machine shops, and improved machinery has made it possible to decrease the average excellence of workmen without reducing the quality of the product.[82]

In order to create this new class of skilled workers, employers set up a training system that was an alternative to the union-controlled apprenticeship system of the past, known as the "short course." The "short course" involved a manager or superintendent taking a worker who had been in a department long enough to get a feel for the process, and giving him or her individualized instruction in some specialized branch of the trade. By using the short course, employers could train workers for specific skilled jobs in a limited period of time. The training period varied, according to the skill being taught, from a few weeks to a year. The secretary of the Milwaukee branch of the National Metal Trades Association described the use of the short course in his district in 1924 as follows:

The handymen are usually helpers desiring to learn more of the trade—are over 21 years of age and usually limit their training to one special line.

And the chairman of a local association of foundrymen reported that same year that

In checking up the situation in this community, the committee found that generally most of the foundries were taking on inexperienced help and developing what has come to be known as specialty molders.[83]

In this way, a new class of skilled workers was created during the first two decades of the twentieth century. These workers were selected by the employers, trained in a short period of time, and then set to work with their job-specific skill. These workers had skills which were good for only one job. They did not have the independence of the nineteenth-century skilled workers, whose skills were transferable to other jobs and other plants. Nor did they have the generalized knowledge of the production process that skilled workers previously possessed. The knowledge they had was that which could serve their employer, but not that which could serve themselves.

Thus, the new skilled workers were a dependent class. The employers had created their dependency on purpose, as advice which appeared in *Iron Age* in 1912 reveals:

Make your own mechanics . . . The mechanics that you will teach will do the work your way. They will stay with you, as they are not sure they could hold jobs outside.[84]

The success of these policies can be judged from the following statement, made by the president of the American Rolling Mill Company in 1927:

Work has become so specialized in these mills that even men in the regular trades, who have not had mill experience, find it difficult to follow their trade until they have served another apprenticeship, which though not a formal one in the narrow sense is nevertheless a real one. So true is this, that furnace helpers and foremen melters of open hearth furnaces, trained in mills making common grades of steel, are unable to fill similar positions satisfactorily in "quality" mills, and, likewise, men trained for these jobs in "quality" mills have almost equal difficulty in mills where the emphasis is placed upon the making of large tonnage of common steel.[85]

2. Changing Role of the Foreman

As the employers expanded their control over the process of production, they realized they had to develop an alternative means for exercising control on the shop floor. Just as they had taken knowledge about production away from the skilled workers, employers also took away workers' authority over their own labor and that of their helpers. Now, the task of regulating production was transferred to the foremen, who previously had authority only over the pools of unskilled workers. Foremen were now seen as management's representatives on the shop floor. To do this, employers had to redefine the job of foreman and retrain the men who held those jobs.

In order to transfer authority to the foremen, the employers had to distinguish them from the skilled workers. This distinction had to be created; it did not evolve out of the new technology. Foremen were recruited from the ranks of the skilled workers—foremanship being the highest position to which a blue-collar worker could aspire. Once there, however, steel employers had to reeducate them as to their role in production. This reeducation began with convincing them *not* to do manual work, which was no easy task. An editorial in *Iron Age* in 1905 quotes one superintendent lecturing an audience of foremen as saying:

"You men have no business to have your coats off when on duty in your shops unless you are warm. You have no business to take the tools out of a workman's hands to do his work. Your business is to secure results from other men's work."

The editorial goes on to say why this is important:

A man cannot work with his hands and at the same time give intelligent supervision to a gang of men, and a foreman who does this is apt to lose the control of his men while he is weakening the confidence of his employers in his ability as a general.[86]

The foreman's job was to direct and correct the work, but never to do the work himself. His authority depended upon that. Foremen, as the lowest ranking "mind" workers, had to be made distinct from the manual workers. One steel company official likened the organization of authority to that of the "army, with the necessary distinction between the commissioned officers and the ranks."[87]

The companies had to give their foremen special training courses in order to make them into bosses. These courses were designed to teach the foremen how to "manage" their men. One such course, at the American Steel and Wire Company, a U.S. Steel subsidiary, spent most of its time on that subject with only a few sessions on production techniques or economics. As described by one of the instructors, the course

includes such subjects as the inherent qualities of the workmen, both physical and mental, temperament, fatigue, emotion, state of mind, and so on, how all these various factors affect the capabilities and efficiency of the men. The management course also includes external environments which affect the man's efficiency, the wage system, employment management, pleasure in work, the human cost of labor, the relations of foremen to the workers, relations of the foremen to the company, and scientific management and subjects of that kind.[88]

This development was not unique to the steel industry. Throughout American industry, special foremen's training courses were becoming prevalent. Dr. Hollis Godfrey, president of the Drexel Institute in Philadelphia, the first private institution concerned solely with foremen's training, said that the purpose of foremen training was to

make the skilled mind worker. The skilled mind worker is a little different proposition than the skilled hand worker, and a great many people are still wandering around in the differentiation between the two . . . From the foreman to the president right straight through, you have got one body of mind workers, and they do but two things: they organize knowledge and then they use the knowledge as organized.[89]

Although foremen did little work, they also did little thinking. Most of their training was designed to teach them how to maintain discipline—techniques for handling men, developing "team work," deciding who to discharge and who to promote. They were the company's representative in the shop, and as the companies consolidated their power over the workers, the strategic importance of the foremen increased.

3. New Types of Managers

Just as the authority that the skilled workers had previously possessed was transferred to the foremen, their overall knowledge about production was transferred to the managers. By adopting new methods for training skilled workers, steel employers took the generalized knowledge about the production process as a whole away from the skilled workers. In their place, employers began hiring a new class of white-collar employees, recruited from the public and private schools and their own special programs. These workers became the bottom rung of the management hierarchy.

Before 1900, most managers in the steel industry were men who had begun at the bottom and worked their way all the way up. Andrew Carnegie had insisted on using this method to select his junior executives. As he once said, boastingly, "Mr. Morgan buys his partners, I grow my own."[90] Carnegie developed a whole partnership system for the management of his empire based on the principle of limitless upward mobility for every one of his employees.[f] He felt that by "growing his own," he not only found those men who had proved their abilities and loyalty to the firm, but also inspired the others to work that much harder. Thus he wrote to Frick in 1896:

Every year should be marked by the promotion of one more of our young men. I am perfectly willing to give my interest for this purpose, when the undivided stock is disposed of. There is Miller at Dusquesne, and Brown, both of whom might get a sixth of one percent. It is a very good plan to have all your heads of departments interested, and I should like to vote for the admission of Mr. Corey; and if there is a sixth left, perhaps Mr. Kerr of the Edgar Thomson Blast Furnaces deserves it. We cannot have too many of the right sort interested in profits.[91]

[f]Although, Carnegie was generous in his disbursement of stock shares and seats on the executive committee, he had no intention of giving up corporate control. All his junior partners had to sign the "iron clad agreement," stipulating that in the event of death or dismissal, their shares would be returned to the Carnegie Steel Company, Limited, for which they would be paid the shares' book value. In this way, Carnegie could reward his "young geniuses" with partnerships and still keep them from challenging his control.

This attitude was well known throughout the Carnegie empire, with the result, as Carnegie's biographer puts it, that "just as Napoleon drove his soldiers on with the slogan that every foot soldier carried a marshall's baton in his knapsack, so Carnegie taught his men to believe that every worker carried a partnership in his lunch pail."[92]

Around the turn of the century, employers began to choose college graduates for their management positions. As one prominent steel official told a member of the British Iron and Steel Institute in 1903:

We want young men who have not had time to wear themselves into a groove, young college men preferably . . . When a college graduate, who shows that he has the right stuff in him, reaches the age of 25 or 30 years, he is ready for a position of trust. When men get older they may have acquired a wider experience, and, therefore, become more valuable as specialists, but for managers and executives we select young men with brains and education.[93]

This was not mere philosophy; the British visitors found on their tour that, of the 21 blast furnaces they visited, "18 were managed by college graduates, the majority of whom were young men."[94]

Employers used publically funded technical colleges to train their new managers. Technical colleges were new, established with the support of the business community and over the protest of the labor movement. As Paul Douglas wrote in 1921:

Employers early welcomed and supported the trade-school, both because they believed that it would provide a means of trade-training, and because they believed that it would remove the preparation for the trades from the potential or actual control of unions.[95]

Some steel employers also set up their own schools to train managers in the arts of steelmaking. For example, the Carnegie Company opened a technical school in Pittsburgh, in 1905. The purpose of the school was "providing instruction in those studies essential to a technical education" to applicants who were high school graduates.[96]

Technical training alone, however, was not sufficient to produce competent managers for steel factories. The young men also needed to know about steelmaking. To meet this need, the steel companies developed a new, on-the-job training program to supplement the formal learning of their young college graduates. This program consisted of short rotations in each mill department under the supervision of a foreman or superintendent, which gave the men experience in every aspect of mill work before they were put in managerial positions. This program was called an "apprenticeship," and although it trained managers instead of workers, it was an apprenticeship by the original meaning of the word. It gave the apprentices knowledge of each stage of the production process and how they fit together. A circular describing the apprenticeship system begun in 1901 at the Baldwin Locomotive Works, which trained both managers and lower-level personnel, stated:

In view of the fact that in recent years manufacturing has tended so largely toward specialization that young men apprenticed to mechanical trades have been able in most cases only to learn single processes, and, as a result, the general mechanic has threatened to become practically extinct, to the detriment of manufacturing interests generally, the Baldwin Locomotive Works have established a system of apprenticeship on a basis adapted to existing social and business conditions.[97]

The visitors from the British Iron and Steel Institute described the prevalence of the new apprenticeship system in their report of 1903:

In a number of the leading American [steel] works, the principals attach importance to binding, as apprentices or otherwise, lads and young men who have had the advantage of a first-class education . . . Indeed, in some cases, as at the works of the Midvale Steel Company, at Philadelphia, my attention was specifically called to the unusually large number of college graduates that were employed on the premises in various positions.[98]

By the 1920s, such methods were nearly universal throughout the industry. Charles Hook, the vice president of the American Rolling Mill Company, a U.S. Steel subsidiary, described his method for selecting and training managers in a speech of 1927 to the International Management Congress:

The condition as outlined respecting the selection of the "skilled" employee is quite different from the condition governing the selection of the man with technical education . . .

Each year a few second- and third-year [college] men work during the summer vacation, and get a first-hand knowledge of mill conditions. This helps them reach a decision. If, after working with us for a summer, they return the next year, the chances are they will remain permanently . . . Some of our most important positions—positions of responsibility requiring men with exceptional technical knowledge—are filled by men selected in this manner.[99]

The prospective managers, in short, were increasingly recruited from the schools and colleges, not from the shops.

In these apprenticeship programs, a distinction was often made between different types of apprentices, distinguished by their years of schooling. Each type was to be trained for positions at different levels of responsibility. For example, at the Baldwin Works, there were three classes of apprentices, such that:

The first class will include boys seventeen years of age, who have had a good common school [grammar school] education . . . The second class indenture is similar to that of the first class, except that the apprentice must have had an advance grammar school [high school] training, including the mathematical courses usual in such schools . . . The third class indenture is in the form of an agreement made with persons twenty-one years of age or over, who are graduates of colleges, technical schools, or scientific institutions ... [100]

Similarly, the application for indenture at the steel works of William Sellers and Company, in Philadelphia, read:

Applications for Indenture as First Class Apprentices will be considered from boys who have had a good common school education ... Applications for Indenture as Second Class Apprentices will be considered from boys who have had an advanced Grammar or High School training ... Applicants for a special course of instruction, covering a period of two years, will be considered from young men over twenty-one years of age who are graduates of colleges, technical schools or scientific institutions. [101]

Thus, formal education was beginning to become the criterion for separating different levels of the management hierarchy, as well as separating workers from managers.

During this period, employers redivided the tasks of labor. The knowledge expropriated from the skilled workers was passed on to a new class of college-trained managers. This laid the basis for perpetuating class divisions in the society through the educational system. Recently several scholars have shown how the stratification of the educational system functions to reproduce society's class divisions. [102] It is worth noting that the educational tracking system could not work to maintain the class structure were it not for the educational requirements that were set up at the point of production. These educational requirements came out of the need of employers to consolidate their control over production.

Within management, the discipline function was divided from the task of directing and coordinating the work. This is the basis for today's distinction between "staff" and "line" supervision. We might hypothesize that this division, too, had its origin in the desire of steel employers to maintain control over their low-level managerial staff.

The effect of this redivision of labor on the worker was to make his job meaningless and repetitious. He was left with no official right to direct his own actions or thinking. In this way, skilled workers lost their status as partners, and became true workers, selling their labor and taking orders for all their working hours.

Part 5: To the Present

Having assumed its modern corporate form by about 1910, the United States steel industry slipped into a period of relatively untroubled calm. The rapid pace of technological change and managerial innovation of the previous 20 years slackened, and the steel employers sat back to let monopoly capitalism flower. Demand for steel was expanding steadily, both domestically and internationally.

Judge Gary managed to stabilize steel prices and developed an informal price-fixing system that prevented steel companies from underbidding each other during recession periods. World War I was a tremendous boon for the steel companies, bringing big windfalls to the stockholders. And, generally speaking, the steel industry suffered no significant "labor troubles." The only exception was the 1919 strike, in which 350,000 steelworkers were out for 4 months, until the steel companies managed to crush them totally.

This calm produced a self-satisfied lethargy among the major steel companies—a lethargy from which the industry has not yet recovered. There were few major technological developments or capital investment programs until the 1960s. New steelmaking technology introduced in other countries was slow to be adopted here. Most notable for its lethargy was the U.S. Steel Corporation, which developed a widely quoted philosophy of "no inventions, no innovations." Although it remained the world's largest producer of steel, U.S. Steel's share of steel capacity in the United States fell from 65 percent in 1901 to 38 percent in 1936. The earnings on its stocks, which had averaged 12 percent between 1901 and 1911, fell to 2.8 percent between 1926 and 1936.[103] By then, the U.S. Steel Corporation had won a reputation among the business community for antiquated management, obsolete plants, archaic pricing policies, and an antediluvian attitude toward organized labor, expressed in blacklists and company spies.[104] As *Fortune* magazine concluded in its series on U.S. Steel in 1936, "The Steel Corporation has been seriously ill."

The labor system set up by the steel employers early in the century also has not changed. The essentials of the system—wage incentives, job ladders, welfare schemes, and a division of labor that kept skills highly job-specific—have lasted to the present.

The only major change in the industry's labor relations has been the union organizing drive of the 1930s, culminating in the establishment of the United Steelworkers of America. The union brought steelworkers job security and raised wages. For the first time, it gave workers a voice in the determination of working hours, working conditions, and fringe benefits. However, the presence of the union did not change the basic mechanisms of control that employers had established. This section deals with the impact of the union on the employers' control of production, and shows that although the union was able to alter the manner in which employers exercised control, it never challenged the heart of this control as institutionalized in the labor system.

Unionization of the steel industry was one of the most dramatic accomplishments of the CIO in the 1930s. By the Depression decade, U.S. Steel's long history of antiunionism and the open shop had led most people to believe that the corporation, and the industry as a whole, was impenetrable. As one historian of the union campaign, Robert Brooks, described it,

For forty years, steel had assumed the leadership of the anti-union movement. As steel had gone, the nation had followed. If steel could be captured for unionism, resistance elsewhere might be broken.[105]

The steel industry was of prime strategic importance to the CIO for several reasons. First, the industry employed hundreds of thousands of people, all of whom were potential dues-paying trade unionists. Second, the industry was central to the nation's economy, and its unionization would give the labor movement a great deal of political, as well as economic, leverage. And third, the open-shop policy of the industry was a direct hindrance to the unionization of other industries. *Fortune* magazine reported in 1936 that U.S. Steel was thought to impose its labor policy not only on the whole steel industry but also on its suppliers, "thus widening the spread of unorganized industry."

Machine works, electrical supply houses, tool makers, manufacturers of steel equipment, could, labor leaders claim, be organized without great difficulty and without great opposition from their operators if it were not that U.S. Steel orders would cease immediately with recognition of the union.[106]

Unionization of steel was of special interest to the United Mine Workers' President, John L. Lewis, who saw steel company-owned mines as a threat to unionism in the coal industry in general.

The story of how the steel industry was finally organized has been told many times.[107] The essentials are as follows. The National Industrial Recovery Act of 1933 contained a clause that said that workers had the legal right to organize. In response, and to ward off any real unionism, the steel companies began to set up company unions, called "employee representation committees," which were mechanisms for airing the workers' grievances without having any power to correct them. However, the steel companies' intention to co-opt union sentiment with these schemes backfired. Many of the company union leaders, elected by the steelworkers, were seriously interested in change and soon realized that the employee representation committees were shams. They began to meet with each other secretly, developing plans to bring real unionism into the industry.

At the same time, John L. Lewis broke with the craft unionism of the American Federation of Labor and set up the Congress of Industrial Organization to organize the mass production industries on an industrywide basis. As part of this effort, he founded the Steel Workers Organizing Committee (SWOC) and placed Phillip Murray, one of his officials from the United Mine Workers, at its head. Together, SWOC and the renegade company unions organized the steel industry, winning their first contract with U.S. Steel in March, 1937. The smaller steel companies held out against the union longer, and put up a bloody fight which culminated in the Memorial Day Massacre in 1938. But in the end, they too capitulated. By 1941, SWOC had won union recognition and signed contracts with all the major steel producers in the United States.

1. Impact of Unionization on the Wage Structure

By the 1930s, the rational wage structure of the steel industry degenerated into hopeless chaos. The basis for many of the job and pay distinctions had been eroded by minor changes in technology and job duties. By the 1930s, wage rates for the same job varied greatly from plant to plant and within individual plants. Furthermore, methods of payment differed greatly within job categories, between jobs, and between plants. Some workers were on straight piece rates, some on piece rates plus bonuses, some on time wages, some on time wages plus incentive bonuses, etc. According to Carroll Daughterly, an economist who studied the impact of the NRA on the industry,

A final point concerning the nature of wage rates in the industry requires emphatic underlining: The wage-rate structure is extraordinarily complex and varied, much more so in fact than those found in most other manufacturing industries.[108]

The different rates and methods of payment were a source of unending dissatisfaction among the steelworkers. Jack Steiber, former member of the Research Department of the United Steelworkers of America, reports that

The union found a ready-made issue in the problem of wage rate inequities and took advantage of the situation to gain members during its organizing drive in the 1930s. According to the union, "the hideous wage structure" of the industry was one of the main reasons for organizing.[109]

Once the union was organized, the issue became even more pressing. Workers began filing grievances about wage inequities and insisting on some form of corrective action. R. Conrad Cooper, Vice President for Industrial Relations of U.S. Steel, said at the time, "The issue of alleged inequities blossomed into an area of major controversy comprising about two-thirds of all grievances, slow-downs, work stoppages, strikes and collateral controversies."[110] Because wage-rate grievances were the overwhelming majority of all grievances once contracts were signed, the union had to come up with a plan for correcting the inequities.

That the dissatisfaction with the wage structure did not take the form of an attack on wage differentials per se, attests to the success of the companies' strategy that lay behind the whole incentive scheme. What workers defined as "inequity" was different payment for the same or similar work. They did not question differences in payment for different work. The divisive nature of the incentive plan led workers to compare their earnings to that of other workers and to perceive their problem as one of inequity among themselves, rather than comparing their earnings to the actual value of what they produced and perceiving their problem as one of inequity between themselves and their employers.

The United Steelworkers of America insisted on doing away with the obvious inequity of different pay for similar work, but did not challenge the basis for the differentials that remained. In the early years, they advised their committees to rate jobs in terms of physical effort, personal skill, hazards, strain, disagreeableness, education, and instruction required, and to weigh these factors in terms of their relative importance in order to devise an "equitable" scale for evaluating individual jobs. As far as actual ratesetting for incentives and bonuses is concerned, they recommended that these be worked out jointly by management and the union. Only occasionally did they question the idea of incentives, piece rates, and bonuses altogether. In an early manual to the committees called "Production Problems," written around 1940, they said at the end of a discussion on piece-rate adjustment,

It is not out of place to state here that any such debatable value to management as piece rates and bonus payments possess are often not worth the ill will and poor practices which these methods radiate. Yet it is important that both workers and executives should know how well they perform their work. This promotes continuing economy of course, but more important, it is usually needed for the complete satisfaction of personal aspiration and individual development. For these purposes, however, production standards are adequate and piece rates are not needed.[111]

During World War II, the issue of wage-rate inequities in the steel industry came before the War Labor Board. The union asked for the elimination of wage-rate inequities by the application of the principle "equal pay for similar work" throughout the industry. This demand was denied by the Board because, as one economist interpreted the ruling, "The Board refused to change its rule that existing wage differentials should be maintained so as not to unstabilize existing pay brackets."[112] The Board ruling of 1944 did, however, say that

The company and the union shall negotiate the elimination of existing intra-plant wage-rate inequities and reduction in the number of job classification in accordance with the following steps:
1. Describe simply and concisely the content of each job.
2. Place the jobs in their proper relationship.
3. Reduce the number of job classifications to the smallest practical number by grouping those jobs having substantially equivalent content.[113]

The Board also stipulated that the wage inequity adjustment should not cost any one company more than the equivalent of a raise of $.05 per hour for all its employees, and that no employee's wage should be reduced as a result of the reevaluation.

As a result of the Board's ruling, the union and the steel companies sat down together in 1945 to reclassify and reevaluate the entire industry's job and wage structure. This herculean task took 2 years to complete, and resulted in a job classification manual for the entire industry, a procedure for classifying new jobs, and a standard hourly wage scale on which all rates would be based. Here we see the formalization of one aspect of the internal labor market—the job hierarchy. The steel manual became the example for job reevaluation programs in other industries, and remains in effect in all major steel companies today.

The job reclassification program reduced the number of job classifications by about one-half, and those jobs it rated according to the following factors:[114]

Pre-employment training	1.0
Employment training and experience	4.0
Mental skill	3.5
Manual skill	2.0
Responsibility for materials	10.0
Responsibility for tools and equipment	4.0
Responsibility for operations	6.5
Responsibility for safety of others	2.0
Mental effort	2.5
Physical effort	2.5
Surroundings	3.0
Hazards	2.0

One of the interesting aspects of this weighting scheme is the relatively insignificant role given to skill factors—indicating once again the lack of important skill differentials between the jobs in steelmaking.

One of the most important results of the program, besides the drastic reduction in the number of job classifications in the industry, was the strict hierarchical order of the job classifications that remained. For example, the following passage describes the effect of the program at U.S. Steel:

[Prior to the program] U.S. Steel alone had had between 45,000 and 50,000 job titles. These were reduced [by the manual] by half, and what was more important, all of these were filed into thirty separate wage-rate classifications. Between each of these was a 3.5-cent-an-hour increment.[115]

A basic hourly rate was set for each wage-rate classification, with even gradations between them. It applied to all hourly rated jobs in the industry and set the minimum wage guaranteed for incentive jobs. Subsequently, the steel companies based the size of the incentive payments on the basic hourly rate as well. The union wholeheartedly supported the entire classification program, which rationalized the basis of the job hierarchies within the industry.

However, no such agreement was ever reached regarding the extra money workers would receive for extra output under incentive plans. In 1947, after the classification manual and the basic hourly rate were agreed upon, the union and the company tried to negotiate a basis for equitably setting incentive rates, based on the determination of a "fair day's work" standard. The parties spent 3 years trying to reach agreement before admitting failure.

The question of wage incentives has remained a source of conflict between the company and the union. For example, George McManus, in his book *The Inside Story of Steel Wages and Prices*, gives the following account of the 1959 contract negotiations in the industry: In addition to some wage demands and demands for tougher sanctions against wildcat strikes, the steel companies

demanded clear acceptance of management's right to develop incentives and establish sound practices. It sought clarification of scheduling rights referring to the speed of work.

Before the question of job reforms arose, an opinion survey showed steelworkers strongly opposed to a strike. Many authorities believe the most minimal terms would have been accepted by the union at this stage . . . The job reform program (proposed by the company) solidified the union. After the list of reforms was published, another opinion survey showed the workers ready to go down the line in resistance to management's blunder.[116]

The resulting strike lasted 120 days—one of the longest strikes in any major American industry.

The issue of incentives took a curious turn during the post-war years. More and more, the nonincentive workers resented the higher earnings of their incentive coworkers, and incentive workers with relatively low earnings demanded rate changes. The union's response was to demand that all workers be put on the incentive plan. As Elmer Maloy, director of the United Steelworkers' wage division, explained in 1953,

the fact that about half of our members are on incentive plans of one sort or another makes the elimination of all incentives quite a problem. We seem to be stuck with it.

Incentives should cover the greatest possible number of employees including maintenance, craft and service employees, if we are to cut down the present dissension.[117]

In short, steelworkers preferred wage incentives to the straight hourly rates simply because it meant better remuneration. The extension of incentive pay had ironically become a way of equalizing pay among different groups of workers. The result, as pointed out by Robert McKensie, was that

under pressure from the union, the steel industry has been forced to extend incentives to coke ovens, blast furnaces, and maintenance operations, not for industrial engineering reasons, but in order to minimize the earnings gap between incentive and non-incentive groups.[118]

The companies, following out the looking-glass logic of the situation, opposed this extension of incentives. From the standpoint of "industrial engineering," they served no purpose because they could not be counted on to increase worker output. As Steiber says,

company industrial engineers were not planning to install incentives in departments like coke ovens and blast furnaces where they were considered unwarranted. Most industrial engineers were of the opinion that workers could exert no positive influence on production in these units and any incentive installed would represent an outright gift.[119]

However, union pressure on this point was increasing throughout the 1950s. By 1956, U.S. Steel was the first steel company to agree to the principle of 100 percent incentive coverage. Since then, other companies have also included more and more workers under incentive plans. Thus, the steelworkers have managed, to a limited extent, to turn incentive pay to their own advantage.

In conclusion, the impact of the union was to rerationalize the wage structure, which it did through the job reclassification program. The result of the program was to build the notion of job hierarchy permanently into the wage structure. The subsequent movement toward equality of pay through extending wage incentives has been a retreat from the principles of the manual, but not a very significant one. The wage incentives are no longer the divisive element in the method of wage payment in the industry—the divisive element is the structure of the hourly rate itself. As Jack Steiber summarizes the impact of the new plan on the industry wage structure,

It was not until the introduction of a common job evaluation system, with complete participation and strong support from the union, that the pattern of uniformity was extended to classifications and rates at all levels of the wage structure. The maintenance of relative occupational differentials among base rates during the post-war period, when market forces and inflationary pressures were operating to narrow differentials, must also be ascribed to union and company influence.[120]

2. Effect of Unionization on Promotion Policies

One of the major accomplishments of the union was the limitation of favoritism as a basis for promotions and layoffs. The union restricted management's ability to use advancement prospects to motivate and manipulate workers, and instead insisted that length of service (i.e., seniority) be used as a basis for upgrading and downgrading. The very first union contract signed between SWOC and the five largest subsidiaries of U.S. Steel, on March 17, 1937, stipulated that

In all cases of promotion . . . the following factors shall be considered . . . (a) Length of continuous service, (b) knowledge, training, ability, skill and efficiency, (c) physical fitness, (d) family status, number of dependents, etc., (e) place of residence.[121]

Since then, the principle of seniority has been modified and refined in every subsequent agreement. Complex seniority systems have been developed, combining plantwide seniority with departmental seniority in a variety of ways, which spell out neatly defined paths of promotion within each plant in the steel industry. For example, in the 1968 contract between the United Steelworkers and the Jones and Laughlin Steel Corporation, 35 pages out of the 155-page agreement are devoted to the issue of seniority. The seniority clause begins with the simple idea that

promotional opportunities and job security in event of promotions, decrease of forces and recalls after layoffs should increase in proportion to length of continuous service.[122]

However, it takes 35 pages of detailed contract language to spell out the exact lines of promotion to which seniority shall apply, the rules regulating intradepartmental and intraplant mobility, the conditions under which seniority shall be modified by other factors, etc. This agreement is typical of all contracts in the steel industry today.

The addition of seniority as a basis for promotion altered the form but not the content of the system that had been established earlier. Although seniority limited favoritism in the granting of promotions, it did not question the hierarchical existence of job ladders which made that promotion system possible. In fact, just as the reclassification program rationalized the steps in the job ladder, seniority rationalized the worker's progress up it. The minutely graded job ladders developed around 70 years ago have survived, intact, to the present.

The British Iron and Steel Industry's productivity team, which visited the United Steel works in 1951, made this observation about promotion in the industry:

The training of American operatives over 18 years of age follows a pattern very similar to that in the British steelworks. It is almost entirely on-the-job training, starting with labouring work with opportunities to learn and perform jobs higher up the ladder of promotion. In a very few instances, there are specific training programmes for certain adult jobs, e.g., crane driving, but usually it is a question of learning by doing jobs under the supervision of existing operatives. In choosing men for promotion, seniority counts most, though ability and physical fitness are taken into consideration. Job security depends on length of continuous service.[123]

Likewise, the International Labour Organization's study, "Vocational Training Promotion in the Iron and Steel Industry," had this to say about promotion policies in the United States:

New workers for production shops usually enter one of the production departments as unskilled workers—either labourers or learners. They may subsequently rise by promotion to posts demanding higher qualifications. Training for production trades is given almost entirely "on-the-job," and workers are promoted from one operation to another as they acquire experience and skill.

As an example of the above, a worker starting as a labourer may advance to cinder snapper, keeper's helper, keeper, blower's helper and finally blast furnace blower. In the open hearth department, a man will start with general cleaning work and advance to door operator, cinder pit man, third, second and first helper and eventually melter. In the finishing mill, the line of promotion might be as follows: pit man, roll hand, manipulator, rougher, and finish roller. *To reach these skilled jobs takes a minimum of four or five years, but usually a much longer time is required.*[124] [Emphasis added]

This report reveals that promotion today, as before, bears little relationship to ability to perform the work, because workers are able to perform the skilled jobs long before they are actually moved into them. Thus, the promotion hierarchy is as artificial today as when it was first created.

Therefore, the establishment of seniority as a criterion for promotion has not affected the promotion system. In fact, seniority has helped to rationalize the system by taking it away from the discretion of the foreman and basing it on principles of fairness. An alternative might have been for the union to press for a system of job rotation, or some other nonhierarchical way of allocating work, using seniority only for purposes of layoffs.

The existence of job ladders has produced continual conflict among steelworkers, as it was originally intended to do. Steelworkers quite rightly regard the seniority list as the determinant of their prospects for advancement in their lifetime. The system, as it was developed, discriminates against some groups of workers, notably blacks and women. And yet, any attempt to change the seniority system meets with the most determined resistance and brings on bitter conflicts between different groups of workers. The job-ladder arrangement has been effective in dividing workers and allowing other kinds of divisions to be institutionalized. [In every case involving Title VII of the Civil Rights Act of 1964 (Equal Employment Opportunity section), the issue of revising seniority lists creates the most dissension. For example, a recent *New York Times* story (1/22/73) describes the racial tension at Bethlehem Steel's Sparrows Point Works resulting from a ruling that the discriminating seniority system had to be changed.]

Clark Kerr, an industrial relations specialist, pointed out the relationship between job ladders and labor "peace" in the postwar steel industry:

The iron and steel industry ... is not particularly famous as a center of strike activity ... It might rank somewhat higher [in its propensity to strike] were it not for the high degree of job differentiation which marks the industry and which both separates one worker from another and creates a ladder for each worker to climb.[125]

3. Impact of Unionization on Welfare Policies

The impressive welfare programs inside U.S. Steel Corporation that were set up after the turn of the century all came to an end during the 1930s. Some of the functions which the welfare programs provided were taken over by the state, as part of the New Deal social welfare programs. Other of the functions became issues for negotiation with the union, rather than being determined and run unilaterally by the company. Thus workmen's compensation, unemployment insurance, social security, and medicare are now provided by the state. Health insurance and pensions are now provided for steelworkers by the union-management contract. Health and safety conditions inside the plant are regulated by contract language, union-management safety committees, and, since 1971, by the federal government's Occupational Safety and Health Administration. The other welfare measures that involved company contributions to the community are now generally defunct. According to the 1951 British Productivity Team Report, "American training schemes and welfare activities are no better than the average progressive British firm."[126]

The transference of the welfare programs from company control to union and governmental control has rid them of their most manipulative features. No longer can a worker be denied a pension for "failing to show a proper interest in the welfare of the corporation." However, many of the union fringe benefits, most notably the pensions, are still based on length of service and as such, still operate to cut down worker mobility between jobs.

In the past decade, the strategy of the union and the labor movement in general has been to press for the federal government to take over all the social insurance programs—such as the current legislative fights for federal insurance of private pension plans, increases in social security benefits, and national health insurance. If they are successful, the effect would be the freeing up the labor market somewhat, by making it less costly for workers to change jobs in the middle of their working lives.

4. Impact of Unionization on Division of Labor

Unionization of the steel industry has also failed to change the redivision of labor through which employers took knowledge about the production process away from the workers. The SWOC did concern itself with the issue of training skilled workers, and it demanded a say in the establishment and operation of training programs. However, in its concern, it did not question the content of the training courses. In a handbook to committees of local unions entitled "Industrial Training" (c. 1940), the SWOC says:

Where unions have been established and collective bargaining relationships exist, there is an opportunity for unions to have a voice in the operation of training programs. They should insist through their representatives on the creation of joint committees to supervise the training programs. With union representation on such committees, they would be able to:

a. See that union members are not discriminated against when opportunities present themselves for advancement.

b. See that employees are given an opportunity for training with a view to advancement, both in acquiring skills and higher wages commensurate with such before new and less-experienced and well-trained employees are hired.

c. Safeguard the seniority rights of the normal working force as well as those new employees who are engaged because of the defense economy.[127]

In contrast, the American Federation of Labor, in 1940, adopted a position on training that insisted on the use of apprenticeship instead of skill-specific training. It read:

Control over training on the job and related supplementary instruction in the school must be provided for through union agreement. This committee should be responsible for the training program. Training on the job includes apprentice training as well as training for specific operations. Apprentice training looking to all-round craftsmen requires study and experience over years. There are no short cuts even in an emergency, but apprentice training systematically carried on over the years is necessary to assure industries an adequate supply of workers for this machine age.[128]

The difference between the SWOC and the AFL positions on training no doubt stems from the fact that the AFL was composed of craft unions, who were ever conscious of the monopoly power of their craft skills, while the SWOC was composed of steelworkers whose craft skills had been taken from them long ago. The steelworkers probably did not consider the possibility that their skills could be other than job-specific. Such was the success of the earlier redivision of labor.

The other side of the coin, as we saw earlier, was the transferring of generalized knowledge to the managers and the use of educational requirements to distinguish managers from workers. The British Productivity Team found in their 1951 visit that this practice was still in force, and still included a version of the "management apprenticeship programs" that were established in the early 1900s.

Recruitment of university graduates for staff positions is a regular practice. One firm visited has been operating for about thirty years what are called "loop" courses for graduates. Broadly speaking, these training courses, which provide knowledge of the production processes and the activities of the firm, are divided into three parts:

(a) Basic knowledge for all trainees (in some works, this includes three months of manual work);
(b) Specialized training to equip the individual to enter a particular field of employment;
(c) Actual training on the job.[129]

A study by the International Labour Organization in 1954 also found that in the United States, "More often than not, future supervisors are taken on by the companies as soon as they leave college and they start their careers with a spell of six months or a year as workmen in one of the departments in the plant."[130]

The International Labour Organization in another study found that steel companies were still concerned with the problem of establishing status relations between supervisors and workers, and solved it by giving "supplementary training which is essential once supervisors have been appointed in order to raise and define their status in relation to their subordinates and to ensure that their activities and those of the management are fully coordinated."[131]

The presence of the union did, however, make some difference regarding the authority of the foremen in the steel industry. The establishment of formal grievance procedures and seniority as a basis for promotion undercut the power that foremen had held on the shop floor. Often foremen reacted by ignoring the contracts altogether. According to the ILO,

A number of American iron and steel plants encountered this difficulty at the time when the United Steelworkers of America were negotiating their first collective agreements with the major companies. Many of them had to re-educate their foremen so as to help them adapt themselves to the new conditions in which they henceforth had to operate. During transitional periods of this kind, complications were inevitable. For example, at the Minnequa plant of the Colorado Fuel and Iron Corporation, a number of problems arose in the early days of the collective agreement because of the ignorance of many foremen concerning the rights and privileges granted to the workers under the agreement. Other difficulties arose from the old mentality which held that the management was always right. These difficulties, according to Rudolph Smith, were largely overcome by means of periodical meetings of foremen and supervisors on the operation of the collective agreement and particularly on the clauses dealing with seniority, promotion, hours of work, etc.[132]

Unionization forced steel management to reeducate their foremen once again.

Part 6: Conclusions

This chapter has traced the origin of the central institutions of the "internal labor market" in the steel industry—hierarchical job ladders, limited ports of entry, inducements to stay on the job, job-specificity of skills, and a sharp division between the physical and the mental work of production.

The bulk of the chapter has focused on the period between 1890 and 1920—the period of transition in the industry from a labor system controlled by the skilled workers to a labor system controlled by the steel employers. In that transition, the breaking of the skilled-workers' union, which was the institutional expression of their control over the production process, was only the first step.

Once the union was destroyed, labor discipline became a problem for the employers. This was the twofold problem of motivating workers to work for the employers' gain and of preventing workers from uniting to take back control of production. In solving this problem, employers were creating a new labor system to replace the one they had destroyed.

All the methods used to solve this problem were aimed at altering workers' ways of thinking and feeling—which they did by making workers' individual "objective" self-interests congruent with those of the employers and in conflict with workers' collective self-interest. The use of wage incentives and the new promotion policies had a double effect on this issue. First, they comprised a reward system, in which workers who played by the rules could receive concrete gains in terms of income and status. Second, they constituted a permanent job ladder so that over time this new reward system could become an accepted fact by new workers coming into the industry. New workers would not see the job ladders as a reward and incentive system at all, but rather as the natural way to organize work and one which offered them personal advancement. In fact, however, when the system was set up, it was neither obvious nor rational. The job ladders were created just when the skill requirements for jobs in the industry were diminishing as a result of the new technology, and jobs were becoming more and more equal in terms of the learning time and responsibility involved.

The steel companies' welfare policies were also directed at the attitudes and perceptions of the workers. The policies were designed to show the workers that it was to their advantage to stay with the company. This policy, too, had both short-term and long-term advantages for the steel employers. In the short run, it was designed to stabilize the work force by lowering the turnover rate, thus cultivating a work force rooted in the community that had much to lose by getting fired or causing trouble. In the long run, the policies were supposed to prevent workers from identifying with each other across industry lines, thus preventing the widening of strike movements into mass strikes. (The prevention of mass strikes continued to be a concern of employers well into this century. The provisions in the Taft-Hartley Law of 1947 that outlaw sympathy strikes and secondary boycotts are some of the most repressive aspects of that law.)

Employers also sought to institutionalize and perpetuate their newly won control over production by redividing the tasks of production so as to take knowledge and authority away from the skilled workers and to create a management cadre able to direct production. This strategy was designed to separate workers from management permanently, by basing that separation on the distinction between physical and mental work, and by using the educational system to reinforce it. This deterred workers from seeing their potential to control the production process.

In brief, then, this chapter has argued that labor market institutions are best understood in their historical context, as products of the relations between classes in capitalist society. Labor market institutions both are weapons in and are produced by the class struggle. Technology plays only a minor role in this process. Technological innovations by themselves do not generate particular labor market institutions—they only redefine the realm of possibilities. The dynamic element is the class struggle itself, the shifting power relations between workers and employers, out of which the institutions of work and the form of the labor market are determined.

Although this chapter has concentrated on the steel industry, the conclusions it reaches are applicable to many other major industries in the United States. The development of the new labor system in the steel industry was repeated throughout the economy in different industries. As in the steel industry, the core of these new labor systems was the creation of artificial job hierarchies and the transfer of skills away from workers to the managers.

Technological innovations in every major industry around the turn of the century had the effect of squeezing the skills levels of the work force, turning most workers into semiskilled machine operators. Paul Douglas, writing in 1921, found that the skill requirements were practically negligible in most of the machine-building and machine-using industries, especially the steel, shoe, clothing, meat-packing, baking, canning, hardware, and tobacco industries. He says, for example,

The wartime experience of the Emergency Fleet Corporation in training workmen for the shipyard trades furnishes interesting proof of how little time is required to master the main principles of a modern trade. Training courses were established in seventy-one yards under the direction of the Fleet Corporation. The men who were thus taught trades were drawn principally from unskilled work and from manufacturing . . . the average training period for all men in the seventy-one yards for which statistics were available was only nineteen days![133]

At the same time that jobs were becoming more homogeneous, elaborate job hierarchies were being set up to stratify them. Management journals were filled with advice on doing away with "dead-end" jobs, filling positions by advancement from below, hiring only unskilled workers for the lowest positions, and separating workers into different pay classes. This advice was directed at the problem of maintaining "worker satisfaction" and preventing them from "restricting output," i.e., fragmenting discontent and making workers' work harder. Thus, the creation of the internal labor market throughout American industry was the employers' answer to the problem of discipline inherent in their need to exert unilateral control over production. Were it not for that, a system of job rotation, or one in which the workers themselves allocated work, would have been just as rational and effective a way of organizing production.

At the same time, employers began a process which they called the "transfer of skill."[134] This meant giving managers the skills and knowledge that workers had previously possessed. They began to use technical colleges and to set up their own programs to train managers in production techniques. This development was aided by the methodology of scientific management, as Paul Douglas pointed out:

The amount of skill which the average worker must possess is still further decreased by the system of scientific management. The various constituent parts of the system, motion study, the standardization of tools and equipment, the setting of the standard task, routing, and functional foremanship, all divest the individual operative of much of the skill and judgment formerly required, and concentrate it in the office and supervisory force.[135]

Likewise, Samuel Haber, an historian studying the progressive period, says, "The discovery of a science of work meant a transfer of skill from the worker to management and with it some transfer of power."[136] Like the creation of job hierarchies, this transfer of skill was not a response to the necessities of production, but was, rather, a strategy to rob the workers of their power.

For the skills which were still needed on the shop floor, employers instituted changes in the methods for training workers that reduced their skills to narrow, job-specific ones. The basic social inefficiency of this policy should be obvious. In an era of rapidly changing products and production techniques, jobs and industries are constantly changing, causing major dislocations in the work force. Therefore, the rational job training policy would be to give people as broad a range of skills and understanding of modern technology as possible, so that they could be flexible enough to weather the shifts in technology and the economy through their capacity to change jobs. Instead, the system of job-specificity creates one aspect of what economists label "structural unemployment" by molding workers to single skill-specific occupations. This policy wastes both individual lives and socially useful labor power.

To varying degrees, the labor movement was aware of these developments while they were occurring. Many unions in the American Federation of Labor developed an early opposition to piece rates, and especially to bonus systems of Halsey, Taylor, and others. In 1903, the International Association of Machinists expressed their opposition to "work by the piece, premium, merit, [or] task," and prohibited its members from accepting such work. In 1906, the Brotherhood of Locomotive Engineers successfully refused to accept the bonus system on the Sante Fe Railroad. In 1907, the Molders Union, the Boot and Shoe Workers, and the Garment Workers all resisted the bonus and premium systems. In general, unions opposed both the piecework and the bonus systems, although an opinion poll of union policies conducted in 1908 to 1909 showed that "unions almost without exception prefer the straight piece system to premium or bonus systems."[137] In 1911, the executive council of the American Federation of Labor passed a resolution condemning "the premium or bonus system [because it would] drive the workmen beyond the point necessary to their safety."[138]

The growing opposition to scientific management in the labor movement went beyond a critique of the speed-up aspects of the bonus system. Samuel Gompers, founder and president of the AFL, was aware that Taylor's system meant the elimination of the role of the skilled craftsmen upon which the entire AFL was based. After reading Taylor's book *Shop Management*, he wrote to AFL vice president Duncan in 1911 that "I have no doubt that it would mean [the destruction of unionism] for it would reduce the number of skilled workers to the barest minimum and impose low wages upon those of the skilled who would be thrown into the army of the unskilled."[139] The machinists' union was one of the more vocal in its fear of this aspect of scientific management.

According to Milton Nadworny, in his book *Scientific Management and the Unions,* the IAM's "Official Circular No. 2"

revealed the craftsman's fear of a system which not only instituted a revolutionary approach to work, but which threatened to reduce his importance in the shop. The machinist, it contended, was no longer required to use his skilled judgment—the planning department provided full instructions; no longer was his "honor" relied upon—the stop watch determined the time of his job. To complete the scheme, the possibility of organized retaliation against the system was prevented because only individual bargaining was permitted.[140]

The Industrial Workers of the World had an even deeper understanding of the new labor system that was emerging and the dangers it posed to the working class as a whole. In the Manifesto of 1905, announcing the IWW founding convention, they warned that

Laborers are no longer classified by difference in trade skill, but the employer assigns them according to the machine to which they are attached. These divisions, far from representing differences in skill or interests among the laborers, are imposed by the employers that workers may be pitted against one another and spurred to greater exertion in the shop, and that all resistance to capitalist tyranny may be weakened by artificial distinctions.[141]

Thus, the IWW understood the full implications of the developments of hierarchy at the point of production. However, they failed, as has every other labor organization in this century, to develop a successful strategy for countering it on the shop floor.

In historical perspective, we can see that the institutions of the labor market were not the inevitable result of modern technology or complex social organization. They came about as part of the process of capitalists taking over production.

Under the old labor market system, the capitalists reaped profits from the production process but did not direct production themselves. The transition that this chapter has described is the process by which capitalists inserted themselves into a central position of control over production. As Karl Marx, in writing about this transition, put it, "In the course of this development, the formal subjection is replaced by the real subjection of labour to capital."[142]

The institutions of labor, then, are the institutions of capitalist control. They could only be established by breaking the traditional power of the industrial craftsmen. Any attempt to change these institutions must begin by breaking the power the capitalists now hold over production. For those whose objective is not merely to study but to change, breaking that power is the task of today. When that is done, then we will face the further task of building new labor institutions, institutions of worker control.

Notes

1. Fitch, John, *The Steel Workers* (New York: Charities Publications Committee, 1920), pp. 141-142.

2. Hogan, William T., *Economic History of the Iron and Steel Industry in the United States*, vol. 1 (Lexington, Mass.: Lexington Books, D.C. Heath and Co., 1971), p. 11.

3. Ibid., pp. 218, 224.

4. Ibid., p. 185.

5. Ibid., pp. 91-94.

6. Ibid., p. 85.

7. Ibid., p. 86.

8. Ibid., footnote, p. 460.

9. Carnegie, Andrew, *Autobiography* (Boston: Houghton-Mifflin, 1920), p. 238.

10. Montgomery, David, "Trade Union Practice and the Origins of Syndicalist Theory in the United States," mimeo., University of Pittsburgh, 1973, pp. 3-4.

11. Bridge, James H., *Inside History of the Carnegie Steel Corporation* (New York: Aldine, 1903), pp. 201-202.

12. Fitch, *The Steel Workers*, p. 102.

13. Doeringer, Peter B., "Piece Rate Wage Structures in the Pittsburgh Iron and Steel Industry—1880-1900," *Labor History*, 9(2), Spring, 1968, pp. 266-267.

14. Great Britain, Iron and Steel Institute, *Journal and Special Proceedings, 1890*, "The Iron and Steel Industry in America in 1890," Vol. 38 (London, 1890), p. 173.

A further description of the non-labor-saving effects of the changing technology can be found in the U.S. Department of the Interior, *Report on the Statistics of Wages in Manufacturing Industries in the Tenth Census* (1880), vol. 20, 1886, p. 115.

15. Sahlin, Axel, quoted in Hogan, *Economics of Iron and Steel*, p. 214.

16. Quoted in Brecher, Jeremy, *Strike!* (San Francisco: Straight Arrow Books, 1972), p. 53.

17. Ibid., p. 62.

18. Robinson, Jesse Squib, *Amalgamated Association of Iron, Steel and Tin Workers* (Baltimore: The Johns Hopkins University Press, 1920), p. 20.

19. Brody, David, *The Steel Workers in America: The Non-Union Era* (Cambridge: Harvard University Press, 1960), pp. 9-11.

20. Jeans, J. Stephan, *American Industrial Conditions and Competition* (London: The British Iron Trade Assoc., 1902), p. 121.

21. Poppelwell, Frank, *Some Modern Conditions and Recent Developments in Iron and Steel Production in America* (Manchester: The University Press, 1906), p. 103.

22. Jeans, *American Industrial Conditions*, p. 503.

23. Ibid., p. 551.

24. Bridge, *History of Carnegie Steel Corporation*, p. 164.

25. Brody, *The Steel Workers in America*, pp. 48-49.

26. Jeans, *American Industrial Conditions*, p. 561.

27. *Report on Conditions of Employment in the Iron and Steel Industry in the United States*, vol. 3, U.S. Commissioner of Labor, 1913, p. 81. (Hereafter cited as *Labor Conditions.*)

28. Jeans, *American Industrial Conditions*, p. 317.

29. Fitch, *The Steel Workers*, pp. 153, 156.

30. Ibid., p. 157.

31. Ibid., p. 159.

32. Ibid., pp. 153, 156.

33. Quoted in Brody, *The Steel Workers in America*, p. 32, in *Labor Conditions*, Chapter 9.

34. *Labor Conditions*, vol. 3, pp. 236-237.

35. Taylor, F.W., *Shop Management* (New York: Harper and Bros., 1911), p. 186.

36. Jeans, *American Industrial Conditions*, p. 58.

37. Ibid., p. 55.

38. "Wage Payment Systems: How to Secure the Maximum Efficiency of Labor," *Iron Age* (May 19, 1910): 1190.

39. Ibid., p. 1191.

40. Taylor, *Shop Management*, p. 52.

41. National Industrial Conference Board, *Systems of Wage Payment* (New York: National Industrial Conference Board, 1930), p. 25.

42. Taylor, *Shop Management*, p. 183.

43. "Union Restriction of Output," *Iron Age* (June 15, 1905): 1901.

44. National Industrial Conference Board, *Systems of Wage Payment*, p. 60.

45. Cotter, Arundel, *The Story of Bethlehem Steel* (New York: Moody Magazine and Book Co., 1916), p. 21.

46. U.S. Labor Bureau, Senate Document No. 521, *Report on Strike at Bethlehem Steel Works, May 4, 1910*, 61st Congress, 2nd Session, 1910.

47. Jeans, *American Industrial Conditions*, p. 62.

48. Ibid.

49. Bloomfield, Meyer, *Labor and Compensation* (New York: Industrial Extension Institute, 1921), p. 295.

50. Ibid., p. 297.

51. Ibid., p. 298.

52. Hook, Charles R., "The Selection, Placement and Training of Employees," Third International Management Congress, Rome, Italy, 1927.

53. Williams, Whiting, *What's on the Worker's Mind?* (New York: Scribner's Sons, 1920), p. 152.

54. "Developing Employees," *Iron Age* (June 14, 1900): 49-50.

55. *Iron Age* (March 30, 1905): 1093.

56. Gary, Elbert, *Addresses and Statements*, vol. 6 (New York: Museums of the Peaceful Arts, 1922), March 29, 1922.

57. Poppelwell, *Some Modern Conditions*, pp. 110-111.

58. Fitch, *The Steel Workers*, p. 142.

59. Brody, *The Steel Workers in America*, p. 107.

60. Fitch, *The Steel Workers*, p. 148.

61. Ibid., p. 15.

62. Ibid., p. 339.

63. Ibid., p. 334.

64. Quoted in Gulick, Charles, "The Labor Policy of U.S. Steel Corporation," *Studies in History, Economics and Public Law* 116(1): 143.

65. Eastman, Crystal, *Work-Accidents and the Law* (New York: Charities Publications Committee, 1910).

66. *Iron Age* (August 3, 1905): 289.

67. Gulick, Charles A., "The Labor Policy of U.S. Steel Corporation," pp. 168-175.

68. Cotter, Arundel, *U.S. Steel: Corporation with a Soul* (Garden City, N.J.: Doubleday, Page & Co., 1921), p. 141.

69. Garraty, John, *Right-hand Man* (New York: Harper & Row, 1960), p. 54.

70. Ozanne, Robert, *Century of Labor-Management Relations at McCormick and International Harvester* (Madison: University of Wisconsin, 1967), chapter 4.

71. Garraty, *Right-hand Man*, p. 11.

72. Garraty, John, "U.S. Steel vs. Labor," in *Labor History I* (1960).

73. *Yearbook of the American Iron and Steel Institute*, 1912, p. 118.

74. Gary, Elbert H., *Addresses and Statements*, vol. 4, (January 21, 1919).

75. Quoted in Montgomery, "Trade Union Practice," p. 8.

76. Taylor, F.W., *Shop Management*, p. 99.

77. Haber, Samuel, *Efficiency and Uplift* (Chicago: University of Chicago Press, 1964), p. 24.

78. Quoted in Ashworth, John H., *The Helper and American Trade Unions* (Baltimore: Johns Hopkins Press, 1915), p. 75.

79. Ibid., footnote on p. 73.

80. "The Modern Apprenticeship System," *Iron Age* (October 24, 1905), 1092.

81. Williams, Alfred Hector, "A Study of the Adequacy of Existing Programs for the Training of Journeymen Molders in the Iron and Steel Foundries of Philadelphia," Ph.D. Dissertation, University of Pennsylvania, 1924, pp. 41-42.

82. *Iron Age* (March 14, 1912): 679.

83. Williams, "Programs for the Training of Journeymen Molders," p. 46.

84. *Iron Age* (November 28, 1912): 1263.

85. Hook, "The Selection, Placement and Training of Employees," pp. 14-15.

86. *Iron Age* (July 6, 1905): 24.

87. Fitch, *The Steel Workers*, footnote on p. 149.

88. "Training the Supervisory Work Force," minutes of the First Bi-monthly Conference of the National Association of Employment Managers, 1919, p. 25.

89. Ibid., pp. 9-10.

90. Hendrick, Burtal Jesse, *Life of Andrew Carnegie* (New York: Doubleday, 1930), vol. 1, p. 297.

91. Quoted in Wall, Joseph Frazier, *Andrew Carnegie* (New York: Oxford University Press, 1970), p. 665.

92. Ibid., p. 666.

93. Jeans, *American Industrial Conditions*, p. 500.

94. Ibid., p. 501.

95. Douglas, Paul, *American Apprenticeship and Industrial Education* (New York: Columbia University Press, 1921), p. 323.

96. *Iron Age* (July 6, 1905): 24.

97. Jeans, *American Industrial Conditions*, p. 351.

98. Ibid., p. 67.

99. Hook, "The Selection, Placement and Training of Employees," pp. 15-16.

100. Jeans, *American Industrial Conditions*, p. 351.

101. Ibid., p. 353.

102. See Bowles, S., and Gintis, H., "I.Q. and the U.S. Class Structure," *Social Policy* (January-February, 1972).

103. "U.S. Steel, Part I," *Fortune* 8(3), March, 1936.

104. Bernstein, Irving, *The Turbulent Years* (Boston: Houghton-Mifflin, 1970), pp. 458-459.

105. Brooks, Robert R., *As Steel Goes* (New Haven: Yale, 1940), p. 244.

106. "U.S. Steel, Part III," *Fortune* 8(5): 136, May, 1936.

107. See Bernstein, *The Turbulent Years*; or Brooks, *As Steel Goes.*

108. Daughterly, Carroll, *Economics of Iron and Steel*, vol. 1, p. 145.

109. Steiber, Jack, *The Steel Industry Wage Structure* (Cambridge: Harvard University Press, 1959), p. 4.

110. Quoted in Steiber, *The Steel Industry Wage Structure*, p. 5.

111. Golden, Clinton S., "Production Standards," Steel Workers Organizing Committee, Pittsburgh, p. 20. The document itself contains no date, but the copy used was obtained by the M.I.T. library in February, 1943, and is the fifth edition, so that we can infer that it was originally written no later than 1940.

112. DeVyver, Frank T., in Warne, Colston, *Labor in Post-War America* (Brooklyn: Remsen Press, 1949), p. 388.

113. "Inter-plant Wage Relationships," U.S. National War Labor Board, Research and Statistics Report No. 29, part 2, p. 22.

114. Robert Tilove, "Steel Wage Rationalization Program," *Monthly Labor Review*, 64:6, (June, 1947): 978.

115. DeVyver, in Warne, *Labor in Post-War America*, p. 391.

116. McManus, George J., *The Inside Story of Steel Wages and Prices, 1959-1967* (Philadelphia: Chilton Book Co., 1967), pp. 15-17.

117. Quoted in Steiber, *The Steel Industry Wage Structure*, p. 224.

118. McKensie, Robert B., "Changing Methods of Wage Payment," in Dunlop, J.T. and Chamberlain, N.W., *Frontiers of Collective Bargaining* (New York: Harper and Row, 1967), p. 185.

119. Steiber, *The Steel Industry Wage Structure*, p. 226.

120. Ibid., pp. 320-321.

121. Hogan, *Economic History of Iron and Steel*, vol. 3, p. 1175.

122. "Agreement between Jones and Laughlin Steel Corporation and the United Steelworkers of America," August 1, 1968, p. 98.

123. "Iron and Steel," Productivity Team report, Anglo-American Council on Productivity, 1952, p. 83.

124. "Vocational Training and Promotion in the Iron and Steel Industry," International Labour Organization, 1952, p. 28.

125. Kerr, C., and Siegel, A., "Inter-industry Propensity to Strike," in Flanders, Allan, *Collective Bargaining* (London: Faber, 1967, footnote on p. 142.

126. "Iron and Steel," Productivity Team report, p. 20.

127. Quoted in "Selecting, Training and Upgrading," National Industrial Conference Board, 1941, p. 8.

128. Ibid., p. 9.

129. "Iron and Steel," Productivity Team report, pp. 83-84.

130. "Human Relations in the Iron and Steel Industry," International Labour Organization, p. 98.

131. "Vocational Training and Promotion Practices in the Iron and Steel Industry," International Labour Organization, p. 37.

132. "Human Relations in the Iron and Steel Industry," ILO, p. 83.

133. Douglas, *American Apprenticeship and Industrial Education*, p. 116.

134. For example, see L.P. Alford's speech to the American Society for Mechanical Engineers, 1922, titled "Ten Years Progress in Management," and the discussion that followed.

135. Ibid., p. 120.

136. Haber, *Efficiency and Uplift*, pp. 24-25.

137. Nadworny, Milton, *Scientific Management and the Unions* (Cambridge: Harvard University Press, 1955), pp. 25-26.

138. Ibid., p. 51.

139. Quoted in Nadworny, *Scientific Management and the Unions*, p. 53.

140. Ibid., p. 56.

141. Quoted in Kornbluh, Joyce, *Rebel Voices* (Ann Arbor: University of Michigan Press, 1968), p.

142. Marx, Karl, *Capital* (New York: International Publishers, 1967), vol. 1, chapter 16.

3

Notes for a Study of the Automobile Industry

Francesca Maltese

What I want to present is a very sketchy, preliminary set of notes concerning the early history of this industry. Although I have just recently begun this research, and therefore it is very tentative, nevertheless I think some of the main trends are clear.

This particular study deals with the Ford Motor Company. This company was chosen because it was the most successful of the early auto manufacturers, and because it led the industry in technological change and concurrent social organization.

The basic relations of production in the auto industry which characterize its production in the first stage from 1900 to 1912 were essentially inherited from the bicycle industry. There are several reasons why it turned out that the automobile industry developed in its early stages with a production process patterned after the bicycle industry (in contrast it might, for instance, have developed from the wagon industry). The automobile had many similar mechanical features, like pneumatic tires, ball bearings, and differential axles. The workers who made these parts were skilled mechanics and machine-tool artisans. The typical bicycle factory of the 1890s was organized around skilled mechanics who assembled the bicycles from parts made in separate metal-working firms, rubber plants, etc. A large number of bicycle manufacturers became interested in automobiles, particularly as the bicycle boom of the 1890s declined. Faced with declining demand, the bicycle manufacturers moved from the dying bicycle industry into the growing auto industry and brought with them the technical skill, organizational plans, and skilled mechanics that formed the basis of early auto manufacture. Many of the bicycle plants had been located in New England. It turned out that many of the auto manufacturers who began to dominate the industry in its earliest stages—from about 1902 to 1906—were located in the Detroit area. As the New England bicycle plants themselves collapsed with the decline of demand, the Detroit producers were actually forced to go to the New England area to recruit the increasingly unemployed bicycle mechanics, for those skilled artisans were the only available workers who possessed the necessary skills to put the first cars together.

The first home of what was to become the Ford Motor Company in fact reflected the productive organization of the bicycle plants. It was a small shop that contained two lathes, two drill presses, a milling machine, a wood planer, a hand saw, a grinding wheel, and a forge. Its labor force consisted of four mechanics, one patternmaker, a draftsman, and a blacksmith. This was in October, 1902. They produced one car by December and then moved their "operation" to a remodeled wagon shop, using an Olds gasoline engine for power to run their equipment. The labor force was increased to about 125 workers, and the company put out 1,700 cars that year. All parts were contracted out. Only the assembly and the designing of some of the parts were done in the shop. In the plant itself, the workers operated as a team. They planned production, solved design problems, and constructed the entire cars together as a unit. That was the way they had learned to build bicycles, and those were the working relations they brought to cars.

The automobile industry was growing rapidly. As demand increased and the market for cars grew even larger with the advent of moderately priced autos, manufacturers had to begin to standardize parts, and in order to do so, had to introduce a series of new machines into the factories. Although there were nearly continual technological changes introduced during this period from 1905 to 1912, they were all incorporated into the traditional work system.

By 1906 the Model N was developed as a car that could be mass-produced because of its many standardized parts. Equipment involved in both assembly and parts production was moved to a newly remodeled plant on Piquette Avenue. The equipment—some of it newly designed—was arranged in a new way with many consecutive operations placed near one another. This was a break with traditional factory layouts where similar operations were placed in the same area. Parts were stockpiled at the most convenient places.

As production increased, Ford found that its own plant was capable of producing 100 cars per day, but that bottlenecks developed because outside parts manufacturers could not meet the increasing demands for their products. Ford was forced to incorporate more and more parts production within its own plant.

In 1908 Ford realized its plans for an easy-to-operate, plain, sturdy car, and the Model T was placed on the market for a price of $850. Within one year 11,000 cars were sold—ranking Ford the number one automobile manufacturer in the country. In order to meet this further expansion of sales, Ford had to continue the experimentation with new technology.

Ford engaged Walter E. Flanders, a well-known factory expert whose innovations spurred production to 10,000 cars in 12 months. Although Flanders only stayed with Ford for one year, his ideas were incorporated into the operations of the new factory at Highland Park that opened in 1910 and went into full use in 1911. Previous production plans were scrapped. Where they had only begun to group consecutive functions at the Piquette plant, in this new plant even machines such as brazing furnaces and cyanide baths, ordinarily "relegated to separate and despised" quarters, were placed in the natural production line. Tools and stock were moved out of the cribs and placed on the floor between assemblers to avoid running back and forth. Ford hired an inventor for the sole purpose of designing machines to speed production. He produced ideas "at such a pace that to get them on paper it took a staff of 200 designers, working day and night." New tools were also being designed to produce parts that were precisely alike. In 1928 Victor S. Clark, in his book *History of Manufacturing in the United States, 1860-1914*, said of the auto industry, "No other single industry has exercised more influence upon the development of machine tools and particularly of special tools...." New machines poured into the factory almost daily between 1910 and 1913. Workers and machines were moved constantly on a moment's notice, crowded in between the growing piles of tools and supplies. Ford kept on developing and trying out new timesaving schemes. Gravity slides were installed next to each operation. When a worker was through with a particular part, he or she merely had to drop it on the slide where it slid to its next destination.

As was said before, all these technological innovations were superimposed on the original organizations of work and workers inherited from the bicycle industry. The pace of innovation had been so rapid that the workers still considered themselves skilled mechanics, and had not yet reduced their expectations about their own work. They seemed to assume that the innovations were temporary and that production would return to its former orientation toward teamwork with skilled mechanics' being the organizers of that production and assembly process. Many assemblers were assigned to teams and moved from chassis to chassis performing their one specialized function. Each gang had a group of helpers and runners to fetch tools and supplies.

In fact, however, order never returned. With each innovation, the process of production got more and more confused. By this time it was almost impossible to walk around a plant. It was so crowded with workers, machines, tools, and stockpiles that a person couldn't move without falling over a coworker or materials. Fights broke out between workers. Workers were pushed to deliver higher rates of production. The absentee rates was 10 percent per day of the entire work force, and the average length of stay was said to be under 18 months.

Workers were further disoriented because their jobs were becoming increasingly specialized, and they were losing their sense of the production process as a whole. Jobs were fractionalized so that a worker could concentrate on a smaller and smaller area of responsibility and improve his/her efficiency in that operation. Numbers of new "Helper" jobs were created so that the assembler would have to make fewer and fewer trips from his or her station to get work materials—further removing the worker from the days when the process of production was experienced from beginning to end. In addition, the increasing specialization of tasks brought more and different kinds of workers into the plant—each one with specific functions. Workers became less and less familiar with the jobs that their coworkers were performing.

The technological solution to the chaotic conditions existing in the factory was, of course, the moving conveyor belt, which was first introduced in 1913 at the Highland Park plant. The principal intent of the new system was to "get the work off the floor." The assembly line set the pace for all workers. Jobs were again specialized, reaching a point where the workers could perform all their duties without moving their feet. Traditional skills were further undermined, and, as two efficiency experts studying the plant in 1914 to 1915 observed,

As to machinists, old-time, all-round men, perish the thought! The Ford Company has no use for experience, in the working ranks, anyway. It desires and prefers machine-tool operators who have nothing to unlearn, who have no theories of correct surface speeds for metal finishing, and will simply do what they are told to do, over and over again, from bell time to bell time.[1]

But while the endless conveyor represented a technical solution to the problem, it by no means implied a complete solution since it was also necessary to ensure that workers would accept the new conditions of employment—to ensure that workers would, to borrow a phrase from the previous quote, "do what they are told to do." There are, in fact, some indications that workers resisted the changes in their jobs, and while these indications do not provide evidence that such opposition created a crisis for the firm, subsequent Ford policies seem clearly to have been designed to ensure that further worker problems would not disrupt the smooth functioning of assembly operations.

In the first place, the installation of the belt appeared to workers as an obviously permanent change. It provided concrete evidence that their illusions about maintaining or recapturing their earlier craft and gang system were futile.

Worker resistance in the Ford factory manifested itself in soaring turnover rates as well. In 1913 turnover increased so greatly that in order to maintain a work force of 15,000, Ford had to hire 500 new workers each day.

Moreover, organized labor had begun to make its presence felt in the automobile industry. The Ford Company's first run-in with "organized discontent" was in 1912, but it wasn't in Detroit. The previous year Ford had purchased the John R. Keim mills in Buffalo, New York, a pressed-steel factory. Although the workers were paid straight wages for Ford work, they received piecework rates on outside contracts. Dissatisfied, the workers called a wildcat strike in September. Trying to escape the problem, Ford merely moved the machinery, management, and loyal machinists to Detroit and converted the mill into an assembly plant.

The Detroit branch of the Industrial Workers of the World (IWW) began its major attempts at organizing auto workers in about 1910. At that time Ford was only the sixth largest employer in the industry, and the Wobblies concentrated their major efforts elsewhere. But the IWW labeled Ford the "Speed-up King," demanded better wages, and disputed the absolute authority of a foreman over the workers. Everyday there were IWW leafleters around the Ford Company. At first Ford merely had them arrested. Finally he resorted to denying Ford workers the right to go outdoors at lunch time. In June, 1913, the Wobblies called a strike of 2,000 workers at the Studebaker plant, indicating that Detroit could no longer rest easily on its reputation as an "open-shop town."

Finally, the period 1910 to 1913 was one of considerable labor unrest in the U.S. generally. Any manufacturers of the time would have looked uneasily at signs of unrest within their industry. As the records of the National Civic Federation show, for instance, most of the large corporations were frightened by the intensity of the Lawrence, Massachusetts strike of 1912, and tried to work with the Lawrence employers to resolve the conflict.

In order to protect itself against any threat of further worker resistance, Ford turned to a conscious labor market strategy to induce workers to accept the new relations of production. In several different ways, Ford systematically sought to create a supply of surplus labor available to the automobile industry. The point of generating such pools of surplus labor was precisely to establish a quick and obvious sanction to workers employed on the line. If they failed to adjust to the new operations, if they failed to perform as specialized semiskilled workers, there would be hundreds of men outside the plant gates, both eager to take their jobs and capable of performing them.

There had not in fact been surplus labor available in Detroit before the assembly line was established. In 1912, the Employers' Association of Detroit—representing producers in all industries—pooled resources in order to increase the flow of labor into the area. Before then, each individual employer had been advertising separately for workers within the Detroit area. The competition for workers simply defeated each individual employer's purposes, for a constant supply of workers was flowing back and forth among plants, further disrupting and confusing production. So, in 1912, the employers abandoned competitive advertising and established a joint fund to finance joint advertisements outside Detroit. Nevins reports that the Association advertised in 191 cities across the country, announcing the availability of work and urging workers to join in the city's growth.

One potential source of labor supply neglected by other manufacturers was that of physically handicapped people. These people were referred to in Ford terminology as "substandard men." Ford began his practice of hiring them sometime around 1913. Since industrial accidents were quite common—in 1917, 1,363,000 workers were injured in the manufacturing industries—this was quite a large pool, and it expanded at the close of World War I.

The second strategy was in many ways the more important and the more successful. In January, 1914, Ford announced the new profit-sharing program, better known as The Five Dollar Day. In 1913 the average daily wage for line workers was $2.34. Although there were many catches connected to earning $5 per day, and it is questionable how many workers actually benefited by this new policy, there is no question that Ford itself benefited tremendously. The morning after the company made the announcement of the new wage and its plans to hire more workers, 10,000 people were lined up clamoring for employment. Even though a riot resulted and police drove people away by turning a fire hose on them, people continued to clog the entrances to Ford's employment office daily. 1913 and 1914 were depression years. As the news spread, people flooded Detroit, hoping for employment at Ford. There can be no question about the intent of the $5-per-day plan. Since it was introduced during years of depression, Ford could obviously have met his demand for labor in the plants by continuing to offer a wage at roughly the previous year's level of $2.34 or even below it. The intention was not to meet the demand for workers, but to create surplus.

Ford also took an active interest in recruiting young workers. As production increased and workers were pushed to work at faster and faster paces, it was found that younger workers could maintain the pace better. In 1916 the Henry Ford Trade School was established "for the benefit of boys whose circumstances compel them to leave school at an early age and go to work." The boys' schooling was divided into two parts—academic and industrial. They spent one week in the classroom and two in the shop. According to the book published by the Ford Company in 1924, "The boys produce a wide variety of Ford parts as well as such delicate precision instruments as gages. . . . Most of the cut-away motors seen in Ford sales rooms are made by the boys out of rejected parts. All work done in the shops is bought by the Ford Motor Company if it passes inspection." In 1924 there were 700 enrolled in the school, and a long waiting list existed. Although none were forced to work at Ford when they graduated, the book states that "most boys prefer to work for the Company."

A further strategy which has continued to the present, but which had its roots in this period, involved the integration of blacks into the production force. In 1910 the U.S. Census Bureau reports that only 569 blacks were employed in motor vehicle and motor vehicle parts industries—constituting only 0.5 percent of the total labor force. More blacks were admitted to the labor force during World War I. By 1920, the black population of Detroit had increased 600 percent—from 5,741 to 40,838. By 1926 Ford employed 10,000 of the total 11,000 blacks employed in the industry in Detroit. Although most of these workers were put to work in the foundry or in other undesirable places, some were hired for the line. It was clear that the company regarded blacks as qualified for assembly-line jobs, and their rapidly growing presence in the city helped increase the total surplus pool.

Overt signs of discontent disappeared from the Ford factories. The efficiency experts, Arnold and Faurote, who studied the Ford Company in 1914 to 1915, summarized the consequences of these strategies:

New regulations, important or trivial, are made almost daily; workmen are studied individually and changed from place to place with no cause assigned, as the bosses see fit, and not one word of protest is ever spoken, because every man knows the door to the street stands open for any man who objects in any way, shape or manner to instant and unquestioning obedience to any directions whatever. . . . Willful insubordination is, of course, absolutely intolerable, and Ford workers must be, first of all, docile.[2]

Notes

1. Arnold and Faurote, *Ford Methods and the Ford Shops.* New York: The Engineering Magazine Co., 1915..
2. Ibid.

Bibliography

Adams, Walter, *The Structure of American Industry* (New York: Macmillan, 1950).

Adcraft Club of Detroit, *Study of the City of Detroit* (Detroit, 1929).

Arnold, H.L. and Faurote, F.L., *Ford Methods and the Ford Shops* (New York: The Engineering Magazine Company, 1915).

Arnold & Schwinn Co., *Fifty Years of Schwinn-Built Bicycles* (Chicago, 1945).

Automobile Manufacturers Association, *A Chronicle of the Automobile Industry in America* (Detroit, Mich., 1952).

Barber, H.L., *Story of the Automobile* (Chicago: A.J. Munson & Co., 1917).

Basset, W.R. and Heywood, J., *Production Engineering and Cost Keeping* (New York: McGraw-Hill Book Company, 1922).

Beasley, Norman, *Knudsen* (New York: McGraw-Hill Book Company, 1947).

Beasley, N., and Stark, G.W., *Made in Detroit* (New York: Putnam, 1957).

Benson, Allan L., *The New Henry Ford* (New York: Funk & Wagnalls Co., 1923).

Brissenden, Paul F., *The History of the I.W.W.* (New York: Columbia University Press, 1920).

Brooks, Robert R.R., *When Labor Organizes* (New Haven, Conn.: Yale University Press, 1937).

Burlingame, Roger, *Henry Ford* (New York: Alfred Knopf, 1955).

Chinoy, Eli, *Automobile Workers and the American Dream* (Garden City, N.Y.: Doubleday & Company, Inc., 1955).

Clark, Victor S., *History of Manufacturers in the United States, 1860 to 1914*, vol. 2 (Washington: The Carnegie Institute, 1928).

Colvin, F.H. and Stanley, F.A., *Running a Machine Shop* (New York: McGraw-Hill Book Company, 1941).

Cunningham, H.M. and Sherman, W.F., *Production of Motor Vehicles* (New York: McGraw-Hill Book Company, 1951).

Doolittle, James R., ed., *The Romance of the Automobile Industry* (New York: The Klebold Press, 1916).

Dunn, Robert W., *Labor and Automobiles* (New York, International Publishers, 1929).

Employers Association of Detroit, *Roster and Classified Business Directory*, (Detroit, Mich.: March 1, 1918), (pamphlet).

Epstein, Ralph C., *The Automobile Industry* (New York: A.W. Shaw Company, 1928).

Faulkner, Harold U., *The Decline of Laissez Faire, 1897-1917* (New York: Rinehart, 1951).

Fine, Sidney, *The Automobile under the Blue Eagle* (Ann Arbor: University of Michigan Press, 1963).

Fisher, Thomas R., *Industrial Disputes & Federal Legislation* (New York: Columbia University Press, 1940).

Ford, Henry, *Moving Forward*, in collaboration with Samuel Crowther (Garden City, N.Y.: Doubleday, Doran & Co., Inc., 1930).

_____, *My Life and Work*, in collaboration with Samuel Crowther (Garden City, N.Y.: Doubleday, Page & Co., 1923).

Ford Motor Company, *The Ford Industries* (Detroit, Mich.: The Ford Motor Company, 1924).

Gambs, John S., *The Decline of the I.W.W.* (New York: Columbia University Press, 1932).

Griffin, Clare E., *The Life History of Automobiles* (Ann Arbor: University of Michigan Press, 1928).

Howe, I., and Widick, B.J., *The UAW and Walter Reuther* (New York: Random House, 1949).

Jacobson, Julius, ed., *The Negro and the American Labor Movement* (Garden City, N.Y.: Doubleday and Co., 1968).

Jones, F.D., and Hammond, E.K., *Shop Management and Systems* (New York: The Industrial Press, 1918).

Kennedy, E.D., *The Automobile Industry* (New York: Reynal & Hitchcock, 1941).

Knoeppel, C.E., *Maximum Production* (New York: The Engineering Magazine, 1911).

Leggett, John C., *Class, Race & Labor: Working Class Consciousness in Detroit* (New York: Oxford University Press, 1968).

Leonard, Jonathan N., *The Tragedy of Henry Ford* (New York: G.P. Putnam's Sons, 1932).

Leonard, J.W., *The Industries of Detroit* (Detroit, Mich.: J.M. Elstner & Co., 1887).

MacDonald, Robert M., *Collective Bargaining in the Automobile Industry* (New Haven, Conn.: Yale University Press, 1963).

Marquis, Samuel S., *Henry Ford, An Interpretation* (Boston: Little, Brown & Company, 1923).

93

McPherson, William H., *Labor Relations in the Automobile Industry* (Washington: The Brookings Institute, 1942).

Miller, James M., *Henry Ford* (Chicago: M.A. Donohue & Co., 1922).

Nevins, Allan, *Ford: The Times, The Man, The Company* (New York: Charles Scribner's Sons, 1954).

Nevins, A. and Hill, F.E., *Ford: Expansion and Challenge* (New York: Charles Scribner's Sons, 1957).

Northrup, Herbert R., *The Negro in the Automobile Industry* (Philadelphia: University of Pennsylvania Press, 1968).

Pipp, E.G., *The Real Henry Ford* (Detroit, Mich., 1922).

Pratt, Charles E., *The American Bicycler: A Manual* (Boston: Houghton, Osgood, and Company, 1879).

Rae, John B., *American Automobile Manufacturers* (Philadelphia: Chilton Company, 1959).

_____, ed., *Henry Ford* (Englewood Cliffs, N.J.: Prentice-Hall, Inc., 1969).

Rauschenbush, Carl, *Fordism* (New York: League for Industrial Democracy, 1937) (pamphlet).

Seltzer, Lawrence H., *A Financial History of the American Automobile* (New York: Houghton Mifflin Company, 1928).

Sennett, A.R., *Carriages Without Horses Shall Go* (London: Wittaker & Co., 1896).

Simonds, William A., *Henry Ford, Motor Genius* (Garden City, N.Y.: Doubleday, Doran & Co., Inc., 1929).

Sinsabaugh, Chris, *Who Me?* (Detroit, Mich.: Arnold-Powers, Inc., 1940).

Sloan, Alfred P., *Adventures of a White-Collar Man* (New York: Doubleday, Doran and Co., Inc., 1941).

Sorenson, Charles E., *My Forty Years with Ford*, in collaboration with Samuel T. Williamson (New York: Norton, 1956).

4

Class Consciousness and Stratification in the Labor Process

Howard M. Wachtel

> "Status-consciousness . . . masks class consciousness;
> in fact it prevents it from emerging at all."
>
> Georg Lukacs, "Class Consciousness," p. 58.

Ask almost anyone and they will tell you that the most prominent feature of Marxian political economy is the analysis of class and class struggle. With such stirring formulations as "The history of all hitherto existing society is the history of class struggles," from *The Communist Manifesto*, how could one think otherwise? Nevertheless, although class, class consciousness, and class struggle do play a prominent role in Marxian political economy, Marx, himself, never produced in one place a complete and comprehensive analysis of class. One reason for this is that the Marxian class categories are accepted as part of the analysis in classical political economy.[a] Marx, however, was not unaware of the analytical complexity and importance of class as he wanted to use the category. Volume 3 of *Capital* ends with two scant pages of an unfinished chapter on "Classes," with Engel's notation that "here the manuscript breaks off."

Although Marx dissected the labor process in the capitalism of his day for purposes of illuminating its contradictions, little has been done since his time in constructing an appropriate analysis of the labor process in monopoly capitalism. A central argument of this chapter is that the transition of capitalism from its competitive to monopoly phase was accompanied by an equally important transition in the labor process. The consolidation of the competitive phase of capitalism produced a homogeneous labor force in which workers were, for the most part, deprived of their skills and forced into relatively undifferentiated and

This material has appeared in the *Review of Radical Political Economics.* (Permission to reprint from publisher and author.)

Many people contributed comments on this paper: Larry Sawers, Ray Boddy, Marty Wolfson, Gordon Welty, Manuel Benedito, Howard Sherman, Dawn Day Wachtel, and members of the editorial board of the *Review* (especially including Amy Bridges and Sam Bowles).

[a]See Marx's letter to J. Wedemeyer (March 5, 1872) in which he says:

> no credit is due to me for discovering the existence of classes in modern society or to the struggle between them. Long before me bourgeois historians had described the historical development of this class struggle and bourgeois economists the economic anatomy of the classes. (Marx and Engels, p. 69)

unskilled jobs. The transition to monopoly capitalism was accompanied by a stratification of labor in which workers became highly differentiated. This alteration in the labor force had its roots both in technological changes and in developments in the social relations of production. And these changes in the labor process have consequences for the development of a working-class consciousness as additional contradictions are evoked by a stratified labor force working in hierarchically organized relations of production.

Objectively, classes are distinguished by their relations to the production process, more specifically whether one produces or appropriates surplus value. However, this objective distinction provides few clues to the dynamics of class relations which form the basis for an analysis of social change. For the purpose of this analysis, class consciousness is a central focus. Though more and more people become proletarianized in an objective sense as capitalism matures—that is, larger proportions of the population produce surplus value and fewer appropriate it—subjectively there appears to be a dimunition in class consciousness as capitalism develops in its monopoly phase. Marx himself did not think that workers would of necessity develop a revolutionary consciousness in all instances. However, his analysis led him to the conclusion that contradictions within capitalism itself would propel workers toward a unified class consciousness.

Central to his analysis was the unification of workers produced by contradictions within capitalism, especially the physical grouping of workers into larger and larger factories and the homogenization of labor in which workers were deprived of their skills and forced to work as "unskilled" workers on undifferentiated tasks that required only raw labor power. However, with the development of monopoly capitalism, labor has become stratified with workers acquiring sharp status differences, a fact which mitigates their identification with a class.

The central issue for understanding contemporary events revolves around an analysis of contradictions within a stratified labor process which perhaps have the potential for eroding the status-identifying aspects of stratification and once again creating a relatively more unified working-class consciousness. These are the analytical and empirical issues which this chapter addresses, particularly the dissection of contradictions within the labor process of monopoly capitalism, the manifestations of these contradictions, and the responses to these contradictions by workers and capitalists (and their agents).

The Analysis of Class in Marx

At the most general level, Marx's conceptualization of class revolves around the concept of *surplus*—its mode of production, its qualitative form, its quantitative changes over time, and the mode of control of the surplus. The most convenient formulation is to view surplus as the production of goods and services in excess of the reproductive cost of labor power (necessary subsistence), modified to take account of some notion of social subsistence, or customary standard of living.

Classes, in Marx's formulation, are defined as the highest level of abstraction in terms of whether one *produces the surplus* or *controls the production of the surplus and lives off the production of that surplus*, the latter class producing no surplus (or even necessary goods and services). For a shorthand notation, we will speak of class division in terms of one class *producing* the surplus and the other class *appropriating* the surplus.

The class formations of precapitalist systems were analyzed by Marx in terms of the social relations surrounding the production and appropriation of surplus, in particular, the peculiar qualitative form which surplus took in those societies as well as its quantitative changes over time. As Marx stated the proposition (volume 1, p. 217),

The *essential* difference between the various economic forms of society, between, for instance, a society based on slave-labor, and one based on wage-labor, lies *only* in the mode in which this surplus-labor is in each case extracted from the actual producer, the laborer. [Emphasis added]

The origins, production, and appropriation of *surplus value* (the unique form of surplus in capitalism) form the point of departure for an analysis of classes in capitalism. These classes, it is important to stress, emerge out of the *production process*, the same as in, for example, slavery or feudalism, and not the *exchange process* as is posited by most mainstream social scientists' definition of "class" which in fact defines "status."

The analysis of the production and appropriation of surplus value lies at the center of Marxian political economy. And the production and realization of surplus value (through the sale of commodities) lie at the core of the dynamic analysis of capitalism—what Marx called the "laws of motion" of capitalism. Important as these questions are, I am forced, by reason of space and logical development, not to treat these issues fully, leaving the reader to pursue other sources for this analysis. (See Marx, Meek, Sweezy, 1968, and Dobb.)

Obviously this categorization of class, as the producers and appropriators of surplus value, is not inclusive in the sense that it does not accurately capture the status of other groups in the society which may in fact form a class. The most prominent example, of course, is the middle class, that group which neither produces nor appropriates the surplus value. Marx tended to abstract from this segment of society, viewing them as playing an inconsequential role in history.[b] Referring to England, Marx wrote (volume 3, p. 885):

---

[b]This is obviously a crude first approximation of a definition of middle class, but one that is usable for purposes of this chapter. For a discussion of the use of abstraction, see Sweezy, 1968, Chapter 1. Marx in his *Class Struggles in France* uses a more variegated definition of class to explain short-term events as does Mao in his "Analysis of the Classes in Chinese Society."

Nevertheless, even here the stratification of classes does not appear in its pure form. Middle and intermediate strata . . . obliterate lines of demarcation everywhere. . . . However, this is immaterial for our analysis. We have seen that the continual tendency and law of development of the capitalist mode of production is more and more to divorce the means of production from labor, and more and more to concentrate the scattered means of production into large groups, thereby transforming labor into wage-labor and the means of production into capital.

In sum, the normal way classes are defined in a shorthand fashion in Marx, as the "relation to the means of production," is seen to have a very specific political-economic meaning, namely, the relations surrounding the production and appropriation of the surplus value.

Class Consciousness

This conceptualization of class in Marx's analysis is solely an *objective* classification, in that it depends entirely on one's relationship to the means of production, or more specifically on whether an individual produces or appropriates the production of the surplus value. It makes no statement whatsoever about the strength of the two classes, their respective degrees of class consciousness, the degree of antagonism of the class struggle, and so forth. All that it does establish are the *objective circumstances* in which workers and capitalists relate to one another in the production process. The next step in the analysis is to see how these objective circumstances contribute to class consciousness and manifest class antagonism. Frequently, the term *classes* in a *subjective* sense is employed to capture the essence of the distinction posed in this section.

In the next few pages I present the analysis of class consciousness and labor market stratification in an abbreviated and summary form, to be expanded as the analysis unfolds.

The term *classes* in a subjective sense implies the existence of a unified economic class that has attained sufficient class consciousness to begin to define its own political position, to control its ideology, and to become an important force in history. This is the point at which Marx's analysis ceased to be a purely analytical-descriptive one of capitalism and became a dialectical analysis of history based on a historical materialist model.

Marx correctly foresaw the increasing proletarianization of the labor force in an *objective* sense—more and more individual artisans and farmers finding themselves forced into wage labor in order to survive the increasing capitalization of all aspects of the economy. This prediction was remarkably accurate; the data on the increasing number of sectors coming under wage labor are irrefutable, along with the concentration and centralization of capital (see Reich, p. 175). Marx also saw the objective grouping of wage laborers becoming more than merely a statistical category. He saw them becoming a class in a subjective sense (a class for itself) in which proletarian consciousness would be assisted by the overall dynamics of capitalist development: the physical unity of workers provided by the large factory, the increasing severity of the business cycle, the increasingly intense struggles over the distribution of surplus value, and so on.

He saw labor becoming united into a class capable of acting for itself on the subjective or consciousness level.[c] If Marx was solely interested in analyzing capitalism in a static sense, he could have been content with the purely objective questions where his insights have been proved accurate. But for a dynamic and dialectical analysis of social change, one needs to integrate both objective and subjective forces, which renders the assignment much more difficult.

For a Marxian analysis of the evolution of workers as a class, there is a dilemma: in an objective sense more and more people are becoming proletarian-ized, while in a subjective sense labor today appears to be more and more politically divided, with apparently only a declining segment having attained anything approaching a proletarian consciousness. The solution to this dilemma lies in an understanding of the principal offsetting tendency to the proletarian-ization of the population in an objective sense: *work stratification. Stratifica-tion*, as used here, refers to objective *divisions among members of a class*. The dynamic response of capitalists to the quantitative growth of the working class and its increasing class consciousness has been to stratify labor. (For shorthand notation, I use the terms *capitalist* and *working class* response to capture obviously more complex dialectical interactions.)

Consequently, while proletarianization and the attainment of a subjective working-class consciousness and unity accompanied the evolution of capitalism, monopoly capitalism appears to be accompanied by a fragmentation of the working class. This has been caused largely by increasing social and economic stratification which has eroded and negated the tendency toward the consolida-tion of a working-class consciousness, while at the same time solidifying the capitalist class through the process of economic concentration and centraliza-tion. Rather than a class united for itself, labor appears to be a class divided within itself. However, the very process of stratification has produced contradic-tions which perhaps have potential for eroding the divisive aspects of worker stratification, a central question analyzed later in this chapter.

To understand the origins and the role of labor market stratification in the contemporary situation, we must place these current developments in their appropriate historical context. The transformation of handicraft workers and artisans to a proletariat parallels the transformation of the economy from one dominated by handicraft production, to one dominated by the factory system

---

[c]This latter analysis is sometimes (mistakenly) taken to be that of the young Marx—his penetrating analysis of alienation and the deteriorating quality of life under capitalism—while stress on the objective forces is (mistakenly) taken for the old Marx. In reality there was one Marx whose analysis necessarily encompassed both objective and subjective forces.

(manufacture), to one dominated by modern industry. In the initial phase of the transformation—from petty commodity production to manufacture—technology had not yet been substantially altered. Essentially, all that had been altered was the organization of production. Sweezy (1972a, pp. 129-130) has commented at length on this transformation:

> The methods and instruments of production in the new factories were essentially those of the artisan workship; but now, owing to the larger number of workers involved and the complete domination of the production process by the capitalist, it became possible to subdivide the work and specialize workers ... Manufacture differs from handicraft production in its organization of the labor process, not in its basic methods and instruments. In handicraft production artisans produce saleable commodities and buy what they need ... Division of labor within the workshop is severely limited ...

This transition from petty commodity production to manufacture was an intermediate stage between handicraft production and the competitive capitalism of modern industry which Marx analyzed. As well, this transition in the organization of production created the basis for the transition of the artisan to a "Marxian" proletariat. It provided an intermediate phase in the development of the type of proletariat which Marx referred to in *The Communist Manifesto*. But this transition in the organization of production produced a particular qualitative dimension in the embryonic proletariat; it created (Sweezy, 1972a, p. 130):

> ... a highly differentiated labor force, dominated, numerically and otherwise, by skilled workers who tend to be contentious and undisciplined but incapable of sustained revolutionary activity. The economy and society based on manufacture is thus inherently change-resistant: it expands under the impact of capital accumulation but does not generate forces capable of altering its structure or, still less, of transforming it into something else.

This labor force, in short, was highly *stratified*; old lines of status hierarchy in work were carried over from petty commodity production, and in some cases, skilled workers continued to exercise substantial control over the work process. The master, the journeyman, and the apprentice no longer had those titles (in some instances), but workers still retained (both objectively and subjectively) those sharp status differences. As a consequence, the necessary ingredients for class unity were absent. It took a further alteration in the organization of production—the introduction of modern industry engendered by some important technological changes—to lay the seeds for the creation of a Marxian proletariat.[d]

---

[d]Marglin has argued that these technological changes were introduced to maximize capitalist control of the production process at the expense of workers. This had the effect of increasing the rate of surplus value produced. The manipulation of existing technologies in the short run is one of the most important devices capitalists have to increase the rate of surplus value. However, epochal transitions are normally accompanied by important technological changes (what Marx called the forces of production) which, for a time, can be

The principal features of this change in the organization of production involved the introduction of new machines which obliterated old skills and a new organization of the labor process which altered the social relations of production, leading to an increase in the rate of surplus value. The deskilled workers began to approximate a mass of *homogeneous* labor with nothing to offer but raw *labor power*. Hence the abstractions which Marx employed in his analysis of this phase of capitalism were quite reasonable; workers were becoming increasingly deskilled and homogeneous, and what they had to offer to the new organization was not work skills but labor power.[e]

The important point here is that the deskilling of the work force and their forced assemblage into large factories were initially instituted by capitalists' use of the new technology for reasons of control over the labor time of workers and for the purpose of increasing and capturing the augmented surplus value (see Marglin). However, it was this process in itself which produced the contradictions which Marx thought would lead to the unification of the working class through an aroused class consciousness.

One of the key elements in this transformation of the working class, which is rarely discussed, is the importance of the integration of workers into new social relations of production. A hypothesis derived from this point is that one of the more important factors which politicizes and radicalizes workers is the abrupt transition from one set of social relations of production into another. Marx witnessed such a transition, and, no doubt, this influenced his observations concerning the potential political role that workers were to play in a socialist revolution. However, the obverse of this hypothesis must also be examined—namely, that stability in the social relations of production over many years and generations depoliticizes workers, reducing their radical outlook. It is interesting to note the following passage from Marx where he recognizes the importance of this point (Marx, volume 1, p. 737):[f]

more important than the control of existing technology by a dominant class. In brief, there is a dialectical interaction between technology and the relations of production whose outcome is a result of the power configurations subsumed in the class struggle.

[e]Sweezy (1972a, pp. 137-138) has commented on this transformation as follows:

machinery does away with, or at any rate drastically reduces, the need for special skills and instead puts a premium on quickness and dexterity. It thereby opens the door to the mass employment of women and children and cheapens the labor power of adult males by obviating the need for long and expensive training programs. There follows a vast expansion of the labor supply which is augmented and supplemented by two further factors: (a) once solidly entrenched in the basic industries, machinery invades ever new branches of the economy, underselling the old handworkers and casting them onto the labor market, and (b) the progressive improvement of machinery in industries already conquered continuously eliminates existing jobs and reduces the employment-creating power of a given rate of capital accumulation.

[f]Engels, in an 1892 letter to the American Socialist F.A. Sorge, makes a similar point (Marx and Engels, pp. 451-452):

The American worker imagines that the traditional bourgeois regime he inherited is something progressive and superior by nature and for all time, a *non plus ultra*. . . .

The advance of capitalist production develops a working-class, which by education, tradition, habit, looks upon the conditions of that mode of production as self-evident laws of Nature. The organization of the capitalist process of production, once fully developed, breaks down all resistance.

The *qualitative* transformation of the work force in modern industry is accompanied by a *quantitative* transformation as well. As modern industry expands and as the drive for accumulation out of surplus value expands, more and more previously independent farmers and artisans become decapitalized and are forced into wage labor in order to survive. So not only is the proletariat transformed qualitatively, it is also augmented quantitatively. But the mere quantitative increase in the proletariat is not sufficient to render it a revolutionary agent in Marx's sense. If one argues that the quantitative growth in the proletariat is all that is required for it to become a revolutionary agent, then this necessarily implies that (Sweezy, 1972b, p. 120)

The proletariat was revolutionary from its birth and that only quantitative predominance was required for it to be able to perform its revolutionary function; for there is nothing in the mere mechanics of the expanded reproduction process to bring about a *qualitative* transformation of the proletariat . . . in Marx's view the proletariat was *not* a revolutionary force from its birth but on the contrary acquired this quality in the course of its capitalistic development.

The proletariat becomes revolutionary in the Marxian sense only when it acquires a *class consciousness.* This notion of class consciousness is one of the more elusive of all concepts in Marxian social theory. And its elusiveness has fostered sloppy analytical usage.

The attainment of class consciousness in Marxian social theory has two elements: an objective and a subjective. The objective side of the coin derives from Marx's analysis of the creation of surplus value in capitalism, the subjective side from the analysis of class consciousness. The analysis implies that capitalists will attempt to maximize their surplus value by attempting to use any means necessary to keep wages low and to increase the productivity of their existing capitals by speed-ups and by lengthening the working day. These tendencies in capitalism, at this stage of immediately postprimitive accumulation, unchecked as yet by any offsetting tendencies, produce the following results (Sweezy, 1972a, p. 138):

Wages are driven down to, and often below, the barest subsistence minimum; hours of work are increased beyond anything known before; intensity of labor is stepped up to match the ever increasing speed of the machinery. Machinery thus

---

The class struggles here in England, too, were more turbulent during the *period of development* of largescale industry and died down just in the period of England's undisputed industrial domination of the world. . . . It is the revolutionizing of all traditional relations by industry *as it develops* that also revolutionizes people's minds. (emphasis in original)

completes the process of subjecting labor to the sway of capital that was begun in the period of primitive accumulation. It is the capitalistic employment of machinery, and not merely capitalism in general, which generates the modern proletariat as Marx conceived it.

While this deskilled homogeneous mass of labor power is rendered weaker economically in this organization of production, Marx thought its political strength would be substantially increased owing to the contradictions inherent in the process itself. Sweezy (1972a, p. 138) has commented on these contradictions as follows:

Old geographical and craft divisions and jealousies are eliminated or minimized. The nature of work in the modern factory requires the organization and disciplining of the workers, thereby preparing them for organized and disciplined action in other fields. The extreme of exploitation to which they are subjected deprives them of any interest in the existing social order, forces them to live in conditions in which morality is meaningless and family life impossible, and ends by totally alienating them from their work, their products, their society and even themselves. Unlike their predecessors in the period of manufacture, these workers form a proletariat which is both capable of, and has every interest in, revolutionary action to overthrow the existing social order.

Stratification of Labor

Although class consciousness is an elusive concept, its importance cannot be underestimated. The Polish sociologist Ossowski would even go so far as to argue that a class is only a class in the Marxian sense when that class attains class consciousness. Ossowski (pp. 152-153) formulates the proposition thusly:

An aggregate of people which satisfies the economic criteria of a social class becomes a class in the full meaning of this term only when its members are linked by the tie of class consciousness, by the consciousness of common interests, and by the psychological bond that arises out of common class antagonisms. Marx is aware of the ambiguity and makes a terminological distinction between *Klasse an sich* and *Klasse fur sich* . . .

Lukacs is one of the few Marxists to have attempted an analysis of class consciousness. But even his important work ("Class Consciousness") leaves one without a precise way to formulate the process of attainment of class consciousness, nor does it provide identifiable indicators of whether class consciousness has been attained or whether class consciousness is growing or declining among the working class over a particular period of time. The proletariat, if it is to aspire to a unified class consciousness (according to Lukacs), must define its own ideology and penetrate its immediate surroundings in order to see its day-to-day problems in terms of the social system, capitalism, of which it is an integral part.[g] In addition, the proletariat must have both the desire for power and the means to develop the organizational experience so that it "can become conscious of the actions they need to perform in order to obtain and organize power" (Lukacs, p. 53). In short, in Lukacs' view, the crucial political question in the attainment of class consciousness requires that the proletariat (Lukacs, p. 76)

> must become a class not only "as against capital" but also "for itself"; that is to say, the class struggle must be raised from the level of economic necessity to the level of conscious aim and effective class consciousness.

Though the *tendencies* toward the development of a unified class consciousness exist in capitalism, there are important *offsets* which arise and can potentially negate the tendencies. The outcome, of course, depends on the relative strength of the tendencies and their offsets.[h]

The offsets to the tendency toward increasing class unity bring us next to the concept of *labor stratification*. The evolution of capitalism, from its phase of modern industry to monopoly capitalism, has been accompanied by a *qualitative* change in the working class, just as the transition from manufacture to modern industry produced a qualitative change in the working class in that historical epoch. While the tendency toward proletarianization of the population in an objective sense has continued (or even accelerated), the *qualitative* character of the working class has changed. *Homogenization* of the work force under modern industry has been supplanted by *stratification* under monopoly capitalism. And, in fact, monopoly capitalism is a phase of capitalism which fosters and facilitates labor stratification. Not only does it control technologies so that it can maximize the status-stratifying dimension of technological change, but the growing surplus value produced enables it, as well, to stratify labor by income, creating what is conventionally called a "labor aristocracy" (Sweezy, 1972b, p. 160):

> In short, the first effects of the introduction of machinery—expansion and homogenization of the labor force and reduction in the costs of production

---

[g]Consider this citation from Lukacs (p. 52):

> if from the vantage point of a particular class the totality of existing society is not visible; if a class thinks the thoughts imputable to it and which bear upon its interests right through to their logical conclusion and yet fails to strike at the heart of that totality, then such a class is doomed to play only a subordinate role.... Such classes are normally condemned to passivity, to an unstable oscillation between the ruling and the revolutionary classes, and if perchance they do erupt then such explosions are purely elemental and aimless.

[h]Marx, his critical interpreters notwithstanding, rarely dealt with the outright *predictions* attributed to him. He was too astute a scientist for crude predictions. Instead, it is the subtlety of the social dynamics produced by the inherent tendencies and their offsets in capitalism that consumed most of his intellectual and political energies.

[value] of labor power—have been largely reversed. Once again, as in the period of manufacture, the proletariat is highly differentiated; and once again occupational and status consciousness has tended to submerge class consciousness.

Paul Romano has described the impact of stratification on workers from his experience as a worker in the late 1940s (Romano, p. 35):[i]

The wage scales and classifications in the shop are extremely numerous. It is a continual battle to reach a higher classification and more money, with one worker competing against another. Much anger is generated between workers and against the company over upgrading or promotions to new jobs. Every time a new job is open, a bitter wrangle takes place. It is not predominantly a question of the nickel raise involved, as it may seem on the surface, but a desire for recognition and a chance for exploitation of one's own capabilities.

The drive toward stratification in monopoly capitalism can be viewed as an offset in part to the growing power of labor exercised through their trade unions. (Once stratification was consolidated, however, trade unions legitimized, reinforced, and supported the stratification of labor.) To the extent that the divide-and-conquer strategy of stratification divides labor along status lines, thereby weakening its class unity, capital prospers. In terms of our earlier exposition of Marxian political economy, capitalists, by stratifying labor, in the short run, increase their rate of surplus value from what it otherwise would have been without stratification, and in the long run reproduce the system itself.

Contemporary radical political economists have written substantially about labor force stratification, and for the purposes of this chapter this previous work needs to be summarized only in the context of the present argument. A useful working definition of labor stratification has been offered by Reich, Gordon, and Edwards (1973, p. 359) as "the historical process whereby political-economic forces encourage the division of the labor market into separate sub-markets ... distinguished by different labor market characteristics and behavioral rules." This stratification emerged historically in the U.S. between about 1890 and 1920 and has been refined and consolidated ever since. In general, this stratification emerged out of the class struggle between an increasingly powerful and proletarianized working class of that period set against the initial consolidation of monopoly capitalist power in the major industrial sectors of the economy. (See Gordon, Edwards, Reich, Part 3.)

Katherine Stone has chronicled these developments in great detail in the

---

[i]Sennett and Cobb, in a series of in-depth personal studies conducted in the 1970's convey a similar impression of the personal indignities and tragedies induced by class and status differences. As they put it, at one point in their analysis (p. 30), "What needs to be understood is how the class structure in America is organized so that *the tools of freedom become sources of indignity.*"

steel industry, showing how a major effort was made in the 1890s to destroy the substantial job control that steelworkers had before the destruction of the steel union led to the system of stratification in the steel industry which exists, largely unaltered, to this day.

Initially, the production of steel was organized around crafts with members of individual crafts capable of rotating among the various jobs in the production of steel. (This discussion is based on Stone.) A substantial degree of job control was exercised by steelworkers through the Amalgamated Association of Iron, Steel and Tin Workers, whose membership reached a peak of 25,000 in 1892. The struggle between capital and labor surrounding control of the production of steel was a violent one involving some of the most bitter and famous of all the labor struggles—notably the Homestead Strike. Following the union-busting period of the 1890s, the membership of the Amalgamated was completely decimated and the union ceased to exist.

Following this, the new labor system introduced unskilled labor into the production process of steel without any important technological changes. Following Marglin's argument, it was the social relations of production, namely the struggle over control of production, that conditioned the type of labor system used in the production of steel rather than any technological developments. But this new mass of homogeneous labor began, itself, to organize in the early part of this century, creating yet another threat to capital's hegemony over the production process. The result was "Taylorism" and the stratification of labor which had the effect of creating (Stone, p.41)

psychological divisions among the workers, to make them perceive their interests as different from, indeed in conflict with, that of their co-workers.

But the newly created job hierarchy was distinct from the earlier labor system of craft control in that skills were specific to a particular job, and the workers were prevented from learning the entire production process. This system reached its peak when, by 1945, U.S. Steel had between 45,000 and 50,000 separate job titles.

Turning to the economy as a whole (and examining labor stratification on a more general level), radical economists have identified several dimensions along which labor is stratified (see Wachtel, pp. 190-191). Summarizing briefly their argument, labor is stratified by industry and occupation (see Bluestone), by race (see Leggett), by sex, and by ethnic groups. The educational system reinforces work stratification by means of the hierarchical differentiation in the school systems (see Bowles). The net effect of all this is to divide labor along status lines, thereby mitigating its class solidarity, while at the same time legitimatizing the inequalities inherent in the functioning of capitalism (see Wachtel).

The impact of this stratification process on consciousness is to divert workers' consciousness from a class orientation and replace it with an identification with one's strata in society, producing status consciousness. This, coupled with the inculcation of hierarchical forms of work organization, is a twin-edged sword which has had profound effects on the American working class.[j]

The important point to note at this juncture is that a proletariat has revolutionary potential only when it attains class consciousness in the sense described by Lukacs. Thus, the "proletarianization" of the population can have two meanings: a purely *quantitative* phenomenon in which more and more people become objectively wage laborers, and a *qualitative* phenomenon in which wage laborers attain a unified class consciousness. Only when the latter occurs, is there a revolutionary potential. Sweezy (1972b, pp. 164-165) argues from a similar position:

In Marx's theory of capitalism, the proletariat is not always and necessarily revolutionary. It was not revolutionary in the period of manufacture, becoming so only as a consequence of the introduction of machinery in the industrial revolution. The long-run effects of machinery, however, are different from the immediate effects. If the revolutionary opportunities of the early period of modern industry are missed, the proletariat of an industrializing country tends to become less and less revolutionary.

This by no means suggests that modern monopoly capitalism is not without its own contradictions. But (Sweezy, 1972b, p. 147),

A social system can be ever so self-contradictory and still be without a revolutionary potential: the outcome can be, and in fact, history shows many examples where it has been, stagnation, misery, starvation, subjugation by a stronger and more vigorous society.

The task for radical political economists today is to investigate contemporary contradictions produced by the change from modern industry to monopoly capitalism and from the homogenization of the working class to its stratification—a task to which we now turn.

The Labor Process in Monopoly Capitalism

Within the hierarchy of contradictions that originate in the production process, Marx identified a principal contradiction between the progressive develop-

---

[j]Consider this remark of the father of scientific management, Frederick Taylor (quoted in HEW, p. 50):

For success, then, let me give one simple piece of advice beyond all others. Every day, year in and year out, each man should ask himself, over and over again, two questions. First, "What is the name of the man I am now working for?" and having answered this definitely then, "What does this man want me to do, right now?"

ment of the forces of production retarded by the stable social relations of production. He used this principal contradiction to explain the *long-term historical transition* between systems, as, for example, in this passage from *Capital* (volume 3, pp. 883-884):

Whenever a certain stage of maturity has been reached, the specific historical form is discarded and makes way for a higher one. The moment of arrival of such a crisis is disclosed by the depth and breadth attained by the contradictions and antagonisms between the distribution relations, and thus the specific historical form of their corresponding production relations, on the one hand, and the productive forces, the production powers and the development of their agencies, on the other hand. A conflict then ensues between the material development of production and its social form.

It is important to note that this principal contradiction is posed at a very high level of abstraction, and its day-to-day manifestations will be difficult, if not impossible, to identify. Nevertheless, it provides a critical insight into major epochal transformations of social systems as between, for example, feudalism and capitalism. We return to this contradiction later in the analysis, but first let us consider several subsidiary contradictions which have somewhat more immediate significance.

There appear to be *two* dominant contradictions involving the working class today.[k] One involves the comparative decline in material insecurity from previous generations of workers and the consequent reorientation of working-class demands, especially but not exclusively among young workers, from issues of wages and old age security to issues of worker control. The other involves a contradiction within bureaucracy and hierarchically stratified jobs, also converging toward a demand for worker control. As the labor process becomes more stratified in monopoly capitalism, supervision and hierarchy proliferate. And at some point resistance by workers to the proliferation of supervision and hierarchy manifests itself in action by workers at the point of production—some spontaneous, some organized—to resist the consequences of the stratification in the labor process. This contradiction in the labor process itself, when coupled with the decline in the disciplining effect of material insecurity, forms the basis for an analysis of current developments among workers in the United States.

As indicated earlier, the stratification of the labor force emerged out of the struggle between capital and labor, receiving its initial impetus from "Taylorism" and its associated stratification of work. But there is a clearly defined outer limit to the amount of work stratification that can be introduced. This

---

[k]A more complete analysis would have to specify what is meant by the "working class" today. For our purposes, however, it will suffice, *as an abstraction*, to include in the working class all blue-collar workers and salaried white-collar workers, excluding managers and officers of corporations and professional employees.

purely physical limit is reached when the number of jobs equals the number of workers, as, for example, in an office with five secretaries when each is given a particular job title with slightly differentiated tasks aligned along some hierarchy. However, this limit is usually not breached, and instead the stratification of jobs stops somewhat short of this boundary. The proliferation of stratification in work implies also a proliferation of supervisory personnel to control the production process. This sets in motion contradictory forces among workers which today have become more manifest, though certainly not limited, to younger workers with higher levels of education. As in so many other instances, Marx, in one of his asides, discusses the role of supervision with surprising contemporaneity (*Capital*, volume 3, p. 384):

this supervision work necessarily arises in all modes of production based on the antithesis between the laborer, as the direct producer, and the owner of the means of production. The greater this antagonism, the greater the role played by supervision. . . . it is indispensable . . . in the capitalist mode of production, since the production process in it is simultaneously a process by which the capitalist consumes labor-power.

These contradictions derive from the logical functioning of monopoly capitalism, especially from the transformation from modern industry to monopoly capitalism which was discussed earlier. First, the tendency for surplus value to rise, coupled with the economic gains won by trade unions (especially in the 1930s), has enabled the working class to capture a share of this rising surplus value. Second, though business cycles have by no means been expurgated, their severity has been muted. Young workers (under 35) lack the socialization of the severe hardship of the Great Depression and consequently respond less docily to threats of firings than do some of their older counterparts. These economic gains, it is important to note, have also been won in part by the trade union movement which capitalized on the crisis of capitalism of the 1930s. [Of course, these gains were a result of a complex of forces, including the panic in the dominant class caused by the severity of this particular crisis, leading to welfare state concessions in order to stabilize monopoly capitalism (see Sawers and Wachtel, pp. 6-18).] Thus, the growth of trade unions, which for a while muted militant worker discontent (Sweezy, 1972a, p. 142), has itself contributed to the creation of the conditions which have led to new contradictions and new working-class demands.

To understand the qualitative dimension of these new working-class demands, we must look at the work situation, especially at the contradiction in the process of labor market stratification, which historically has been an important weapon in the hands of capitalists and managers, used to weaken the strength of working-class movements. The commodity fetishism of markets in capitalism is now joined in bureaucratic economic organization by an "office fetishism"—"an aspect of exploitative relations . . . hidden behind the office," having the effect of creating "a mystification of the activities of officeholders" (Horvat, 1969, pp. 11 and 13). But the internal logic of the functioning of bureaucracy contains its own inherent contradiction (Horvat, 1969, p. 16):

A completely bureaucratized organization would require that the number of rules be almost as great as the number of concrete decisions. Since this is impossible and the number of rules is much smaller, an important element of imprecision and unpredictability creeps into the organization. To cope with this defect, those in authority tend to multiply rules, whose sheer number and increasing inconsistency with each other have a strong negative effect on those who are required to observe these rules, and this drives them to inactivity.

The intersection of these two contradictions—the decline in the work-disciplining aspect of economic insecurity and the proliferation of hierarchy, work rules, and work supervision—becomes manifested in the type of worker uprisings typified by Lordstown[1] (where the average age of the workers was under 25) and is revealed in the decline in worker productivity that took place in the late 1960s. (On the Lordstown strike, see Rothschild.)

The issue of worker productivity is a central one for capitalism, involving the basic production relation that determines the distribution of the rewards of net output at the point of production. It is particularly important for the profitability of the firm, faced as it has been recently with substantial international competition. In the late 1960s and early 1970s we heard a great deal about the "productivity crisis." Between 1968 and 1969 the percentage change in productivity was barely positive (officially stated at 0.4 percent), down from the meager productivity increases of 2.9 and 2.1 percent in the two previous years (U.S. Department of Labor, p. 240). Between 1969 and 1970 it was not much higher (only 1.0 percent), but thereafter has risen sharply to 3.6 percent and most recently, between 1971 and 1972, to 4.2 percent. These figures are important because the one short-term weapon that capital has is to speed up the production process, thereby increasing labor productivity. [At the General Motors Vega plant in Lordstown (which cost some $100 million to build), workers were expected to produce 100 cars per hour, while the normal line speed in other plants was only *60* cars per hour (see Rothschild, p. 19).] This speed-up coincided during this period with the maturation of the two contradictions isolated for investigation here. To speed up requires more supervisory personnel to discipline workers into their new rate of work. Superimposed upon a declining willingness of workers newly integrated into this wage labor system, the imposition of increased hierarchy and supervision to increase labor productivity led to the Lordstown-type worker uprising. (The same contradictions and patterns of response emerged in Europe at about the same time; see Bosquet.)

---

[1]An important strike in 1972 involving a highly stratified and automated General Motors Vega factory and young workers drawn from rural and semirural towns.

Another quantitative indicator of developments in the labor process is unit labor costs, which are a combination of the amount of compensation a worker receives each hour and the amount of output the worker can produce each hour (labor productivity). Between 1959 and 1965 unit labor costs in manufacturing actually *declined* by *3.2 percent*—that is, it cost the employer some 3.2 percent less to produce each unit of output in 1965 than it did in 1959 (all data are taken from U.S. Department of Labor, p. 242). This is caused by a combination of comparatively large increases in productivity and low increases in wages. But between 1966 and 1972 unit labor costs *increased* by *23.3 percent*—that is, it cost the employer over 23 percent more to produce each unit in 1972 than it did in 1966. Though wage increases are part of the reason for this sharp increase in unit labor costs, sharp drops in productivity increases play an equally important role.

The combination of productivity declines and the failure of speed-ups to increase productivity via the traditional weapon of increased stratification and supervision led to real concern during this period. Especially important were the data showing the United States with the lowest rate of productivity increase between 1965 and 1972 among all its major trading competitors.[m] This led to the formation of so-called Productivity Councils and a rash of studies proclaiming the decline in the "work ethic."

Summing up these concerns for industry and reflecting a no-compromise attitude about worker control, Joseph E. Godfrey, general manager of the (in)famous General Motors Assembly Division, remarked: "Within reason and without endangering their health, if we can occupy a man for 60 minutes we've got that right." (See Salpukas.) Marx could not have described the struggle over work time and the "ownership" of a worker's labor power better! Godfrey goes on to reveal another critical point about worker productivity. The year-to-year changes in productivity involve primarily rearrangement of the existing technology by speed-ups rather than the introduction of fancy new machines: "A typical example would be to rearrange a man's work area so that he no longer has to walk to get needed parts but can simply reach for them. With the time saved, the worker might be asked to put on an additional part" (Salpukas). James Roche, chairman of the board of General Motors, put the matter more succinctly, in his *Christmas Message* to General Motor's 794,000 employees (quoted in Gooding, pp. 69-70):

[m]Data from Peter Flanagan's *International Economic Report* (reported in "Productivity and World Competition") show:

Country	% Change in Productivity, 1965-1972
United States	20.0
Great Britain	36.6
Italy	41.5
West Germany	42.0
France	53.3
Japan	130.3

The company did not seek extra effort beyond a "fair day's work," but did expect increased output per manhour from better equipment and methods and most importantly by the *cooperation of labor.* [Emphasis added]

Today, somewhat of a new twist has been added to the struggle, namely the use of *advertising* to try to convince workers about the need for productivity increases. Recently, the National Advertising Council announced a $10 million advertising campaign, in the words of former Commerce Secretary Peter Peterson, to try to persuade workers that "productivity is not a 12-letter dirty word representing certain people getting exploited by others" (quoted in Bernstein, 1973b). As a personnel director of a $1 billion corporation puts it (quoted in Gooding, p. 7), "now it is much harder teaching new employees their jobs, because not only do you have to teach them the job, you have to teach them about work."

Judson Gooding, an editor of *Fortune* and chronicler for the advanced segment of management on these issues, reports that the quit rate at Ford was 18 percent in 1969, reaching a height of 25 percent in some plants. And absenteeism doubled at Ford and General Motors between 1960 and 1970, amounting to an average of 5 percent, reaching a high of 10 percent on Fridays and Mondays (Gooding, pp. 69, 72). In response, "Some GM plants, groping for a solution, have even tried rewarding regular attendance with Green Stamps, or initialed glasses that over the months . . . form a set." But as a General Motors official commented, "If they won't come in for $30.50 a day, they won't come in for monogrammed glasses" (Gooding, p. 112). Work quality, as well, has suffered (Gooding, p. 18):

At one Ford assembly plant, the manager . . . had to keep 160 repairmen busy fixing defects on brand-new cars just off the assembly line a few feet away, where 840 men labored imperfectly to assemble those same cars.

The response initially to these productivity struggles, or more appropriately job control struggles, proceed in most instances, however, along the lines suggested by our earlier model: increasing the intensity of work in order to increase labor productivity and thereby increase surplus value. The state has ratified this policy in their wage guideposts and the wage controls. Wage increases are tied to labor productivity increases which, on a year-to-year basis, involve primarily the speed-up in the use of existing technology (Marx's increase in the intensity of labor) rather than in the introduction of glamorous new technologies.

Thus the contradiction in the labor process is complete: worker discontent—manifested in absenteeism, turnover of jobs, sabotage, and declines in productivity—derives from the hierarchy and irrationality of bureaucratic management (the absence of worker control) which exacerbates the tendency toward the decline in worker productivity due to the proliferation of both inconsistent work rules and supervisory personnel. But capitalists respond in the system's most logical fashion by trying to increase worker productivity through speed-ups, enforced by even more work rules and more supervisory personnel.[n] Lacking the previous strength of the disciplining threat of firings, young workers (especially) resist and respond with militant wildcat strikes such as occurred at Lordstown and with more passive forms of resistance such as absenteeism, turnover, slowdowns, sabotage, and poor work quality.

In short, the rise in material security for workers won by trade unions out of the growing surplus value and the stratification of workers by capitalists as a response to this worker organization (and ultimately legitimized by trade unions) have been the instruments for the creation of new work situations and "new workers" which have now created new contradictions. Without employing a dialectical methodology, the authors of the government-sponsored report *Work in America* (HEW, p. 12) concluded (dialectically) that "It may be argued that the very success of industry and organized labor in meeting the basic needs of workers has unintentionally spurred demands for esteemable and fulfilling jobs." The manifest response of the relevant parties to these contradictions will be examined in the next section of this chapter.

Worker and Corporate Response to Contradictions in the Labor Process

The decline in labor productivity and the concern among corporate leaders with the decline in work discipline (labeled the decline in the "work ethic") have recently led to governmental and foundation financial support for studies on "what ails the blue-collar worker,"[o] culminating with the introduction of legislation (S. 736) in the United States Senate by Senator Kennedy and eighteen of his colleagues which provides for "research for solutions to the problem of alienation among American workers and to provide for pilot projects and provide technical assistance to find ways to deal with that problem . . . " (see Committee on Labor and Public Welfare).

Though the statistical survey results of these various studies are interesting, we should be wary of reading too much political significance into them, and we must be careful in interpreting their results in relation to the question of class consciousness. In general, these studies report widespread work dissatis-

[n]This is the initial response of capital and the one most consistent with the basic production (and therefore) power relations of capitalism. However, if these speed-up schemes are resisted by workers, a dialectic then arises in which capital proclaims the inherent "inhumaneness" of speed-ups and responds with "human relations" or "job enrichment" schemes. We return to this point later.

[o]See Herrick and Quinn; Herrick; Sheppard and Herrick; and U.S. Department of Health, Education and Welfare.

faction among all occupations, income levels, ages, races, and sexes. However, the intensity of dissatisfaction on all dimensions is greater among young workers (under 30). The most dissatisfied group of workers in the Sheppard-Herrick study (p. 4) are black workers under age 30, followed by workers under age 30 who have some college education, and women workers under age 30. And these tendencies are fairly constant over all income groups among young workers earning up to $10,000 per year (Sheppard-Herrick, p. 5). Young workers exhibit "less authoritarian" attitudes (measured on a conventional social psychological scale) and therefore are less "disciplined" in hierarchical work structures and less eager to cooperate with supervisors (Sheppard-Herrick, chapter 7). Of the issues that concern young workers, job control—including job rotation, quality of work, and worker participation—are more important than wage and security issues (Sheppard and Herrick, chapter 7). Herrick and Quinn (p. 22) ranked job characteristics most closely associated with job satisfaction and found that of the top ten characteristics, only one could be considered a wage or security issue (greater paid vacation), the remaining characteristics being associated with job control.

The HEW report reached a similar conclusion (p. 12):

Satisfaction, then, is a function of the content of work; dissatisfaction, of the environment of work. Increases in productivity have been found to correlate in certain industries and occupations with increases in satisfaction, but not with decreases in dissatisfaction. Hence, hygenic improvements may make work more tolerable, but will not necessarily raise motivation or productivity. The latter depends on making jobs more interesting and important.

The report of the U.S. Department of Health, Education and Welfare *Work in America* reached similar conclusions with regard to the higher level of disaffection among young workers. It attributes this to the following (p. 49): (1) young people have higher expectations as a result of their higher levels of education;[p] (2) the greater material security for young people "makes them less tolerant of unrewarding jobs"; (3) "all authority in our society is being challenged"; (4) "many former students are demanding what they achieved in part on their campuses . . . —a voice in setting the goals of the organization";[q] and (5) "young blue-collar workers, who have grown up in an environment in which equality is called for in all institutions, are demanding the same rights . . . as university graduates." Summing up the present failures of the human relations school of management (in which workers are treated better without changing the jobs or who controls them), the HEW report concludes (p. 18):

[p]In 1960 only 26 percent of white and 14 percent of black artisans and operatives had completed four years of high school. By 1969, 41 percent of white and 29 percent of blacks in those jobs had completed four years of high school (HEW, p. 34).

[q]"In 1968 over half (56 percent) of all students indicated that they did not mind the future prospect of being "bossed around" on the job. By 1971 only one out of three students (36 percent) saw themselves willingly submitting to such authority" (HEW, p. 44).

Simplified tasks for those who are not simple-minded, close supervision by those whose legitimacy rests only on a hierarchical structure, and jobs that have nothing but money to offer in an affluent age are simply rejected. For many of the new workers, the monotony of work and scale of organization and their inability to control the pace and style of work are cause for a resentment which they, unlike older workers, do not repress.

In sum, two themes emerge from all the studies: first, that job satisfaction is more closely associated with job control rather than wage and security issues; and second, that workers (especially young workers) see job dissatisfaction firmly rooted in hierarchically stratified work situations. Both of these findings are consistent with our previous discussion of contradictions among the working class in monopoly capitalism today. Further, we find that the most dissatisfied groups—young blacks, young women, and young workers with some college education—contain workers who are entering into *new* social relations of production or are entering social relations of production far below their expectations and the expectations that society's ideology fosters. This is much the same as petty commodity producers becoming wage laborers and entering into new social relations of production, with the consequent radicalization of those workers in the period Marx was analyzing.

All the studies find these tendencies more severe among young workers. Sheppard and Herrick (p. 119) go so far as to say that "the young worker has different work values than do middle-aged and older workers." Gooding (p. 10) likens the young worker to his university counterpart:

The most important changes are taking place among young workers, and there is a perceptible parallel between them and the students who have made their wishes known on university campuses.

The "stick" of more hierarchy, supervision, and stratification in work in order to increase productivity by enforcing a speed-up are not the only devices which capital has tried when faced with work discipline problems. They have some "carrots" in their bag of tricks as well. Earlier in this century, as a response to the workers' opposition to the excesses of Taylorism, a "human relations" school of management flourished in which the idea was to make the jobs more pleasant while not altering the control over the production process. Today, complementing these human relations experiments are experiments in workers' participation, frequently called "job enrichment" schemes. But the central question is, *Who is getting rich from job enrichment?* The Saab auto factory has taken to advertising its new assembly group (as opposed to assembly line) production process under headings such as "Bored people build bad cars" and "For years, most car makers tried to produce cars faster and cheaper. We're trying to produce them slower and better."

There is little question in the minds of capitalists and their managers that job enrichment of the workers' participation sort is good business (especially in view of the fact that the old hierarchical system became bad business). The job enrichment "movement" has been receiving increasing attention in the popular press. An article in *Readers Digest* (Armbrister, p. 231) proclaims: "Worker alienation means low morale and productivity." And (Armbrister, p. 232) "employers are realizing that people are capable of doing far more than their jobs either require or allow. . . ." *Newsweek* magazine also had an article typical of this genre, entitled "The Job Blahs: Who Wants to Work?" HEW (pp. 188-201) reports on dozens of experiments in various forms of workers' participation.

Workers' skepticism over who gets rich from job enrichment has been revealed recently in two reports from the pollster Louis Harris. In one (Harris, 1973a) *74 percent* of all hourly-wage workers interviewed thought stockholders would benefit "a lot" from productivity increases, *71 percent* thought management would benefit a lot, while only *29 percent* thought consumers would benefit a lot, and only *17 percent* thought employees would benefit a lot. [Typical of recent newspaper headlines is "Closure Threat Spurs 32% Productivity Increase in Steel Plant" (Bernstein, 1973a), and the article goes on to recount how workers' participation in production increased productivity and "saved" a plant from closing. Though the article is mute on this point, I doubt whether workers' wages were increased by 32 percent!] At the same time (Harris, 1973b), 85 percent of all people interviewed thought business should enable people "to use their creative talents fully" (up from 73 percent in 1966), but only 41 percent thought business was "enabling people to use creative talents fully" (down from 65 percent in 1966).

Such experiments in workers' participation as we are witnessing today are not new in our history, and they usually arise in response to a crisis in the old form of production caused by worker resistance. Blumberg (Chapter 5) reports on dozens of experiments earlier in this century with workers' participation schemes. In nearly all instances these schemes were introduced during a period of crisis in the production process and eliminated once the crisis had been overcome and because workers started (gradually) to wrest more and more control from management. Almost without exception, these schemes of workers' participation produced sustained increases in rates of productivity change. Blumberg concludes (p. 123):[r]

There is hardly a study in the entire literature which fails to demonstrate that satisfaction in work is enhanced or that other generally acknowledged beneficial consequences accrue from a genuine increase in workers' decision-making power. Such consistency of findings . . . is rare in social research.

---

[r]Melman, in comparing similar Israeli firms organized on the Kibbutz worker management principal with those organized along traditional lines, finds the worker managed firms to be more productive.

This returns us to a principal contradiction of capitalist production, namely the contradiction between the progressive development of the means of production being retarded by the less progressive social relations of production, rooted, as they are, in property relations. In the present context, there is ample evidence that the forces of production (productivity) are retarded by the relations of production (the hierarchical structure of stratified jobs). Workers are manifesting an antagonistic response to hierarchically stratified work relations. Moreover, a more profound inhibition to the further expansion of the means of production arises under capitalist social relations of production—namely, the retardation of technical innovation by workers who stand to lose (individually) rather than to benefit from technical innovation since they do not control the distribution of the fruits of technical innovation.

What we are witnessing is an attempt to mediate this contradiction, reducing its antagonistic edge, by restructuring (perhaps temporarily, perhaps permanently) work, by altering *slightly* the control of the production process. History has shown that such timid steps towards socialist *form* without socialist *substance* are less likely to be successful in contrast to their success under socialism. (Gorz and Mandel discuss the workers' control movement in the context of the struggle for socialism.) If left solely within the bounds of capitalism, such changes in work will constitute a most important reform, but a reform within capitalism nonetheless. But the question is, can you be a little bit socialist or have a little bit of workers' control? Or does a dialectic arise in which workers are propelled by their experiences toward higher and higher demands for the elimination of capitalists and managers as a class once workers realize that it is they who are most central to production and the managers who are an artifact of capitalist hierarchical control and work stratification and who become superfluous once stratification and hierarchy in work are eliminated? As Mandel (p. 346) puts the case for workers' control demands: "The program of anticapitalist structural reform . . . cannot be carried out in a normally functioning capitalist system; it rips this system apart; it creates a situation of dual power; and it rapidly leads to a revolutionary struggle for power."

In short, the social organization of the enterprise must reproduce a workers' consciousness consistent with the capitalist relations of production embodied in work hierarchy and job stratification. A "noncapitalist" social organization of the enterprise—embodied in job rotation, worker participation in decisions, reduced hierarchy and stratification—may erode the very worker consciousness required to reproduce the capitalist relations of production. If this should happen, then one can expect increased militancy within the working class at the point of production, reflecting a challenge to the decisionmaking hegemony of capitalists and their managers.

Several caveats about this analysis are warranted. First, we do not know if the same level of dissatisfaction (and its distribution among workers) is unique to the present working class or whether it was common to other generations too. It is fairly widely accepted that trade union leaders in the past, as well as today, have negotiated away job control demands of rank-and-file workers in exchange for wage and security concessions. (William Serrin has provided a very detailed account of how this occurred in the 1970 UAW strike against General Motors.) Second, we do not know what political form (if any) these discontents will take. If they remain rooted in economic concerns, then the politicization needed for class consciousness will not arise.

The political direction of workers in response to current contradictions is still uncharted, though rank-and-file caucuses are certainly one significant development. We have already seen how one giant monopoly capitalist company (General Motors) has responded to the situation and how their workers have responded. But not all corporate elites respond by increasing the intensity of labor and the number of supervisory personnel. Gooding (chapter 6), HEW (pp. 188-201), and Sheppard-Herrick (chapter 11) detail many experiments with job enrichment and worker participation designed to mute this new form of worker discontent. Gooding (pp. 15, 17) is quite explicit when it comes to the reasons for responding creatively:

It would seem preferable by far to introduce the improvements in work conditions before they are demanded, at the pace and time chosen by management, rather than being forced to make radical changes, under union pressure, at times not of managements choosing. . . . The choice comes down to moving with the exigencies of the times—not mollycoddling but accommodating the demands of people for more control over their environments—or existing in a grim atmosphere of discontent or active hatred.

On the other side, trade union officials, with few exceptions, have not been responsive to these new worker demands. Sheppard and Herrick (p. 189) asked employers and union officials whether they believed workers are "very or somewhat satisfied with their opportunity to do interesting and enjoyable work." In contrast to the low proportions of workers who thought they do interesting work, 85 percent of employers and 58 percent of union officials thought workers were satisfied with their work conditions. Typical of the union reaction is that of Frank Pollara, assistant research director of the AFL-CIO (quoted in Gooding, p. 179):

Motivation, as I understand it, is an abstract concept that has very little relevance, very little pertinence, very little meaning for the industrial world today.

Other union leaders, notably Irving Bluestone of the UAW, have responded in a more progressive fashion (Bluestone, p. 17):

A departure from the miniaturization of the job embraces the idea of bringing the democratic institution of society into the work-place. Participatory management at all levels, worker decision-making . . . are combined . . . with the opportunity to exercise a meaningful measure of autonomy and to utilize more varied skills.

In sum, with the relative decline in material insecurity among workers today compared to that of previous generations, workers are now concentrating on nonwage demands of the job control sort. Coupled with the proliferation of work stratification, the relative decline in material insecurity has led to intensified job dissatisfaction, manifested in sporadic outbursts which cripple production and an overall decline in labor productivity. Initially, capital responds with a larger dose of the same medicine, namely increased work supervision, hierarchy, and work speed-ups. But part of the problem is caused by the very character of the labor process under monopoly capitalism which is characterized by work speed-up, hierarchy, and supervision. So the medicine of monopoly capitalism merely feeds the disease. Failing these remedies, some of the more advanced segments of the monopoly capitalist managers suddenly discover the innate virtues of job enrichment and worker participation. The important question for radicals, beyond an understanding of this dynamic in the labor process, is whether a taste of worker participation offered by corporate managers to ride out the immediate crisis can be contained, or whether once put into place, workers' participation develops a dynamic of its own which leads to more radical working-class demands for an embryonic form of socialism appropriate to the character of advanced monopoly capitalist economies.

The critical political question, which touches on an issue beyond the scope of this chapter—namely, the transition to socialism in advanced monopoly capitalist countries (see Horvat, 1972)—revolves around several developments.

1. Will the new contradictions in the labor process outlined in this chapter generate a politicization of workers, creating a working-class consciousness which enables workers to unify themselves politically, thereby transcending the disunifying elements of stratification?

2. If workers do become politicized, then will they develop a radical or reformist class consciousness?

3. Can workers, as a corollary of point 2, begin to define their own radical ideology and political programs, within their own organizations, transcending their day-to-day work situation in order to see their problems as *systemic* rather than personal?

Answers to these three questions will portend crucial political developments over the next decade.

Along all these dimensions, the contradictions will, no doubt, become more severe as international competition places increased "productivity pressure" on domestic production. The first (and most logical) response by capitalists will follow the lines suggested by the theory developed earlier, namely speed-ups and the intensification of the use of labor. To discipline workers, we can expect even more unemployment created via the "political business cycle." But these developments are secondary in the sense that they are external forces which impinge upon a set of contradictions (and exacerbate them) already inherent in the production process under monopoly capitalism. And the new dimension added by monopoly capitalism to the traditional contradictions of competitive capitalism inheres in the labor stratification process. Combined with a relative decline in material insecurity won from earlier working-class struggles, the disciplining force of alienated work is now less powerful. However, the outcome of these contradictions in terms of a politicized working class must await the actual practice which radicals and others engage in over the next years as well as the outcome of the challenge from radical rank-and-file caucuses which have been mounted in trade unions against their established leadership.

Bibliography

Armbrister, Trevor, "Beating Those Blue-Collar Blues," *Reader's Digest* (April, 1973): 231-240.

Bernstein, Harry, "Closure Threat Spurs 32% Productivity Increase in Steel Plant," *The Washington Post* (February 11, 1973a): E5.

_____ , "U.S. Work Ethic: A Cherished Virtue or a Theoretical Dream?" *The Washington Post* (January 1, 1973b): A3.

Bluestone, Barry, "The Tripartite Economy: Labor Markets and the Working Class," *Poverty and Human Resources* (July-August, 1970): 15-35.

Bluestone, Irving, "Democratizing the Workplace" (mimeo, June 22, 1972).

Blumberg, Paul, *Industrial Democracy: The Sociology of Participation* (New York: Schocken Books, 1969).

Bosquet, Michel, "The 'Prison Factory'," *New Left Review* 73 (May-June, 1972): 23-34.

Bowles, Samuel, "The Integration of Higher Education into the Wage Labor System," appearing in this volume.

Committee on Labor and Public Welfare, *Worker Alienation, 1972* (Washington: U.S. Government Printing Office, 1972).

Dobb, Maurice, *Political Economy and Capitalism* (London: George Routledge and Sons Ltd., 1937).

Gooding, Judson, *The Job Revolution* (New York: Walker and Company, 1972).

Gordon, David M., Richard C. Edwards, and Michael Reich, "Labor Market Segmentation in American Capitalism," (mimeo, 1973).

Gorz, Andre, "Workers' Control is More Than Just That," in Gerry Hunnius, G. David Garson, and John Case, *Workers' Control* (New York: Random House, 1973), pp. 325-343.

Harris, Louis, "Productivity Gains Held in Suspicion," *The Washington Post* (February 19, 1973a): B16.

———, "Toughness with Business Favored Short of Takeover," *The Washington Post* (February 12, 1973b): A14.

Herrick, Neal Q., and Robert P. Quinn, "Who's Unhappy?" *Manpower* (January, 1972): 3-7.

———, "The Working Conditions Survey as a Source of Social Indicators," *Monthly Labor Review* 94(4): 15-24, April, 1971.

Horvat, Branko, *An Essay on Yugoslav Society* (New York: International Arts and Sciences Press, 1969).

———, "The Transition to Socialism," presented at URPE conference, American University, April, 1972 (mimeo).

Jenkins, David, *Job Power: Blue and White Collar Democracy* (Garden City: Doubleday and Co., 1973).

"The Job Blahs: Who Wants to Work?" *Newsweek* (March 26, 1973): 79-89.

Leggett, John C., *Class, Race and Labor. Working-Class Consciousness in Detroit* (London: Oxford University Press, 1968).

Lukacs, Georg, "Class Consciousness," in Georg Lukacs, *History and Class Consciousness* (Cambridge: The M.I.T. Press, 1971), pp. 46-82.

Mandel, Ernest, "The Debate on Workers' Control," in Gerry Hunnius, G. David Garson, and John Case, *Workers' Control* (New York: Random House, 1973), pp. 344-373.

Marglin, Stephen A., "What Do Bosses Do? The Origins and Functions of Hierarchy in Capitalist Production" (mimeo, 1971).

Marx, Karl, *Capital*, Volumes 1 to 3 (New York: International Publishers, 1967).

——— and Frederick Engels, *Selected Correspondence* (Moscow: Progress Publishers, 1955).

Meek, Ronald L., *Studies in the Labor Theory of Value* (London: Lawrence and Wishart, 1956).

Melman, Seymour, "Industrial Efficiency under Managerial vs. Cooperative Decision-making," *Review of Radical Political Economics*, 2(1): 9-34, Spring, 1970.

Ossowski, Stanislaw, "The Marxian Synthesis," in Edward O. Laumann, Paul M. Siegel, and Robert W. Hodge, eds., *The Logic of Social Hierarchies* (Chicago: Markham Publishing Co., 1970), pp. 149-168.

"Productivity and World Competition," *The Washington Post*, April 30, 1973, p. A22.

Reich, Michael, "The Evolution of the United States Labor Force," in Richard C. Edwards, Michael Reich, and Thomas E. Weisskopf, eds., *The Capitalist System* (Englewood Cliffs, N.J.: Prentice-Hall, Inc., 1972), pp. 174-183.

———, David M. Gordon, and Richard C. Edwards, "A Theory of Labor Market Segmentation," *American Economic Review* 63(2): 359-365, May, 1973.

Romano, Paul, *Life in the Factory* (Boston: New England Free Press, n.d.).

Rothschild, Emma, "GM in More Trouble," *New York Review of Books* (March 23, 1972): 18-25.

Salpukas, Agis, "G.M.'s Toughest Division," *New York Times*, April 16, 1972, sec. 3, pp. 1, 4.

Sawers, Larry, and Howard M. Wachtel, "Activities of the Government and the Distribution of Income in the United States," delivered at the 13th General Conference of the International Association for Research in Income and Wealth (Balatonfured Hungary, September, 1973).

Sennet, Richard, and Jonathan Cobb, *The Hidden Injuries of Class* (New York: Alfred A. Knopf, 1973).

Serrin, William, *The Company and the Union* (New York: Alfred A. Knopf, 1973).

Sheppard, Harold L., and Neal Q. Herrick, *Where Have All the Robots Gone?* (New York: The Free Press, 1972).

Stone, Katherine, "The Origins of Job Structures in the Steel Industry," (this volume).

Sweezy, Paul M., "Karl Marx and the Industrial Revolution," in Paul M. Sweezy, *Modern Capitalism and Other Essays* (New York: Monthly Review Press, 1972a), pp. 127-145. Copyright © 1972, Monthly Review Press. Reprinted by permission of Monthly Review Press.

————, "Marx and the Proletariat," in Paul M. Sweezy, *Modern Capitalism and Other Essays* (New York: Monthly Review Press, 1972b), pp. 147-165.

————, *The Theory of Capitalist Development* (New York: Monthly Review Press, 1968).

Tse-Tung, Mao, "Analysis of the Classes in Chinese Society," in Mao Tse-Tung, *Selected Works*, vol. 1 (Peking: Foreign Languages Press, 1967), pp. 13-21.

U.S. Department of Health, Education and Welfare, *Work in America* (Cambridge: The M.I.T. Press, 1973).

U.S. Department of Labor, *Manpower Report of the President, 1973* (Washington: Government Printing Office, 1973).

Wachtel, Howard M., "Capitalism and Poverty in America: Paradox or Contradiction?" *American Economic Review*, 62(2): 187-194, May, 1972.

Part II:
Labor Markets

5 Notes for a Theory of Labor Market Stratification

Michael J. Piore

This chapter is designed to develop a series of concepts which I believe to be helpful in the understanding of socioeconomic mobility and, in particular, the problems associated with such mobility or lack thereof, in the United States during the past decade. This development starts from the *dual labor market hypothesis* introduced several years ago in an attempt to understand the labor force problems of disadvantaged, particularly black, workers, in urban core areas.[1] That hypothesis has proved an attractive way of organizing operating experience in low-income labor markets and, for this reason, has attracted adherents among manpower practitioners and academicians oriented toward this community. It has not, however, lent itself readily to the organization and analysis of existing labor market data and has thus tended to frustrate rigorous empirical examination.[2] This chapter represents, in part, an attempt to expand and clarify the initial hypothesis with a view toward overcoming these limitations. It is not, however, meant to be limited to that hypothesis alone; and, indeed, it is hoped that the concepts developed here will contribute to a more general conceptual apparatus for the analysis of economic mobility.

The chapter is divided into three parts. The first part is an attempt to define the mobility problem and to develop the basic conceptual apparatus critical to an understanding of it. This part is, in turn, divided into three sections. The first reviews the initial dual labor market hypothesis, broadens that hypothesis to recognize, in addition to the primary and secondary sectors, a division of the primary sector into an upper tier and a lower tier, and links these three segments of the labor market to the sociological distinction between middle-class, working-class, and lower-class subcultures. The second section proposes the concept of *mobility chains* and uses this concept to redefine the distinction among the three basic segments of the labor market. The third section attempts to explain the construction of mobility chains in terms of the process of *automatic, incidental learning.*

The second part of the chapter examines the problem of changing mobility patterns and restructuring mobility chains generally. In the third part, the specified constraints imposed by technology, on the one hand, and the home environment (or the subculture), on the other, are examined.

Part 1: The Basic Concepts

1. Labor Market Segments

The basic hypothesis of the dual labor market was that the labor market is divided into two essentially distinct segments, termed the *primary* and the *secondary* sectors. The former offers jobs with relatively high wages, good working conditions, chances of advancement, equity and due process in the administration of work rules, and, above all, employment stability. Jobs in the secondary sector, by contrast, tend to be low-paying, with poorer working conditions and little chance of advancement; to have a highly personalized relationship between workers and supervisors which leaves wide latitude for favoritism and is conducive to harsh and capricious work discipline; and to be characterized by considerable instability in jobs and a high turnover among the labor force. The hypothesis was designed to explain the problems of disadvantaged, particularly black, workers, in urban areas, which had previously been attributed to unemployment. It implied that the basic problem was that they were somehow confined to jobs within the secondary sector, and the reported unemployment rates were essentially a symptom of the instability of the jobs and the high turnover among the labor force which held them rather than a literal inability to find work. The relative stability of jobs and workers in the two sectors also appeared to be the critical explanatory variable in understanding the origins of the two sectors, and the other characteristics may be viewed as derivatives of this one factor.[3]

A broader view of the labor market suggests that the dual labor market hypothesis focuses too narrowly on the problems of disadvantaged workers, and that there are distinctions among primary jobs which are in many ways as important as the distinction between the primary and the secondary sectors. At the very least, it seems useful to recognize a distinction within the primary sector between an *upper* and a *lower* tier. The descriptions of jobs and workers used in development of the dual labor market hypothesis are really characteristic of the lower tier alone. The upper tier of the primary sector is composed of professional and managerial jobs. Such jobs tend to be distinguished from those in the lower tier by the higher pay and status and the greater promotion opportunities afforded. They are also distinguished by the mobility and turnover patterns, which tend to more closely resemble those of the secondary sector; except in contrast to the patterns of that sector, mobility and turnover tend to be associated with advancement. Upper-tier jobs, also like those of the secondary sector, are distinguished by the absence of the elaborate set of work rules and formal administrative procedures which characterize lower-tier employments. But the personalized relationship between worker and supervisor which substitutes for these rules in the secondary sector seems to be replaced by an internalized code of behavior. Formal education in the upper tier seems to be an essential requisite for employment, and educational requirements which can often be circumvented elsewhere in the economy, varying with economic conditions and easily substituted by the equivalent in informal training or experience, tend to be absolute barriers to entry. Finally, upper-tier work seems to offer much greater variety and room for individual creativity and initiative, and greater economic security. These last characteristics differentiating the upper and lower tiers seem to be underlying many of the complaints of middle-income groups over the last several years, and the distinction between the upper and lower tiers speaks to the problems of this segment of the labor force much as the dual labor market explains those of disadvantaged workers.[4]

The characterization of the secondary sector and the upper and lower tiers of the primary sector suggest the distinctions made in the sociological literature between the lower-, working-, and middle-class subcultures. The labor market divisions seem quite clearly related to these subcultures and possibly are, in the same way, anchored in them. The characteristics of the subcultures vary over the life cycle of the individual; the parallel to the labor market segments is closest at the adult phase of the life cycle, the age when individuals have typically been married and have children.[5] The working-class subculture at this stage is anchored in a stable, routinized life-style. Life centers in an extended family unit and in a set of relationships in a peer group drawn from friends developed in childhood and adolescence. Individuals tend to define themselves and their roles in terms of these relationships. Work is viewed as an instrument for obtaining the income necessary to support the family and participate in peer group activities; education is seen as an instrument for obtaining work. In all these respects, the subculture appears supportive of work in the lower tier of the primary sector, which seems, like the basic life-style, to be stable and routinized. The priority accorded family life enables one to bear the lack of challenge on the job, whereas the challenge, were it to exist, might distract from family activities.

The working-class subculture contrasts with that of the middle class. Here, the line between the family, on the one hand, and work and educational activities, on the other, is blurred. The extended family obligations of the working class are narrowed to the nuclear unit, thus reducing the potential for conflict with work. Both work and education are viewed, at least ideally, as ends, rewarding in themselves, as well as a means for obtaining income. The friends with whom the family passes its leisure time are often drawn from work and based upon common professional interests. In these respects, the middle-class subculture is well adapted to the support of upper-tier work patterns; the nuclear family and professional friendships facilitate geographic and social mobility and permit intellectually demanding and time-consuming jobs. The view of education is supportive of extensive prework schooling far removed from the payoff and of no immediate relevance.

The lower-class subculture deviates from that of the working class in a way which appears similarly adapted to the employment patterns of the secondary labor market. Lower-class men have a highly personalized conception of themselves, divorced from and independent of a network of relationships with family and friends. Such relationships thus tend to be volatile, short-lived, and unstable, and their life tends to be characterized by an effort to escape routine through action and adventure. It is thus a pattern consistent with the erratic employment of the secondary labor market as well as with other characteristics such as the personal relationship between worker and supervisor.

In sum, then, the basic labor market strata appear to reflect a threefold division between a secondary sector and a primary sector, split into an upper and a lower tier. The characteristics of work in the three divisions are closely related to the sociological distinctions among the lower-, working-, and middle-class subcultures. The bulk of this essay is devoted to an attempt to clarify the meaning of those strata and to understand the process through which they are generated. It will be argued in the next section that the strata essentially reflect differences in what are termed *mobility chains* and that these differences should in fact be taken as their defining characteristics.

2. Mobility Chains

The concept of a mobility chain represents an attempt to formalize the intuitive notion that socioeconomic movement in our society is not random, but tends to occur in more or less regular channels. These channels are such that any given job will tend to draw labor from a limited and distinct number of other particular points. As a result, people hold jobs in some regular order or sequence. We shall term such a sequence a *mobility chain.* The points along a mobility chain may be termed *stations*: they generally include not only jobs but also other points of social and economic significance. Thus, people in a given job will tend to be drawn from a limited range of schools, neighborhoods, and types of family backgrounds; and conversely, people leaving the same school or neighborhood will tend to move into one of a limited set of employment situations.

The prototype of mobility chain is the type of line of progression in blue-collar manufacturing jobs.[6] Entry into such lines is typically confined to a small number of relatively low-skilled jobs. The remaining jobs are arranged in a hierarchical sequence; each job in the sequence is filled by promotion from the job directly below it and cannot be entered directly. These lines of progression—or *seniority districts*, as they are more generally known—are very often negotiated with a trade union and institutionalized in collective agreements. But a close examination suggests that they are reflective of more basic forces relating one job to another, and that their existence as paths through which movement regularly occurs predates the advent of unions—in fact, they often exist today in nonunion plants. Analogies to blue-collar lines of progression can be found in managerial jobs in large enterprises, which also tend to fall into definite sequences which, while not quite institutionalized, tend to be customary.[7] Similar sequences of movement between jobs emerge even in unstructured craft markets where there are no formal institutionalized linkages between the enterprises in which the sequential jobs are found.[8] Casual observation suggests the existence of sequences of this kind for higher-level professional careers which span enterprises. Indeed, the strong intuitive appeal of the concept appears to derive from the fact that most social scientists sense that the careers of their colleagues fall into a set of discernible paths of this kind.

Mobility chains may be identified both in a very specific, narrow sense, and on a broader typological plane. Manufacturing lines of progression are examples of specific mobility chains. In many plants, the jobs spelled out in the collective agreement could be further traced to the schools from which the labor was drawn and, through the schools, to particular neighborhoods. Even when chains cannot be extended in this very specific way, they can at least be traced to general types of schools, neighborhoods, and family types.

The three labor market segments identified in the preceding sections may be redefined as a broad typology of mobility chains. The distinction between these segments, which was originally based upon the types of jobs and workers, thus becomes dependent upon types of job sequences through which individuals pass in the course of their work lives. This redefinition serves, I think, to clarify many of the empirical problems to which the dual labor market hypothesis gave rise, since it is now clear that a particular job might lie on more than one type of mobility chain. The empirical issues should center, in other words, not on a single job, but on the precedent jobs from which the individual comes and the subsequent jobs to which he or she gains access.

In redefining the market segments in this way, it is relatively clear that the critical distinction between the primary and the secondary sectors is that the mobility chains of the former constitute some kind of career ladder along which there is progress toward higher-paying and higher-status jobs. This is true in both the upper and lower tiers and constitutes the rationale for speaking of the two tiers together as the primary sectors. In the secondary sector, by contrast, jobs do not fall into any regular progression of this kind: they are held in a more or less random fashion, so that a worker coming into a job may take the place of another person moving to the job which the first worker just left. These random mobility chains are rooted in the lower-class families, neighborhoods, and schools. Similarly, the preemployment stations on the upper- and lower-tier mobility chains would consist of working-class and middle-class institutions.

It is less clear at this stage of the analysis what distinguishes the job stations along the mobility chains of the two tiers. It will be argued later, however, that the important distinguishing characteristics are the extensive formal education prior to employment in the upper tier and the turnover patterns along the mobility chains in that tier, particularly the degree of geographic and social distance that those turnover patterns entail. These, in turn, reflect differences in the kind of traits required to perform work in the two sectors.

Several types of work are not easily encompassed within this simple typology, particularly when linked to the sociological subcultures. Perhaps the most glaring exception is craft jobs, which are generally thought to be held by working-class types; but in terms of job stability, variety, and, although perhaps less often, in terms of pay, advancement, and supervision these often resemble upper-tier (or middle-class) jobs. A second exception is certain routine white-collar jobs which nonetheless involve an important educational component such as clerical work, as well as certain jobs whose incumbents would generally be classed as middle class but which involve a degree of routine characteristic of the working class. An attempt will be made below to explain these deviant patterns.

The general typology developed here also tends to be a better description of male jobs than of female jobs, and of urban, industrial employment as contrasted to rural and particularly preindustrial labor markets. No attempt is made here to overcome these limitations.[9]

3. Productive Traits and Automatic Incidental Learning

The structure of mobility chains appears to be understandable in terms of individual worker traits and the process through which they are acquired and changed. The relevant worker traits range from very concrete skills, such as the performance of specific manual motions on a machine or certain kinds of useful reasoning (such as addition and multiplication), to more amorphous behavioral traits, such as the punctuality, regularity of attendance, ability to lead others, to follow instructions, and to accept supervision. Although diverse, each of these attributes appears to be encompassed by a definition of traits as *behavioral patterns which will be reproduced in response to a given stimulus in a particular type of environment.*

Not all traits, however, represent equivalent levels of knowledge or understanding. The behavior which is valued on the job can be produced by traits of two different kinds. The behavior may be produced as a direct response to the stimulus offered by the environment, in which case it may be termed a *specific trait.* Alternatively, the behavior may be derived from a rule (or set of rules) which enables the individual to deduce from the environment and the stimulus what the correct response may be, although that particular combination of circumstances may never have been encountered before. Such sets of rules may be termed *general traits*.

Specific traits are acquired in a process which we shall call *automatic incidental learning*. This is the process through which people tend to acquire a set of traits appropriate to the environment in which they are living or working automatically, simply by the fact that they are around and incidental to the activity in which they are directly engaged. The paradigm of this process is training on the job in the process of production.[10] Such training is automatic in the sense that it occurs without the consciousness of the individuals involved, so that it is often termed "learning by osmosis." It is incidental to the activity in which the individual is directly engaged and to which the institution is devoted, i.e., production. Similar learning occurs at home where it is incidental to family life and leisure activities and in the school, where it is incidental to formal classroom instruction.

The learning process appears understandable in terms of an amalgam of concepts derived from learning theory, social psychology, and the process of socialization as understood by sociologists.[11] The productive traits themselves may be thought of as habits in the sense that that term is understood in learning theory, i.e., patterns of behavior and thought acquired through a process of reinforcement and changed by extinction. The reinforcements, however, are of several kinds. Certain of these reinforcements are very crude kinds of physical pressures and economic rewards, analogous, if not precisely equivalent, to those used in classical learning experiments such as those of Pavlov. Such pressures are inherent in any work environment, although in some they are more directly linked to job performance than in others. Thus, for example, the learning of efficient manual movements on a machine is frequently reinforced by the fact that inefficient movements are awkward and physically uncomfortable. It is similarly reinforced in some plants by a piecework system which links economic reward directly to individual units of output.

A second component of the learning process involves what in classical learning theory would be termed a *secondary reinforcement*, the tendency of imitation. Most people seem to have an acquired tendency to develop habits directly by imitating the behavior of others around them, generally without conscious effort and in the absence of any other direct reinforcement.

The third component of the learning process is related to the development of social groups. Such groups tend to form in any stable situation in which the same individuals come into regular and repeated contact with each other. The members of such groups develop a common set of behavioral patterns which they tend to elevate to the position of the group's norms and to treat as ethical precepts, adherence to which is viewed as a matter of right and wrong. New individuals entering environments in which these groups exist then tend to adopt the norms as habits, either because group pressure is used to enforce adherence and that pressure operates as a reinforcement or because a tendency to conform to group norms in a new environment is itself an acquired principle of behavior which acts, like imitation, as a secondary reinforcement. The learning involved in imitation and in conformity to groups' norms creates a tendency for individual productive traits to be a function of the traits of those people with whom they have social contact and seems to underly the process which sociologists call socialization.

Given the character of the environment, the speed with which the individual adjusts to it, i.e., acquires traits appropriate to effective operation within it, depends upon the traits which he or she brings to it. If these traits are congruent with those required by the new environment, then obviously no adjustment is required. If the traits are in conflict, then they must be extinguished before they can be replaced, and this prolongs the adjustment process. When conflicting traits are innate or very firmly rooted, adjustment cannot take place, and the individual may be completely barred from entry into the environment. Adjustment may also be forestalled when the individual must operate simultaneously in two environments requiring conflicting traits as, for example, when he or she holds two different kinds of work or when the home environment is very different from the work environment. The work of extinction in one environment is then overcome by reinforcement in the other. To the extent that traits are acquired (rather than innate), however, and workers move through environments sequentially, the traits which an individual carries with him or her will depend upon the previous environments through which he or she has passed, and, given the character of the new environment, the sequence of past environments thus become the major determinant of the adjustment process.

If the learning process which we have been describing explains the development of specific traits, how are general behavioral traits generated? Basically, there would appear to be two alternatives. First, general traits may be *induced* from a series of specific traits. In this case, the individual learns a series of different responses to a set of similar situations, and ultimately comes to recognize a general principle which distinguishes these environments and leads to the proper response in new situations not previously encountered. Second, the individual may learn the general rules directly through some kind of process of instruction. This is presumably the function of formal education. Education, of course, does not always serve this function. In fact it can be argued that general traits are always acquired through induction and that what school learning actually does is establish a background which facilitates induction from a relatively few specific behavioral patterns of general rules which would otherwise emerge only after exposure to a much wider range of experience. In any case, it appears that schooling is virtually never sufficient in and of itself to develop general traits; and whether because one needs practice to develop facility in their application or because schooling, although it facilitates induction, does not substitute for it, experience on the job seems to be a critical element of training in virtually every occupation.

The importance of posteducational experience suggests one final element of learning: general rules—or the facility to acquire them if that is what is learned in school—can *decompose* into a set of specific behavioral traits, if after they are learned, they are not exercised. Such decomposition will occur, for example, if after leaving school, an individual is confined to a limited range of situations, repeating the same behavioral patterns which come, so to speak, to be learned by rote, independently of the general principles from which they supposedly, and perhaps did in fact initially, derive.

It is in the distinction between general and specific traits that the basic difference between the upper and lower tiers of the primary labor market seems to lie. The traits displayed by workers in lower-tier jobs tend, as a rule, to be specific. They are, in other words, habits in and of themselves. The learning process, therefore, depends upon the ability of the individual to mold herself or himself to a specific set of surroundings in which the same behavioral patterns arise repeatedly. It is for this reason that lower-tier jobs place a premium upon stability and routine, and work tends to be repetitious, lacking inherent interest, and generally failing to command the conscious attention of the worker. It is for this reason, too, that formal education is relatively unimportant in such jobs, and formal education requirements are frequently circumvented.

In the upper tier, productive traits tend, by contrast, to be deduced from a set of general principles, and mobility chains are constructed, in like contrast, so as to produce these principles and develop facility in their application. This accounts for the role of formal education in upper-tier mobility chains. It implies that the relatively high mobility in the upper tier serves the function of exercising the general principles learned in school and preventing their decomposition into specific traits.

Craft mobility chains may be understood in these terms as a variant of the lower-tier mobility chain. What distinguishes a craft job from other working-class jobs in the United States (in Europe the term *craft* is used somewhat differently) is the number of specific tasks which a craftsperson, as compared for example to a production worker, has mastered. As these tasks accumulate, a certain number of craftsworkers induce general principles from them, and many of these people go on—especially in the construction trades, but also in such trades as machinists, tool and dye making, cooks, chefs, etc.—to become supervisors, independent entrepreneurs, designers, and inventors.[12] This accounts for the fact that craft mobility chains tend to lead into those jobs which are typically thought of as middle class. On the other hand, the crafts tend to be working class in that the basic learning process is specific: formal education, even when it becomes important, invariably tends to accompany on-the-job training rather than, as in most middle-class careers, preceding it. While it is clear from any contact with the trades that certain artisans are working from a set of general precepts, it is also clear that for many others the skills will never amount to more than an array, however vast, of specific traits. The particular approach to knowledge, as well as the character of associations on the job and in leisure home activities for even those artisans who do develop general skills, explains why they tend to remain working class in attitude and outlook despite the fact that the income and status of their position is often equivalent to the middle class.

The other important deviation consists of workers who are middle class in background and outlook but whose careers exhibit very little of the mobility characteristic of the upper tier and whose work tends to be uninteresting and routine. They may be interpreted as people who began in upper-tier-type mobility chains but whose general skills decomposed into a set of specific traits because they were applied in only a limited number of tasks. It is not possible to identify this phenomenon with a single type of career or occupation recognized in common parlance as one can in the case of the craft pattern. A number of bureaucratic careers in the civil service do seem to follow this model. In other cases, however, the careers in which this is involved tend to be ideosyncratic; certain individuals get blocked at some point and remain behind in a job which for them becomes increasingly routine, while others, moving through a similar set of stations early in their careers, rise to higher positions which involve a greater variety of work. The difference may be due in some cases to distinctive characteristics of individuals; in the other cases, it may be simply a matter of chance that an individual, because of an unusual period of stability in an otherwise variable work load or some peculiarity in opportunities for promotion (a sudden dearth of vacancies or unusually stiff competition), remains so long with a set of tasks that her/his general skills decompose.

This last pattern, which we are explaining as a deviation from the dominant upper-tier pattern by decomposition, is to be distinguished from a number of white-collar career paths which involve essentially repetitive work, such as lower-level clerical and sales jobs. These, I would argue, only appear to be upper tier because of the association of the latter with the middle class and because of a tendency to draw a parallel between the middle and the working classes, on the one hand, and white-collar and blue-collar jobs on the other. Because the work is basically repetitive and the traits required are specifically learned, the jobs belong essentially to the lower tier. If the typology developed here fails to contain them, it is due less to its epistomological foundations than to the fact that it is designed largely to explain male careers and fails to adequately characterize the careers of women, who dominate many of these employments.

Part 2. The Construction of
Mobility Chains

From the point of view of social policy, the critical issue, of course, is not simply that mobility chains exist and can be distinguished in these ways, but why they are constructed as they are and how they can be changed. The answers to these questions lie in further examination of the process of "automatic, incidental learning." That process is not simply one of learning but, more fundamentally, one of adjustment between the individual and any new environment which he or she enters. It implies that, through physical reinforcements, imitation, and conformity, an individual entering a new environment will eventually be molded to it, subject only to the constraints imposed by his/her innate characteristics and by other environments in which he/she must operate simultaneously and which, therefore, interfere with the extinction of antagonistic traits. Understood in these terms as a process of adjustment, it is clear that it is not peculiar to movement between jobs along lower-tier mobility chains where specific productive traits are developed. A similar adjustment between the individual and the new jobs which she or he enters must occur in upper-tier mobility chains when there is a disparity between the traits required by the work environment and those carried by the individual and in the secondary sector. It also occurs in movement between nonwork environments: in moving from the family to the school, between schools, and from school into a first job.

The process of adjustment, however, is one which carries costs, both to the individual and to the institution in which it occurs. The costs to the individual arise because learning depends upon the reinforcement through the administration of pleasure and pain. The cost to the institution is generated by the tendency of the individual to disrupt the environment in which he or she is operating until he or she has accommodated to it.

This suggests that the construction of mobility chains can be cast as a conventional problem of cost minimization: jobs (or, more broadly, stations) are formed into chains, it implies, so as to minimize the amount of adjustment involved in movement from one station to another. To complete the theory along these lines, one would want to translate the concept of "adjustment" into monetary costs (or, possibly, opportunity costs) and recognize that certain wage differentials could compensate for excessive adjustment costs. Thus a chain might be formed involving an adjustment process more costly than some other alternative if the differentials in the wage bills of the two alternatives were greater than the added cost. But, basically, this approach leads one to imagine an economy tending toward a steady state in which jobs form into a set of least-cost chains along which the requisite supply of labor is generated, and disturbances which strain the ability to supply required labor through the original channels initiate a search for some new set of least-cost alternatives. In any subsector of the economy—or any particular job—the other jobs in the economy would form some rank order according to the cost of mobility from them into the job in question, and as demand increased progressively, these jobs would be tapped in succession.

The difficulty with this approach is that it ignores several facets of automatic incidental learning which suggest that the cost of movement between two jobs will decline rapidly toward zero with the amount of movement which takes place and the period of time over which it has occurred. Under these circumstances, the savings to be had from adjusting to an increase in demand in a "least-cost" fashion may be quite small and ephemeral; the pressures to do so would be correspondingly reduced and quickly eliminated if, as seems likely, the various alternatives are not readily apparent and can be discovered only through an extensive search process which itself carries costs. The door is then open for a variety of other factors to determine the evolution of mobility chains. And a theory of mobility is at least obliged to identify the circumstances under which other factors are likely to dominate. Ideally it would specify these other factors as well. For these purposes, the properties of the learning process which lead the cost of mobility to decline with movement must be specified. These are basically as follows.

First, the dependence of learning on imitation and conformity makes it possible to construct mobility chains along which learning precedes movement. This will occur if there is contact between people at successive stations along a mobility chain. People of one station can then be introduced to the skills and behavioral traits required for the next station before they actually make the move and before these traits can have any effect one way or the other on the efficiency of the productive process. In the extreme, a person will be able to absorb all the traits required to perform the next job in a mobility chain before moving into it. But even where this person cannot absorb all the traits, such prior exposure tends to reduce the cost of adjustment. To the extent that the prior learning depends upon some underlying tendency to imitate and conform (rather than the direct administration of physical and psychological reinforcements), it is not only costless to the institutions in which it occurs but also painless to the individual involved.

Certain jobs fall naturally into this relationship where prior learning occurs. The apprentice learns from the journeyman in this way in construction; the stockboy learns from the stock clerk in a shoe factory. In the academy the Ph.D. candidate learns to teach as a student in the classroom. But, for the evolution of mobility chains, the critical point is that some of the contracts upon which this prior learning depends are generated by the mobility process itself. Thus, for example, in schools graduates often come back to teach at their own high schools, and this tends to reinforce a channel of mobility between certain high schools and certain colleges as students in high school acquire the specific training and broader norms which their teachers bring from college. As more of the high school teachers are drawn from a given college, the amount of adjustment which their students must go through to accommodate to college life declines.

Backflows of this particular type are probably relatively rare, but there is one kind of backflow which occurs regularly—that between the work environment and the home environment. This implies that when a new flow of labor between, for example, a job and a neighborhood is opened up, the opportunity for prior learning is created for other people in that neighborhood. The cost of adjustment for the children and friends of the first movers should be less than the initial cost of movement, and, to this extent, any pattern of movement, once initiated, will tend to be self-perpetuating and reinforcing. To this extent also the opportunities of whole groups of people are at stake when a new source of labor is opened up.

As we have used the concept, environments, to the extent that they are composed of people, are essentially defined by the characteristics of the individuals within them. Thus, the general principle at stake in the existence of regular backflows is a tendency for the donor environment to evolve toward the recipient environment as movement between them occurs. There is a corresponding tendency for the recipient environment to evolve toward the donor. Such a tendency is implicit in the postulate of *imitation* as a basic behavioral characteristic of individuals. Thus, just as new individuals will tend to adopt the behavioral traits of older workers by imitating their behavior, there will be a tendency for older workers to adopt the behavioral traits of new workers in the same way. When the number of new entrants is small in relation to the body of experienced workers, the effect of the former upon the latter is likely to be trivial. But when the number of new entrants becomes relatively large, their effect upon other workers begins to be important, and the burden of adjustment will no longer be borne solely by the entering individuals. Since the traits of the entering individuals reflect the characteristics of the environment from which they come, any tendency of the receiving environment to move toward the traits of new entrants implies a tendency for it to move toward the donor environment as well.

In sum, then, the movers tend to mediate between the donor environment and the receiving environment and, in the process of doing so, to bring the characteristics of the two environments closer to one another. The process is in many ways analogous to the mutual attraction exerted by two bodies of matter. As movement of individuals occurs between them, they should move toward each other and, eventually, collide or, *mejor dicho*, merge. The distance which each environment moves, moreover, should be a function of their relative sizes. This follows from the fact that, for any given amount of movement, the influence of the movers upon others in the environment should be proportionate to their numbers relative to the total population. The amount of change which occurs in the two environments will, of course, be a function of a number of other variables as well. Perhaps most importantly, it will depend upon the constraints—economic, technical and social—upon each of the environments involved. These specific constraints are examined in the next part of this chapter. Before turning to this, however, two more general points about constrained evolution may be made.

The first relates to the way in which extraneous characteristics, or traits, become barriers to movement. The basic argument is that when two environments consistently interchange people, the characteristics required to operate effectively within them will tend to evolve toward each other. In the case of job environments, however, one would expect the evolution to be constrained, and the tendency thwarted when those characteristics are economically dysfunctional. Job environments are, after all, located in economic institutions which permit such adjustments to proceed unrestrained only at the risk of their own demise. On the other hand, when the characteristics are economically irrelevant, or when their economic relevance is obscure, one would expect the evolution to proceed unrestricted. Thus, when there are regular flows of labor between two environments, all sorts of extraneous relationships between the donor and receiver are likely to grow up which, while they have nothing to do with the initiation of the flow, will act as a barrier to the entry of outsiders. An example is language: in much production work, it does not matter what language is spoken—it may not even be necessary that a single language be spoken. But if the work place starts to draw workers, all of whom speak the same language, language will eventually come to constitute a barrier to entry.

The existence of this phenomenon is particularly important in understanding how formal education and schooling affects mobility patterns. An educational environment is supposed to develop a set of traits in the people who pass through it which have a particular economic function. We have argued that it does in fact do so for upper-tier primary jobs, and that for the lower-tier primary jobs, its role in this regard is largely a myth. But, in addition to the functional traits, schools tend to develop a set of other traits which are of no particular functional importance. That is to say, at least initially, these traits do not affect the efficiency with which work is done. If all, or virtually all, the people moving into a given work environment pass through the schools and acquire these traits, however, then (because environments tend to evolve toward each other) the economically irrelevant traits will tend to be incorporated in the work environment. When this occurs, the school does become a prerequisite for entry into the work environment. If this is what has occurred for lower-tier primary jobs in the United States—and I think a good case could be made that it has—then one's attitude toward educational policy and job requirements becomes a good deal more complex than that suggested by our characterization of lower-tier mobility chains as involving learning of specific traits on the job. In particular, it suggests that in attempting to change patterns of mobility, formal education cannot be treated as simply a screening or rationing device, however valid that view of formal education may be in understanding the origins of existing mobility patterns.

A similar point may be made in relation to the role of education in upper-tier chains where we have argued that it performs a critical function. The tendency for environments to evolve toward each other, by incorporating whatever traits are carried by the people who pass through them, suggests that the *informal* learning which occurs in the schools, and the on-the-job learning which occurs along upper-tier chains after school, may eventually come to constitute as real a barrier to movement as the formal education which explains the original construction of these chains.

A second point which emerges from consideration of the process through which environments evolve toward each other has to do with the way in which mobility chains are constructed and changed. A basic problem for policy is the attempt to gain access to the initial station on a mobility chain for a new group of workers. This is essentially what we have been trying to do for "disadvantaged" workers; it is a process which has operated historically as the vehicle for social mobility of immigrants from abroad. It may be described as an attempt to attach a new station to the bottom of an existing mobility chain. If successful, it leads to a process whereby the initial station on the old mobility chain and the new station which is being attached to it evolve toward each other. Thus, in the case of black workers from the ghetto gaining access to white jobs, one hopes that the initial group of blacks placed in those jobs will set off a process through which the ghetto environment becomes better suited to the development of productive traits prior to employment and, by the same token, that the work environment becomes better adapted to the traits of ghetto workers.

In this process of evolution, however, the higher stations on the mobility must act as a constraint upon the evolution of the initial station toward the new source of labor. If they do not act as an effective constraint and the initial station evolves freely, a point may be reached when that station becomes so different from the subsequent stations on the chain that it is effectively detached from the chain, and entry begins to occur at the second station rather than at the first. This is what seems to have happened with a number of jobs newly opened to blacks in the last decade: it appeared that people were gaining access to the initial station on a mobility chain in the primary market, but the end result was that the station adapted the characteristics of the secondary jobs from which the new workers had come and was simply detached from the mobility chain.

Something of the same thing may have occurred historically as the working class has attempted to use education to gain access to upper-tier primary jobs. As long as the schools are dominated by students drawn from middle-class backgrounds and the number of working-class students is small, then the latter are forced to adapt (or, more exactly, socialize) to the middle-class view of education and the educational process, a view which, as we have seen, is supportive of the function that education performs in upper-tier mobility chains. Thus, there is some relatively small number of working-class students who can use a given school as a vehicle for social mobility. When large numbers of such students attempt to do so, however, as has historically been the case in the United States, then they swamp the educational environment and impose their own values and norms upon it. These norms are not, as we have seen, conducive to upper-tier jobs; they lead to schools which emphasize rigid disciplinary rules, and specific, functional knowledge in the same way that these things are emphasized in lower-tier jobs. The process is, in other words, very much the same as that which occurs in the attempt at black mobility: the environment which once served as an initial station on the mobility chain (in this case the schools) evolves so far toward the environment from which it is drawing a new source of entrants (working-class families) that it becomes detached from the original mobility chains (leading to professional and managerial jobs).

Part 3: The Underlying Determinants of Mobility Chains: Technology and Social Class

The considerations of the preceding section, while useful in assessing certain aspects of public policy in the last ten years, shed little light in and of themselves upon the underlying determinants of existing mobility chains and, in particular, upon the question of what generates the basic segments into which the labor market appears to divide. It is not possible to provide a definitive answer to this question, but the logic of the problem and a variety of scattered pieces of evidence drawn from sociological studies and the labor market research of my own and others suggest the following series of hypotheses about technology and class subcultures. These hypotheses may be developed in terms of the traditional problem of adjustments in the demand for and supply of different types of workers. Suppose, in other words, that there is a structural imbalance in the labor market: that, while the total number of workers is equal to the total number of jobs, the composition of the two does not match: certain types of workers are in excess supply while there is excess demand for other types. How is balance then restored? Does the composition of the labor force shift or does demand adjust so that the types of workers in excess supply can be employed in the available jobs? In our terms, there are basically three types of workers who should be recognized for this exercise: workers to fill jobs in the secondary sector, in the lower tier of the primary sector, and in the upper tier of the primary sector. The supply for these types of labor is rooted in class subcultures: the demand in the technology. Each may be examined separately.

1. The Technology

Conventional theory suggests that adjustment in the demand for labor may be basically of two kinds: the first is a shift in the composition of the demand for the final product which, unless all products use different types of labor in the same proportions, will result in shifts in the composition of labor demand; the second kind of adjustment is a change in the techniques utilized to produce a given final output. The speed with which these adjustments occur should be influenced by the extent to which the techniques of production and the composition of final output are frozen in fixed capital equipment which acts to inhibit change. These adjustments are generally thought to be triggered by changes in relative prices and wages, and any constraints upon their rate of change will also act to inhibit adjustment.

My own studies of the border line between the primary and secondary markets suggests that this conventional picture leaves out an important dimension of the technology, particularly as it relates to the segments of the labor market which have concerned us. Most industries appear to be operating as if they consistently faced a choice between two different techniques of production.[14] One of these techniques, reminiscent of Adam Smith's pin factory, breaks the work down into a series of highly specialized, individual tasks: the tasks are then assigned singly to workers who perform them, frequently with considerable mechanical aid. As a result, this technique tends to involve a relatively large complement of capital equipment. The production and maintenance jobs which this technique generates lend themselves to incorporation into the kind of mobility chains and specific learning processes which characterize the lower tier of the primary sector, although a complement of professional and managerial personnel drawn from the upper tier is required and the bottom stations on the lower-tier chains can be detached and assigned to workers drawn from the secondary labor market.

The alternative technique is one which utilizes a much more general set of skills: work is less finely divided into a set of individual, carefully defined tasks, and considerably less capital equipment is employed in production. The jobs generated by this technology tend, on the whole, either to be quite unskilled and involving menial work and obvious but nonroutine judgment, or, alternatively, to require highly trained craftsworkers and generally trained professionals. There are very few intermediate positions. As a result, the jobs do not lend themselves to construction of career ladders, and employment tends to bifurcate into two groups: workers drawn from the secondary sector holding the unskilled jobs and another group drawn from the crafts at the top of the lower tier or professionals drawn from the upper tier.

The choice between these two techniques appears to be dominated by three variables: the degree of standardization of product demand, the stability of that demand, and its certainty. The specialized, capital-intensive technique lends itself to production for a standardized market where demand is either stable or, if it does so, fluctuates in a predictable manner and within sufficiently narrow limits that the fluctuations can be met through inventory changes without interrupting production. Under these circumstances, both the capital and labor involved in production remain fully employed. When, on the other hand, there are wide or unpredictable fluctuations, the capital investment required by the first technique is deterred. It is also difficult to specialize the labor force, and the employment of people who can transfer to other activities when output declines is promoted—hence the reliance upon craftsworkers, the secondary sector, or the upper tier, all of whom possess the characteristic of transferability. Variability in the nature of the product acts like variability in final demand to favor general, as opposed to specifically or narrowly, trained labor for reasons which are fairly obvious. It is less obvious why the lack of a standardized product should deter fixed capital investment, but this does seem to be the case.

Most industries seem to use the two techniques simultaneously, and although they are sometimes found only in different firms, or at least in plants of the same firm, they can often be found operating side by side in the same plant. This is because, even when the degree of standardization, stability, and predictability necessary to justify the specific technique are generally met, there tend to be variations above the stable base of demand which are sufficiently random so that the investment required to meet them through the specific technique is not justified. Conversely, even when the bulk of demand is so unpredictable that only the employment of highly mobile factors of production can be justified, there is generally some minimal level of demand which is sustainable and which it pays to meet through specialized production. Industries organize differently to meet these two components of demand. In some industries, certain firms will pick out the stable portion and refuse to increase production above that level. Their customers must, therefore, wait in line, and when the line gets long, they are drawn off by other firms who utilize the more general, less intensive technology. Components of the machine and tool and dye industry seem to work in this way. In other industries, a single firm will meet both the fluctuating and the variable portions of demand, and the two techniques can be seen operating simultaneously side by side. One large paint brush manufacturer which I recently visited exemplified the second case.

Industries also divide between the two techniques according to the degree of standardization of the product, again sometimes by firms and other times within the same firm. Thus, for example, in the garment industry there is a division between the low-priced market which produces long runs of standard items (and within that, certain segments like the work-cloth segment, where there is little variation in output from year to year) and the high-priced, high-fashion segment where these runs are short and fashions change extremely rapidly. The restaurant industry, to take another example, divides between a standard segment, running from sandwich shops at the bottom of the price range to steak houses at the top, and a variable segment composed of haute cuisine and, to a lesser extent, banquets and catering.

A final point which seems important in understanding the relationship between the techniques is that, although the two techniques operate simultaneously, there also appears to be an important process in time whereby the specific technique evolves out of the general technique. What seems to occur is something like the following: when a previously variable output stabilizes, the workers associated with its production find themselves spending full time at what was initially thought to be a temporary assignment. Those workers who stay under these circumstances find their general skills degenerating into a set of specific traits. Many generally trained workers refuse, for this reason, to remain, and their departure forces management to find replacements, often through internal promotion, which the stabilization of demand permits. Once the internal promotion channels are opened, it becomes possible to attract and hold workers in unskilled entry positions; in this way, the unskilled jobs are transferred from the secondary to the primary market. It is this kind of evolutionary process through which the types of labor change.

A similar, but in some ways more important, evolution occurs in the technology. Once production stabilizes, a whole series of technological changes begin to take place. When the product is similar to that produced elsewhere, the new technology can be "borrowed," and these changes involve an explicit decision to introduce equipment already in operation elsewhere. When the product is unique and such borrowing cannot occur, the process is similar but less dramatic. Once people are working continually at the same thing, different tasks begin to be separated out and distinguished. This facilitates the development of mechanical substitutes for human actions through a series of changes which are individually often no more than minor modifications in existing equipment. In other words, the fact that the technology is specialized and the operations separately identified, apparently enables people to perceive the opportunities for improvement in a new way. In sum, then, what occurs is a gradual evolution of the specialized technology from the general technology over time. The evolution is an intellectual process which must then have an inherent dynamic, or pacing system, of its own. The speed with which it occurs can probably be increased by economic pressures but only within limits. In looking at a cross section of industries, therefore, one would expect that the number of jobs which lends itself to lower-tier mobility chains, relative to those in the upper tier and in the secondary sector, would be a function not only of the stability and certainty of demand at any moment of time, but also of the length of time which demand had possessed these characteristics.

Together, what these points about the technology suggest is that, for the adjustment of demand to the composition of supply, the critical variables are the standardization, stability, and certainty of demand for the product. Changes in this direction generally in the economy as a whole, or through changes in the composition of product demand, will favor jobs which lend themselves to incorporation into lower-tier mobility chains. Because such chains tend to involve fixed capital investment, however, there will be a certain irreversibility in the process. It is easier for the economy to move toward lower-tier mobility chains than away from them.

2. The Supply of Labor:
Class Subcultures

The class subcultures are such that secondary jobs can be filled by labor drawn from the lower class, or by working- and middle-class *youth*. The latter pass through a period of adventure and action-seeking in adolescence and early adulthood before settling down into the routine family life, stable employment, and, in the case of the middle class, professional career training. During this period they have many of the characteristics of lower-class workers: they are not seeking and could not sustain a commitment to a career ladder. Employees seeking career workers will not hire them. They are thus forced, if they are to work at all, to accept the types of work available in the secondary sector; and, within the limit of certain social and geographic restrictions, these youths tend to share many of the employments of the secondary sector with lower-class adults. The fact that they do is one of the additional humiliations of lower-class status in American society. In any case, to the extent that these youths are a significant segment of the secondary sector, their number constitutes one of the major constraints upon the supply of labor for secondary work.

The other constraint is the number of people emerging from the lower class. There is no want of theories to explain the lower-class subculture.[16] To examine them here would constitute a considerable digression. Instead, we put forth a single hypothesis: that lower-class subculture is most fruitfully viewed as derivative of the subculture of the working class and that the process of derivation is closely linked to that of migration. This hypothesis is suggested by the fact that the fundamental difference between the two subcultures emerges only in adulthood: in adolescence, the life-styles of the working and lower classes are very similar. The lower-class pattern, thus, appears to be a carry-over into adulthood of a mode of behavior which, among the working class, is confined to adolescence. This implies that the roots of lower-class culture are to be found in an examination of the process of transition from adolescence to adulthood which occurs among the working class.

That transition appears to be characterized by three basic elements:

1. Family formation (getting married and having children)
2. The stabilization of employment patterns
3. The transition in the character of peer group activities.

This last item seems to be a particularly important element both in supporting the adolescent life-style and in its abandonment. The peer group tends to be composed of friends acquired in the school or neighborhood and carried throughout life. These friends engage in the adventures of adolescence together. Most of them then marry, have children, and obtain stable employment at about the same time, and the fact that they do changes the whole character of the activities in which the group engages and the norms which it establishes and to which its members adhere. Thus, the peer groups tend to support and encourage the transition out of adolescence.

If the working-class transition is characterized in this way, the failure to complete it, which seems to typify the lower class, might be traced to any one of the components: a lack of stable employment, a failure to form a family, or the lack of a supportive peer group.

The process of migration through which the American labor supply traditionally has been fed is disruptive to all three factors. Migrants have generally come from rural agricultural communities in Europe, Latin America, or, especially recently, the black South. These communities are composed of a network of extended family and peer group relationships not unlike those which characterize the urban working class and to which the subculture of the latter is sometimes traced. Most migrants leave home, however, at more or less the time when they would be passing through adolescence and into adulthood. In migrating, they leave behind their childhood peer group and thus lose whatever supporting role that group might play in the transition: they often leave behind as well (at least temporarily) a wife and young children, thus tending to attenuate the influence of family formation upon the stabilization of life-styles; sometimes (although after a migration stream is started and there are relatives at the destination, this is less important), the extended family network in which working-class activity—and presumably a considerable amount of the social pressure to settle down—is located is lost. Finally, the process of migration and reorientation at the destination reduces the opportunities for stable employment.

At the destination, migrant communities seem to be accompanied by a considerable amount of flux, which prevents the development of stable relationships and reduces the prospect for a successful transition even for the children born in the cities. People are forever moving around from one neighborhood to another as new members of the family arrive and living accommodations have to be expanded. Children are frequently sent home to be cared for by grandparents during periods of economic hardship. Particularly for blacks and Puerto Ricans and especially with the reduced cost of transportation of recent years, whole families may return home for extended visits, for vacation, or in cases of emergency, in search of employment, and the like. This continual flux inevitably undermines the transition to the stable routine life-style of the working class for those who are themselves engaged in it. But it probably also constitutes a threat to the transition of those who are not themselves directly involved, for it disrupts peer group relationships for those who remain in the neighborhood quite as effectively as it does for those who move in and out. Since employers tend to judge people in terms of the characteristics dominant among the ethnic groups to which they are attached, membership in an ethnic group which, because of the amount of reverse migration, has a reputation for job turnover increases the difficulty of finding acceptance in stable employment.

The American experience with immigrants has been one in which the society is fed by a series of waves of migrants from different origins with cultural, racial, and linguistic barriers separating them from each other. It seems likely, therefore, that part of what appears to be an assimilation or acculturation process is actually related to a cycle of stabilization. In the early stages of any new migration, the ethnic community is dominated by the flux of migration, and this flux prevents the adult transition to a routine life cycle. As the community ages, there begins to develop a second generation of people, some of whom are rooted in the neighborhood with an extended family network growing up around them; but as long as this group is small relative to the population of more recent migrants, the latter tend to determine the character of the community in such a way as to minimize the prospects for a successful adult transition. Eventually, however, the number of people rooted in the destination becomes so large relative to the inflow of new migrants that *they* begin to dominate the atmosphere of the ethnic community, whose members then start to move in significant numbers from a lower- to a working-class subculture. In the United States, the transition has been hastened by the fact that changes in immigration laws and events in the home country have often acted to cut off the flow of new migrants and reduce the possibilities for returning home.

The basic hypothesis, then, is that the size of the lower class and hence the supply of workers to fill secondary jobs are a function of the rate of in-migration of ethnic and racial groups, and of the size of the stock of second- and third-generation members of these groups relative to the inflow of new members. As the new migrant stream declines, both absolutely and relative to the second and third generations, there should be a decline in the supply of workers for secondary jobs and an increase of the supply of workers for jobs in the lower tier of the primary market. Finally, because of the sensitivity of the transition to a routine life-style to the availability of stable work and the interaction among individuals through the peer group, it is likely that, given the rate of inflow of new migrants and the relative size of older members of the community, the rate at which the community generates primary workers is also directly influenced by the availability of primary jobs.

In sum, then, the basic hypothesis is that the lower-class subculture is a derivative of the working-class pattern in which people fail to make a transition into a routine life-style pattern as adults; that the transition is associated with family formation and with the availability of stable jobs not only to the individual but also to enough other members of his or her peer groups so that the groups' norms change in such a way as to support the changes in the individual life-style; that the process of migration and the presence of large numbers of recent migrants in the community are disruptive of the transition because they inhibit family formation, peer group development, and maintenance of stable employment; and, thus, that the migrant process is a major determinant of the relative numbers of the lower and working classes.

3. The Adjustment Process

It should now be possible to bring the preceding analysis of demand and supply together into an overall picture of the adjustment process. The basic hypothesis is essentially that the underlying determinant of the division into different types of mobility chains is the structure of technology. This dictates a core of jobs that lend themselves to the building of lower-tier mobility chains. The jobs at the bottom of these mobility chains can, but need not, be detached and formed into a secondary sector. The technology which generates these core jobs also has a much smaller complement of work, which lends itself to upper-tier mobility chains. Around this core is a second technology, associated with the uncertainty and instability of demand, which generates a job structure that does not lend itself to lower-tier mobility chains, but instead to secondary jobs and upper-tier mobility chains. Thus, in terms of adjustment, the technology permits variation along two dimensions: (1) the distribution of demand between the core and the periphery, and (2) the attachment or detachment of jobs in the core at the bottom of the lower-tier chains. There is possibly a third dimension in that certain jobs may be built into either lower- or upper-tier chains depending upon whether the rules of hiring and tenure in those jobs force sufficient movement to prevent a set of general traits from deteriorating into specific applications of them. Finally, to the extent that different products generate different proportions of the jobs types, adjustment can also be affected by changes in the composition of final demand.

The supply side of the market consists of a series of individuals coming out of lower-class, working-class, and middle-class institutions. What I have argued in this text is that youths from all three backgrounds are adapted essentially to secondary work, and the number of youths in the labor force constitutes one determinant of the supply of secondary workers. As these groups age, the middle-class flows tend to move into the upper tier, and the working class into the lower tier, leaving the lower class in the secondary market. A central hypothesis of the analysis, however, is that the lower-class adult life-style is essentially a derivative of the working-class style. That derivation is a complex function of several variables. But one of these variables is the availability of stable employment to youths at the point of transition to adulthood. Lower-class workers at this stage of their lives are particularly adjustable to one or the other kinds of job structures, depending upon what kind of work is available. The other important determinant of the derivation is the process of migration. The lower-class subculture is a product of the early stages of a migration such that as a given migration stream ages and the proportion of recent migrants declines, a working-class subculture in the racial and ethnic group involved in the migration is restored. The rate at which this process proceeds should then be a function of the relative availability of primary and secondary jobs. If there is an excess demand for secondary workers, new migration should be encouraged or the stabilization of older migrant communities retarded, or both. If there is an excess supply of secondary workers, then, conversely, the stabilization of older migrant communities should be hastened and new migration retarded.

It would be nice to understand adjustments in the upper tier of the primary market in a similar clear-cut manner. Certain postulates about these jobs can be deduced, but I feel less confident about their validity. One postulate is that bottlenecks in the upper tier will lead to an increase in the size of the core economy through standardization and mechanization. The assumption is that although the core economy requires a complement of upper-tier workers, the input of such workers per unit of output is less than on the periphery. A second postulate is that the spread of higher education has created a permanent excess supply of upper-tier workers, at least within wide limits, and a variation in demand results in variations in the rate of promotion (or mobility) and, hence, in the relative number of potential upper-tier workers whose general knowledge decomposes through lack of exercise into specific behavioral traits. The most general postulate is that both factors are operative: there is a potential supply of upper-tier workers created by the output of the educational system. If supply exceeds demand, a part of that supply simply falls back into, in effect, the lower tier. If demand exceeds supply, the adjustment comes through the distribution of work between the core and the periphery.

Thus, in sum, adjustment can take place on either the demand or the supply side of the market. On the demand side, it will have to occur through changes in the distribution of output between the periphery and the core, or through changes in the composition of final demand. It can also occur by detaching jobs at the bottom and top of lower-tier mobility chains, filling the former with secondary workers and moving the latter to the upper tier through systematic rotation of labor. On the supply side, the main avenue of adjustment between secondary and primary workers is the rate at which new migrant communities can be expanded and the aging of older communities retarded. The supply of upper-tier workers depends heavily upon the output of the school system, and this appears to introduce a certain asymmetry of responses. It is difficult to expand supply beyond the upper bound which that output imposes, but an excess supply will simply fall into the lower tier through specific employments which that sector has to offer. This, it will be noted, is not a theory which says anything about a price system, and to introduce it here would require a much expanded format. It should be pointed out, however, that certain of the adjustment mechanisms could be triggered by price changes while others would operate effectively without a price trigger.

Notes

1. Michael J. Piore, "On-the-job Training in a Dual Labor Market" in Arnold Weber et al., *Public Private Manpower Policies* (Madison, Wisc.: Industrial

Relations Research Association, 1969); "Jobs and Training" in Samuel Beer and Richard Barringer, *The State and the Poor* (Cambridge: Winthrop Publishers Inc., 1970) and Peter B. Doeringer and Michael J. Piore, *Internal Labor Markets and Manpower Analysis* (Lexington, Mass.: D.C. Heath, 1971), Chapter 8. See, more generally, David M. Gordon, "Economic Theories of Poverty and Unemployment," mimeo, National Bureau of Economic Research, January, 1971.

2. There is nonetheless a certain amount of evidence bearing upon this hypothesis—certainly the most ingenious of which is David Gordon, *Class, Productivity, and Class: A Study of Labor Market Stratification* (Unpublished doctoral dissertation, Harvard University, May, 1971). Among the other work that has direct bearing, see also Robert E. Hall, "Prospects for Shifting The Phillips Curve," *Brookings Papers on Economic Activity* (3): 659-702, 1971; Arthur J. Alexander, "Income, Experience and the Structure of Internal Labor Markets," Rand Corporation, 1971; and Bennett Harrison, *Education, Training, and the Urban Ghetto* (Unpublished Ph.D. dissertation, University of Pennsylvania, 1970).

3. See, particularly, Michael J. Piore, "On-the-job Training in a Dual Labor Market."

4. Michael J. Piore, *Upward Mobility: Job Monotony and Labor Market Structure*, M.I.T. Working Paper No. 90, September, 1972.

5. The following on class subcultures draws heavily upon Herbert J. Gans, *The Urban Villagers* (New York: The Free Press, 1962), Chapter 11. My understanding of lower-class subculture and its relationship to the labor market has also been much shaped by Elliot Liebow, *Tally's Corner* (Boston: Little Brown, 1967).

6. See Doeringer and Piore, *Internal Labor Markets*, Chapter 3.

7. See, for example, Theodore Alfred, "Checkers or Choice in Manpower Management," *Harvard Business Review* 14(1): 151-169, January-February, 1967; Edith T. Penrose, *The Theory of Growth of the Firm* (New York: Wiley, 1959); and William H. Whyte, *The Organization Man* (New York: Doubleday Anchor Books, 1956).

8. David P. Taylor and Michael J. Piore, "Federal Training Programs for Dispersed Employment Occupations," in Stanley Jacks, ed., *Issue in Labor Policy: Papers in Honor of Douglass Vincent Brown* (Cambridge: M.I.T. Press, 1971).

9. I think that these limitations can be overcome, particularly those relating to female employment, by reference to the differences between male and female roles in various subcultures, but it seemed that to try and do so in this essay would take us too far afield.

10. See Peter B. Doeringer and Michael J. Piore, "Labor Market Adjustment and Internal Training," *Proceedings of the 18th Annual Meeting*, Industrial Relations Research Association, New York, December, 1966, pp. 250-263; and Michael J. Piore, "On-the-job Training and Adjustment to Technological Change," *The Journal of Human Resources* 3(4): 435-449, Fall, 1968.

11. The following summary draws heavily upon George A. Kimble, *Hilgard and Marquis' Conditioning and Learning* (New York: Appleton-Century-Crofts, 1961); Neal E. Miller and John Dollard, *Social Learning and Imitation* (New Haven: Yale University Press, 1941); and Alexander P. Hore, *Handbook of Small Group Research* (New York: Free Press of Glencoe, 1962).

12. See Taylor and Piore, cited in note 8.

13. Some large organizations deliberately maintain pyramidal promotion ladders—and the civil service is perhaps a special case of this—but the shape of these ladders does not explain why some individuals, when passed over for promotion, remain in the organization while others leave to find jobs which will exercise their range of general skills.

14. Cf. Robert T. Averitt, *The Dual Economy* (New York: Morton and Co., 1968). Averitt's distinction between the center and the periphery corresponds very closely to that between the two technologies developed here. He is primarily concerned with industrial organization, but it is easy to see why the differences in labor utilization should be related to the organizational differences which he describes.

15. The following draws heavily upon a study of the labor market for recent migrants in Boston in which I am presently engaged. It is also influenced by Gans, *Urban Villagers.* See, in addition, Jeffery Piker, *Entry into the Labor Force* (Institute of Labor and Industrial Relations, University of Michigan-Wayne State, December, 1968); and Eugene B. Brody, ed., *Behavior in New Environments* (Beverly Hills: Sage Publications, 1969).

16. Charles A. Valentine, *Culture and Poverty* (Chicago: The University of Chicago Press, 1968).

6 The Economic Effect of Career Origins

Howard Birnbaum

Much emphasis in recent discussions about the distribution of income in the United States has concerned the effect of formal education and other skill training programs. This emphasis is found both in governmental policies to train and retrain the poor and in the emphasis of economists on human capital theory.[1] This concern with marginal productivity considerations assumes individual investment decisions are the crucial determinant of productivity, and hence of earnings.

As an alternative to that view, labor market segmentation theories[2] view the labor market as separated into different sectors with minimal worker mobility between the sectors. Framed in an institutional setting, the focus of these theories is on the demand side of the labor market, for it is these institutional, job, and firm characteristics such as working conditions and opportunities for on-the-job training and advancement, which, the segmentations theorists argue, define the sectors. With wages fixed by the job and technology,[3] the income distribution implications of these theories are derived from knowledge about the distribution and mobility of workers between the sectors. A crucial assumption is that little intersector mobility exists. Then, the income distribution pattern is fixed by the distribution of jobs and enterprise-employer demand considerations. Their conclusion is that only altering the structure of demand and of the opportunities offered by the job structure can alter the distribution of income.

The contradictory implications of these theories are obvious. For the human-capital proponents, the key is the individual skill development process. For the segmentation proponents, it is not individual choice, but the opportunity set limiting choice which is crucial.

Although human-capital theories are customarily developed and focused around an examination of individual responses, they are also compatible with views that consider differences between job structures as an important considera-

Primary financial assistance for this research was provided by the Manpower Administration, U.S. Department of Labor, under Research and Development Grant No. 71-25-71-02. Additional financial assistance was provided by the National Institute of Education, U.S. Department of Health, Education and Welfare under Research and Development Grant No. NE-6-00-3-0202. This research does not necessarily represent the official opinion or policy of the Departments of Labor or Health, Education and Welfare. The author is solely responsible for its contents. This research has benefited from the useful criticisms of Peter Doeringer and Zvi Griliches.

tion in explaining variations in individual outcomes. Segmentation theories quite precisely include in their analyses the responses of individuals to various kinds of job structures, allowing for an interaction of supply-and-demand considerations. These segmentation theories focus heavily on an analysis of the sources of differences in job structures. One place where the two approaches intersect is in considering the effect of the characteristics of jobs to which individuals respond and which heavily influence individuals' acquisition of marketable traits. This chapter attempts to clarify the nature of the effect of the "job experience" by focusing on the effects of career origins.

At least some of the problem in evaluating the operation of the labor market is due to the confusion and measurement problems surrounding the concept of job experience (commonly called the "job"), for it is the characteristics of the job ("job traits") which the segmentation theories posit as opposite to the human resources of the individual ("people traits") in the income determination process. Appropriate evaluation can occur only after the meaning of job experience is understood. As a step in that direction, this chapter first develops an analysis of career origins as a measure of the effect of the job experience. Then a category of job experiences is developed. Finally, these categories are used to suggest the potential magnitude of the limits which the job experience may place on the labor market experience of individuals.

Career Origins and the Skill Development Process

Both the segmentation and human capital theories emphasize, albeit in somewhat different fashions, that skill development and on-the-job training are important determinants of the distribution of earnings.[4] The economic significance of job experience and of career origins stems from this emphasis.

Individuals may learn from every job, developing specific and general skills and augmenting and altering their measured and unmeasured human resources. Since jobs differ in both quantity and quality of opportunity for acquiring skills, the opportunity potential of every job for developing more human resources is important in determining future income streams. This training differential can translate into widening income differentials, for the same training does not necessarily translate into the same earnings payoff. For example, the dollar value of a unit of additional training depends on whether the individual can use her/his training. Someone who completes a training program one year before the retirement age of 65 may not be able to find an employer who is willing to use the individual's new skill for just that one year. But someone who completed the program at age 25 might get hired at a higher wage.

While differential experience in various jobs and job ladders produce different income streams *partly* because individuals face different learning opportunities for developing cognitive task skills, differences in income streams may *also* arise from individuals' moving along different job ladders which alter affective personality traits such as reliability, responsiveness to authority, and discipline, rather than, or in addition to, cognitive skills.[5]

The following examples suggest other possible relationships between training and earnings. Worker X, who starts with a skill advantage which can be translated into one year more of on-the-job training than that of worker Y, but is otherwise identical in qualifications, receives a wage differential of amount *A* in the first year. If X and Y continue to receive the same training, but X is simply one year ahead on the training ladder, and if both X and Y have similar training and promotional opportunities, X will always remain one year ahead of Y, but only one year ahead. So their wage differentials will reflect only this one-year differential, as shown in Figure 6-1.

However, because of the initial unit skill advantage, X may be placed in advanced training, e.g., an apprenticeship program. Then X is acquiring on-the-job training faster than Y, who became, for example, a dishwasher. Now, their initial wage difference because of their initial skill difference will continue to grow. While the individuals started out only one unit of training apart, as long as there is a difference in accumulating training, this difference in training and earnings increases.

So, because different jobs have different opportunities for developing cognitive and affective skills, starting wage differentials can become translated in the future into even larger differences. The examples also emphasize the difficulty of correctly measuring training and accumulated human resources. Even though both X and Y were in the labor force the same number of years—which is the standard proxy variable for on-the-job training—where X received valuable training, Y "wasted" her/his training time.

Both human-capital and segmentation theories similarly relate the influence

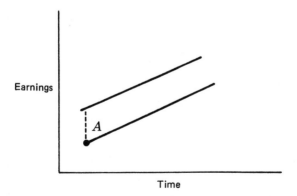

Figure 6-1. Age-Earning Profiles with Training Differential.

of training via on-the-job experience to the accumulation of measurable and unmeasurable human resources. By offering different opportunities to the individual to change his/her human resources, the job structure influences earnings. While changes in the individuals' skills are the apparent cause of differences in earnings, the underlying mechanism is differences in overall job experience. If measures which could correctly and totally measure the development of all marketable resources during the entire work history of an individual were available, then these measures could be used to estimate the effects of the job structure over and above the effects of the human resource variables developed prior to entry in the labor force. Unfortunately such measures are unavailable, and proxies must be found. A measure of career origins is suggested below as an appropriate proxy. While this measure is most appropriate to the logic of the labor market segmentation theories,[6] in the case of the human-capital argument, it provides a minimum estimate of the effect of the job structure.[7]

Employment considerations and career origins are best incorporated into the human capital framework by Rosen.[8] His model of the labor market is based on an implicit market for learning opportunities. Since different job experiences offer different opportunities for learning, and also have equalizing wage differences, "maximization of lifetime wealth is a problem of optimal capital accumulation and implies a choice of an optimum sequence of progression of work activities over working life,"[9] simultaneously determining both lifetime earnings and occupational patterns of workers. Initial job experience is a basic determinant of future earnings opportunities because career origins lay out a set of different learning opportunities. So initial "jobs with a 'future' really carry with them an implied pattern of lifetime work activity and income."[10] While individuals can switch jobs, the switching is related to initial position. So while the available data cannot adequately measure the job history, the association between initial and later positions will allow a measure of initial position to pick up a minimum estimate of the effect of the job structure.

Because of their emphasis on barriers to mobility, the segmentation theories more directly relate the economic significance of career origins to the economic impact of overall job experience. These theories emphasize that individuals come with histories, which make their human resources very durable and unmalleable. Where Rosen implicitly assumed that the optimal sequence of job progression was always feasible, the segmentation theories argue that barriers to mobility mean that previous work activities rule out certain future possibilities. Rather than emphasizing worker choice, as do the human-capital theories, the segmentation theories emphasize that once career origin is determined, opportunities for future job movement can narrow because of discrimination, limited opportunities for training, certification, promotion, and the differential development of "affective" personality traits. Lack of mobility and the importance of promotional and on-the-job training opportunities imply that career origins may be important determinants of career ending.[11]

So far it has been argued that differential skill, training, and promotional opportunities in individuals' early job experiences can lead to permanent earnings differentials. If jobs can be classified on the basis of opportunity for development, and if the effect of job experience can be isolated from the effect of the resources of the individuals in those jobs, then the economic effect of the job experience can be estimated.

An Economic Approach to Jobs

When economists have considered jobs, they have emphasized working conditions, unionization, wages, industry, and establishment of skills. A definition of job experience is developed here, based on skills and the skill development process, for both the human-capital and the segmentation theories agree on this emphasis on skill, when *skill* is broadly defined as the ability to perform tasks. Then skill reflects both personality traits emphasized by the segmentation theories, e.g., dependability, and the more customary specific task traits emphasized by the human-capital theories, e.g., cutting a straight line with a saw.[12]

Since every job entails a variety of tasks and since different jobs may involve overlapping tasks, dividing jobs into job categories on the basis of skill relationships entails looking at all the particular job tasks of a specific job. For example, the job "secretary" encompasses more than operating a typewriter. And jobs other than secretary may also involve typing. Skill-related job tasks belong to the same *skill family*. Different skill-related job tasks belong to a different skill family. For example, typing belongs in one skill family, while driving a tractor belongs in another. And job tasks in the same skill family differ according to the *level* of skill each involves, where "level" refers to the position of an imaginary learning curve. For example, the job "carpenter" encompasses a higher skill level than the job "apprentice carpenter."

Jobs differ not only in level of skill, but also in the range of skill families they encompass. The range and scope of the skill families a particular job encompasses are called the *breadth* of the job. This definition allows for overlap of job tasks. For example, while an accountant must be able to perform all the tasks of a bookkeeper, the "breadth" of his/her skills is much greater as he/she performs additional job tasks in the other skill families. Hence, on-the-job training and promotional opportunity involve improvements in both level and breadth of skill.

The *content* of any particular job, then, refers to a bundle of skill families used in the job task as well as to the level of skill in each of the particular skill families. Jobs are related to each other on the basis of whether they encompass the same, similar, or related skill bundles and are at the same, similar, or different levels. So both a doctor and a dentist are at the same level of similar skill bundles. Both can be opposed to an intern who has a similar bundle, but is at a lower level. There are then dimensions on which elasticities of substitution, training, promotional opportunities, and the requirements of a particular job, as well as mobility patterns, can be computed and compared.

This categorization allows for a spectrum of larger groups called *job sectors* to be aggregated from these considerations. The level of aggregation into the three job sectors chosen for this research corresponds closely to the three modes of work emphasized by the revised dual labor market theories, the upper and lower tiers of the primary sector, and the secondary sector.[13] Those jobs which involve similar numbers of skill bundles, even though they may be different skill bundles, and which involve being at the same level on each bundle, may be classified into a particular job sector. Therefore, lawyers and doctors are placed in the same job sector, while nurses and orderlies are in a different job sector. While the skills might belong to different skill families, the magnitudes of the training and promotional opportunities would be the same for jobs in each job sector. Since the effect of job experience on earnings comes from training and promotional opportunties, measuring the effect of the job experience, then, entails measuring the effect of these job sectors.

Appropriately measuring job content as distinct from the human resources of the individual in the job is crucial and difficult. The following two examples illustrate the problems. One problem is to measure accurately the "real" factor substitution possibilities and other technological considerations, as opposed to the "observed" patterns. Suppose it is observed that all ex-farmers become carpenters. This change could be because farmers enjoy working with their hands, and so find a job which also involves this, i.e., carpentry. Or the change could be because the skills which a farmer develops are easily transformable into those needed by a carpenter; i.e., building a barn is similar to building a house.

The second example further brings out the problem of distinguishing "job" traits from "people" traits by assuming that an accurate description of the "real" technological considerations of job content exists. Then, for example, among the technological considerations found for the job of furniture mover will be strenuous work activity. To satisfy this "real" requirement requires a strong person. This example suggests that because individuals are chosen for suitable characteristics, the job title may reflect the workers' embodied, but otherwise unmeasured human resources, rather than the content of the job. The problem is that not only do workers respond to the job experience, but the job title may also describe the worker.

However, before the effect of the job structure can be measured, the job sector classification scheme must first be operationalized.

Classification into Job

In this section the United States Census occupational classifications are provisionally divided into four job sectors and two residual categories on the basis of "level" and "breadth" of skill.[14] The effect on earnings of an individual starting her/his work history in a job in one of these job sectors will be the effect of career origins and will be the test of the economic effect of the job structure.

The census titles were classified into one of four job sectors: F1, F2, F3, F4, or one of the residual categories: FARM and P. F1 is composed of jobs which have both a high level and wide breadth of skill, where "level" refers to the position on an imaginary learning curve and "breadth" refers to the number of skill families encompassed. F2 includes those jobs with middle ranges of level and breadth of skill. Those jobs which involve no or very low levels and breadth of skill were placed in F4. There do exist certain jobs which have a level of skill different from their breadth. For instance, apprentices have a similar breadth of skill as journeymen, yet their level is lower. So F1 and F2 can have subgroups which are composed of those jobs with a higher measure of one criterion, but a lower measure of the other. Only two jobs were found in the F1 subgroup. These are placed in F2. The F2 subgroup which had a middle level or a middle breadth of skill but whose other criterion was low was labeled F3. Obviously rural activities such as farming were placed in the residual category FARM. The other residual category, P, consists of those jobs which, for one reason or another, simply did not fit into any classification. These included, for example, job titles which encompassed very wide and heterogeneous tasks, such as "occupation not reported," or job titles which were defined according to ability, yet unrelated to skill in the sense used here, such as musician. Table 6-1 shows several examples of the classification scheme.[15]

The Validity of Measures of Job Sector

This section presents an initial look at the 1966 National Longitudinal Survey of Men, 45 to 59 years old, to see if there is any validity in the job sector categorization and in the emphasis placed on career origins.[16]

To illustrate the amount and type of mobility existing within and across job sectors, a sample of 160 individuals who started in job sectors F1 to F4 was randomly selected from among the individuals in the 1966 National Longitudinal Survey. Forty individuals for each level of initial job sector were chosen in order to see if there were any patterns in job history. The results were quite revealing.[17]

The high-skill F1 starters not only tended to remain in F1, but virtually always maintained the same job title throughout their work careers, e.g., lawyers remained as lawyers. Among the middle-skill F1 starters, there were two patterns. (1) Some few individuals started and ended their careers in different, unrelated jobs—a plumber became a taxi driver and an insurance agent became a teacher. (2) But orderly career progression is clearly dominant for F2 starters: a

Table 6-1
Classification into Job Sectors

Level of Skill	Breadth of Skill		
	Wide	Middle	Low
High	Architects (F1) Managers–Manufac- turing (F1) Physician (F1)	Photographers (F2)	n.a.*
Middle	n.a.*	Journeyman (F2) Surveyor (F2) Manager, Food Establishment (F2) Nurse, Registered (F2)	Cook (F3) Physician's Attendant (F3) Truck Driver (F3)
Low	n.a.*	Apprentice (F3) Nurse, Practical (F3)	Elevator Operator (F4) Janitor (F4)

*n.a. (not applicable)–no job titles found in this classification.

draftsman became a machinist and then a foreman; a machinist became a foreman. Among the lower-skill F3 starters, there were again two patterns. (1) More individuals now seem to start and end their careers in different, unrelated jobs–a telephone lineman became a meat cutter; a knitter became successively a bartender, then an attendant, and ended as a manager. (2) However, there were still some individuals who seemed to follow logical career progressions either moving up a job ladder–like the apprentice machinist who became a journeyman machinist, and ended as a foreman–or remaining in the same job title–the barber remained a barber. Among the unskilled F4 starters, there appeared to be little career pattern except job switching. Most ended in jobs little different or "better" than the ones in which they started–a laundry operative became successively a professional attendant, then a charman, and ended as a porter; a porter became successively an assembler, a laborer, and finally ended by not reporting his occupation. But even here in the bottom starting sector, some few individuals did move up, although not too far and to apparently unrelated jobs–as the office boy who ended as a cabinet maker. The conclusion reached from these patterns of job movement is that career origins may perhaps serve as an adequate proxy for the entire work history.

Further evidence about the importance of career origins is presented in the intragenerational mobility matrix in Table 6-2 from sector of first job to sector of current job, that is, 1966. The percentages in the table relate to row totals

159

Table 6-2

Intragenerational Mobility Matrix of 1966 National Longitudinal Survey: Outflow Percentages by Row: First Job Sector (F1 to F4) to Current Job Sector (C1 to C4)

First Job Sector	C1: Highly Skilled	C2: Moderately Skilled	C3: Low-skilled	C4: Unskilled	CFARM: Residual	CP: Other Residual	Row%	Number of Individuals in Row
				Current Job Sector				
F1	72.9%	14.6%	6.3%	0.0%	0.0%	6.3%	2.8%	96
F2	24.9	45.3	8.6	6.5	0.8	14.3	7.1	245
F3	9.1	25.9	34.8	16.3	1.2	13.0	21.9	754
F4	5.5	23.2	24.4	27.2	1.4	18.4	28.1	970
FARM	2.0	14.1	20.0	33.1	13.2	0.0	21.7	748
P	9.1	22.1	20.2	18.2	1.4	29.1	18.5	639
Column %	9.4%	22.9%	23.3%	22.2%	3.9%	18.4%		

and are outflow percentages. For example, of the 96 individuals (28 percent of the sample) who started their work history in a highly skilled F1 job, 72.9 percent were currently in a highly skilled job in 1966 (see Table 6-2.)[18] None ended either in the unskilled category, C4, or in the FARM category.

Before looking at the cell entries, the row and column percentages should be noticed. Over half the individuals start in the bottom two classified job sectors, the low-skilled F3 and the unskilled F4 job sectors. Only 10 percent start in the highly skilled F1 and moderately skilled F2 sectors. So, few individuals start at the top. However, 20 to 30 years later, as is expected, much upward movement to these top jobs has occurred. By 1966, 9 percent of the sample had moved into or remained in the highly skilled F1 sector, and 23 percent had moved into the moderately skilled F2 sector. While the percentages of individuals who ended in the low and unskilled job sectors are close to the starting percentages, this apparent identity is due to individuals who started in FARM jobs moving into these bottom job sectors, replacing those individuals who rose to more skilled job sectors.

Turning to the cell entries, a picture of limited but significant opportunity for mobility exists: 73 percent of the individuals who start in the highly skilled F1 job sector remain there. Most who leave go to the moderately skilled F2 job sector, although 25 percent advance to F1. Much more mobility exists in the bottom two classified job sectors. Only one-third of those individuals who start in the low skilled F3 job sector remain there. While 16 percent fall into the unskilled F4 sector, over 25 percent rise to the moderately skilled F2 sector. Even more mobility appears to exist for the unskilled F4 starters. While 27 percent remain, one-fourth rise to the low-skilled sector, while another fourth rise to the moderately skilled sector.

An analysis of this table could only tell whether significant differences in movement exist between different job sector relationships. Whether the mobility present in Table 6-2 is sufficient to make the career-origin measure of job experience inadequate or the emphasis of the segmentation theories on barriers to movement inappropriate can only be answered by ascertaining whether wage differentials due to starting job do exist.

The Empirical Significance
of Career Origins

The hypothesis is that the position of the individual's first job with respect to the four job sectors affects his or her later earnings. Since earnings are assumed to be at least roughly related to skills, then individuals who have more of an opportunity to acquire and use these skills will receive higher earnings. So starting in a job sector with more opportunity for skill training and promotional advancement should have a positive return relative to starting in jobs with less opportunity. This would hold despite the fact that individuals should be willing to pay a premium for these highest payoff jobs if barriers to mobility are sufficient to restrict the equalizing tendencies.[19]

While the job sectors F1 to F4 were categorized on the basis of jobs already possessing greater or lesser level and breadth of skills, it is assumed here that opportunity for further skill development and job advancement in any job sector is proportional to the level and breadth of skill of the sector. The premise upon which this assumption is made has been suggested by Ben Porath.[20] He argues that more complicated job situations have more room for on-the-job training. When jobs are similar and simple, he suggests, learning opportunities quickly disappear. When jobs are more complicated, greater learning opportunities prevail.[21]

Since high-skill F1 jobs are the most complicated and involve continual learning through exposure to new situations, they also have the most opportunity for development. Those jobs entailing frequent repetition of simple, routinized tasks in the F4 sector offer the least opportunity for development. The hypothesis then becomes the following: individuals in the high-skilled F1 sector with the greatest opportunity for development should get a positive return to starting in that sector, relative to individuals who start in the minimal opportunity, unskilled F4 sector. Starting in a sector with intermediate levels of opportunity, in F2 or F3, should result in an intermediate return. This return to the job structure is over and above the returns to the individual's other human resources.

The hypothesis may be tested in the usual earnings equation framework as follows. Let earnings be a linear function of the usual measures of human resources, including, for example, education, age, and experience. These human resources may be summarized by the vector of individual traits, X. Then,

$$Y = a + bX \tag{6.1}$$

where Y is a measure of earnings

X is a vector of human resources

If career origins have an impact on later earnings, then including measures of career origins in addition to the measures of human resources should result in statistically and economically significant coefficients. This hypothesis can be tested by including dummy variables F1, F2, and F4, which take a value of 1 if the individual started his/her work history in that job sector, and 0 otherwise, in the earnings equation in addition to the vector of human resources, as in Equation (6.2).[22]

$$Y = a + bX + c1F1 + c2F2 + c4F4 \tag{6.2}$$

The null hypothesis then becomes that $c1 = c2 = c4 = 0$: starting sector as measured by F1 to F4 does not affect the level of earnings. The alternative hypothesis is that $c1 \neq c2 \neq c4 \neq 0$—that career origins are associated with later levels of earnings. The data were from the 1966 National Longitudinal Survey of Men of ages 45 to 59.[23] The subsample of the 1966 NLS used in this empirical work consists of only those men in the labor force who reported suitable information for all the variables used in these regressions, e.g., education, age, earnings, career history, etc., and who were not self-employed either in 1966 or at the time of their first job.[24]

The major characteristics of the NLS subsample and the variables used are listed in Table 6-3. For the most part, the definition of the variables follows standard practice.[25] Earnings is the natural logarithm of hourly earnings.[26] Education is years of completed schooling. Race is a dummy variable: 1 = White, 0 = otherwise. The location variables are also dummies: SMSA (1 for currently living in an SMSA, 0 otherwise); REG (1 for currently living in non-South area of U.S., 0 otherwise); HEALTH is also a dummy variable (0 = any sort of health limitation or handicap, 1 = otherwise); AGE is in years. The experience variable is REX: the number of years in current job. It is used to capture on-the-job training and is different from the usual measure of experience, i.e., total number of years in the labor force. But because cross-sectional age-earnings and total experience-earnings profiles are flat for men of this 45-to-59 age range, the age and total-experience variables are unlikely to have an impact on earnings. Preliminary regressions found these measures insignificant, and they are omitted from results reported here.[27]

Equation (6.1) includes those variables which are customarily included in earnings equations: education (ED), race (RACE), experience (REX, REX2), health (HEALTH), and the location variables (SMSA, REG):

$$E = -.1989 + .0471ED + .0200REX - .0003REX2 \qquad (6.3)$$
$$(.0333)\ (.0021)\quad\ (.0020)\qquad\ (.0000)$$

$$+ .2315SMSA + .1071HEALTH + .2500RACE + .1662REG$$
$$(.0175)\qquad\ (.0188)\qquad\quad (.0184)\qquad\quad (.0170)$$

$$R^2 = .392$$
$$RSS = 622.62$$
$$SEE = .439$$

The estimated coefficients in Equation (6.3) are similar to estimates of the effect of these human resources found in other earnings equation studies.[28] This human-resource framework must now be augmented to include measures of starting sector in order to test the effect of career origins.

Equation (6.4) includes the F1, F2, and F4 measures of career origins in the earnings equation. The residual job sector classifications, FARM and P other unclassified jobs, are also included to make full use of the NLS sample.

$$E = -.0863 + .0361ED + .0202REX - .0003REX2 \qquad (6.4)$$
$$(.0391) \quad (.0024) \qquad (.0019) \qquad (.0000)$$

$$+ .0651RD + .2204SMSA + .1094HEALTH + .2476RACE$$
$$(.0266) \qquad (.0172) \qquad (.0185) \qquad (.0182)$$

$$+ .1708REG + .3833F1 + .1447F2 - .0125F4 - .0974FARM$$
$$(.0169) \qquad (.0487) \quad (.0324) \qquad (.0211) \qquad (.0240)$$

$$+ .0006P$$
$$(.0232)$$

$$R^2 = .409$$
$$RSS = 643.50$$
$$SEE = .432$$

The difference between Equations (6.3) and (6.4) is due to the inclusion of the starting-sector measures. The previously included variables remain the same. In an F test with degrees of freedom, $F = (5,3437)$ is the appropriate statistical test on the joint inclusion of the starting-sector dummies. The calculated F is 8.89. This is opposed to a critical value at the .05 significance level of $F(5,3437) = 2.21$. So the hypothesis that $B_{F1} = B_{F2} = B_{F4} = B_{FARM} = B_P = \phi$ is rejected, and the sector dummy variables are statistically significant.

While these sector dummy variables are statistically significant, their effect on the standard error of estimate is to reduce it by less than 2 percent. While these sector variables do not narrow the dispersion of earnings, their statistical significance in conjunction with their economic significance does support the career origins view of the operation of the labor market.[29] The effect of sector of origin on differences in earnings, holding all other variables constant—that is, taking into account differences in education, location, experience, etc.—is to raise the high-skill F1 starters' earnings by 40 percent and to raise the middle-skill F2 starters' earnings by 15 percent, relative to starting in the low-skill F3 sector.[30]

Segmentation theories lead one especially to expect differences between the low and unskilled sectors. Yet these sector coefficients were economically insignificant, for starting in the unskilled F4 sector reduced earnings by only $0.03 per hour.[31] In part, this may be due to faulty measures of job sector and work experience (as discussed in footnote 29). Future research should investigate this apparent indistinction between the low and unskilled sectors.

However, this lack of distinction between the bottom sectors is not to say that career origins do not make differences in earnings. Starting in the high- and medium-skill sectors is positively associated with earnings relative to starting in jobs with less opportunity for training and promotion. Depending on the reader's own perspective, these results can be framed to support either a human-capital or a labor market segmentation outlook. But what is clear is that

Table 6-3

Means and Standard Deviations of Variables: All Men, 45 to 59, in Subsample of 1966 NLS*

Variable	Mean or Fraction in Subsample	Standard Deviation	Symbol in Subsequent Work
Age (years)	51.26	4.23	AG
Race (1:White; 0:otherwise)	.69	.46	RACE
Education (completed years of schooling)	9.39	3.92	ED
Total years of experience	36.49	8.49	CEXP
Total experience, squared	1,403.2	659.87	CEXP2
Current years of experience	14.45	11.31	REX
Current experience, squared	336.62	497.59	REX2
Now living in an SMSA (1:yes; 0:no)	.72	.45	SMSA
Current region of location (1:non-South; 0:South)	.65	.48	REG
Current health (1:no limitations; 0:otherwise)	.80	.40	HEALTH
ln of hourly earnings, dollars	.98[†]	.56	E
ln of median yearly income of current occupation	8.41[‡]	.41	LRY
ln of median yearly income of father's occupation when respondent was 15	8.06	1.01	LFAY
Starting job in high-skill sector F1	.028	.16	F1
Starting job in middle-skill sector F2	.071	.26	F2
Starting job in low-skill sector F3	.219	.41	F3
Starting job in unskilled sector F4	.281	.45	F4
Starting job in sector P, residual	.185	.39	P
Starting job in sector FARM	.217	.41	FARM

*N = 3,451.

[†]$e^{.98}$ = $2.66.

[‡]$e^{8.41}$ = $4,493.

starting in these skilled jobs is associated with a rise in earnings above and beyond the effect of the individual's measured human resources.[32]

To test whether sector of career origin was important despite race, separate black-white earnings equations were estimated.[33]

If the coefficients of the measures of starting sector are still of statistical and economic significance, then it may be concluded that this impact is not due to racial differences, but rather is due to job differences or other "unmeasured" people differences. Equation (6.5) is the white earnings equation comparable to the overall Equation (6.4). Equation (6.6) is the black earnings equation.

$$E = .2033 + .0196REX - .0002REX2 + .0630RD \qquad (6.5)$$
$$(.0487)\ (.0024) \qquad (.0000) \qquad (.0324)$$

$$+ .0421ED + .1747SMSA + .1102HEALTH + .0925REG$$
$$(.0030) \qquad (.0202) \qquad (.0221) \qquad (.0209)$$

$$+ .3657F1 + .1177F2 - .0057F4 - .1021FARM + .0019P$$
$$(.0527) \qquad (.0356) \qquad (.0253) \qquad (.0288) \qquad (.0264)$$

$$R^2 = .281$$
$$RSS = 437.93$$
$$SEE = .431$$
$$N = 2,367$$
$$\overline{E} = 1.1274$$

$$E = -.1258 + .0250REX - .0004REX2 + .0781RD \qquad (6.6)$$
$$(.0664)\ (.0035) \qquad (.0000) \qquad (.0453)$$

$$+ .0232ED + .3060SMSA + .1104HEALTH + .2986REG$$
$$(.0039) \qquad (.0325) \qquad (.0031) \qquad (.0291)$$

$$+ .4291F1 + .2160F2 - .0373F4 - .0946FARM - .0238P$$
$$(.1484) \qquad (.0941) \qquad (.0389) \qquad (.0429) \qquad (.0478)$$

$$R^2 = .394$$
$$RSS = 191.66$$
$$SEE = .423$$
$$N = 1.084$$
$$\overline{E} = .6574$$

The calculated F statistic for the homogeneity of the entire relationship was 7.63, as opposed to a .95 critical F statistic of 1.74 at $F(13,3425)$. Hence the null hypothesis that the white and black equations are the same is rejected. While there are racial differences in the determinants of the level of earnings (for example, note the differences in the location coefficients), the most important result for the job hypothesis is that the coefficients on the starting-sector dummy variables hardly change, and they retain the same pattern of statistical and economic significance. So starting sector is important above and beyond racial differences.

Conclusion

Career origins are crucial, it has been argued here, for they are the beginning of a dynamic process which continually affects the level of earnings. While there were problems in the classification of occupations, a definite pattern of results did emerge which supported the emphasis on career origins. For the overall sample and for the black and white samples, starting in the high- and middle-skill sectors was consistently associated with increases in later levels of earnings. The potential magnitude of the return of starting sector on later levels of earnings is as large as 50 percent for white high-skill starters and 10 percent for white medium-skill starters. So at least for that part of the labor market where careers are most explicitly defined, job experience does matter.

This interpretation is contingent upon a very basic assumption, that the F1 to F4 measures of starting sector were measures of the job and not of the people who took those jobs. This issue of job measurement interpretation must be faced directly. Human-capital proponents can argue that the apparent economic and statistical significance of the measures of starting job do not result from forces emphasized in the starting-job argument, and that this formulation tests only whether there are left out measures of human resources in the usual earnings equation framework which omits measures of career origins. The correct interpretation of rejecting the null hypothesis here, so goes this line of argument, is simply that the individuals in F1 had more unmeasured human resources than the individuals in F4. Unmeasured by any other variables, these differential resources are captured by the dummy variables, for the job measures are but disguised measures of "people" characteristics. While the surrogate measures of the individual's human resources (e.g., education) capture some of the total stock of human resources, they are after all only surrogates, and do not measure all an individual's resources. The job in which the individual starts his or her career also acts as a surrogate measure. The fact that an individual started in a high-skill sector means, so goes this argument, that he or she simply had more human resources to start out.

Better tests of this revealed human-capital argument are now being formulated. For example, if there were a time period during which large changes occurred in the "job structure" while the "people structure" remained relatively constant, e.g., during the Depression, then differences in the effect of career origins between this period of changes in the job structure as compared with the effects of career origins in a normal period could be examined. The test here is whether the Depression starters, who started in "worse" jobs than they "should" have started in, were able to recuperate from their initial job limitation. Preliminary results suggest that individuals starting in the middle, low, and unskilled sectors during the Depression may not recuperate. These results suggest that initial job limitations kept these individuals from rising to levels commensurate with their initial human resources. The conclusion, then, is that at least some of the association of career origins with earnings is due to the job structure.

Notes

1. The best survey of the human capital theories is in Mincer, Jacob, "The Distribution of Labor Income, A Survey with Special Reference to the Human Capital Approach," *Journal of Economic Literature*, March, 1970.

2. These theories are surveyed in Gordon, David, *Theories of Poverty and Underemployment* (Lexington, Mass.: D.C. Heath, 1972).

3. Thurow, Lester C., "Education and Economic Equality," *Public Interest*, Summer 1972.

4. This emphasis is placed on skill development by both theories is developed by Birnbaum, Howard, "Determinants of Earnings: The Economic Significance of Job Experience and the Effects of Cohorts on Age-Earnings Profiles," Chapter 1, unpublished Ph.D. dissertation, Harvard University, 1974.

5. Gintis, Herbert, "Education, Technology, and the Characteristics of Worker Productivity," *American Economic Review*, May 1971. Katherine Stone (this volume) has also argued that persons who pass along different job ladders may go through individual steps which produce no differential skills and whose specified positions have nothing to do with differential requirements and yet still end up on differential income streams.

6. Piore, Michael, "Toward a Theory of Labor Market Stratification," (this volume) develops these ideas in terms of "mobility chains."

7. Rosen, Sherwin, "Learning and Experience in the Labor Market," *Journal of Human Resources*, 1972.

8. Rosen, ibid.

9. Rosen, ibid., p. 341.

10. Ibid.

11. Piore, Chapter 5 (this volume).

12. Piore, Chapter 5, carefully distinguishes these different kinds of skills.

13. Piore, Chapter 5; Gordon, David, "Steam Whistles to Coffee Breaks," *Dissent*, Winter 1972; and Birnbaum, see note 4. They develop historical and industrial structure reasons why these three levels of skill bundles and experience opportunities best measure the major dimensions of segmentation in the labor market.

14. Because no appropriate measures of level and breadth of skill are available, this method cannot be implemented with complete accuracy. Yet while there exists no accurate list or description of the necessary information, there does exist a vast literature and also much unwritten knowledge. The following classification procedure was developed to benefit from this knowledge. A first rough classification was made on the basis of general impressions, derived

from reading the relevant literature and from a multitude of discussions with various "authorities" on the subject. Included among the useful sources were: Moore, Wilbert F., *The Professions* (New York: Russell Sage, 1970); Scoville, James, *The Job Content of the United States Economy, 1940-70* (New York: McGraw-Hill, 1969); Scoville, James, *Manpower and Occupational Analysis: Concepts and Measurements* (Lexington, Mass.: Heath, 1972); *Occupational Outlook Handbook* (Washington, D.C., U.S. Department of Labor, Government Printing Office, 1970); and *International Standard Classification of Occupations* (Geneva: International Labor Organization, 1969). Refinements were then made by comparing these job sectors with other occupational measurement devices, especially the *Dictionary of Occupational Titles* (Washington, D.C.: U.S. Department of Labor, Manpower Administration, Government Printing Office). This comparison ensured that no grave oversights were made. The final criterion was internal consistency of the groups. Several alterations of the categorizations were tried in the empirical work to evaluate the robustness of the result of this provisional classification. No significant change ever resulted. Furthermore, the results found here were compared to several related attempts at classification, and seem quite reasonable, e.g., Gordon, David, "Class, Productivity, and the Ghetto," unpublished Ph.D. dissertation, Harvard University, 1971; Friedman, Marcia, Chapter 2, "The Structure of Employment," Columbia University mimeograph, 1973; and Bowden, Leslie, "Occupational Mobility of Young Men," Ph.D. dissertation in progress, M.I.T. Similar procedures can be found elsewhere in economic literature, e.g., Eckstein, Otto, and Thomas Wilson, "The Determinants of Money Wages in American Industry," *Quarterly Journal of Economics*, August, 1967.

15. Further discussion of this procedure and a complete categorization of the census titles into their appropriate job sectors is in Birnbaum, "Determinants of Earnings," Table I, Appendix A.

16. The National Longitudinal Survey (NLS) is the data base for the empirical work in this paper. For further discussion of the data see Birnbaum, "Determinants of Earnings," Chapter 3.

17. The entire job histories of these 160 individuals are presented in Birnbaum, "Determinants of Earnings," Table II, Appendix A. A small random sample was chosen in order to read the full pattern of their entire case histories. To digest the case histories of the entire 5,020 men NLS sample would not have been possible.

18. The classification for jobs was the same for both first and current job. "Fx" refers to the first job. "Cx" refers to current 1966 job.

19. See the discussion of the crossing of age-income profiles in Mincer, op. cit., and Mincer, Jacob, "Schooling, Age, and Earnings," *National Bureau of Economic Research*.

20. Ben Porath, Yoram, "Some Aspects of the Life Cycle of Earnings," unpublished Ph.D. dissertation, Harvard University, 1967.

21. Ibid.

22. The F3 variable is suppressed to avoid singularity.

23. For further discussion see *The Preretirement Years*, Vol. 1, Parnes, H., et al., Manpower Research Monograph No. 15, United States Department of Labor, 1970.

24. These restrictions reduced the 1966 NLS from 5,030 observations to 3,451. By far the largest reduction was due to omitting self-employed individuals, for 19 percent of the total NLS were self-employed in 1966. This reduced the sample to 4,100 individuals. Slightly over 12 percent more of the original sample, 609 men, were eliminated because they were not in the labor force at the time of the survey. So once these basic cuts were made, only a trivial amount were finally eliminated for not reporting the crucial variables of interest.

25. See, for example, Griliches, Zvi, and W.M. Mason, "Education, Income, and Ability," *Journal of Political Economy*, May/June 1972.

26. Mincer, "Schooling, Age, and Earnings." The Mincer survey article develops the justification for the semilogarithmic formulation.

27. Similar results using the same data were found by Freeman, Richard B., "Occupational Training in Proprietary Schools and Technical Institutes," Harvard Institute of Economic Research, Discussion Paper No. 337, November, 1973.

28. See for example Freeman, "Occupational Training," and Luft, Harold, "Poverty and Health: An Empirical Investigation of the Interactions," unpublished Ph.D. dissertation, Harvard University, 1973.

29. In part, this minor effect on the dispersion of earnings may be due to misclassification of job titles into incorrect sectors. For example, if some low-skill jobs were incorrectly classified as unskilled, and vice versa, then the apparent difference, between starting in one sector or another would have been minimized.

In an effort to see if there were obvious misclassifications, "outlying" observations were analyzed. *Outliers* were defined to be individuals whose predicted earnings deviated from their actual earnings by more than one standard error of estimate. Predicted earnings were found by multiplying the individuals' actual characteristics by their estimated coefficients. The only pattern to emerge was that the more nebulous job titles, such as salesmen, mimeo operatives, laborers, and attendants dominated the outliers—both the outliers who did better than predicted and the outliers who did worse. For example, 17 of the 51 white low-skilled outliers whose actual earnings were more than one standard error *below* their predicted earnings were "salesmen." And 11 of the white low-skill outliers whose actual earnings were more than one standard error of estimate *above* their predicted earnings were "salesmen." This analysis of outliers suggests that many of the categorized job titles in the low and unskilled sectors were too heterogeneous and encompassed what in actuality was a wide range of job tasks and work experiences. A better original breakdown, for example, might have had at least two types of salesmen.

Misclassification could have occurred either in the F1 to F4 job sector classification or in the U.S. Census classification of their 296 job titles. One effort was made to regroup job titles on the basis of outlier information. It, too, yielded unsatisfactory distinctions between the low and unskilled sectors. A major research effort at correctly categorizing job experience is needed.

30. The overall sample mean of hourly earnings is $e^{.9798}$ = \$2.66. Starting in sector F1 raises this to $e^{1.3631}$ = \$3.91 for a 40 percent increase. Starting in sector F2 raises earnings to $e^{1.1145}$ = \$3.05, for a 15 percent increase.

31. F3 earnings were $e^{.9798}$ = \$2.66. Starting in F4 reduced this to $e^{.9773}$ = \$2.63.

32. In order to reduce the unmeasured component of human resources, other measures of the individuals' human resources which were available in the NLS were tested to see whether they contributed to the earnings determination process. Measures of "ability" at the time of first job and motivation at the time of the same were included in the earnings equation. The proxies for initial ability were a measure of the father's ability—the natural logarithm of the median income of the father's job when the individual was 15—and also skill at the time of entrance into the labor market, as measured by the natural logarithm of the median income of the first job of the individual. The measure of motivation is presumably a constant over time. These variables were never, either individually or in combinations, of statistical or economic significance. Nor did they ever alter any of the coefficients of the sector dummy variables. These results coincide with other research into the effect of unmeasured ability. For example, Griliches and Mason, "Education, Income, and Ability," have concluded that the direct and indirect effects of I.Q. on current income are very small.

33. If the sample of individuals who started in the low-skilled job sectors was dominated by black observations, while the sample of individuals who started in the more skilled sectors was dominated by white observations, then this apparent significance of career origins might be attributed to unmeasured differences in black-white levels of human resources.

This possibility is certainly present in the NLS data. The following table displays the percentages of blacks and whites in this subsample by starting job sector. While almost 4 percent of the white subpopulation started in the high-skill sector, only 1 percent of the black population started there. And since there are over twice as many whites as blacks in this sample, white domination is overwhelming in the high-skill sector—90.6 percent of the individuals starting in the high-skill sector are white. So the apparent significance of sector may be due to racial differences.

	Total Sample % of Population	F1: High Skill	F2: Medium Skill	F3: Low Skill	F4: Unskilled	FARM	P
				Percentage of the White and the Black NLS Population by Sector of Job Origin			
Blacks	31.4	0.8	2.2	16.4	34.4	32.7	13.5
Whites	68.6	3.7	9.3	24.4	25.2	16.7	20.8

Racial Domination in Advanced Capitalism: A Theory of Nationalism and Divisions in the Labor Market

Harold M. Baron

Racial domination has proved to be the most explosive issue in the United States during the last generation. Based on an analogy with the sophisticated fashion in which modern capitalist nations have been able to dissipate the potentially disruptive forces of class conflict, one would expect that racial antagonisms would long ago have been made manageable in the most advanced capitalist nation in the world. Obviously there is a very deep-seated and powerful set of forces operating to maintain the subjugation of Black people.[a] This chapter seeks to comprehend these forces by developing a theory to explain the system of racial domination as it operates within the United States today.

Within the last two-thirds of a century a truly astounding transformation has taken place in the socioeconomic order of the Black community and the racial system that dominates its conditions of existence. A dependent peasantry, i.e., one not owning its own land, has been converted into an urban people. In a short span of 60 years, the typical world of Black people in America changed from that of tenant farmers immersed in the traditionalism of preindustrial society to a very modern one of wage workers within a metropolitan order dominated by large corporations and bureaucratic organizations. This dialectical transformation in internal relationships has not diminished the Black community's identity as a community. Indeed this identity has heightened. Simultaneously, while the relation to White society has drastically changed in specifics, it still maintains the form of racial subordination. The structure and dynamics of these new specifics of racial control are the subject of this inquiry.

The continuing solidity of the Black social formation is highlighted by contrast with the massive ethnic communities that migrated from Europe in various waves from the middle of the nineteenth century to the 1920s (Blauner, 1972, pp. 61-70). These European groups also underwent the social metamorphosis from the traditional peasant society to that of modern capitalism. However, after two or three generations the immigrant ethnic communities lost most of their distinctive old-world cultural forms and social cohesion. In varying

This chapter is part of a larger project on the persistence of institutional racism that has been financed in part by the Russell Sage Foundation. The comments and criticisms of Paula Baron, David Gordon, and Eric Perkins on an earlier draft have been very helpful.

[a]The terms "Black" and "White" will be capitalized in the text where their usage indicates a nationality as the referent.

degrees they have amalgamated into the dominant culture.[b] What cultural distinctiveness they maintain tends to be a direct carryover of traits from the old country rather than traditions which retain their vitality through transformation and growth in relationship to their new conditions. The Black community, on the other hand, gives no indication of disappearing. In linguistic, musical, and literary forms it is generating a vibrant culture that is simultaneously rooted in the past Black history and innovative in terms of the present Black experience. The racial demography of any major city continues to bear testimony to the social solidarity of the Black community as well as to the continuing rigidity of de facto racial segregation in a wide range of institutional situations. Within metropolitan White society, there has also been a great deal of inventiveness—in this case, an inventiveness regarding the fashioning of new modes of racial control.

In the shaping of this new phase in the life of the Black community, the decisive factor has been the Black working class, and there is every indication that it will continue to be decisive in the future. The essential dynamics underlying the transition from a peasant to an urban people are those of the changing demand for Black labor (Baron, 1971). Vis-à-vis the Black community, wage workers, the large majority of which are in blue-collar jobs, comprise almost the total labor force. That which is distinctive about Black urban culture has been forged out of the lives of working people. During the course of the 1960s upsurge of the Black liberation movement, the initiative passed out of the hands of the middle class into those of the working class, including those sectors that are most marginal in the labor market. Vis-à-vis the total American society, the Black working class is proving itself to be the most combatative and the least co-opted sector of the proletariat. The actions of Black workers serve to energize other working people and to mobilize political activity among popularly oriented groups. This unique role of the Black working class means that it must be central to an analysis of the modern racial situation.

The position of the Black community in America can be properly understood only within the development of capitalism on a national and a worldwide scale. The racial system, in both its institutional and ideological forms, originated in the slaving operations that were part and parcel of beginnings of capitalism and preceded industrialism. Today, in the midst of advanced capitalism, racial domination, with its specific features drastically modified, is still operative. As in the history of class society, the situation of the racial groups is a unique combination of stability and change. "The structure remains the same; conjunctural features are often profoundly modified" (Mandel, 1970, p. 159). We

[b]The claim here is not that these ethnic ties are without import. For instance, they have given distinctive shape to urban politics and working-class history (Allswang, 1971; Gutman, 1973). The point is that in the present metropolitan society the ethnic communities are no longer strong or cohesive enough to be of major significance *as communities* in the shaping of economic and political relationships.

must ground our comprehension of the present situation in the materials and forces that it inherited from the past, but we are not justified in reducing the dynamics and dialectics of the present to just the momentum of this heritage. By the same token, a reduction of the rich complexity of the racial scene to a current psychological or economic mechanism is a theoretical abstraction that is unwarranted and quite harmful in the development of an effective antiracist praxis.

Theoretical clarification of the unique position of the Black community and the operation of the system of racial domination requires an examination of a number of the major features of American society. A major social element at any particular time in its history is shaped by the intersection and interaction of a number of social, political, and economic structures. The particular structures that this analysis will concentrate upon are: (1) the economic system, primarily the relations of production as they are organized within advanced capitalism; (2) racism as an international and national determinant of status and exploitation; (3) nationality as a form of the organization of social, political, and economic relations, with special attention to the distinctiveness of Blacks and Whites. *The most significant conclusion is that a new mutually reinforcing relationship has developed between the American racial system and the segmentation that is characteristic of labor markets under advanced capitalism.*

It is important that the order of progression in this chapter's argument be outlined to the reader because it is a complicated one. Further, because this chapter is eventually intended to be the theoretical part of a larger study on racism within present-day America, the more ample development of points and their detailed illustration are necessarily quite condensed here. Since the theorizing here is carried on within the tradition of Marxist thought, we start out with a digression from the main theme of racial domination in order to establish exactly how Marxian categories will be employed. In keeping with the essential methodology of Marxism, we have modified and extended certain concepts to encompass social relations that have emerged or become more salient within this century. The substantive inquiry then moves on to an examination of the interaction between racism and nationalism both historically and currently.

On Marxist Categories and Dialectics

This detour into some of the elements of Marxist theory is necessary to establish the grounds of the whole argument, especially with an American readership which tends to be unfamiliar with Marxism. Further, given our general intellectual tradition of empiricism and deductive simplicity, we tend not to grasp the many-faceted nature of Marxist categories. They are quite different and more complicated than the components in a mechanical schema of economic causation that some people take Marxism to be. The inclusiveness of Marxist theory is also more specific and formulated than the generalized theory of multiple causation to which many historians subscribe.

American social science and economic theory remain true to their origin and follow the fundamental postulate of Enlightenment philosophy. The basic concept from which these theories are constructed is that of an atomistic individual, rationally seeking his or her self-interest. To the contrary, in Marxism the fundamental categories are always social relationships or contradictions—that is, they are dialectical in form. The specification of a relational complexity does not always lend itself to neat definitions and frequently requires considerable elaboration. Since Marxism shows that our knowledge of society is derived from people's activity within their social relations, the concepts of this philosophy of praxis often become clearer if we trace them through the contexts of their origin and development.

The Marxist theory of historical materialism is inclusive so that, as it were, there are no significant social factors that are exogenous to the model. However, this inclusiveness is not achieved at the expense of reducing one major element into being a function of another one. The constitutive elements are dialectically related. This means that they interact with each other within the broad limits of an historically conditioned and evolving framework—in other words, according to the laws of historical development. Simultaneously, each of the major elements has a history or logic of its own that gives it a distinctive mode of reaction and development. A particular factor, such as a cultural heritage, is at once determined by and a determinant of the total socioeconomic configuration.[c]

The development of Marxist (or any other) theory is conditioned by the particular features of the social relationships within a given society and by the practical social activity being conducted either to maintain or to change that society. Therefore, the decisive struggles of the Black liberation movement in the past dozen years have revealed whole new dimensions of the system of racial domination in America. These political struggles have made it possible to bring into theoretical focus many of the aspects of racism that have emerged within the metropolitan setting of advanced capitalism. The validity of these new

[c]The complete social formation can only be understood in terms of the interplay (reinforcements and contradictions) between the subsidiary formations that constitute the whole dialectic. To a certain extent these subsidiary formations have their own distinctive laws, or conditions of development, that can be known only through a careful examination of the contradictions within and between them. Explanations that stress the accidental character of the relation between major social factors do this by avoiding the conclusions that follow from inclusive theoretical specifications. Accordingly, their categories leave the laws of the subsidiary formations unconditioned by the primacy of the whole dialectic. On the other hand, economic determinism makes an *a priori* overspecification and tends to absorb the whole historical dialectic into the logic of the most decisive subsidiary formation, the mode of economic production. This determinism denies the validity or the distinctiveness of the laws of cultural, social, political, and national determinations.

elements of theory, as in the case of all other social theories, is to be measured not only by its ability to generalize the known facts coherently and concisely but more importantly by its applicability in guiding further practical activity and struggle for the improvement of society.

Base, Superstructure, and Nation

The capitalist mode of production, nationalism, and racism are symbolically related in their historical origin and their current function. However, the nature of their interrelation is far from clearly understood, even within the Marxist tradition which has strongly asserted their interdependence (for recent work see Hroch, 1968; Kiernan, 1965; Miliband, 1969; Poulantzas, 1973; O'Connor, 1973). The failure to comprehend the interaction of these forces has proved to be a great stumbling block for political movements in their practical work, to say nothing of the confusion it has caused in the realm of theory. Yet, taken together these societal relationships have largely been constitutive of the history, first of the North Atlantic civilization and, then, of the entire world. Industrial society, imperialism, modern-state capitalism, and fascism have been shaped by one configuration or another of nationalism and racism in relation to a capitalist productive system. Even in socialist countries, to a far greater extent than they usually admit, national imperatives still largely determine their particular histories.

The classic Marxian model for the historic development of a whole society is delineated in terms of a base and superstructure. The economy or mode of production constitutes the base upon which metaphorically the rest of the society is erected. This economic foundation in turn is made up of the forces of production, i.e., the accumulated capital goods, skills, and technology, and the social relations of production, i.e., the class relations that people enter into in order to produce goods and to appropriate them. The decisive motor force of history in the long run is the contradiction in the base between the forces of production and the relations of production, which takes the form of class struggle. Other contradictions do occur between the base and the superstructure or various aspects of the superstructure. However, the decisive function of the superstructure is to reinforce the control of the dominant economic class over the whole of society.

This superstructure contains the other elements of society—the noneconomic social relations, such as those of family and community, ideology, art, politics, and the state. In capitalist society the state is, so to speak, the capstone of the structure, guaranteeing the dominance of the bourgeois over the rest of society and the survival of a particular national bourgeois versus other bourgeois.[d]

---

[d]Many applications of the base-superstructure model mechanistically apply this metaphor as though they were exercises in architectural engineering. For cautions against this interpretation see Williams (1973) and Thompson (1965, pp. 351-353). Unfortunately, Thompson almost throws out the baby with the bath water.

In light of the decisive position of the state, it is valuable to follow the usage of Enlightenment writers and Hegel in distinguishing between the state and civil society, i.e., the nonstate or private elements of society including the economic ones. Among modern Marxist theoreticians Gramsci has especially employed the distinction between the state and civil society. For example, his term *hegemony* refers to the class dominance that is exercised by the prevalence of the *Weltanschauung* of the ruling class among all elements of civil society. In contrast, the dominance through the state is exercised ultimately by coercive means or by the consensual acceptance of this power which is usually called legitimacy.

Nation is one further concept that has received considerable practical and tactical concern within the Marxist tradition but has been theoretically slighted. All capitalist societies (and all socialist societies) have taken place within a national form. Every base and superstructural configuration has a set of boundaries within which it functions. These boundaries—or as one writer has termed them, "conditions of production" (Borochov, 1937, pp. 135-141)—are a combination of cultural, ideological, social, and territorial elements that together make up a national integument for the operation of the base and superstructure. The functional efficacy of the combination of these elements, rather than the absence or presence of any one element, is the key criterion for the present or potential existence of a nation. For example, a few federal nation states, such as Switzerland and Belgium, have been able to encompass different cultural and linguistic groups, albeit with certain abiding conflicts. Zionism has shown the possibility of a type of nationalism that originated without a territorial base. In modern African nations, the state, whose boundaries have followed those of the colonial administrative units they have superseded, in effect has called a nation into being from a diversity of ethnic groups. The existence of a linguistic or cultural group does not preordain the coming into being of a nation. Indeed, in the course of modern European history not every nationalist movement resulted in the autonomy of its people (Hroch, 1968, pp. 16-19). Assimilation did sometimes occur, especially in areas like France and Britain where capitalist development was the most advanced.

As capitalist and urban relationships dissolve the old social bonds of kin and local community, nations provide the basis for a new type of mass cohesion or peoplehood that is not in conflict with the impersonal conditions of the capitalist marketplace. The localistic loyalties to the primary groups in traditional societies are not compatible with the mobility, the scale of operation, or the calculation of self-interest that make for a viable capitalist order. The nation came to provide an overriding definition of loyalty and culture that was not inextricably linked with kinship and villages (Gellner, 1964, pp. 151-155). Mass armies, mass communication, mass education, and mass markets are correlatives of the modern nation.

The classic founders of sociology paid great attention to the transition from status to contract or from community to impersonal association that was a key social feature of the development of capitalism. What they neglected in this case was requirement of these new social forms for a new encompassing formation—the nation—that could define both their internal cohesion and their external boundaries giving shape to the novel and much more abstract duties and rights. The nation also provides the expanded frame of operation for the market itself, that is, both the market for wage labor and the market for commodities (Berdahl, 1972; Deutsch, 1966, pp. 47-55). Finally, the boundaries of the nation and the state tend to be coterminous and reinforcing. In fact, as Rousseau and Hegel perceived in the early phases of modern national development, a nation exists on the basis of citizenship rights rather than traditional rights, and the sovereign state is the ground of these citizenship rights. (For further development and illustration of this point see Bendix, 1969, chapters 3 and 4.) Therefore a modern nation is never fully functional unless it has its own state apparatus. However, a single state apparatus might govern more than one potential nation.

At this point it is necessary to clarify the usage of some of our terminology. *Nationalism* refers to the ideological, cultural, and political movements that agitate for the establishment of a nation or modifications within an established nation (see Smith, 1971, n. 17, p. 303). *Nationality* and *nation* refer to the social, economic, and political complexes whose boundaries they define and give shape to. A nationality might not be politically independent, while the term *nation* is usually employed with the implication that a high level of autonomy and/or sovereignty has been obtained.

Eric Hobsbawn (1972, p. 384) has noted that "Nationalism is probably the most powerful political phenomenon of our century, and one whose importance continues to grow, but analysis has found it remarkably hard to come to grips with it." Within Marxian analysis, *nationalism* is an underdeveloped concept, particularly as it applies to mature capitalism. Marxist writings on nationalism, arising out of revolutionary praxis, have oriented themselves on particular problems. None of the key formulators of Marxism wrote a systematic theoretical analysis on the topic. Marx and Engels basically addressed themselves to the question of what national forms would hasten capitalist development in order to set the stage for a socialist revolution. Prior to World War I, Lenin's writings on nationalism focused on the necessary conditions for creating a working-class alliance across national lines within the Tsarist and Austro-Hungarian multinational empires. Both Lenin and Marx maintained such a strong internationalist norm for the working-class movement that concern for nationalism appears as a kind of tactical concession on their part, at best as a necessary detour on the road to proletarian internationalism. [Davis (1967) provides a good review of the Marxist treatment of the national question up to 1917.]

Post-war Leninist and Maoist writings did treat nationalism within the context of colonial liberation movements as a distinctive formation—as an anti-imperialist force which was not completely reducible to class forces. Consequently, the Leninist movements' ability both in theory and in practice to deal with the interrelation of class and national forces within the struggles of oppressed peoples has provided them with increasing prestige in the Third World during the last half-century.

Nationalism as a force in itself within developed capitalism, however, has been slighted. When it has been considered, it has generally been dealt with in terms of the chauvinism of imperial nations vis-à-vis colonized and neocolonized peoples. The functions of the nation in maintaining the conditions of production and the internal coherence of the advanced capitalist countries have been glossed over. Even in the case of fascism, where the operations of nationalism were most explicit, Marxism did not elaborate any inclusive theory regarding it. No theory of the nation comparable for example, to the theory of the state has been developed. Nevertheless, the imperatives of national maintenance provide a specifiable set of general conditions for the operation of advanced capitalist systems (and emerging socialist ones), just as much as there are somewhat different historical laws for national liberation.

Relative Congruency

Within the Marxist tradition, the mutual reinforcements and contradictions between the elements of the base-superstructure-nation model have never been definitively codified. Marx and Engels dealt with this issue on a concrete, instance-by-instance basis in their historical writings. Lenin (1917, Section 7), with the concept of the *uneven development of capitalism*,[e] made a more general formulation that proved strategically very valuable in dealing with the contradictions of the world capitalist system. More recently Althusser (1969, chapters 3 and 4) has developed the concept of *overdetermination* to designate the multiplicity of different structural relations that are fused together to constitute a concrete social formation. Ernest Gellner, a non-Marxist theoretician, has made the category of uneven development a key to his explanation of twentieth-century African and Asian nationalism.[f]

In order to address this issue of the relations of the elements within a base-superstructure-nation formation, it is useful to introduce a new term of

[e]This concept primarily refers to the fact that capitalism develops at varying rates in different countries and in different sectors of a single country. The resulting disparities create tensions and exacerbate contradictions within particular nations and within the world system of capitalism.

[f]"Essentially nationalism is a phenomenon connected not so much with industrialization or modernization as such, but with its uneven diffusion. The uneven impact of this wave generates a sharp social stratification which, unlike the stratifications of past societies, is (a) unhallowed by custom, and which has little to cause it to be accepted as in the nature of things, which (b) is not well protected by various social mechanisms, but on the contrary exists in a situation providing maximum opportunities and incentives for revolution, and which (c) is remediable, and is seen to be remediable, by national secession." (Gellner, 1964, p. 166)

relative congruency. Congruency designates that while the major elements within a social formation operate with a degree of autonomy according to their own history and internal relationships, a particular element provides the supportive conditions of the other major elements in that society. The political and social structures function in a manner that is symmetrical with and reinforcing of the structure and dynamics of the economic base, and vice versa. Certain ideologies, personality types, governmental forms, etc., are more supportive of the development of a particular set of economic relationships. The mutual reinforcement between Reformation Protestantism and emerging capitalism, as has been demonstrated in the work of Weber and Tawney, provides an excellent example of congruence.

The major structures within a social formation do not fit into some kind of smoothly functioning whole. Indeed they are never totally congruent. Under varying conditions more or less disparity exists between these elements, even to the extent that they relate as antagonistic contradictions. Accordingly, we qualify our term to be *relative congruency*. This concept is dialectical in that it necessitates simultaneously looking at both reinforcing and conflicting relationships. Relative congruency is not intended to have an abstract meaning, for it is usable only concretely within an historical context and with a specification of a relation of elements within the base-superstructure-nation model of Marxism.

Revolutionary situations develop from the impacting of a number of incongruencies. Althusser (1969, p. 99) assesses this situation in regard to the contradiction between two antagonistic classes which

cannot of its own simple, direct power induce a "revolutionary situation," nor *a fortiori* a situation of revolutionary rupture and the triumph of the revolution. If this contradiction is to become *"active"* in the strongest sense, to become a ruptural principle, there must be an accumulation of "circumstances" and "currents" so that whatever their origin and sense (and many of them will *necessarily* be paradoxically foreign to the revolution in origin and sense, or even its "direct opponents"), they "fuse" into a *ruptural unity:* when they produce the result of the immense majority of the popular masses *grouped* in an assault on a regime which its ruling classes are *unable to defend*.

Let us now turn to some of the many forms in which contemporary capitalist society is structured, namely, racial domination, advanced capitalism, and the nation under advanced capitalism.

Racial Domination[g]

Along with the modern nation and state, racism is a major social formation which grew symbiotically with the nascent capitalist system.[h] Specifically,

[g]Following Robert Blauner's usage, the term *racial domination* will be used to refer to the institutional arrangements of subjugation, and *racism* will refer to the ideological movements and formulations that relate to the system of domination. This section has benefited from two of Blauner's unpublished essays.

racism developed as part of the imperial expansion of Europe which started with the fifteenth-century voyages of discovery and reached its culmination with the mid-twentieth-century world domination by the major capitalist powers. Within this overall development there were two distinct, but related, processes in the elaboration of racism. First was the domination by the European powers of the peoples of Asia, Africa, and Latin America by colonial rule and other mechanisms. On a world scale, colored peoples were exploited by whites and subordinated to them. Second, within the larger process, plantation and settler societies were established, especially in the New World. The plantation labor force was usually provided by black slaves forcibly exported from Africa. A racist social order was fashioned around the focus of controlling and regulating this labor force. In terms of the domestic development of the United States, the second process has been far more important.

Although the immediate productive relations of this slave system were not capitalistic, i.e., did not involve wage labor, the plantations were totally dependent upon merchant capitalism for the supply of slaves, its major force of production. This plantation system also bore a unique relationship with European capitalist societies that provided the markets for the distribution of commodities produced. In turn, European capitalism was dependent upon the trading of slaves and slave production of goods as a major source of the original accumulation of capital and for the enlargement of commodity markets. Upon the base of this slave plantation system, an elaborate social, ideological, and moral order—or superstructure—was erected. In those cases where a mother country or dominant social system was primarily of a feudal-manorial form, that unmistakably delineated the distinctions between social estates; as Marvin Harris (1964, chapter 7) has shown for Brazil, the incongruency between it and the plantation systems it controlled was not as great as where the dominant system was thoroughly grounded in an individualistic capitalism. Under the latter conditions, as in the United States, the plantation order was forced to develop a more systematic and institutionally exclusive elaboration of racism since it lacked as clear-cut and ready-made a social definition of servility.

In the United States the stigmatization of all Black people, slave and free, spread way beyond the bounds of the plantation system, not only in the South but in the free states of the North as well. The racial subordination of Black people assumed a certain dynamic that was partially independent of the plantation system and was eventually to survive its demise. Worldwide, the colonial division of Africa and Asia in the latter part of the nineteenth century stimulated a more extensive elaboration of racial doctrines among Europeans

[h]The complexity of this interrelationship is indicated by Kiernan's (1965, p. 34) conclusions regarding the absolutist State in the sixteenth and seventeenth centuries: "In France and England, political and economic ascendancy went together and reinforced each other. There the home province and its burghers knew how to profit by the wealth pumped into the metropolis by governmental and court nobility. In these conditions, in fact, may be seen the matrix of modern capitalism: like nationalism, less the creator than the creation of the modern State."

and North Americans. While the main force of this new racialism was directed toward the mobilization of a consensus for the subjugation of the colored peoples of the earth, it also played a role in generating internal cohesion within the imperial nations. The survival imperatives of these countries, which were rent by class strife, required at least an aura of common community. The mass sentiment of racial solidarity and nationalism was to a considerable extent the result of the engineering of class resentment into xenophobia (Semmel, 1968).

Within a broad world perspective, colonialism generates races just as capitalism generates classes. Racial domination represents a global system of hierarchy and exploitation. Wallerstein (1972, p. 222) makes a distinction between racial discrimination which operates within relatively small-scale social organizations and the status-group category of race which has become "a blurred collective representation for an international class category, that of the pro-letarian nations." The United States' racist system obviously operates through mechanisms of discrimination, but it is also part of that international status hierarchy. To add to the complexity of this situation, Black people in the United States are also part, albeit on a restricted basis, of the dominant imperial nation in the world system. The contradictions involved in this set of circumstances are central to this chapter.

Advanced Capitalism

In response to the tremendous shocks the world capitalist system encountered in the Great Depression, World War II, and post-war reconstruction, a major adaptation has taken place in the structure of the socioeconomic order within the more developed capitalist nations. This new stage of advanced capitalism is essentially characterized by the following: private ownership and control of the means of production; economies dominated by hierarchically organized large corporations; accelerated and regularized technological innovation; a permanent war economy; an enlarged state apparatus that interpenetrates both the economy and a growing sphere of social life; and an overwhelmingly urbanized society tied together by market, or other similarly impersonal, relationships.

Congruent changes have taken place throughout the whole of advanced capitalist society (although a whole range of new incongruencies is now in the process of emerging). Social forms, ideologies, personalities, and life-styles have evolved, more or less, into forms that are compatible with the modifications in the mode of production. Later in the chapter the economic aspects of the organization of work in advanced capitalism will be considered, but right now certain political features of class conflict and nationalism are the objects of our focus.

As Marx demonstrated a century ago, the capitalist mode of production brings into being a working class that of necessity exists in struggle with, or in contradiction to, the capitalist class. Based on the experience of the dramatic rupture of the French Revolution, the violent working-class confrontations, such as the Paris Commune of 1871 and the Russian revolt of 1905, and the Bolshevik Revolution, orthodox Marxism has conceived of the class struggle as being a highly antagonistic one. Theoretically Marxism has not been as clear regarding class contradictions under the conditions when the major elements of a social formation are more congruent. Mao Tse-tung (1937, Section 6) in making a distinction between antagonistic and nonantagonistic contradictions provides a framework for addressing this issue:

Contradiction and struggle are universal and absolute but the methods of resolving contradictions, that is, the forms of struggle, differ according to the differences in the nature of the contradictions. Some contradictions are characterized by open antagonism, others are not. In accordance with the concrete development of things, some contradictions which were originally non-antagonistic develop into antagonistic ones, while others which were originally antagonistic develop into non-antagonistic ones.

At a certain stage in the development of the leading capitalist countries, the originally antagonistic class contradiction became essentially a nonantagonistic one. This period roughly corresponds to Lenin's stage of imperialism which links the economic and political division of the world with the growing dominance of monopoly capital within the metropoles of the imperial powers. The theory of imperialism did not devote a great deal of attention to the corollary domestic superstructural developments in the imperial nations. The analysis of these features was basically limited to the growing parasitism among the rentier class and the co-optation of a labor aristocracy through deception and bribery (Lenin, 1916 and 1917, Section 8), both of which were based upon vast profits gained at the expense of the colonial territories. The internal ramifications of the labor co-optation were not given sufficient attention, for the successes of working-class struggle in trade unions and parliaments necessarily established a network of operations within the capitalist framework. E.P. Thompson (1965, pp. 343-344) illustrates this point with his description of the British labor movement in the second half of the nineteenth century:

As they improved their position by organization within the workshop, so they became more reluctant to engage in quixotic outbreaks which might jeopardize gains accumulated at such cost. Each assertation of working-class influence within the bourgeois-democratic state machinery, simultaneously involved them as partners (even if antagonistic partners) in the running of the machine. Even the indices of working-class strength—the financial reserves of trade unions and co-ops—were secure only within the custodianship of capitalist stability.

Thompson's use of "antagonism" here would obviously fall into Mao's category of nonantagonistic contradiction.

For a certain period of time, the working class of the developed capitalist nations became a somewhat stable subordinate interest in the established order, but it could only maintain that secondary position through constantly, albeit usually legitimate, contesting for its rights. During the stage of advanced capitalism, the working-class position moves into a more developed form of normalization through the mechanisms of the welfare state, well-established collective bargaining, high wages, and the emergence of new life-styles centered on mass communications and mass consumptions. In the histories of the leading capitalist nations, class strife has been the most intense (the class contradiction has been the most antagonistic) when there has been a piling of incongruencies within the whole social formation, usually during initial industrialization or a major war. Advanced capitalism has succeeded in temporarily generating a relatively more congruent order. It appears that we are now, after a 30-year interval, undergoing a breakdown of some of the congruency within advanced capitalism. Therefore, we can expect that the class contradiction will once more become antagonistic. Any new class strife will not be a reversion to pre-World War II forms, but will shape itself in terms of specific incongruencies within advanced capitalism.

Reformist and conservative theories attempt to explain this new situation with claims that class contradictions never existed or that, if they did, they have now become so muted as to be indistinguishable from a number of other conflicting interests in the society. In response, many Marxists will assert the theory of a labor aristocracy unfortunately in a way that is more moralistic in condemnation than scientific in understanding. It is one thing for Lenin to have put forth this position in 1916; it is quite another thing to persist in it, as many Marxists have for over 50 years. "To explain a historical fact that has endured for nearly a century by the corruption of the leaders and the deception of the masses is, to say the least, hardly in conformity with the method of historical materialism." (Emmanuel, 1972, p. 179).

One of the sources of the increased incomes of the working class comes from the huge economic surpluses generated through the regularization of technological innovation and the systemization of management within the large corporations. The other sources are the vast profits and the high wages that the capitalists and the workers in the developed countries gain at the expense of the underdeveloped world. The source of these latter items are in profits from the export of capital and gains from unequal terms of trade. Both of these processes require a well-integrated nation and a strong state apparatus.

The Nation in Advanced Capitalism

The history of national development for the advanced capitalist countries appears to have proceeded through three stages: (1) The establishment of the capitalist state. (2) The era of imperialism in which the working class won recognition as a subordinate interest on the bourgeois order; mass suffrage, mass newspapers, and mass education are well instituted; and there is an elaboration of an ideology of expansive nationalism. (3) Advanced capitalism in which the state increasingly becomes the regulator of economic and social life and the guarantor of a wide range of economic rights.[i]

This new nation-state is the instrumentality of the planning and the monetary and fiscal policies that stabilize the advanced capitalist economy. Inclusion in the economic relations provides a wage that is vastly greater than that of a comparable worker in an underdeveloped country. To a certain degree, but by no means to the extent that some, like Emmanuel (1970), would argue, the nation-state becomes the bargaining unit for dividing up the gains from the exploitation of the third world. The welfare activities of the state also reinforce the saliency of the nation as it furnishes the framework for the various benefits that tie the divergent interests and classes together. "As the process of interaction evolves, the entire institutional structure of the state becomes set in a matrix of economic nationalism." (Myrdal, 1967, p. 135; see also chapters 10 and 11; see also Shafer, 1972, p. 259) Additionally, there is a qualitative increase in the saturation of the population with mass communications, especially through electronic media and in the length of schooling, which in the United States now involves almost everyone into young adulthood.

The outbreak of World War I in 1914 was the key test of strength of nationalism versus the proletarian internationalism in the phase of imperialism. In the developed capitalist countries, the reinforced nationalism proved that it could prevail when almost all the European working classes and their political organizations rallied to the defense of their respective fatherlands. Fascism was a transitional form of nationalism between the second and third stages. It faced backward in that it arose and was successful in situations in which there was a relatively large incongruity between a capitalist mode of production and precapitalist features of the political culture. It faced toward advanced capitalism in the way it elaborated state interpenetration of economic and social life.

Nationalism, as an ideological movement, is not so strident today in advanced capitalist countries for the very reason that it is so well institutionally grounded in the all-pervasive bounds of the modern nation-state and ritualized in everyday life. However, in crisis situations it can easily break out as racism or xenophobia. During the Cold War era, anticommunism operated as a nationalist mechanism to squelch internal dissent and mobilize a consensus behind a protracted struggle for world hegemony. For the present we can conclude that nationality is a form of allegiance that takes precedence over class. An interview in Northern Ireland that Conor Cruise O'Brien (1972, p. 307) recounts makes this point most tellingly:

---

[i]Lenin (1964, p. 39), judging the imperialist system to be on the brink of overthrow, did not foresee any further development of nationalism in the mature capitalist countries. "In the Western countries the national movement is a thing of the distant past. In England, France, Germany, etc. the 'fatherland' is a dead letter, it has played its historical role, i.e. the national movement cannot yield here anything progressive, anything that will elevate new masses to a new economic and political life."

... one Belfast shop-steward, a Communist, told me that after years of trying to bring politics (i.e., left-wing politics) *into* the works, he was now devoting the same energy to keeping politics *out*, because politics inevitably meant sectarian conflict. He also described how management and shop-stewards in this major plant were actually in a kind of collusion to engineer confrontations between "management and workers," in order to take men's minds off "the real conflict" which was capable of blowing the works apart, ruining men and management together. The "real conflict" which the carefully contrived "class struggle" ballet sought to avert, was that between Protestants and Catholics.

Congruence of Nationalism and Race

An explication regarding the nature of Black and White nationalisms within the United States is required at this point. In the first place, it is not claimed that these nationalisms are based on separable socioeconomic entities that are functionally self-sufficient nations on the order of France and Germany, for example. For this reason we shall refer to their institutional basis as nationalities that exist as significant formations within an overarching American *nation*. We do claim that these nationalities are sufficiently structured to provide the framework for a wide range of institutional operations, decision-making procedures, and primary loyalties of persons. Racial distinctions in the United States are something more than the sum of discriminations. They are now grounded in the nationality conflict between the dominated community and the dominating community, making the antagonism a deeply rooted one. (In addition to the Black nationality, Puerto Rico exists as a more classic colony with a potential of full nationhood. In the Southwest a Chicano nationality is emerging. This chapter limits itself to an examination of Black-White relationships.)

Racial domination in America has not always existed in its present nationalistic form. An evolution has taken place. The operations of these nationalities can be seen more clearly through a brief review of the highlights of their historical development. First let us look at White nationalism.

In North America the control of the Black slave population was inextricably linked to the development of citizenship for the lower orders of the White population. These dynamics are well illustrated by Fredrickson's summary of recent studies on colonial Virginia (1974):

Only at the end of the [seventeenth] century, when the supply of white servants dried up just as black slaves were becoming increasingly available at prices planters could afford, did anything like a true color line begin to develop. The gradual change in the labor force on the plantations—from mixed but predominantly white to almost exclusively black—and the accompanying rise of a white yeomanry composed largely of ex-servants can be seen as necessary preconditions for a flourishing Southern racism. Once racial distinctions could be made to correspond to social and economic divisions, it was easy and advantageous to set blacks apart as a totally different and inferior people.

This new social structure was also the basis of a kind of pseudo-equality among whites, for the class division that remained between rich planters and subsistence farmers could be obscured by a sense that, unlike the blacks, whites all shared in the rights of free Englishmen and even, in most cases, the possession of property. . . . On this foundation of black subjugation and white opportunity a racially circumscribed democracy could gradually develop.

As sectional conflict grew in the nineteenth century, the solidarity of all Whites was even more developed by the embattled political leadership, and distinctive elements of the Southern subculture were shaped by the hegemony of the plantocracy over the much more numerous nonplanter whites.

While the major root of White nationality lay within the civic order that was fashioned in order to maintain the system of racial domination in the areas of the slave plantations, another source of this nationalism came from the yeoman farmer territories largely in the old Northwest, but also including some of the upland areas of the South. Yeoman racism (and also that of many urban workers) looked upon the planters and their Black slaves as competitors. Accordingly, their brand of racism did not seek to secure a system of racial domination; rather, it looked to the exclusion of the Black from the nation. "Significant in Republican and free-soil thinking of the late 1850's and well into the Civil War, it appears, was a militant racial nationalism, an expectation of white expansion into every corner of the nation, with the disappearance of the Negro as the inevitable corollary." (Fredrickson, 1971, pp. 147-47).

In the Civil War the South made a nearly successful attempt to protect its racial order by creating an independent national order buttressed by its own state apparatus. Although the South lost its bid for national independence, the social, ideological, and political lines of cleavage that had been generated to control the Black slave labor force were so sharp that they did prepare the ground for a new type of nationality cleavage—this time directly along the lines of race. The Radical Republicans were the only politically significant White group that was racially inclusive in its definition of the American nation and citizenship. The Radicals were also notable for their nationalism in opposition to regionalism and localism, and for their support of an active state (Montgomery, 1967, pp. 78-86). Their political defeat in the middle of Reconstruction marked the end of the one significant chance that merger would take place between the burgeoning racial nationalities.

The main line of the development of modern White nationality goes back to the regional base of the nineteenth-century South, where Blacks as a servile class were excluded from any citizenship in the slave period and from effective citizenship in the post-Reconstruction era. In the old South, whiteness meant inclusion in the nation. While racism ideologically and behaviorally was country-wide, the economic base was regional—first in the plantation system and then in the peonagelike sharecropping and tenancy operations. A castelike status was developed to regulate the economic exploitation of the Black agrarian worker. In the twentieth century the economic base of the Southern system was eroded by the demand for Black labor in the metropolitan centers, first in the established ones of the North and then in the growing ones of the South. This process was intensified and made irreversible with the mid-twentieth-century expulsion of the Black peasantry from the land when it became economically and technologically expedient to do so (Baron, 1971, pp. 19-31).

Although in the metropolitan centers special advantage was taken of the new Black workers regarding pay, work conditions, and job security, no distinctive *form* of economic subsystem was erected upon the special relations with this labor force. Accordingly, no important sector of the capitalist class developed a direct stake in the racial control of labor comparable to that of the nineteenth-century planter class. However, given the pervasiveness of racism and its sanction by the state, the growth of the Black metropolitan population brought about an intensive evolution of new social forms that elaborated the distinctiveness of White and Black civil societies. The new institutional expressions of these racial societies were characteristically urban, embedded in such key metropolitan systems as the labor market, the housing and land markets, the schools, and local government. While White civil society relies upon the labor of Black workers for its economic institutions, in other areas of direct social contact it has remained fairly insulated racially (Baron, 1969).

Vis-à-vis the Black community, a strong interclass national solidarity of Whites was promoted by the exercise of control and domination over Black institutions and Black subsectors within the major metropolitan systems. As the size of the urban Black communities grew, not only did various White groups gain advantages from their exploitation and subjugation, but the continuing viability of a wide range of White institutions—from central business districts and major universities to ethnic residential neighborhoods—became dependent on their insulation from the Black community and the intensification of barriers that kept Black people in a subordinate status. White national solidarity operated to regulate the Black community, especially in times when Black people were pushing for developmental objectives that were disruptive of institutional stability within White society. In addition, the White solidarity that was generated by targeting attention on an external object fostered a consensual meeting ground for otherwise conflicting forces. Along this line, racism worked to develop a commonality of perceived interests among White workers and employers.

In the state apparatus there is a prevailing racial bias toward the interests of the dominant White nationality. However, within the last decade, in response to the pressures of the civil rights and Black liberation movements, the state has diminished its active role as an organizer of racism. It even engages to a limited extent in ameliorative equal-rights operations, but the essential inertia of the state is sufficient to sustain the now well-established urban racism.

There are two strategies of White nationalism. The internal debates on race questions have become a contest regarding which of these strategies should prevail. The conservative strategy calls for the maintenance of the status quo in order not to threaten the viability of the nation through shocks and disorganization. The liberal strategy calls for an equalitarian opening up to include those Blacks who will assimilate to the norms of the White nation. Over the long run, the liberal strategy looks to the disappearance of Black people as an historic people. Neither _of these strategies can address themselves to the further development of those sectors of the Black people that they cannot control through the hegemony of the institutions of White society. Historically this factor has fostered the long-run dominance of the conservative tendency over the inclusionist tendency.

Since a reader in the 1970s is much more likely to accept the reality of Black nationalism, we do not have to devote as much space to this topic as we did to White nationalism. In the trammels of slavery a distinctive Afro-American culture was forged. In the United States the direct carryovers from Africa were not as strong as they were in the Caribbean or Brazil, so that essentially new Black institutions of the family and religion were fashioned by the slave and the small, free Black communities. This new subculture not only was conscious of its distinctiveness within America but constantly rediscovered its links to Africa (Drake, 1970, pp. 12-51).

For the brief decade of Reconstruction after the Civil War, the possibility existed for the grounding of a Black nation along classic lines. Black people constituted a majority in a great crescent of territory that extended from the Carolinas to Louisiana and centered on the fertile land of the black belt. An independent peasantry would have been the seed bed for the nurturing of a national bourgeoisie. Instead the overthrow of Reconstruction froze Black people into a quasi-colonized status. Before an assertive Black bourgeoisie emerged, Blacks were expelled from agriculture and, thereby, lost an extensive and contiguous territorial base. Nevertheless, nationalist movements have frequently sprung up from the Black community. They have arisen during periods of great dislocation for Black people when there has not been a powerful White movement addressing some of the issues confronting them. Such periods occurred within the defeat of Reconstruction that saw the explicit nationalism of the Exodusters and the implicit nationalism of Booker T. Washington, the post-World War I era with the rise of Garveyism, and the recent flourishing of Black nationalism in the 1960s. Today Black people are dispersed, the majority being encapsulated as minorities in the central cities of some 50 large metropolitan areas. Under these demographic conditions the consolidation of an administratively viable national homeland is extremely difficult, if not impossible.

Black capitalism has never become more than a marginal operation that employs only a small portion of the Black labor force. It does not provide the kind of strong economy required of an independent, or even semiautonomous, nation existing within the territorial confines of the present United States. Today the primary economic foundation of the Black nationality lies in the distinctiveness of its working class. However, this proletarian base, which is limited rather well by established labor market and other social institutions, cannot be segmented off from White institutions, for it is largely employed by the giant corporations and public bureaucracies that are the key elements in the whole American economy. Therefore, neither the growing Black proletariat nor the stagnant Black entrepreneurial class provides an easily separable economic base. In an analogous way, no institutional network that could serve as an incipient state apparatus, on the order of the colonial Indian civil service or the North African military service, has emerged. [The nearest development of a network that could have served as the womb of an incipient state apparatus formed around Booker T. Washington and his coterie in the first decade of this century (see Meier, 1963).]

The Black nationality is most strongly structured in the noneconomic sectors of civil society. Distinctive Black social, cultural, and ideological formations have evolved over the centuries in America. They have been adapted to modern urban conditions within the last 70 years, giving coherence to the lives of Black working people. The movements of the 1960s have strengthened the dialectical relationship between the working class and the other elements of Black society. The long-run significance of these factors is heightened because it is in the area of civil institutions that White society is undergoing the greatest weakening.

A Model of Racial Nationalities

In order to crystallize our understanding of the national character of present-day racism, it is helpful to codify the racial relationships in a simple model.[j] The purpose of our model is to make the essential features regarding the current system of racial domination stand out. By using this approach we shall have to neglect many secondary elements. It is appropriate to add these other features back into the model only after we have clearly established the essence of the system.

---

[j]It is helpful to clarify the use of models within the methodology of historical materialism. Although models can be useful in delineating the decisive relationships that are operative in a particular period or area of life, they are no substitute for the actual integrity of history or everyday life. The English historian E.P. Thompson (1965, pp. 349-350) has provided a dialectical illumination of this question:

A model is a metaphor of historical process. It indicates not only the significant parts of this process but the way in which they are interrelated and the way in which they change. In one sense, history remains irreducible; it remains *all* that happened. In another sense, history does not become history until there is a model: at the moment at which the most elementary notion of causation, process, or cultural patterning, intrudes, then some model is assumed.

History and everyday life *are*. They are not illustrations of some model. At the same time they are not unknowable. Only with a model that has some degree of validity are they intelligible and subject to purposeful action.

A geometric analogy of our model of the national character of modern American racism is depicted in Figure 7-1. It has four basic overall structural elements: the total configuration that represents the overall American nation, the White nationality, the Black nationality, and the ruling class. Regarding the characteristics of the national elements, a few features of the model should be noted in addition to the more general previous discussion. The graphic figure emphasizes social structure solely for clarity of visualization. The functioning of the economic and political (state) structures in regard to the racial nationalities will be explicated in the text. The total configuration is a triangle, implying a society that is hierarchical with a relatively small dominant group and with increasing proportions as the status scale is descended.[k] The White nationality, occupying almost all the American social structure except at the lowest reaches, has a status configuration that closely approximates that of the whole.

The *race line* that divides Whites from Blacks meets certain qualifications. It touches both legs of the triangle so that there is no White who does not have

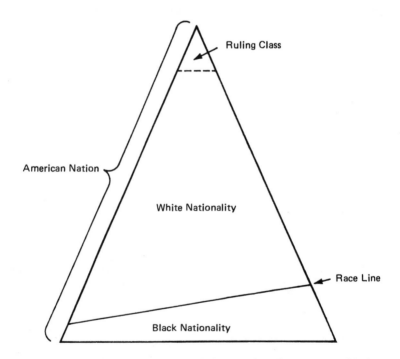

Figure 7-1. Schema of Racial Nationalism within the American Nation.

[k]Some kind of diamond-shaped configuration that certain stratification experts have argued is more appropriate to the present-day United States would not change the basic dynamics. The society would still be hierarchical with a small dominant group (Mayer, 1963; Coleman and Neugarten, 1971).

some Blacks beneath him or her. This condition is one that has held historically from the seventeenth century to the present. Theoretically this condition might not be absolutely necessary to the preservation of a national type solidarity among the Whites, but in practice it has been functionally significant. The fact that the race line has a slope greater than zero indicates the stratification within the Black community and that some Blacks are better off than some Whites. This slope also reflects some of the realities of the Black nationality. Internally there are leadership groups that provide coherence and direction. Further, since the White groups cannot sufficiently penetrate the Black community to maintain all the social controls necessary for their domination, they have to promote the prestige and status of certain Blacks who can perform these functions as their surrogates. In actuality this line does not have to be strictly linear but might have a somewhat greater slope toward the upper end that would indicate a small number of Blacks with something higher than a lower-middling status.

The ruling class is that small social group that controls and directs the major corporations, owns the bulk of the wealth, and in whose basic interests the state is operated. William Domhoff (1970, 1974) has shown decisively that the present-day ruling class is a socially cohesive group (although he might somewhat underestimate its willingness to co-opt new talent). A ruling class cannot exercise power on an arbitrary basis. It makes and enforces decisions under the constraint of those conditions (or laws) that sustain its power and aggrandizement. In the case under consideration, these conditions are in a general sense the laws of development of advanced capitalism as regards both economic growth and the maintenance of the nation-state.

The dominance of the ruling class is expressed through its control over the disposition of the country's economic surplus, and its ability to subordinate other objectives to the continuous quest to increase the mass of that surplus. The most important forms in which the surplus is realized are corporate profits and the cash flows of wealthy families. This control of the economic surplus implies the subordination of other social classes, but in this initial stage of our model we do not have to specify much regarding the control of the subordinate White classes. The imperatives of a viable national framework require the maintenance of the following: a state that promotes the stability of corporate operations domestically and internationally; a system of order that balances in the interests of subordinate classes; a national "civic religion" that sustains the allegiance of most sectors of society.

Let us now examine the function of the race line from the position of the ruling class. In the period of slavery and the succeeding peonage-type tenancy, a politically and economically significant section of the ruling class had a direct stake in the race line as a mechanism for appropriating the economic surplus through the enforcement of a more intensive form of labor exploitation than could take place within White society. Under these conditions the race line was more horizontal, and the barriers represented by it were especially strong, as the ruling class (or a politically powerful sector thereof) had a direct economic interest in, at minimum, maintaining the size of this special labor force. Since this was the period in which White nationalism developed, the race line, of course, also had other important social and political functions that were internal to the White sector.

Once the White and Black nationalities were established and grounded in a whole range of institutional and ideological forms, the special economic surplus extraction features of racial controls in the agrarian sector could drop to secondary importance, and yet the overall system of racial subordination could remain intact. This process did occur in the twentieth century with the combination of a growing demand for Black labor as part of the industrial proletariat and the shift in production techniques in Southern agriculture. Comparative studies of racism and industrialization in South Africa and Brazil reinforce this conclusion. [On Brazil see Bastide (1957, 1965) and Fernandez (1969). On South Africa see Adam (1971) and Jordan (1973).] As Herbert Blumer (1965) has summarized,

The picture presented by industrialization in a racially ordered society is that industrial imperatives accommodate themselves to the racial mould and continue to operate effectively within it. We must look to outside factors rather than to a maturation of these imperatives for an explanation of the disintegration of the racial mould.

After a certain stage in the homogenization of the productive processes to the basis of wage labor, the ruling class can lose its essential economic stake in the system of racial oppression. In South Africa where racist divisions prevail juridically and in formal labor market designations, major enterprises retain a calculable stake in racially intensified economic exploitation; therefore, they can base long-term planning upon this consideration. However, in the United States where the major sectors of the labor market operate through the outward forms of uniform standards (we shall qualify this statement later), it is hard for large corporations and bureaucracies to make significant plans regarding the economic gains of racism through the relative underpayment of Black labor. Under these American conditions, the slope of the race line becomes increasingly indifferent to the ruling class *from the considerations of surplus accumulation.* In contrast to the old planter class, the modern corporate controllers are not constrained by survival needs to exercise immediate racial controls for the purpose of castelike economic exploitation, although the option of special exploitation might still be pursued when the political context makes it feasible. In fact, if other national considerations could be excluded, the ruling class might well prefer a diminution of racial controls. They could use the extreme individuation of persons that a corporation-dominated society fosters in order to break up the troublesome and now aggressive cohesiveness of the Black community.

Within the range of the ability of the ruling class to set its policy objectives, the slope of the race line and its intensity as a barrier are set by considerations of maintaining its political and social dominance within its national settings. On the basis of empirical observation these conditions appear to be: (1) the race line does not intercept the line that defines the ruling class; (2) the race line does not shift in such a manner as to disturb the ruling class's dominance within the White nationality or within the American nation as a whole; (3) direct control of the Black nationality is of secondary importance to the ruling class and is subordinated to the second point. These propositions require some elaboration.

There is no theoretical reason that would determine the absolute exclusion of Blacks from the ruling class. There were a few successful Black plantation owners in the old South although they were not socially integrated into the planter class. Today considerable encouragement is being given to the development of Black managers and professionals, but there is no move to bring color into the ruling class itself. Some liberal sectors of the ruling class might be willing to attempt such co-optation if the pressures were great enough. On the other hand, the racial exclusiveness of the ruling class is dictated by its own internal standards of solidarity and prejudice, and by leadership demands placed on it as the dominant group within the White nationality.

Since the social and ideological forms within the White nationality and the whole nation are rather similar, conceivably inclusive White nationality could be totally dissolved into the American structure, and the basic socioeconomic system would remain operative. However, such a dissolution does not seem to be under way. Appeals to racism become important solidarity mechanisms to be exploited either in factional fights or in crisis periods and, thereby, continuously reinforce the distinctiveness of White society. This point can be illustrated through the use of the bussing issue by the Nixon campaign in the 1972 elections or in a more strident form in the Nazis' use of the master race doctrine. Further the unity generated on the basis of racial dominance operates to mitigate potential conflict inherent in the hierarchical arrangements of the corporate and bureaucratic institutions that are the major components of the state capitalist system.

From an external perspective, the existence of Black communities as alien and dominated enclaves poses threats to the continued operation of a wide range of White institutions. These might be ruling-class-controlled institutions that are adjacent to an expanding ghetto, as in the case of major urban universities or central business districts which contend with the Black community for urban land. Or they might be institutional preserves of lower social strata, such as ethnic and working-class neighborhoods or racially protected job classifications. In either case, or in any ranging between the two, White nationalism is called upon as a socially mobilizing defense mechanism. The ruling class and middle class tend to be more subtle and sophisticated in their use of racial nationalism, while the working class tends to be more direct and obvious.

It is appropriate here to modify our consideration of consensual homogeneity regarding racial matters in the White community. In reality there are many kinds of conflicts in White society. While over the long run class contradictions are the most decisive form of these conflicts, they also exist within different strata of a specific class or even between sectors of the ruling class on the grounds of divergent interests or approaches to strategy. Likewise, but not on as extensive a basis, there are frictions and oppositions between elements in the Black community. At various times one contending White group will seek to strengthen its position by allying with the Black community or some significant section of it. Conflicting White groups frequently counter these moves by appealing to racism and White solidarity. If this tactic works out successfully, it simultaneously thwarts the White group that made the interracial move and increases the strength of a broad range of racial controls that are necessary to the definition of White nationalism.

There is no preordination as to which White group will reach out for Black support and which one will make the racialist counterthrust. This mechanism has been operative over a long period of American history. When poor farmers and working-class groups have attempted interracial alliances, e.g., during the Populist movement of the 1890s or in trade union organizing during the New Deal, the response of employers and the ruling class has been to promote racism as a means to break up the movement. The opposite also holds: upper-class moves for political alliances or the expansion of their employment of Black labor into previously forbidden occupational preserves have been met by lower-strata campaigns for racial exclusion in jobs, neighborhoods, and the political process.[1] It should be kept in mind that whatever White group sought interracial accommodation or alliance, it always ended up casting the Blacks into a subordinated position in their relationship.

If we return to our model, we note that the ruling class directly dominates the whole nation and the White nationality. It may exercise control over the Black nationality either directly or through the mediation of other elements in White society and cooperating groups in Black society. The national configuration defines Blacks as a subordinate nationality group. Therefore, from a ruling-class perspective, barring upsetting conditions, the objectives of its control over Blacks are set as a residual of the imperatives of control over the whole American nation and the White nationality. The whole of the White group has a certain direct claim on ruling-class objectives. The Black group receives attention only in terms of what is necessary for the other two national entities, but not in terms of strictly Black objectives. Black claims on the setting of priorities and the making of important decisions are only operative to the extent that members of the group are able to exert influence in the overall national context. This

---

[1]O'Connor (1973, pp. 51-58) describes the strategies developed in response to the black movement in the 1960s as being those of a social-industrial complex whose success "requires that gains from technical progress be redistributed; they must devolve to monopoly capital and competitive sector workers, not to monopoly and state sector workers."

influence is quite limited, and has resulted only from Black social and political struggles. While some sectors of the White community would just as soon see Black people banished, the ruling class cannot afford to adopt this position because it has a vested interest in Black people as a source of labor for their corporate enterprises.

It was asserted earlier that from considerations of the accumulation of economic surplus the slope of the race line per se was growing to be a matter of increasing indifference to the ruling class. However, from considerations of maintaining national control, the position of the race line has strong implications. As we shall discuss later, nationality divisions facilitate the division of the advanced capitalist labor market into primary and secondary sectors. Of greatest importance is the fact that any major shift in this line causes considerable shock waves throughout the whole of the White community. The solidity and rigidity of White nationalism is sufficiently strong that the effects of racial dislocations are rapidly transmitted from one sector to another. In the last quarter-century, disturbances in the existing racial arrangements, more so than any other factor, have threatened the ruling class's dominance and social hegemony over their fellow Whites.[m] The overhanging threat of disruption in the given pattern of racial accommodation has profound administrative implications because the uncertainty it generates reduces the predictability that is necessary for the operation of technocratically oriented giant corporations and bureaucracies. *In terms of these national considerations, the ruling class is constrained to minimize the shocks to the racial order by seeking an equilibrium that as nearly as possible maintains the race line where it already is at any particular time.*

Contrary to the strategic needs of the ruling class for stability, historical exigencies operate to disrupt the racial balance. These disturbers of the racial balance can be categorized under three forces:

(1) Economic shifts that arise from technological, administrative, and demographic imperatives. These changes are usually mediated through market mechanisms, and the most important ones are the shifts in the demand for Black labor such as were occasioned by the mechanization of Southern agriculture.

(2) Pressures from Black nationalism for self-development and self-determination. This category includes not only the more political-type operations that range from civil rights negotiations to urban uprisings, but also the survival pressures of the Black community to keep its institutional integrity, to expand its living space, and to increase its employment and educational opportunities.

(3) Pressures of White nationalism. The White concentration on the maintenance of the racial status quo means that new pressures on this account are usually counterreactions to shifts that originate from one of the first two causes, e.g., the organized resistance to racial transition in urban neighborhoods. These

---

[m]During the 1960s both Republican (Phillips, 1969) and Democratic (Scammon and Wattenberg, 1970) staff analysts concluded that the key domestic issue was the "social question," a euphemism for White hostility to concessions made to Black people.

pressures may originate from any stratum of White society whose path to the access of resources or prestige puts it into competition with Blacks.

Under these conditions the ruling class is hard put to maintain a static equilibrium. The possibility of a racial stasis was eliminated by the great increases in demand for Black labor that were generated during the two World Wars in the urban industrial sector of the economy. Pragmatically, the ruling class's preferred strategy has to be one of seeking a dynamic or smoothly shifting racial equilibrium, i.e., a system that is able to reduce the shocks to a manageable frequency and to incorporate them into the existing order in a nondisruptive manner. Such a strategy can be best pursued by fostering a series of small incremental changes that are mediated by a market mechanism, or in nonmarket spheres mediated through protomarket-type mechanisms such as electoral politics. Next in preference is the strategy of fostering the development of a sufficiently large Black bourgeois leadership that has a vested interest in the structure and order of the overall multinational configuration. (For statistical evidence indicating the current application of this approach, see Freeman, 1973b.) Although much rhetoric is expended on the promotion of Black capitalism, this is not considered to have significant strategic potential. The real resources for the development of the bourgeoisie are expended on the training of professionals, technicians, and lower- and middle-level management. Finally, efforts are directed to a replication of the incorporative strategy that was successful with the White working class. The better-off sections of the Black proletariat are conceded improved working conditions, higher incomes, and increased consumptive opportunities. In spite of the increased efforts put into ruling-class strategies aimed at gradual and nondisruptive change in both the slope and the intensity of the race line, the inherent dynamics of the racial nationalisms, to one degree or another, tend to frustrate the achievement of this objective.

Control over the shifts in the race line can be exercised by policies of concession or repression. In actual practice, the policy is usually a mixture of the two. Enough concessions are offered to be meaningful to some Black people. Enough repression is concomitantly exercised to force the rest of the Black people to acquiesce in that level of concession. The concurrence of concessions with shifts in the race line that derive from technological and demographic imperatives creates some blurring of racial distinctiveness, particularly at the physical and social boundaries of the Black community. Some jobs and services, more usually those of lower social status, are available biracially on a fairly stable basis. More frequently neighborhoods, jobs, schools, etc., that are in the process of transfer from the White to the Black sector have biracial personnel in the period of transition. One form of concession emerging in the United States is cultural co-optation. As in the Portuguese colonial system, persons who adapt to and adopt the culture of the dominant power are no longer designated by the racial label of "native" and are accorded citizenship in the metropolis. Most Whites consider this process to be an extensive form of concession and categorize it as integration.

Sanctions in order to smooth racial adjustments are not always imposed against Blacks. Civil rights laws and judicial decisions provide, in a muted form, for the exercise of authority over Whites. Direct sanctions are sometimes threatened but rarely exercised. When racial adjustments might diminish certain White privileges in a specific area, they are often compensated for by concessions or the granting of advantage in some other area.

The state is the primary instrumentality for the regulation of the race line's stability or its smooth shifting, while the shocks that disturb the line's equilibrium generally originate in civil society. Even though direct racial regulation is no longer constitutional, much of the state's racial policy is directed to maintaining the status quo in this area through the protection of vested property rights and traditional social privileges. In the face of the frequent disturbances of the racial equilibrium within the last 25 years, a whole body of federal and local statutes, regulations, and court decisions has arisen to provide an orderly process for changing the relationships of racial domination. At some times, this state action has maintained a smooth control over affairs; at other times it has been met by disorder in such forms as White backlash and Black urban uprisings. The work of the state machinery has had to be bolstered within civil society by the efforts of blue-ribbon leadership, intellectuals, foundations, and universities in order to assert the hegemony of the doctrine of gradual racial change.

Much of the state's strategy for the nondisruptive, incremental shifting of the race line is implemented through its broad welfare and benefits policies. Since the national setting provides the framework for planning and welfare operations under state capitalism, the overlapping nationalisms in the United States provide a complicated context within which to operate. Although governmental programs are formulated in the language of juridical equality for all, functionally they respect the variety of nationalist realities. De facto the benefits are biased to the advantage of the higher status groups and Whites in general. Where the federal laws and administrative rulings do not accomplish this purpose directly, the mediation of local power groups and state and local governments accomplished it indirectly. Benefits to rich and middle-class groups are considered a matter of right. Welfare to Blacks and poor people is so administered as to carry the stigma of dependency. Federal housing policies illustrate this situation very clearly. They have encouraged the growth of Black ghettos and White suburbs. They have removed Blacks from the vicinity of prestigious White institutions through urban renewal. While giving subsidies in the form of tax breaks to better-off homeowners, they create the aura of the pariah for Black people in public housing projects.

Divisions in the Labor Market

The argument so far has shown that from the perspective of a ruling class, based on the control of large-scale corporate and bureaucratic operations, a castelike system for regulating Black labor is neither necessary nor particularly desirable for the rationalization of its management of the labor force. In terms of the base-superstructure model, the question, therefore, arises: Is there any important congruence between the overall national structure of race and the economic base of American society? The lack of a base in the relations of production would indicate a considerable weakening of the race structure in the near future. (Indeed, in the South during the last 25 years, the breakup of the old agrarian economic relations set the conditions for the civil rights movement and the breakup of the Jim Crow system.) In view of the long-run influence of the economic base in the shaping of social relations, the most probable expectation is that a lack of congruence between racial domination and the relations of production under advanced capitalism would lead to a diminution of racial definitions. To the contrary, on the metropolitan scene race consciousness and national consciousness are growing among Blacks, and operationally it remains very efficacious among Whites. Therefore, we must examine carefully the economic basis of racial nationalisms.

In the metropolitan labor markets, there are in effect two systems that segment the labor market so as to define the subordination for Black workers. Historically one system is the direct outgrowth of the old plantation-based, castelike status of Black workers. This is the division of the labor market into distinctive Black and White sectors. The other system is that of the modern-type labor hierarchy, based upon the organizational needs of large economic units and the relationship of these giant enterprises to the rest of the economy. Out of this latter set of conditions another form of labor market segmentation develops between a primary sector with decent-paying, steady employment and a secondary sector with marginal jobs. In addition to the direct racial subordination that is grounded in these two patterns of labor market segmentation, discrimination rooted in ideological, psychological, and other social structures operates to the detriment of Black workers.

Racial segmentation in urban labor markets has a strong continuity going back to the slave era. Not only did slaves in the cities form a specially subjugated work force, but free Blacks, both in the North and in the South, were ascribed a stigmatized status that derived from the caste position of their brothers and sisters in bondage. After abolition the labor constraints upon the Black agricultural caste were somewhat relaxed, but they continued to set the norms for the employment of Blacks in the cities. The freed men and women were largely confined to jobs that were servile, dirty, and low-paying. Frequently these positions became known as "Negro jobs." Under these conditions the racial dualism of the metropolitan labor markets emerged full blown with the large Black in-migrations during the labor shortages of the two World Wars.

The sharp restriction in European immigration in the 1920s made industry more reliant upon the reserves of workers among the Black peasantry[n] both for the general expansion of capitalist production and for the less desirable jobs in the increasingly hierarchically organized work forces of the large corporations. The emergence of the Black proletariat as a distinctive decisive social form took a considerable period of time. In the late 1920s Carpenter (1927) could claim that the difference between Black and immigrant workers was only one of degree. However, four years later Herman Feldman in writing on personnel administration (1931, p. 288) was more prescient and singled out Blacks as the "major racial situation in the country" whose relationship to industry was prototypical for other darker peoples.[o] The Great Depression, which was harsher on Black workers and diminished their status relative to White workers (Ashenfelter, 1970), marked a temporary setback in the formation of the Black proletariat. The conclusive establishment of the Black working class as a major force both qualitatively and quantitatively did not occur until the conjuncture of the prolonged labor shortage that essentially ran from World War II through the Korean War with the wholesale displacement of tenants and sharecroppers from Southern agriculture. In a parallel movement an urban-oriented Black nationalism developed first in the Garvey movement of the 1920s and renewed itself from the latter part of the 1950s onward. Concurrently White nationalism moved from being primarily a Southern issue to being a countrywide phenomenon.

This racial dualism is manifest in a dominant sector of the labor market in which firms recruit White workers and White workers look for jobs and a smaller sector in which firms recruit Black workers and Black workers look for jobs (Baron, 1969, pp. 146-147; see also Baron and Hymer, 1968):

There are distinct sets of demand and supply forces determining earnings and occupational distribution in each of the white and black sectors of the job market; the two sectors also differ as to practices and procedures for the recruitment, hiring, training, and promotion of workers. . . . Black workers are hired by certain industries, by particular firms within these industries, and for particular jobs within these firms. . . . Within establishments that hire both blacks and whites, the black workers are usually limited to specific job classifications and production units. An accurate rule of thumb is that the lower the pay or the more disagreeable and dirty the job, the greater the chance of finding a high proportion of Negroes.

Within the racial division of the labor market, the black subsector is in a subordinate position. Jobs are distributed between black and white workers in a way that gives white workers the first opportunity for employment. Expansion

---

[n]Numerically the white farm population, which continuously declined from 1920 on, formed a larger labor reserve, but in contrast to the black peasantry this group did not provide the human material for any unique urban social group.

[o]Feldman was a most astute analyst of the social and personnel needs of the modern corporate organization. He codified a set of guidelines for the racial practices of management and personnel officials that include most of the major features of the corporate policies adopted in the 1960s (pp. 303-305).

of employment opportunities for the black workers occurs only during periods of tight labor markets when certain jobs transfer either partially or fully to the black sub-sector.

Under the political pressures from the Black community in the last few years there has been some blurring of the boundaries between the racial sectors, but the fundamentals of the description still hold.

The subordination of the Black workers within this dual system supports underpayment and speed-up in relation to comparable standards in the White sector. This extra exploitation is most marked in marginal firms and declining industries. For many of the individual firms in these categories, wage discrimination has become a condition for survival, and they have a vested interest in its maintenance. Since these companies tend to be low-profit operations, they do not usually realize these gains from discrimination. In the cases where they operate with high-cost, inefficient, and obsolescent technology, the low wages are never realized as profits, for the labor is underutilized in terms of modern production possibilities. In the other cases not limited by these constraints, the employing firm usually faces a highly competitive market and does not realize the advantages of discrimination as profits, but passes them on via lower prices for its goods and services. High-profit oligopolistic firms and consumers indirectly reap the fruits of the lower cost of Black labor. Since these gains are mediated through a chain of market transactions, it is hard for a specific large corporation to calculate its payoff from the wage discrimination in the low-profit firms.

Giant corporations which operate with uniform personnel practices and trade union contracts find it difficult to pay Black workers less or to speed them up more on an immediate racial basis, except in those numerous instances where it is possible to isolate them in certain production facilities or job categories. Taylor (1968) showed a racial differential in pay for janitors and material handlers in the Chicago labor market. In individual firms the wage rates were uniform, but those firms which hired large numbers of Blacks in these jobs were able to pay less. While this practice is still very common, it was more prevalent 10 or 15 years ago. It is being somewhat attenuated by external pressures for equal employment opportunity and by imperatives internal to the management of the large firm that requires an administrative system that at least has the appearance of evaluating individual characteristics and performance. While particular production and service units within the large corporation, like some smaller firms, can develop a profit interest in racial discrimination, from the long-run perspective of the whole corporation racism is not a major profit factor. [For a review of some of the empirical literature on wage discrimination, see Gordon (1972, pp. 114-115; also Gwartney, 1970a, 1970b).] The total gain from direct racial discrimination that can be realized in the production of goods and services is at most between 1 and 2 percent of the total national wage bill, or on the order of the firms' costs for workmen's compensation and unemployment insurance. This sum hardly appears to be of significant enough magnitude for corporate leadership to calculate that it is sufficient grounds for maintaining the racial system with all its potential for social disruption and the high costs for repression and welfare controls.[P] The discussion here has been cast in terms of the strategic interests of the ruling class. While the economic gains of racial control might be a secondary factor to the ruling class or the White nationality as a whole, to the Black community this form of discrimination alone amounts to a penalty of 15 to 25 percent in its wage income.

Racial dualism also permits certain groups of White workers, especially skilled ones, to limit entry to their fields, and, thereby, to preserve higher wage levels and employment security. In larger firms this discrimination gives preference to Whites in the entrance to progression ladders. On the other hand, management can use racial divisions to foster antagonisms among its employees and to weaken the bargaining position of its work force as a unit.

Simultaneously with the entry of a large number of Black workers into the metropolitan labor markets, another type of segmentation was taking place. The emergence of the large corporation as the decisive institution in the economy imposed a reorganization of work relations. In preindustrial society and to a large extent in the first phases of industrialization, the processes of work were organized along customary artisan and craft lines in which a great deal of the control over the flow of activity was vested in the workers. Gradations of remuneration and authority were largely based upon traditions of status and social estate. In the industrial era the introduction of power-driven machinery, followed by instrumentation and then automation, imposed new forms of regulation and rationalization in the work process. The large corporation had to carry this trend further, not only tying together a much broader and more complex set of productive operations but also linking them with sales effort, distribution, and planning. A systemization and normalization of productive relations went hand in hand with the gaining of oligopolistic positions in national and international markets.

Constantly changing technical and administrative imperatives, not tradition, became the dominant factor in the organization of work. The big corporation had to develop a hierarchy based upon these new principles to maintain order and direction over its thousands or tens of thousands of employees. As part of the ordering of the large firm's realm, the working conditions of the majority of its employees were stabilized. Rising wages, pension plans, seniority, extensive

---

[P]This point is illustrated by the consent decree entered into by nine major steel companies, the United Steelworkers Union and three federal agencies. The decree provides for $31 million in back pay mainly to minority workers, plantwide seniority which facilitates progression for workers who have been locked into "negro jobs," and quotas for upgrading Black, Chicano, and women workers. This decree obviously was accepted because it headed off agitation and organization by Black workers that was troublesome to both companies and unions. It specifically denies further redress, campaigns for which were being organized in a number of mills.

written work regulations (either in a personnel manual or a trade union contract) were all part of the development of what is now called the *primary sector* of the labor market. In contrast, many of the medium-sized and small employers make up a *secondary sector* of less desirable jobs that are still largely administered on the conditions of less complex and less hierarchical organization of work which are more characteristic of the earlier phases of industrialism. Michael Piore (1971, pp. 90-94) makes the distinction:

One sector of that market, . . . the primary market, offers jobs which possess several of the following traits: high wages, good working conditions, employment stability and job security, equity and due process in the administration of work rules, and chances for advancement. The other, or secondary sector, has jobs which, relative to those in the primary sector, are decidedly less attractive. They tend to involve low wages, poor working conditions, considerable variability in employment, harsh and often arbitrary discipline, and little opportunity to advance.

Obviously not all jobs in large firms are in the primary sector, nor are all jobs in small firms in the secondary sector. But the modern corporations at the core of the economic system basically define the primary labor market for today's working class. The peripheral firms upon which the secondary labor market is based are necessary for the overall operation of the economy and often function to the long-run advantage of the major corporations (Averitt, 1968). Each sector of the labor market develops its own labor force, and there is a relatively low rate of intersectoral transfer of workers.

A body of literature analyzing the primary-secondary segmentation of the labor market has been in the process of development over the last half-dozen years. This work arose out of investigations of poverty that sought to explain low income in terms of the operation of labor market institutions themselves rather than by attributing all the causes to outside factors, usually personality ones, that the employees or employers bring to work. These investigations show that the productive relations of advanced capitalism and a civil society with significant inequalities in income, status, and education provide sufficient conditions to explain most of the segmentation along the primary-secondary axis. Under these conditions the labor market will intensify the divergence between workers in the two sectors. As the work of Vietorisz and Harrison (1973a, 1973b) has shown, *this theory of labor market segmentation does not require any racial assumptions.*

It should be obvious that a much larger proportion of the jobs in the Black sector of the labor market, as compared to the White sector, is also located in the secondary sector. In some metropolitan areas with large Black and Latin populations, these two groups might now provide a majority of the workers in the secondary labor market. This overlap is not fortuitous. It is the conjuncture of two different structures determining the same reality in a mutually reinforcing manner. In concrete cases it is frequently impossible to disentangle the combined effect of these two modes of segmentation. (In other concrete cases there is a fusion of more than one mode of structuring social relations. For instance, in the organization of work there is often a combination of some precorporate forms of labor market segmentation with the primary-secondary type of segmentation.)

The combination of racial with the primary-secondary segmentation compounds the immobility, low wages, and poor working conditions of the large number of Black workers who participate in the secondary labor market. On the whole they are considerably worse off than the White poor and near poor who work in the secondary sector. In the primary sector, when jobs become identifiable as "Black jobs," they often become separated from the normal promotion ladder, are subject to speed-up, or begin to lag in wage increments—that is, they begin to take on many of the characteristics of jobs in the secondary sector.

A number of recent studies illustrate the way that the Black sector of the labor market overlaps with the secondary sector, yet maintains its distinctiveness. Using data for the year 1969, probably the year most favorable for the relative status of Black workers, Hall and Kasten (1973, p. 783) show that 58 percent of the 17- to 22-year-old male Black workers were in occupational categories largely in the secondary labor market, compared to only 36 percent of the Whites of this age. Among 23- to 27-year-old males, 48 percent of the Blacks and 15 percent of the Whites were in secondary jobs. Wage data demonstrate that within the secondary labor market there is a marked difference in the position of the Black worker. The younger group of Black workers earned 82 percent as much as the White peers, while the older group of Blacks earned just about the same as the younger ones, and only 71 percent of the wage of the comparable White age group. (Wages in Hall and Kasten's categories 1 and 2 combined by weighted averages.) At the same time there is evidence that younger Blacks with good educations have gained better access to the primary labor market, at least when the general employment situation was very tight.

Improvements in the relative earnings and occupational positions of Black workers have been caused by a combination of long-run shifts out of agriculture and domestic service, the pressures of Black political movements, and the extended economic boom of the 1960s. The most marked gains have been made by those able to move into some of the primary sector's better jobs, especially recent Black college graduates. Somewhat paradoxically, the other grouping of Blacks who have improved their relative positions are in those demographic categories where Whites have the highest rates of secondary labor market participation. Women and workers of both sexes under 35 are the two groups of Blacks who have made the most improvement vis-à-vis comparable White groups (Freeman, 1973a, pp. 83, 114-15, note also the printed discussion; Ashenfelter, 1970; Blinder, 1973). This development is consistent with the primary-secondary structure of the labor market. Adult White males have by far the highest proportion of participation in the primary sector. They realize the greatest perquisites of this position only after they have been in their jobs or professions long enough to gain the full advantage of seniority and progression ladders. Therefore, the White males' occupational status and earnings typically rise for a long portion of their careers. Blacks and women, being largely situated in the secondary sector, tend to have a much flatter earnings profile over the course of their employment history.

A new congruence has been forged between the racial nationalisms—an increasing proportion of which are operative in the social sphere—and the labor market segmentation that takes place under advanced capitalism. The primary-secondary division in the labor market has provided an economic base to racial discrimination at just the time that the older agrarian caste system was dying out and its successor of racial dualism in metropolitan centers was attenuating somewhat. Under the old plantation system there was a very close congruence between the economic base and the superstructure of the racial system. While with the new form of labor market segmentation there is not nearly as close a fit of economic controls and racial nationalism, the existence of even this lesser congruence between the structure of the decisive sectors of the economy and the racial formations works to reinforce the whole system of White national dominance in a novel way.

A couple of examples can illustrate the codetermination of racial nationalisms and the relations of production. Since we have already made clear the impact of shifts in the demand for Black labor under racial conditions, let us look at instances where the dynamics of race shape conditions in the labor market. In a number of large cities, most notably New York, nonprofessional hospital work is being unionized, and what were some of the worst jobs in the secondary sector of the labor market are beginning to assume many characteristics of jobs in the primary sector. The essential impetus in this process came from the energy and leverage developed by the civil rights and Black-power movements in the 1960s. The key trade union initiator in this instance was Local 1199, which had the willingness and ability to channel these forces into effective militant organizing and labor market bargaining.

In another case, expansion and contraction in the creation of new primary market jobs for Blacks operated through the mediation of the state according to the resultant pressures of the nationwide racial conflicts. In response to the protest movements and urban uprisings during the 1960s, the Kennedy and Johnson administrations greatly expanded federal programs in health, welfare, and education. The number of Black professionals, technicians, and semiprofessionals in these fields increased tremendously as a result of these new jobs and the breaking down of hiring barriers. For example, between 1960 and 1969 Blacks moved from comprising 4 percent of all health professionals and technicians to 8 percent. Among teachers Blacks rose from 7 to 10 percent of the total. The Nixon administration reversed field and followed a strategy of openly appealing to the burgeoning White nationalist backlash. The policy of "benign neglect" toward Blacks was involved in the freezing or the rolling back of programs that had provided the great increase in federally aided Black professional employment. By 1972 the percentage of Blacks among all professionals had ceased growing, and among teachers it had even declined (U.S. Department of Commerce, 1970, p. 43; 1973, p. 51).

The relatively good conditions of the primary sector of the labor force did not come about just through the corporate leadership's rational calculation of its advantage. Trade union organizing within industry and political contestation for welfare and other benefits helped force this organization of work into being. The welfare state and primary-secondary segmentation in the labor market developed as mutual correlates in the process of the civic inclusion of the working class within advanced capitalism. In effect, there are two levels or degrees of working-class inclusion. The workers in the primary sector are clearly more privileged and are recognized as a more significant vested interest. As a group, they are not limited to the direct benefits associated with their current job. They can also expect more vigorous efforts by the state on their behalf in case they are displaced from their employment, e.g., take the major efforts to place the large number of unemployed aerospace engineers at the end of the 1960s. The secondary-sector workers, although they earn considerably more than the mere subsistence wages of the nineteenth-century proletariat or workers in the Third World, are second class, receiving considerably lower economic rewards and fewer political concessions than workers in the primary sector. Politically and socially, the workers of the primary sector have been able to maintain a limited subhegemony over the whole working class, largely through their dominance in the trade union movement.[q] This subhegemony simultaneously involves a certain subordination of the secondary workers and provides them some support in improving their conditions through minimum wage and welfare legislation.

From the perspective of the employers and the state, the secondary sector operates as a regulator of the level of concessions that are made to the primary-sector workers. The substitutability of workers from the secondary sector functions both as an economic alternative and as a negotiating weapon in the making of wage bargains with primary-sector workers. Within any given set of production possibilities, there is a limit to the quantity of benefits—higher wages, better working conditions, lower unemployment—that can be conceded to workers and still leave the sufficiently large and continually growing accumulation of capital necessary to keep the possessing class in control over the disposition of the economic surplus (Glyn and Sutcliffe, 1972). Along with

[q]Trade union membership is more important to Black workers for their inclusion in the primary sector than it is to White workers. Among Black blue-collar workers, trade union members earn 42 percent more than nonunion members. The relative advantage for White unionists is only 19 percent. However, the Black union members' year-round earnings are the same as the White nonunion workers (U.S. Department of Commerce, 1973, p. 55).

other methods, such as direct political and economic contestation, the existence of the secondary sector serves as a mechanism for maintaining a ceiling on the working class's share of the national income. This mechanism operates both by holding down the wage cost for the large pool of secondary workers and by the competitive threat that this group presents to the more privileged portion of the working class.

In terms of functionally maintaining the ruling class's control over an economic surplus that is a stable or increasing proportion of the national income, the combination of the Black and secondary sectors of the labor market provides a stronger regulation of the rationing of working-class income and benefits. (Other forms of discrimination, such as sexism, serve a similar function, for a disproportionate number of women are located in the secondary sector of the labor market.) While the differences between the primary and secondary subclasses are reinforced by some noneconomic social forms, the racial division is bolstered by the whole range of nationality forms. The subordination of the Black workers in the secondary sector provides a much clearer demarcation of status than that which is based on economic relations alone. Accordingly, the barriers to enter the primary sector are much greater for these Black workers. Further, in metropolitan areas the whole secondary sector begins to be cast according to the norms for Black workers, and the Whites who compete in this area of the labor market are subject to the regulation that comes from such a derivative ascription of racial designation.

The subordinated sectors of the labor market provide a modern version of Marx's industrial reserve army of surplus population, unemployed and half employed, that allows the expansion of the labor force in boom times without a proportionate increase in wage rates. This mechanism freed the process of capital accumulation, and the necessary work force accompanying it, from the limits of the natural growth of population (Marx, n.d., Volume 5, pp. 690-701). Historically, the major source of the industrial reserve army was displaced small farmers and agricultural workers. In the United States a large share of this reserve army came by immigration from Europe. Under advanced capitalism, the secondary and Black sectors of the labor force provide an analogous function. Only now this new reserve is largely incorporated into the industrial system and the urban social world, constituting what Arthur Okun (1973, pp. 208, 237-242) has called "a reserve army of the underemployed." Okun has very interestingly shown how the segmentation of the labor market insulates the wage structure from serious disorganization in periods of cyclical upturn with tight labor markets.

The congruence between nationalism and primary-secondary labor market segmentation is not unique to advanced capitalism in the United States but is also to be found in Western Europe. There the highly developed capitalist countries, with the exception of Italy, have essentially exhausted their own agrarian labor reserves. They are now importing a large part of their secondary labor force across national lines—Britain from the old empire, France from North Africa and the Iberian peninsula, Germany from Southeast Europe and Turkey. The similarities with the American racial scene has given *Fortune* magazine (Ball, 1973) the occasion to gloat:

Until recently, Europeans could (and did) congratulate themselves on not having all the social problems familiar to Americans, associated with a large, identifiably different, and unassimilated minority at the bottom of the economic ladder. But the time for self-congratulation is over. Europe—and the U.S.-based multinational corporations doing business there—must now deal with the tensions and dislocations created by a massive importation of unskilled foreign labor.

At least, 7.5 million "guest workers" are employed in Europe. They make up 11 percent of the work force in Germany and 27 percent in Switzerland.

Importation of immigrant workers is not new in the history of European industrialism. The Irish have been coming to England for well over a century, and large numbers of Polish miners worked in the Ruhr 70 years ago. Previously, the foreign workers were only temporary in a boom period or were not sharply differentiated from the indigenous unskilled labor force and assimilated into the general population over a generation or two (Bodeman, 1974).[r] With modern management methods and large-scale production the segmentation of the European labor markets into primary and secondary jobs has proceeded apace. Welfare nationalism in extending schooling has raised the age for entering the labor force and by increasing pensions has lowered the age for leaving the work force. The resulting employment gap is being filled by immigrant workers moving into both the secondary sector and physically harder jobs in the primary sector. (In the case of the younger immigrant worker without family the host state saves most of the social costs of welfare benefits.) An amazing similarity exists between the employment pattern of the "guest workers" and Black Americans in regard to industries, job classifications, and concentration in particular urban centers. Although both groups are subject to a great deal of fluctuation in employment, they occupy permanent niches in the economy.

W.R. Boehning (1972, pp. 54-71) has developed a model to explain this European development on the basis of assumptions about liberal "post-industrial society." Although his theoretical premises are quite different from those in this chapter, his conclusions regarding the key role of labor market dualisms corroborate our analogy between the European and American situations:

A post-industrial society facing the first instances of endemic labour shortage has two options open to it. Firstly, it could pursue a revolutionary manpower policy by adapting its social job structure to post-industrial requirements, i.e. to pay a

---

[r]The distinction between a partially literate, localistically oriented German peasant and a Polish peasant of similar characteristics 75 years ago is much less than that between a well-schooled, nationally oriented German worker and a peasant from Turkish Anatolia today.

truly economic wage for undesirable jobs, taking into account the fact that market forces are largely inapplicable on the labour "market" and that wage structures are determined socio-politically. Secondly, it could fill these jobs with foreign workers admitted not for settlement but for the specific purpose of filling the supposedly temporary shortages on the labour market (the *Konjunctionpuffer* approach). The alternative to the first option, namely, to permit large-scale unemployment and a considerable drop if not reversal in the real growth of the economy in order to stop the flight from the undesirable jobs, is not feasible politically because it would catapault the party in power out of government (this alternative would not fit with the second assumption). The alternative to the *Konjunctionpuffer* option would be to have a settlement immigration related to economic needs. No government in a country which is not traditionally a country of immigration and which deliberately set out to invite aliens to settle inside its borders on purely economic grounds, would survive the onset of this immigration. Permanent settlement migration is usually not even considered because the labour shortage problem is seen as essentially short term.

In Europe as in the United States, the division in the work force on national lines becomes an important sociopolitical reinforcer of the secondary labor market. The majority of the European "guest" workers are imported on a temporary basis without their families. They are denied political rights and social acceptance; they are aliens not included within the host nation. In economic downturns the European capitalists have a luxury not enjoyed by their American counterparts: they can export their labor surplus back to their home countries. However, as foreign workers tend to stay for longer periods or even settle permanently, domestic racism and xenophobia increase (Nacht, 1969). In Great Britain the immigrant labor force includes many colored peoples from the empire who got in before the current legislative restrictions. Since the old legislation granted them citizenship, they are not walled off by juridical definitions of nationalism. Therefore, racism per se has become especially pronounced in Great Britain. As the "guest workers" are marked off within the labor force, they and their families are marked off in the general population by discrimination on the basis of nationality, race, language, and religion—especially for Moslems who are outside the tradition of European Christianity. The European ruling classes have responded with strategies similar to those of their American counterparts. They simultaneously guarantee the augmentation to the labor force of workers with a second-class status and condone the sharp divisions that this generates in the working class (Castles and Kosack, 1972).

Implications

One of the great strengths of the current work on labor market segmentation is that the theory is institutionally inclusive. The factors generating the segmentation can be explained in terms of economic dynamics. In contrast, the traditional neoclassical economists have to perform on a theoretical merry-go-round. Either the factors causing racial discrimination are considered as external to the rational economic process, or they are conceptually imported as psychological utilities, as in the case of Becker's (1957) very influential, but tautological, "taste for discrimination." [For a critique of Becker's theory see Thurow (1969); for empirical tests of his hypothesis with negative results see Franklin and Tanzer (1970) and Flanagan (1973).]

However, a good thing can be carried too far. Those working on the theory of labor market segmentation would be well warned to pay great attention as to where they draw the limits to the endogenous features of their theories. Because there is a certain degree of congruence between the divisions of the primary and secondary labor markets and those of the racial structure, it cannot be assumed that the one can be collapsed into the other. More specifically, the most significant feature of racial domination in this epoch, i.e., its nationality form, cannot be specified as endogenous factors within a labor market model. There is a danger here of falling into a mechanistic type of economic determinism that gives an overwhelming primacy to a causal schema in which the labor market sets the essential conditions for the maintenance of the whole racial system. While in certain eras, e.g., the plantation slavery era, such a causal model had greater validity, it does not necessarily hold for all periods.[s]

What is called for here, as in social theory in general, is a dialectical mode of thinking. Its conceptualizations have to maintain simultaneously the distinctiveness of specific systems and the concreteness of their interaction and mutual determination within the whole that is history. Racial nationalisms and advanced capitalism's mode of production do not occur as pure forms. Along with other complex political, social, and cultural systems, they operate in a combined way, in a conjunctural unity, to shape the course of history and everyday life. This history does not unfold according to some laws of mechanics. Within the potentialities inherent in existent circumstances and relations, according to Gordon Childe's felicitous phrase, "man makes himself." The achievement of rational goals through this process requires a human practice that is guided by a rational understanding of its own history and its own actions.

The ultimate test of the significance of the theories put forth here is their ability or inability to help shape effective strategies of action. But a careful consideration of this issue would require another essay, and even this would have limited meaning apart from the practical work and struggle to change the conditions of racial oppression. Still this theoretical analysis does immediately imply certain themes regarding strategy and tactics. By specifying the concrete conditions of the Black nationality within the United States, the analysis should

[s]Also almost all the writings on labor market segmentation have not given adequate theoretical or empirical attention to the role of the state. No consideration of any major feature of advanced capitalism is adequate unless it takes into account the workings of the state within the economy.

minimize the reliance on analogies—which have been valuable but often over-extended—with the colonial and neocolonial nations in the Third World. The context of overlapping nationalisms in the United States indicates that meaningful tactics might well be specialized to a particular nationalistic context, but the strategies that guide these tactics ought to take into account the determining factors within all three relevant national frameworks—Black and White nationalities and the inclusive nation-state. The theory also points to the decisiveness of the Black working class and its potential for leadership in the Black liberation movement. Concurrently the Black proletariat is also part of the inclusive American working class. Because of its extra exploitation, its lesser degree of co-optation, and the strength and coherence it gains from being part of the Black nationality, the Black proletariat is in the position to be politically the most aggressive force in the whole working class.

At the same time, this analysis focuses on problems within the Black community: The differences between the primary and the secondary sectors of the labor force within it especially have to be considered in the formulation of programs and strategies. In addition, the theory should illuminate for Black strategists the internal dynamics of White society and the American nation. Hopefully, this will be of help in assessing the conditions affecting alliances, conflicts, and negotiations with various White groups.

Since Black nationalist consciousness has already been made quite explicit by recent historical events, this theorizing should have greater significance for White groups that recognize the necessity for the overthrow of the system of racial oppression. They are forced to deal with the reality of Black nationalism as more than just a cultural expression. Regarding their own strategies, they have to face up to White nationalism as a concrete and rather inclusive historical force that is well grounded in the material conditions of life. The dynamics of the White nationality impose conditions of operation that cannot be willed away through moral condemnation. Until antiracist White forces learn how to master some of the contradictions within the White nationality so as to build their own strength, they will not present themselves as a very attractive group for Blacks to ally with. Division of the White labor force between the primary and secondary sectors requires very careful consideration for the shaping of strategy and tactics. White workers in the secondary sector potentially have stronger bonds with Black workers and might, as is occurring in parts of the South today, join with some of their militants. Perhaps the primary political questions within the White working class are how to minimize the division between primary and secondary workers and how the secondary workers can gain a stronger determination over the strategy of the working class as a whole.

Bibliography

Adam, Herbert, *Modernizing Racial Domination* (Berkeley: University of California Press, 1971).

Allswang, John M., *A House for All Peoples: Ethnic Politics in Chicago, 1890-1936* (Lexington: University of Kentucky Press, 1971).

Althusser, Louis, *For Marx* (New York: Pantheon, 1969).

Ashenfelter, Orley, "Changes in Labor Market Discrimination over Time," *Journal of Human Resources*, Fall, 1970.

Averitt, Robert T., *The Dual Economy: The Dynamics of American Industrial Structure* (New York: W.W. Norton, 1968).

Ball, Robert, "How Europe Created Its 'Minority Problem,'" *Fortune*, December, 1973.

Baron, Harold M., "The Demand for Black Labor: Historical Notes on the Political Economy of Racism," *Radical America*, March-April, 1971.

———, "The Web of Urban Racism," in Louis L. Knowles and Kenneth Prewitt, eds., *Institutional Racism in America* (Englewood Cliffs: Prentice-Hall, 1969).

———and Bennett Hymer, "The Negro Worker in the Chicago Labor Market," in Julius Jacobson, ed., *The Negro and the American Labor Movement* (New York: Doubleday, 1968).

Bastide, Roger, "The Development of Race Relations in Brazil," in Guy Hunter, ed., *Industrialization and Race Relations* (London: Oxford University Press, 1965).

———, "Race Relations in Brazil," *International Social Science Bulletin*, 1957.

Becker, Gary, *The Economics of Discrimination* (Chicago: University of Chicago Press, 1957).

Bendix, Reinhard, *Nation-Building and Citizenship* (Garden City: Doubleday & Co., (Anchor), 1969).

Berdahl, Robert M. "New Thoughts on German Nationalism," *American Historical Review*, February, 1972.

Blauner, Robert, *Racial Oppression in America* (New York: Harper & Row, 1972).

Blinder, Alan S., "Wage Discrimination: Reduced Form and Structural Estimates," *Journal of Human Resources*, Fall, 1973.

Blumer, Herbert, "Industrialization and Race Relations," in Guy Hunter, ed., *Industrialization and Race Relations* (London: Oxford University Press, 1965).

Bodeman, Michael, "Comments on Oppenheimer's 'The Subproletariat,'" *The Insurgent Sociologist*, Spring, 1974.

Boehning, W.R., *The Migration of Workers in the United Kingdom and the European Community* (London: Oxford University Press, 1972).

Borochov, Ber, *Nationalism and the Class Struggle: A Marxian Approach to the Jewish Question* (New York: Poale-Zion, 1937).

Carpenter, Niles, *Nationality, Color and Economic Opportunity in the City of Buffalo* (New York: The Inquiry, 1927).

Castles, Stephen, and Kosack, Godula, "The Function of Labor Immigration in Western European Capitalism," *New Left Review*, May-June, 1972.

Coleman, Richard P., and Neugarten, Bernice, *Social Status in the Cities* (San Francisco: Jossey-Bass, 1971).

Davis, Horace, *Nationalism and Socialism* (New York: Monthly Review Press, 1967).

Domhoff, G. William, *The Higher Circles: The Governing Class in America* (New York: Vintage, 1970).

––––––, "State and Ruling Class in Corporate America," *The Insurgent Sociologist*, Spring, 1974.

Deutsch, Karl W., *Nationalism and Social Communication*, 2d ed. (Cambridge: M.I.T. Press, 1966).

Drake, St. Clair, *The Redemption of Africa and Black Religion* (Chicago: Third World Press, 1970).

Emmanuel, Arghiri, "The Delusions of Internationalism," *Monthly Review*, June, 1970.

––––––, *Unequal Exchange: A Study of the Imperialism of Trade* (New York: Monthly Review Press, 1972).

Feldman, Herman, *Racial Factors in American Industry* (New York: Harper & Brothers, 1931).

Fernandez, Florestan, *The Negro in Brazilian Society* (New York: Columbia University Press, 1969).

Flanagan, Robert J., "Racial Wage Discrimination and Employment Segregation," *Journal of Human Resources*, Fall, 1973.

Franklin, Raymond and Tanzer, Michael, "Traditional Microeconomic Analysis of Racial Discrimination: A Critical View and Alternative Approach," in David Mermelstein, ed., *Economics: Mainstream Readings and Radical Critiques* (New York: Random House, 1970).

Fredrickson, George M., *The Black Image in the White Mind* (New York: Harper & Row, 1971).

––––––, "Why Blacks Were Left Out," *New York Review of Books* February 7, 1974.

Freeman, Richard B., "Changes in the Labor Market for Black Americans, 1948-72," *Brookings Papers on Economic Activity* 1973a.

––––––, "Decline of Labor Market Discrimination and Economic Analysis," *American Economic Review* May, 1973b.

Gellner, Ernest, *Thought and Change* (Chicago: University of Chicago Press, 1964).

Glyn, Andrew and Sutcliffe, Bob, *Capitalism in Crisis* (New York: Pantheon, 1972).

Gordon, David M., *Theories of Poverty and Unemployment* (Lexington, Mass.: Heath, 1972).

Gutman, Herbert G., "Work, Culture, and Society in Industrializing America, 1815-1919," *American Historical Review* June, 1973.

Gwartney, John, "Changes in Nonwhite/White Income Ratio–1939-67," *American Economic Review* December, 1970a.

————, "Discrimination and Income Differentials," *American Economic Review* June, 1970b.

Hall, Robert E. and Kasten, Richard A., "The Relative Occupational Success of Blacks and Whites," *Brookings Papers on Economic Activity* 1973.

Harris, Marvin, *Patterns of Race in the Americas* (New York: Walker, 1964).

Holsbaum, Eric, "Some Reflection on Nationalism," in P.J. Nossiter et al., eds., *Imagination and Precision in the Social Sciences* (London: Faber and Tabert, 1971).

Hroch, Miroslav, *Die Vorkaempfer der nationalen Bewegung bei den Kleinen Voelkern Europas* (Prague: Universita Karlova, 1968).

Jordan, Kenneth, "Industrial Pressure on Racism," *The Nation* September 17, 1973.

Kiernan, V.G., "State and Nation in Western Europe," *Past and Present* July, 1965.

Lenin, V.I., *A Caricature of Marxism and Imperialist Economism*, 1924, in *Collected Works*, 75 vols. (Moscow: Foreign Languages Publishing House, 1964), Vol. 23.

————, *Imperialism, The Highest Stage of Capitalism*, 1917.

————, *Imperialism and the Split in Socialism*, 1916, in *Selected Works*, 12 vols. (New York: International Publishers, 1943), Vol. 11.

Mandel, Ernest, "Workers under Neo-Capitalism," in David Mermelstein, ed., *Economics: Mainstream Readings and Radical Critiques* (New York: Random House, 1970).

Marx, Karl, *Capital* (New York: Modern Library, n.d.), Vol. 1.

————, and Frederick Engels, *Selected Works*, 2 vols. (Moscow: Foreign Languages Publishing House, 1951).

Mayer, Kurt B., "The Changing Shape of the American Class Structure," *Social Research* Winter, 1963.

Meier, August, *Negro Thought in America, 1880-1915: Racial Ideologies in the Age of Booker T. Washington* (Ann Arbor: University of Michigan Press, 1963).

Miliband, Ralph, *The State in Capitalist Society* (New York: Basic Books, 1969).

Montgomery, David, *Beyond Equality: Labor and the Radical Republicans, 1862-1872* (New York: Vintage, 1967).

Myrdal, Gunnar, *Beyond the Welfare State* (New York: Bantam, 1967).

Nacht, Marc, "Racisme et immigration," in Patrice de Camarmond and Claude Duchet, eds., *Racisme et Société* (Paris: Maspero, 1969).

O'Brien, Conor Cruise, *States of Ireland* (London: Hutchinson, 1972).

O'Connor, James, *The Fiscal Crisis of the State* (New York: St. Martin's Press, 1973).

Okun, Arthur M., "Upward Mobility in a High-pressure Economy," *Brookings Papers on Economic Activity* 1973.

Phillips, Kevin P., *The Emerging Republican Majority* (New York: Arlington House, 1969).

Piore, Michael, "The Dual Labor Market: Theory and Implications," in David M. Gordon, ed., *Problems in Political Economy: An Urban Perspective* (Lexington, Mass.: Heath, 1971).

Poulantzas, Nices, *Political Power and Social Classes* (London: Weidenfeld, 1973).

Scammon, Richard M. and Wattenberg, Ben J., *The Real Majority* (New York: Coward-McCann, 1970).

Semmel, Bernard, *Imperialism and Social Thought* (Garden City: Doubleday and Co., 1968).

Shafer, Boyd C., *Faces of Nationalism* (New York: Harcourt Brace Jovanovich, 1972).

Smith, Anthony D., *Theories of Nationalism* (New York: Harper & Row, 1971).

Taylor, David P. "Discrimination and Occupational Wage Differences in the Market for Unskilled Labor," *Industrial and Labor Relations Review* April, 1968.

Thompson, E.P., "The Peculiarities of the English," in Ralph Miliband and John Saville, eds., *The Socialist Register, 1965* (New York: Monthly Review Press, 1965).

Thurow, Lester C., *Poverty and Discrimination* (Washington: The Brookings Institution, 1969).

U.S. Department of Commerce, Bureau of the Census, *The Social and Economic Status of Negroes in the United States.* Current Population Reports, Series P-23, No. 29, n.d.

_____ , *The Social and Economic Status of the Black Population in the United States.* Current Population Reports, Series P-23, No. 46, 1973.

Vietorisz, Thomas and Harrison, Bennett, "Labor Market Segmentation: Institutionalization of Divergence," unpublished paper delivered at Conference on Labor Market Segmentation, Harvard University, March 16-17, 1973a.

_____ and _____ , "Labor Market Segmentation: Positive Feedback and Divergent Development," *American Economic Review* May, 1973b.

Wallerstein, Immanuel, "Black Africa: Race and Status Group," in Ernest Q. Campbell, ed., *Racial Tensions and National Identity* (Nashville: Vanderbilt University Press, 1972).

Williams, Raymond, "Base and Superstructure," *New Left Review* November-December, 1973.

Woodman, Harold D., "Economic History and Economic Theory," *Journal of Interdisciplinary History* Autumn, 1972.

8

Stratifying by Sex: Understanding the History of Working Women

Alice Kessler-Harris

The Framework of Interdependence

The sexual division of labor is one of the most pervasive and effective bases on which the labor market is segmented. Its success rests on the use of ideological arguments to justify sex roles and to resist efforts to change them. This chapter will attempt to make explicit the assumptions that surround sexual roles in the labor market. It will explore the various ways in which sexual stratification has occurred over time in the United States, and demonstrate how effectively ideas have simultaneously sustained and obscured discrimination against working women. Because ideological constraints and limits on aspiration regulate the participation of all workers and influence the entire operation of the labor market, exploring the boundaries of women's work force participation should tell us something about the subtle nature of segmentation mechanisms.

√The relationship between changing ideas about women and divisions in the work force involves several important elements. First, the segmentation process, as it affects women, reflects both the economic interdependence of individuals within the family and the ideological and economic relationship of the family to the surrounding culture. Most recent literature acknowledges that inducements for women to work are mitigated by their primary relationships to the family, but stops short of asking about the family's changing relationship to the political economy.[1] In a brilliant essay, Eli Zaretsky addressed himself to this fundamental problem. He explored the consequences of changing economic needs for individuals within families, concluding that the family could not be understood except as part of the surrounding economic structure.[2] Where, as in capitalist society, families have served as stabilizing agencies, transmitting the particular values necessary to sustain the economic system, women have played special roles. Their childrearing and socializing functions as well as their household maintenance were critical. As long as most work took place within the home, few women felt any tension between their work and family roles. The growth of industry in the eighteenth and nineteenth centuries encouraged many employers to seek ways to use potentially profitable female labor power in their factories. To do this without undermining women's primary allegiance to the family has

A shorter version of this chapter will appear in *Liberating Women's History*, edited by Berenice Carroll, to be published by the University of Illinois Press (Fall 1975).

remained a continuing problem of employing women in the labor force. The struggle to contain the tension between the need for certain kinds of labor power on the one hand, and perceived women's roles in a changing family on the other is a recurring theme of this chapter. It provides a dynamic explanation for the variety of ways women have been integrated into the labor force and their varying consequences for women of different classes and ethnic groups.

∨ A second element in women's paid labor force participation has been the way in which socialization and culture influence perceptions of roles so that they appear to be inevitable and unchangeable. Since even in the best of times women were expected to function in quasi-subservient ways, to restrict their aspirations, and to possess certain nurturing qualities, these became the boundaries of their job opportunities. Only exceptional women could consciously resist the psychological and cultural attributes into which they were overwhelmingly socialized. And though it happened, not infrequently, that poor working women demanded better pay and working conditions, only rarely did they question the family structure that was the instrument of their oppression.[3] Widespread convictions that women's proper work was within the family explain their particularly poor position in the labor force throughout the nineteenth and twentieth centuries. Until the present, only financial necessity has driven most women into the paid labor force, but as with men, class differences have to some extent determined job opportunities, and values derived from traditional immigrant families often influenced perceptions of job possibilities.

A third theme in the problem of sexual stratification is rooted in the changing economic needs of employers. These operated in a dialectical relationship that comprehended the function of ideology in sustaining societal goals as well as changes in family-centered social values on the one hand, and structural economic change on the other. The use of technology to increase labor productivity and the changing organization of work have been critical variables in inducing women of different strata to enter or leave the labor force. The changing demands of the labor market explain much of the slow accommodation of educational institutions and family patterns to the demands of women.

The pattern of women's historical participation in the work force is rooted in all these factors. It is, in part, a function of the ideology of the family, and therefore of the roles that women, like men, are convinced they must play. That ideology emerges both from the objective needs of families and from a complex of societal goals that derive from a changing political economy. Women are used in the work force in ways that relate the ideological justifications of a whole society to its immediate labor force needs. These together provide part of the complex reality that translates back into class divisions among working and nonworking women, and into specific policies that affect women workers. What follows is an attempt to sketch out these changing relationships in the United States, to break through the mystification process, and to explore the social realities of the millions of women who have always worked.

Regulating Respectability

The family had been a keystone of social order in puritan New England. The Massachusetts Bay Colony self-consciously encouraged families to be "little cells of righteousness where the mother and father disciplined not only their children, but also their servants and any boarders they might take in."[4] Unmarried men and women were required to place themselves in the home of a family in order to be guided by them. Family members were encouraged to supervise one another in order to guard the morals of the community as a whole. John Demos sums up his study of the Plymouth colony by noting that the family functioned as a business, a school, a training institution, a church, and often as a welfare institution. "Family and community," he concludes, ". . . formed part of the same moral equation. The one supported the other and they became in a sense indistinguishable."[5] The middle and southern colonies did not differ markedly.[6]

While the functions of the family changed toward the end of the eighteenth century, certain assumptions remained. A preindustrial society assumed that, except among the privileged few, all family members would work as a matter of course. So widely accepted was this practice that colonial widows often took over businesses left by their deceased husbands, and in at least one instance an innkeeper, deprived of the services of a wife, recently buried, was denied permission to operate his tavern.[7] Widows and orphans with no other means of support were set to work by the community. In her pioneering work on women in industry, Edith Abbott notes that "court orders, laws and public subscriptions were resorted to in order that poor women might be saved from the sin of idleness and taught to be self-supporting."[8] But work for women was so closely identified with home and family that when Alexander Hamilton in his famous report on manufactures suggested putting women and children to work in incipient manufacturing enterprises, his idea was scorned. The curse of idleness was insufficiently threatening to justify removing women from their homes.

The heavy burden of household production and the interdependency of family life and economic survival encouraged little revolt against these roles. Family and work were bound together in an integrated and stable whole. But as the agrarian society of the eighteenth century moved into the early industrialization of the nineteenth century, new economic conditions produced a need to reaffirm and articulate "proper" places for women. At first, mills took over the spinning, and the fiber was handed out to women to weave in their homes. When weaving machinery became more complex, both processes were moved to the factory. It seemed natural that women should follow. The new mill owners sought their labor supply among widows and children who needed to work, as well as by hiring whole families. Removing women from their homes did not prove appealing to a largely agrarian population with a coherent conception of women's roles, and independent farmers were reluctant to adapt to the discipline of the factory. Mill owners complained constantly of the difficulties of finding an adequate labor supply.[9]

The unmarried daughters of New England farmers seemed to be the only alternative. Could one reconcile the moral imperative of the home with the use of these young women in factories? It was the genius of Francis Cabot Lowell to conceive of a way of doing so. He appealed to the young single daughters of farm families to fulfill their family responsibilities by engaging in hard work away from home. For the mill which finally opened in Lowell, Massachusetts, in 1821, he proposed carefully supervised boardinghouses for women who would spend a few years before marriage at the mills, and offered salaries which were to be saved for their trousseaux, to help pay off mortgages, or to send a brother through college. At the same time, parents were assured that their daughters would experience the hard work and discipline that would make them into better wives and mothers. The mills at Lowell and elsewhere in New England attracted a reliable labor force that was easily disciplined in industrial routines and cheaper than male labor. In return, they offered a training ground in morality.

The mill owners' need coincided with their conviction that they were providing a service for the nation. Mill owners repeatedly stated "that one of their prime purposes in launching the textile industry was to give employment to respectable women to save them from poverty and idleness."[10] They argued that they were preserving republican virtues of hard work and raising the moral and intellectual tone of the country.[11] The mill women themselves, at least in the early years, determined to preserve their own respectability in the eyes of the public. In a manner reminiscent of the early Puritans, they "supervised" one another, ostracizing those whose morals were in question.[12]

But the need to maintain high wages and good working conditions proved too much for employers to bear. Within a few years Lowell women complained of excessively long hours, wage cuts, and extra work. Occasional strikes and rumblings of discontent became audible from Pawtucket, Rhode Island, to Paterson, New Jersey, and Philadelphia, Pennsylvania. In 1828, factory women in Dover, New Hampshire, "turned out" for the first time, marching through the streets to the ridicule of onlookers.[13] Repeated complaints in the 1830s received no response. When Lowell workers organized themselves into the Female Labor Reform Association in 1845, the mill owners abandoned their moral stance. Taking advantage of increasing Irish immigration, they rapidly eliminated the old work force. In 1845, only 7 percent of the employees in the eight Lowell mills were Irish. By 1852, more than half of the work force was foreign-born. The pattern was repeated in Holyoke, Massachusetts, in New Hampshire and in Connecticut. The protected New England mill woman swiftly disppeared.

The pages of the *Lowell Offering*, a factory-supported paper, reveal how completely an alternative cheap labor supply took precedence over the employers' oft-pronounced morality. Some operators continued to believe as late as 1849 that corporation owners would raise wages so as "to attract once more the sort of girl who had made the industry what it was."[14] Skeptics felt that the mills had lost the respect of the community because standards of morality and the old spirit of mutual surveillance had declined. Caroline Ware, historian of the textile industry, assesses the position of the employers: "Necessity had forced them to gain and hold the respect of the community in order to attract the requisite workers and they were only too eager to be relieved of that necessity by the advent of a class of labor which had no standing in the community and no prejudice against mill-work."[15] Native-born females simply stopped applying for jobs. One Massachusetts paper remarked in 1852 of the Chicopee mills that "foreign girls have been employed in such numbers that what American girls are employed there experience considerable difficulty in finding society among their workmates congenial to their tastes and feelings."[16]

Although only about 10 percent of all women worked in the paid labor force, the mills depended on their labor. In the mid-forties about one-half of the factory population was female. In textiles, shoes, and hats their numbers were even higher. From 80 to 90 percent of the operatives in some mills throughout New England were women.[17] As the numbers of working women rose, the proportions who came from nonimmigrant families declined. In part this was the result of the development and institutionalization of a new regulating device: the domestic code which established proper roles for women and toward which poor and immigrant women could only aspire.

The source of this major ideological transition remains imperfectly understood, but its elements are fairly clear. The growth of industry, a developing laissez-faire ideology, and a concurrent redefinition of the home and family required more constricted women's roles and resulted in sharper divisions in the self-concept of middle- and working-class women. Industrialization and urbanization slowly increased the number of men who worked in impersonal factories beyond the immediate surroundings of home and community. Because men were removed from contact with children during the lengthy and exhausting day, women assumed responsibility for training children to fill future labor force needs. Simultaneously, the old puritan ethic which stressed morality, hard work, and community gave way to laissez-faire economic policies that emphasized individualism, success, and competition. Men who worked hard and strove for success required wives who were emotionally supportive and who could competently supervise the household.

Ideas about what women should do conformed to these new societal requirements. Their clearest expression occurred first among the prosperous and growing urban middle class. In what historian Bernard Wishy calls a reappraisal of family life that took place after 1830, motherhood rose to new heights, and children became the focus of womanly activity. Mothers were asked to give up wealth, frivolity, and fashion in order to prepare themselves for a great calling. "The mother was the obvious source of everything that would save or damn the child; the historical and spiritual destiny of America lay in her hands."[18]

Simultaneously, the woman became a lady. Meek and passive, modest and silent, women were expected to submerge their wills into those of their husbands and fathers. Piety, purity, and submissiveness became the ideal. The art of home-making now reached professional proportions, with some educators arguing that women must be trained to that end. There could be no higher calling.[19]

The public schools that multiplied in the 1830s and 1840s admitted girls readily. Discipline, respect for authority, adherence to routine, and the rudiments of reading, writing, and arithmetic were as essential to their future lives at home as to the lives of men.[20] Most children left school before they had completed the fourth grade. But girls often stayed on. They were not, after all, expected to go out into the world to make their living, and schooling beyond the initial socialization process was not seen as vocational preparation. With occasional exceptions, colleges, even the lyceums that offered community lectures, remained adamantly closed to females until the 1860s when the pressure of feminism opened them.

In its most dramatic form, the developing ideology described the female as functioning only within her crucial sphere. Aileen Kraditor notes, "it was not that social order required the subordination of women, rather . . . it required a family structure that involved the subordination of women."[21] One popular nineteenth-century schoolbook argued, "When a woman quits her own department . . . she departs from that sphere which is assigned to her in the order of society, because she neglects her duty and leaves her own department vacant. . . ."[22] Though many strong voices objected to the constraints, they received little support from the majority of middle-class women who were persuaded that they were functioning usefully. In return for an ideology that glorified their roles and perhaps offered some power within the family, women were denied a broad range of social and economic options. By the mid-1850s, the only sanctioned occupations for women were teaching and, when genteel poverty struck the homes of the respectable, dressmaking.

As ideas about "proper roles" for women became institutionalized in the first part of the nineteenth century, they had severe consequences for the vast numbers who could not meet their rigid prescription. By defining the role at home as the measure of respectability, the domestic code sharpened class differences. In this period of early industrialization, more women than ever before could aspire to display the perquisites of the "lady"—elegant dress, servants, and the absence of an economic contribution to household maintenance. These requirements excluded from respectability most women who had to work in the paid labor force and created for them a set of perhaps unattainable aspirations centered on the family. Factory work and domestic service slid rapidly down the scale of status. Immigrants, Black women, and the destitute who toiled at necessary jobs found no focus for their aspirations at work and no protection from exploitation in an ideology that excluded them from respectability. Yet their presence in the labor force had a number of tangible benefits for employers.

First, the existence of the middle-class feminine ideal of domesticity provided employers with a docile group of women who, convinced that marriage and work were incompatible and that their real calling lay in marriage and child-rearing, had only a transient interest in their jobs. The desire for respectability provided working women with a set of aspirations (equivalent to upward mobility for men) which mitigated class consciousness and complaints about present exploitation. A Knights of Labor organizer, Leonora M. Barry, summed up the problem in 1887: "if there is one cause more than another that fastens the chains on . . . working women it is their foolish pride, they deeming it a disgrace to have it known that they are engaged in honest toil."[23]

Second, the belief that women belonged at home permitted employers to exploit working women by treating them as though their earnings were merely supplemental. Until the end of the nineteenth century, women customarily received about one-third to one-half of the prevailing wages for men, a sum seldom sufficient even for a single woman to support herself.[24] John Commons estimated that while in 1914, a living wage for a single person was defined as $8 per week, only 25 percent of all female wage earners earned that much, and half took home less than $6 per week. A 20 percent unemployment rate further reduced these wages.[25] The assumption that women belonged at home occasionally led employers to ask that the help received by women living at home be taken into account in calculating "living wages." Department store managers pointedly refused to hire salesclerks who did not live in families for fear that financial need would drive them to the streets.[26] The same assumption led employers to refuse to train women to perform skilled jobs, exacerbating their poverty and offering them no choice but to remain unskilled labor.

Third, employers benefited by competition between men and women. Working men argued that women workers held wages down. Repeatedly in the 1830s, and with growing stridency thereafter, they insisted that wages paid to them would be higher if women were excluded from the work force. In 1836, a National Trades Union Committee urged that female labor be excluded from factories. After explaining that the natural responsibility and moral sensibility of women best suited them to domesticity, the report argued that female labor produced "ruinous competition . . . to male labor" whose final end would be that "the workman is discharged or reduced to a corresponding rate of wages with the female operative." The report continued:

One thing . . . must be apparent to every reflecting female, that all her exertions are scarce sufficient to keep her alive; that the price of her labor each year is reduced; and that she in a measure stands in the way of the male when attempting to raise his prices or equalize his labor, and that her efforts to sustain herself and family, are actually the same as tying a stone around the neck of her natural protector, Man, and destroying him with the weight she has brought to his assistance. This is the true and natural consequence of female labor when carried beyond the family.[27]

The president of the Philadelphia Trades Association advised women to withdraw altogether from the work force: "the less you do, the more there will be for the men to do and the better they will be paid for doing it, ultimately you will be what you ought to be, free from the performance of that kind of labor which was designed for man alone to perform.[28]

Male fears of displacement or of reduced wages seemed justified. While men and women normally did not compete for the same jobs, employers often substituted one for the other in response to changing technology and labor market conditions. New England textile factories, whose workers were 90 percent female in 1828, were only 69 percent female in 1848.[29] The proportion of Massachusetts teachers who were male had dropped from about 50 percent in 1840 to 14 percent in 1865.[30] By 1865, the labor press was complaining of "a persistent effort on the part of capitalists and employers to introduce females into its various departments of labor heretofore filled by the opposite sex."[31] The feared consequence would be to bring down the price of labor "to the female standard, which is generally less than one half the sum paid to men." Employers sometimes trained women to act as strikebreakers. According to a Senate report, a Chicago newspaper publisher "placed materials in remote rooms of the city and secretly instructed girls to set type and kept them there until they became sufficiently proficient to enter the office. . . ."[32] Silk manufacturers testified in 1910 that "as long as there are women horizontal warpers, . . . [the manufacturers have] a strong defense against the demands of the men."[33]

A fourth effect of attributing proper roles to women was to keep women out of unions. Since many felt their work life to be temporary, women had little incentive to join in a struggle for better conditions. Leonora Barry complained in 1889 that in the absence of immediate discomfort, the expectation of marriage blinded many women to the long-range advantages of unions.[34] But the hostility of employers and of male coworkers may have been decisive. Because unions would negate the advantages of low wages and docility, employers would not tolerate them. A government report issued in 1910 noted that the moment a woman organized a union, "she diminishes or destroys what is to the employer her chief value. Hence the marked objection of employers to unions among women."[35]

Men's attitudes toward organizing women varied with their particular circumstances. Sensitive to the competition engendered by employers who used women as strikebreakers or to undercut wages, workers frequently saw clearly the economic role women in fact played in the nineteenth-century labor market. But they rarely repudiated conventional ideas about the social role that women were expected to play. On the other hand, male trade unionists offered support to women attempting to unionize about as often as they struck to protest the hiring of females. In the 1830s Baltimore's journeymen tailors, New York's bookbinders, and Massachusetts' cordwainers all encouraged their female counterparts to unite for better working conditions.[36] The National Labor Union in the late 1860s persistently urged women to organize, and the Knights of Labor, in its halycon period in the early 1880s, organized about 50,000 women into local units.[37] Yet these instances can be measured against examples of many craft unions that well into the twentieth century had constitutions calling for suspending members who trained, or worked with, women. Women who repeatedly, and often successfully, organized themselves throughout the nineteenth and early twentieth century still faced the problem of securing recognition for their unionizing efforts. As union structures developed nationally at the turn of the century, their brother trade unionists often refused to admit them to national membership. Philadelphia candy workers, Norfolk waitresses, and New York printers pleaded in vain for admission to their respective national unions. If the men did not reject them outright, they procrastinated until the women succumbed to pressure from their employers.[38] A consistent pattern appears only toward the end of the century with the emergence of arguments that since women were working anyway, it was safer to have them in unions than outside them. The International Typographers admitted women under duress in 1869, and the Cigar Makers began to admit them when competition threatened their own jobs.[39]

Finally, the "cult of true womanhood" glorified the family structure and contributed to a stability that encouraged, even coerced, the male head to work harder in order to support his family and provide for his wife. For one's wife to be working meant that the husband had failed. The need to secure the wife's position on a pedestal helped to isolate men in an endless search for upward mobility and financial success. The idea that women should be able to stay at home—the better to mother their children—justified hard work, long hours, economic exploitation, and a host of other evils for male workers. A New York *Post* writer in 1829 accurately summed up a prevailing attitude when he asserted that the only way to make husbands sober and industrious was to keep women dependent by means of insufficient wages.[40]

The moral imperative that confined women to their homes served many purposes. It maintained social order by providing stable families. It kept most married women out of the labor force, confining them to supportive roles in relation to the male work force. It helped to ensure that those women who did work would stay in the labor force only briefly, remaining primarily committed to their families and satisfied with low-paid jobs. The special position of women as the least-paid and least-skilled members of the work force induced hostility from unskilled male labor. Afraid that women might take their jobs, some workingmen might have been afraid to demand justice from intransigent employers.[41]

Overflowing Tensions

For most of the nineteenth century, notions about the proper roles of women effectively contained the tension between the need for labor and the need for stable families. If those who worked on farms are excluded, then less than 20 percent of all women worked in the paid labor force before 1900. Of these, 70 percent were domestic servants in 1870, and 24 percent worked in textile mills and the developing garment industry. Together with tobacco-making, these areas comprised most of women's participation in the nonagricultural work force before 1900. Within these trades, women were the lowest-paid workers and performed the least-skilled jobs. Poor rewards and unpleasant working conditions discouraged all but the poorest from working. The entry into the labor market was thus naturally regulated, and many left the work place with relief when marriage and motherhood offered an acceptable escape.

Toward the end of the century, changes in the structure of work and the economy began to alter this seemingly harmonious balance, encouraging women to enter the labor force in ways that directly challenged their family roles. Increasing numbers of women in the labor force and the deteriorating conditions under which some women worked reflected the failure of ideas about women's proper roles in keeping them out of the work force in the face of labor market demands. At the same time, a mature industrial society encouraged changes in the nature of families in ways that led affluent women to become dissatisfied with constrained roles and to seek new outlets. The resulting tension called forth new definitions of social roles and new compromises in the ways that women could be employed.

The nature of the compromise emerged from the transition from competitive to monopoly capitalism, whose greatest thrust was concentrated in the years from 1890 to around 1920. Its outlines are by now familiar. Small competitive businesses dependent on local markets and a local labor supply gave way to the giant impersonal corporation whose markets were national and whose workers were increasingly drawn from rural towns and villages to large industrial centers. As the size of plants expanded, impersonal relations replaced an old paternalism; jobs became increasingly specialized and the number of workers employed in skilled labor declined. Control over workers, which had formerly been a result of community sanctions and loyalty, was achieved by a developing hierarchy of employees and reinforced by the persistent availability of a large surplus of labor. Workers responded to the denigration of their skills, to economic insecurity, and to the pressures of steadily worsening work conditions by forming labor unions. The period around the turn of the century witnessed bloody strikes in railroads, coal, steel, and the garment industries. They were decades in which it seemed, to some, plausible to unite all "producers" to resist corporate encroachment on humane relationships in the name of profits. In the end, economic rationalization and corporate efficiency won the day. The early twentieth century witnessed a modification of laissez-faire policies in favor of government regulation in a corporate state.

Accelerating job specialization in the factory, which raised the demand for unskilled and semiskilled labor, increased employment opportunities for women.

In addition, the developing bureaucratic hierarchy and corporate structure demanded increasing numbers of office workers who had limited skills and few job-related aspirations. The proportion of women in the nonagricultural labor force rose dramatically. In 1880, 12.8 percent of all women had worked in nonagricultural jobs. By 1900, the figure had climbed to 17.3 percent, and by 1910, to 20.7 percent. There the figure stabilized.[42] By 1910 one of every five gainfully employed workers was female. Within the ranks of working women, the proportions working as domestics decreased steadily. More than 60 percent of all working women (including farm workers) were so employed in 1870. By 1910, only a little more than one-quarter of all employed women worked as servants, and by 1920 the figure had dropped to 18.2 percent. In contrast, the percentage of women who worked in factories increased from 17.6 percent in 1870 to 20.3 percent in 1890 and 23.8 percent in 1920. The proportion who worked in offices climbed from little more than 5 percent to more than one-quarter of all working women in 1920.[43] Some industries depended heavily on unskilled and semiskilled female labor. Fully 40 percent of the vast complex of textile workers, for example, was female in 1910.[44]

Less dependent in post-Civil War America on skilled workers, employers took advantage of the plentiful labor supply offered by immigration to reduce wages and to coerce hard work out of vulnerable employees. As trade unions sprang up and strikes spread, public attention was drawn to their grievances. Newspaper exposés and government investigations noted the injurious effects on all workers, but especially on women, of harsh working conditions and of wages insufficient to keep body and soul together. Investigators worried incessantly about the morality of working women. Some pointed to spreading prostitution as one consequence of low industrial wages. Others insisted that it was their business to determine "in what particulars ... employment exerted pressure upon the feminine character."[45] Still others argued that stunted and warped young women endangered the health of unborn children and that working mothers were forced to leave children to roam the streets all day with "latchkeys" strung about their necks. Pressure for legislation to protect these women began to build up.

Simultaneously, it became apparent both to the investigators and to male workers that women were finding it increasingly necessary to work. Sickness, accident, and death rates among industrial workers reached all-time heights between 1903 and 1907. Unemployment fluctuated cyclically. Despite rises in real wages after 1897, they remained too low to meet normal family needs. Perhaps as a consequence, the proportion of married women in the nonagricultural work force almost doubled between 1890 and 1920.[46] Workingmen now voiced new fears that women would undermine the wage standards and work opportunities of the male labor force. While occasional trade unions, especially in industries where women were heavily concentrated, made sporadic attempts to organize them into trade unions, most supported legislation that would effectively limit women's opportunities to work by raising their wages, regulating their hours, and prescribing the kinds of jobs in which they could be employed. Adolph Strasser, secretary of the Cigar Makers Union in 1879, was only a few years ahead of his time when he said, "we cannot drive the females out of the trade but we can restrict their daily quota of labor through factory laws."[47]

The changing nature of the immigrant population adds another dimension in explaining women's increasing participation in the work force and the continuing breakdown in prescribed social roles. Primarily Southern and Eastern European, Catholic and Jewish, new immigrants were channeled into the bursting ghettos of expanding cities. Anxious to help their families achieve economic security, women from preindustrial origins who had not been socialized into nineteenth-century America and whose traditions incorporated both strong family loyalty and strong work orientations, regularly contributed to family incomes. Married women took in boarders or sewing at home. Unmarried women worked as dressmakers and in factories as well as in other people's houses. Among gainfully employed women, the proportion who were immigrants or their daughters increased steadily until 1910, when it began to drop.[48] Aware of the threat to stable family life, reformers undertook movements to "Americanize" immigrants. Beginning in the 1890s and continuing through the 1920s, they were especially concerned with the health and domestic aptitude of present and future mothers. The social settlement for example, tried with some success to resocialize immigrant women through classes in the arts of homemaking, bathing and caring for children, sewing, and cooking. Although they also made enormous efforts to improve factory conditions, many settlement residents were convinced that mothers belonged at home.

But the tension between the desire to keep women in families and the disruptive consequences of the need for labor was equally apparent among some middle-class women. While social values dictated leisure and an absence of work for women, enforced idleness bred a challenge to social order. For the wealthy married woman, affluence, servants, and a decline in the birthrate all added up to boredom. Some middle-class women developed symptoms of hysteria in response; others insisted on an education or threw themselves into charitable activities.[49] Excess energies spent themselves in ways that often had consequences for working women. Those who sought suffrage allied themselves with working women, breaking down momentarily the class barriers that had consistently divided them. Affluent women who became involved in the trade union movement not only contributed to the success of women attempting to organize themselves, but revealed the common disabilities that linked the two groups. Those who became reformers and social settlement residents investigated and exposed abuses against children and women in factories, publicizing, in consequence, the conditions on which their own leisure rested.[50]

Still a third group crossed class lines more dramatically. Attracted by new jobs opening in offices, they chose to work. Large numbers of women who came from groups not previously employed began to search for jobs. In 1890 only 35.3 percent of all women who worked were native-born daughters of native parents. By 1920 this figure had soared to almost 44 percent, while the proportion of native-born daughters in the population had increased only slightly.[51] The dramatic increase in the proportion of native daughters accompanied enormous shifts to the clerical sectors of the work force.[52] The needs of employers for people who were, at one and the same time, relatively well educated and relatively poorly paid seems to have created a new labor market. In part, this was met by rising educational levels among immigrant daughters who had traditionally worked, but in part it was met by native white women entering the labor market for the first time.

The expansion of acceptable jobs for women between 1900 and 1920, and the spread of gainful employment beyond the very poor, contributed to attacks on conceptions of "proper roles." Leading feminists, like Charlotte Perkins Gilman, questioned women's economic dependence; the suffrage campaign mounted in intensity and solicited support among industrial workers of both sexes; unskilled women in factories and department stores redoubled their efforts toward unionization.[53] The interests of working women and their middle-class sisters joined in groups like the proliferating working girls' clubs, in the Consumers Leagues, and in the Women's Trade Union League. Their goals coalesced around the desire of working women for better conditions, shorter hours, and more equal pay—and the concern of the more affluent that work not detract from the health and morality of their working sisters and thus undermine the still essential family. The groups united under the banner of protective legislation.

Protective legislation acknowledged the increasing place of women in the work force while attempting to control implicit changes in women's social roles.[54] It recognized that women had two jobs, one of which had to be limited if the other were to be performed adequately. Yet legislation institutionalized the primary role of social reproduction by denying that women were full-fledged members of the working class. It extended an ideology of "proper roles" to working-class people on the one hand, while loosening the bonds of propriety from the arms of some middle-class women. Protective legislation thus provided a device for dividing workers along gender lines and stratifying the work force in a period when homogeneity in levels of skill threatened to lead to developing class consciousness and to give rise to class conflict.[55]

The new body of laws was rooted in the potentials inherent in an expanding technology and increasingly productive labor force. Large-scale corporate enterprise and the rapid expansion of capital led many corporations to seek new ways to invest their economic surplus and to stimulate the consumption of the goods they produced. This had two opposing consequences for women. On the one hand, slowly rising wages and better working conditions for some workers encouraged wives to remain at home. On the other, expanding labor productivity influenced the structure of the family. As society became more urban, households began to produce less of their food and clothing and to rely more heavily on consumer goods. Declining work for women in the household encouraged those whose husbands did not earn sufficient income to consider paid labor as a realistic alternative. Specialization and the division of labor meant that children were frequently trained outside the home, altering further the functions of women within the household. On balance, the early twentieth century witnessed a steadily rising proportion of women in the nonagricultural labor force.

Protective legislation which began about 1900 reflected these changes. Institutionalizing "proper roles" for women who worked in factories and shops at one and the same time insulated them from their male coworkers and reduced the jobs available to them. It had little effect on the new office clerk who normally did not work at night, or in ill-ventilated factories, or lift heavy weights. Working women found themselves subject to an increasing barrage of legislation limiting the hours of work, establishing minimum wages, and regulating the sanitary conditions under which they could work. These laws had the immense advantage of ameliorating the worst conditions of women's work, while offering to conserve the health and energy to rear present and future families. Their supporters quite specifically argued that legislation was in the best interests of the state. Oregon, for example, preceded its minimum wage law with a preamble: "The welfare of the State of Oregon requires that women and minors should be protected from conditions of labor which have a pernicious effect on their health and morals, and inadequate wages ... have such a pernicious effect."[56] Men did not benefit from minimum wage laws in this period, and courts repeatedly struck down legislative restrictions on hours which applied to men.

At the same time, legislation had a significant impact on the work force as a whole. In reducing the economic desirability of female employees, it limited competition with males. In the words of one authority, "The wage bargaining power of men is weakened by the competition of women and children, hence a law restricting the hours of women and children may also be looked upon as a law to protect men in their bargaining power."[57] Workingmen favored a minimum wage legislation for women because it effectively reduced a downward pull on their wages.[58] The newly established Women's Bureau of the Department of Labor took great pains in the 1920s to prove that women were not displaced by factory laws.[59] While technically that seems to have been true, the Bureau interviewed a number of employers who indicated that restrictive legislation rendered them unable to consider women for otherwise suitable jobs.[60] Despite job shifts that provided new opportunities, women's rate of labor force participation remained stable until the late 1930s.[61]

With rare exceptions, employers did not suffer. Legislation was slowly and tentatively achieved, with due regard for the interests of manufacturers whose businesses were likely to be hurt. Sanitary and health regulations often went unenforced. By and large, regulation was opposed only by small manufacturers represented in the National Association of Manufacturers, whose interests in any event often contradicted those of the corporations and labor unions that both came to approve and lobby for protecting women.

Working women were confused about the legislation, and the trades unionists among them took contradictory positions in the early years of the twentieth century, finally opting for protection when organization seemed impossible. By the 1920s when most industrial states had some legislation limiting hours and regulating night work, conflict came to a head. Some feminists, largely business and professional women, protesting the assumption that women had special roles that required state protection, advocated an Equal Rights Amendment to the Constitution whose effect would be to eliminate the body of legislation so painstakingly built up. Women trade unionists, the Women's Trade Union League, and the Women's Bureau led the fight against the Equal Rights Amendment.[62] One woman supervisor in a Virginia silk mill expressed the conflict well: "I have always been afraid," she wrote, "that if laws were made discriminating for women it would work a handicap upon them." By 1923, she had changed her mind: ". . . it would in time raise the entire standard, rather than make it hard for women."[63] Business and professional women, led by the Women's Party, supported the E.R.A. Many professional women's clubs forthrightly condemned labor laws for women.[64]

As the number of women in the work force rose and the kinds of jobs open to them became more varied, segmentation among different groups of working women increased. Women considered certain kinds of jobs more appropriate than others. Rose Schneiderman, an immigrant who later became a trade union organizer, recalls that when, at the age of sixteen, she left her department store job to become a sewing machine operator, her mother was "far from happy. She thought working in a store much more genteel than working in a factory."[65] Waitresses, considered by many in the early twentieth century as the most degraded of workers, had their own hierarchies. Those who worked where liquor was sold, and where tips were larger, were despised by the others.[66] As with men, employers used language and race to build barriers around employees. Garment industry employers deliberately hired women who spoke different languages to inhibit communication in the workshop.[67] Tobacco processors most frequently hired black women only to strip tobacco—a job white women would take only as a last resort.[68]

Schooling played a major role in segmenting women. New office jobs required not only facility in reading and writing English, but a command of typing, stenography, simple bookkeeping, the typewriter, and other business machines. In the early years of the century, manufacturers set up schools to train young women in the use of their products. Occasionally employers subsidized women who went to classes run by organizations like the Women's Educational and Industrial Union, which offered to teach department store employees such subjects as English, arithmetic, hygiene, history of manufactured goods, art of politeness, and store diplomacy.[69] But most employers relied on an expanding network of manual or vocational training programs to discipline young women for the work world and to endow them with necessary skills. Beginning with the first vocational training school for women in 1899 and capped by the federal Vocational Education Act in 1917, these programs channeled suitable candidates into acceptable jobs. They preserved the dichotomy in women's two roles intact by almost universally offering training in domestic science along with typewriting.

By the end of the 1920s the pattern had been confirmed. Most male and female workers were segregated from each other, largely by prevailing norms about proper roles, but increasingly by protective legislation and by an educational structure that reflected those norms and channeled women into jobs deemed appropriate. Within the female work force, separate segmentation mechanisms were fairly widespread. Enticed by the image of the glamorous flapper, single women went to work in offices, department stores, and factories roughly according to their socioeconomic status. Schools and professional agencies opened their doors to those destined to become teachers, social workers, and nurses. Some women entered graduate school and became lawyers or doctors. But married women and poor women were encouraged to remain at home unless absolutely necessary, and industrial employers, discouraged by minimum wages and short hours, often looked elsewhere for labor. That compromise satisfied both employers, who had an abundance of immigrant labor, and workingmen who worried less about female competition.

But the compromise was never very effective. It began to flounder on the questions raised by women who confronted changes in their own roles at home and who, married or not, increasingly sought to work. It was finally scuttled by the insatiable demand for office workers.

The Compromise Collapses

The depression of the 1930s obscured the long-term trend, but could not challenge the essential compromise worked out in the preceding decades. If relative poverty inhibited consumerism and encouraged women once more to exercise economy and increase their productivity in the household, the continuing shift in job structures confirmed women's marginal but essential position in the work force. Rising unemployment led to pressure to eliminate some married women from the state and federal civil service, yet many wives sought jobs to eke out family incomes. To some extent, men entered traditionally women's occupations like teaching. But, remarkably, women held onto the jobs that had been sex-role stereotyped. It is noteworthy not that women gained few jobs in the 1930s, but that they lost none.[70]

Wartime prosperity succeeded the Depression, and women entered the labor force in large numbers. Though they breached sex lines in every imaginable job category, women faced at wars' end a major propaganda campaign to force them back into their homes.[71] Appeals to familial duty were only partially successful. Many women resigned their jobs, but a residue remained at work to be joined later by a steadily mounting number.

These women heralded a changing economy that, since World War II, has simultaneously opened new jobs and altered the nature of families and of women's functions within them. Within the family, increased affluence and improved household technology as well as expanding consumer services have altered the kind of work women do at home, reducing their functions as producers but increasing their roles as consumers. Despite changes in household technology, rising standards of house care may have increased the actual time spent at household tasks. Longer life spans for men and women and declining birthrates have reduced the proportion of time spent in child-rearing. For some sectors, relative affluence has reduced the need to instill values of thrift, hard work, and the need for education, raising questions about how to socialize children.[72] Official policy still acknowledges the traditional central role of the family as a stabilizing agency. But young people and women are beginning to explore alternatives that reflect doubt about old values.[73]

At the same time, job structures have shifted dramatically from primarily blue-collar and manual labor before World War II, to white-collar and service work in the post-war period.[74] The expanding sectors—teaching, social work, the human services, health, publishing, and advertising—are all extensions of family functions and have long been acceptable areas for women. While the spread of mass education and the demand for office workers of various kinds have led women to enter the labor force, on the one hand, the concomitant need that these workers not seek advancement or high compensation has encouraged the belief that their work experience is and ought to be secondary to their home roles. Popular magazines, advertising, prevalent truths about child-rearing, and the glorification of femininity have conspired to support this belief. But low-level clerical and secretarial jobs may be opening faster than they can be filled by the available pool of single or childless women.[75] Short of a dramatic rechanneling of men into office jobs, which would involve major adjustments in social values, large-scale bureaucracies will be forced to make allowances for women with children.

The problem is already evident in the changing composition of the work force. Female workers are becoming older, better educated, less likely to take time off for childbirth, and more likely to be married and to have children. Fully 40 percent of all women over 16 now work, and two-thirds of the women in the labor force are married; 42 percent of the paid labor force is now female.[76]

Because jobs have expanded in precisely those sectors in which women have been working, women have begun to reevaluate their commitments to the home and to seek occupational mobility. Women with seniority rights and prior experience become discontent when they are consistently overlooked for top jobs. For many women, the need for a job has given way to the demand for a career, and marriage is no longer an escape from the world of work.

Changing families and new job structures expose more clearly than before the fundamental tension between the demands of the labor market and the belief that social order is vested in the family. Women who are uncomfortable with confused family patterns and limited work force options have begun to question their "proper roles." Ideas that assign them to secondary places in the work force seem unacceptable. The feminine mystique seems no longer able to contain the contradiction. In contrast to the past when only exceptional women agitated for more responsible jobs and release from their family roles, protest against the concept of roles is now becoming generalized. It is evident in attacks against images of women in advertising, on television, in popular magazines, and in movements to alter textbooks and clothing styles. While working women have frequently asked for higher wages and better working conditions, their failure to achieve them is explained by the continuing strength of ideas about women's roles. Some recognition that these ideas are losing credibility may be indicated by government-instituted affirmative-action programs and pressures to admit women to prestigious colleges and professional schools.

Some ways of containing these new challenges are already being tried. A few jobs are being opened up to women, and occasionally wages are being equalized. But the percentage of women holding prestige jobs has not increased, and on the whole, women's wages have not risen comparably to those of men.[77] Predictably, the issue of competition between men and women has undermined key questions about the nature of work and has produced something of a backlash now known as "reverse discrimination." One can expect these reactions to worsen in the event of economic recession. But the most subtle and debilitating response has been its class-based nature. As in the early twentieth century, legislative responses are institutionalizing gains for the affluent and well-educated, while excluding most others from the work force. Recent federal legislation encourages women who can afford the cost of child care or household help to work while current executive action deprives those who are poor, but not on welfare, of federally financed day-care centers.[78] Affirmative-action programs have benefited professional and business women far more than clerks and secretaries. Yet office workers have begun to organize, and trade union women are beginning to talk about joint action.

The enormous number of women now working raises questions about whether their commitments to jobs will undermine the basis of the traditional family. Rising divorce rates, the recent Supreme Court decision on abortion, public affirmations of homosexuality, all testify to increasing conflict about the traditional role of the family and erosion of confidence about its social necessity. The decline of the family as an economic unit, valuable for the social insurance it provides, may herald women's freedom from it. Women who challenge the necessity for a sexually stratified work force could expose the segmentation process which divides all workers. They could provoke other less well-defined groups to scrutinize their own particular sources of stratification. But if family roles have changed to the extent that society can afford to let women out of their homes, sexual stratification may give way only to be replaced for women by the traditional mechanisms of segmentation along class and race lines.

Notes

1. See, for example, Valerie Kincaide Oppenheimer, *The Female Labor Force in the United States: Demographic and Economic Factors Governing Its Growth and Changing Composition*, Population Monograph Series No. 5 (Berkeley: University of California, 1970); James A. Sweet, *Women in the Labor Force* (Seminar Press, 1973); John Shea, Ruth Spitz, Frederick Zeller, et al., *Dual Careers: A Longitudinal Study of Labor Market Experience of Women*, Center for Human Resources Research, vol. 1 (Columbus: Ohio State University Press, 1970); Juanita Kreps, *Sex in the Marketplace: American Women at Work* (Baltimore: Johns Hopkins, 1971).

2. Eli Zaretsky, "Capitalism, the Family, and Personal Life," *Socialist Revolution*, 3 (January/April, 1973): 69-125. For an extended discussion of the implications of changes in household production—an issue only touched upon in this essay, see Wally Secombe, "The Housewife and Her Labor under Capitalism," *New Left Review* 83 (Jan.-Feb., 1974): 3-24.

3. Examples of those who raised these questions range from Ann Hutchinson in 1635 to Frances Wright, Charlotte Perkins Gilman, and Emma Goldman.

4. Edmund Morgan, *The Puritan Dilemma* (Boston: Little, Brown, 1958), p. 71; also see John Demos, *A Little Commonwealth: Family Life in Plymouth Colony* (New York: Oxford, 1970), p. 78.

5. Demos, *A Little Commonwealth*, p. 186.

6. Arthur W. Calhoun, *A Social History of the American Family from Colonial Times to the Present* (New York: Barnes & Noble, 1945), vol. 1, p. 201.

7. Demos, *A Little Commonwealth*, p. 89.

8. Edith Abbott, *Women in Industry* (New York: Appleton, 1910), p. 34.

9. Caroline T. Ware, *The Early New England Cotton Manufactures: A Study in Industrial Beginnings* (Boston: Houghton Mifflin, 1931), p. 198. Hannah Josephson, *The Golden Threads: New England's Mill Girls and Magnates* (New York: Duell, Sloan & Pearce, 1949), p. 22; Oscar Handlin, *Boston's Immigrants: 1790-1880* (New York: Atheneum, 1971 [1941]), pp. 74-76; Reinhard Bendix,

Work and Authority in Industry: Ideologies of Management (New York: Wiley, 1956), p. 39.

10. Josephson, *The Golden Threads*, pp. 63 and 23; see also John Kasson, unpub. Ph.D. dissertation, "Civilizing the Machine: Technology, Aesthetics, and Society in Nineteenth Century American Thought," (New Haven: Yale, 1972); and Holland Thompson, *From the Cotton Field to the Cotton Mill: A Study of the Industrial Transition in North Carolina* (New York: Books for Libraries Press, 1971 [1906]), p. 52 for a similar example of paternal employment in the South. About one-half of the employees in the New England textile mills were recruited in this way. That an undetermined number of the women who worked in the mills were self-supporting or responsible for families of their own fails to undermine the rationale.

11. Kasson, p. 41.

12. Ibid., pp. 53-55.

13. John B. Andrews and W.D.P. Bliss, *History of Women in Trade Unions*, vol. 10 of the Report on Condition of Women and Child Wage Earners in the United States, Senate Doc., #645, 61st Congress, 2nd Session (Government Printing Office, 1911), p. 12. Hereinafter cited as Andrews and Bliss.

14. Ware, *The Early New England Cotton Manufactures*, p. 231.

15. Ibid., p. 234.

16. Quoted in Constance McLaughlin Green, *Holyoke Massachusetts: A Case History of the Industrial Revolution in America* (New Haven: Yale University Press, 1939), p. 31 fn.

17. Abbott, *Women in Industry*, p. 90.

18. Bernard Wishy, *The Child and the Republic* (Philadelphia: University of Pennsylvania Press, 1972), p. 28.

19. Ruth Miller Elson, *Guardians of Tradition: American Schoolbooks of the Nineteenth Century* (Lincoln: University of Nebraska Press, 1964), p. 309; Siegfried Giedion, *Mechanization Takes Command: A Contribution to Anonymous History* (New York: Norton, 1969 [1948]), p. 514; for discussions of the nineteenth-century woman, see also Barbara Welter, "The Cult of True Womanhood, 1820-1860," *American Quarterly* 18 (Summer, 1964), and Glenda Gates Riley, "The Subtle Subversion: Changes in the Traditionalist Image of the American Woman," *The Historian* 32 (February, 1970).

20. See Michael B. Katz, *The Irony of Early School Reform: Educational Innovation in Mid-Nineteenth Century Massachusetts* (Boston: Beacon Press, 1968), for a general discussion of schools in this period. Arguments for domestic education for women are widespread, but see especially any of Catherine Beecher's numerous works; Elson, *Guardians of Tradition*, p. 309; and Gerda Lerner, "Women's Rights and American Feminism," *American Scholar* 40 (Spring, 1971): 238.

21. Aileen Kraditor, *Up from the Pedestal* (Chicago: Quadrangle, 1968), p. 13. Kraditor continued: "The home was the bulwark against social disorder, and

woman was the creator of the home . . . she occupied a desperately necessary place as symbol and center of the one institution that prevented society from flying apart."

22. Quoted in Elson, *Guardians of Tradition*, p. 309.

23. Andrews and Bliss, p. 118.

24. See Green, *Holyoke*, for example. Helen Sumner, *History of Women in Industry in the United States*, vol. 9 of the Report on the Condition of Women and Child Wage Earners in the United States, Senate Doc. #645, 61st Congress, 2nd Session (Government Printing Office, 1910), p. 28, reports that the *Workingman's Advocate* in 1868 complained that women only got one-quarter of men's wages. This source will be hereinafter cited as Sumner, 9.

25. John R. Commons, et al., ed., *A Documentary History of American Industrial Society*, vol. 6, the Labor Movement (Glendale: A.H. Clark, 1910), p. 195; Emilie Josephine Hutchinson, *Women's Wages: A Study of the Wages of Industrial Women and Measures Suggested to Increase Them* (Providence: American Mathematical Society, 1968), pp. 24, 25; Handlin, *Boston's Immigrants*, p. 81, notes that women earned an average of $1.50 to $3.00 per week, while men earned from $4.50 to $5.50.

26. *Wage Earning Women in Stores and Factories*, vol. 5 of the Report on the Condition of Women and Child Wage Earners in the United States, op. cit., pp. 13, 22. Hereinafter cited as Report 5; Commons, *A Documentary History*, p. 210.

27. Commons, *A Documentary History*, pp. 282, 284.

28. Andrews and Bliss, p. 48.

29. Elizabeth F. Baker, *Technology and Women's Work* (New York: Columbia University Press, 1964), p. 17. See also Sumner, 9, p. 51, who indicates that the number of women dropped to 40.6 percent in 1900.

30. Katz, *The Irony of Early School Reform*, p. 12. There is a discrepancy in the figures Katz presents in the Appendix (p. 224) and those presented in the text. I have used the more conservative figures here. See also Hutchinson, *Women's Wages*, pp. 34 and 158.

31. Quoted in Sumner, 9, p. 29.

32. Andrews and Bliss, 10, p. 104.

33. *The Silk Industry*, vol. 4 of Report on the Conditions of Women and Child Wage Earners, op. cit., pp. 40, 41.

34. Andrews and Bliss, 10, p. 122.

35. Hutchinson, *Women's Wages*, pp. 159-160; Andrews and Bliss, 10, p. 151; also see p. 179 for the cigar industry. The report attributes the decline in membership that occurred among women after 1902 to deliberate hostility by employers.

36. Andrews and Bliss, 10, pp. 39, 41, 46, 47, 57; and Sumner, 9, p. 61, fn.

37. Commons, *A Documentary History*, 9, p. 205; Andrews and Bliss, 10, p. 17.

38. Boone, *The Women's Trade Union League*, pp. 166, 167. Margaret Rankin to Margaret Dreier Robins, March 30, 1919.

39. Andrews and Bliss, 10, pp. 103, 94.

40. Quoted in Sumner, 9, p. 26.

41. The same moral code seems to have had a better impact on middle-class women for whom it not only provided justification for opening up educational institutions to them, but also provided a basis for the suffrage argument at the end of the nineteenth century.

42. These figures are for females over 16. See Joseph A. Hill, *Women in Gainful Occupations: 1870-1920*, Census Monographs, 9 (Government Printing Office, 1929), p. 19. Oppenheimer, *The Female Labor Force*, pp. 2-6, has an excellent discussion of the debate over the increase after that date.

43. Hill, Ibid., p. 40.

44. Sumner, 9, pp. 59, 60; see Carroll D. Wright, *The Working Girls of Boston* (New York: Arno, 1969 [1889]), for a breakdown of women in manufacturing in Boston in 1880.

45. *Relation of Occupation and Criminality among Women*, Report on the Condition of Women and Child Wage Earners, vol. 15, op. cit., p. 93. Hereinafter cited as Report, 15. Report, 5, pp. 34, 70; Department store owners were defensive about the question of morality. One, for example, insisted of his employees that "the majority must be good girls from sheer physical necessity. They cannot live a fast life after 6 o'clock for successive days and weeks and be in proper condition to do their work in the store. If they are busy at night when they should be taking their rest they are soon in such shape that they cannot attend to business and are discharged." Report, 5, p. 32.

46. Among those who worked, 12.1 percent were married in 1890 and 19.8 percent in 1910. The percentage of married women who worked increased from 3.3 in 1890 to 6.8 percent in 1910. Donald Lescohier, "Working Conditions," in John Commons, *History of Labor in the U.S.: 1896-1932*, vol. 3 (New York: Macmillan, 1918), p. 37; and Hill, *Women in Gainful Occupations*, pp. 76, 77.

47. Caroline Manning, *The Immigrant Woman and Her Job* (New York: Arno, 1970 [1930]), passim. See also Barbara Klaczynska "Why Women Work: A Theory for Comparison of Ethnic Groups," unpublished paper delivered at the American Studies Association Meetings, San Francisco, 1973.

48. Hill, *Women in Gainful Occupations*, pp. 101-102, 94. Part of this pattern can be explained by population shifts. The proportion of immigrants and their children in the population as a whole increased slightly until 1910. But the proportion of foreign-born women who were working outpaced it. Between 1910 and 1920, the proportion of immigrants in the population dropped slightly, but the decline in the relative proportion of working women who were foreign-born far exceeded it. See table accompanying fn. 51. U.S. Census Office, *11th Census of Populations*, Part 2 (Washington: Government Printing Office, 1890), p. clx; *14th Census of Populations*, vol. 3 (1920), p. 15.

49. The work of Carroll Smith-Rosenberg is important in illuminating the problems of middle-class women in the nineteenth century. See for example, her article written with Charles Rosenberg, "The Female Animal: Medical and Biological Views of Women in Nineteenth-Century America," *Journal of American History* 60 (September, 1973). Good perspectives on the forces driving the late nineteenth-century middle-class woman can be obtained from any of a number of autobiographies and biographies, including Vida Scudder, *On Journey* (New York: Dutton, 1937); Mary Kingsbury Simkhovitch, *Neighborhood: My Story of Greenwich House* (New York: Norton, 1938); Josephine Goldmark, *Impatient Crusader: Florence Kelley's Life Story* (Urbana: The University of Illinois Press, 1953); Allen F. Davis, *American Heroine: The Life and Legend of Jane Addams* (New York: Oxford, 1973).

50. Allen F. Davis, *Spearheads for Reform: The Social Settlements and the Progressive Movement, 1890-1914* (New York: Oxford, 1967) describes the work of some of these people. The results of their efforts are found in such books as Helen Campbell, *Prisoners of Poverty: Women Wage Workers, Their Trades and Their Lives* (New York: Garrett Press, 1970 [1887]); and Elizabeth Butler, *Women and the Trades: Pittsburgh, 1907-1908* (New York: Charities Publication Committee, 1909), and Butler, *Saleswomen in Mercantile Stores: Baltimore, 1909* (New York: Russell Sage, 1912).

51. The shift occurred largely at the expense of Negro women and immigrant women, as the following table indicates.

Comparison of Working Women in Each Group, by Percentages, with Their Proportion in the Population as a Whole, 1890-1920

	Proportion of each group engaged in gainful occupations				Proportion of each group in total population			
	native born of native-born parents	native born of foreign parents	Foreign born	Negro	native born of native-born parents	native born of foreign parents	Foreign born	Negro
1890	35.3	20.9	20.4	23.4	55.03	18.37	14.4	12.2
1900	36.7	22.6	17.4	23.2	53.9	20.6	13.4	11.6
1910	38.3	22.0	16.1	23.9	53.8	20.5	14.5	10.7
1920	43.8	24.9	13.4	17.6	55.3	21.4	13.0	9.9

Source: Hill, pp. 85, 94, 102, 110 and U.S. Census, *11th Census* (1890), p. clx; *14th Census* (1920), p. 15. Orientals and Indians excluded.

52. Hill, *Women in Gainful Occupations*, pp. 90, 96, 39-41. See also Chapter 11, this volume, by Margery Davies.

53. Good descriptions of this ferment can be found in William Chafe, *The*

American Woman: Her Changing Social, Economic and Political Roles, 1920-1970 (New York: Oxford, 1972); and Eleanor Flexner, *Century of Struggle: The Woman's Rights Movement in the United States* (New York: Atheneum, 1970 [1959]).

54. John R. Commons and John B. Andrews, *Principles of Labor Legislation*, rev. ed. (New York: Harper, 1927), p. 30, has a statement of the general principles of protective legislation. Elizabeth Faulkner Baker, *Protective Labor Legislation*, vol. 66, Studies in History, Economics and Public Law (New York: Columbia University, 1925), contains a summary of laws and court decisions to 1925.

55. See Chapter 1 (this volume) for a description and analysis of this process.

56. Hutchinson, *Women's Wages*, p. 81.

57. Commons and Andrews, *Principles of Labor Legislation*, pp. 69, 30.

58. Hutchinson, *Women's Wages*, p. 161.

59. After an extensive study, based on an investigation that threatened to split the Bureau itself, the Bureau issued a bulletin in 1928 entitled *The Effects of Labor Legislation in the Employment Opportunities of Women.* Much of the debate was chronicled by the press in reporting the meetings of the Women's Industrial Conference in January, 1926. See especially the New York *Times*, Jan. 20, 1926; Boston *Globe*, Jan. 20, 1926; Washington *Evening Star*, Jan. 21, 1926; and New York *Herald Tribune*, Jan. 27, 1926.

60. The following difficulties recorded by a Women's Bureau interviewer of her coversation with a California can manufacturer are not atypical of the negative comments expressed by employers affected by protective legislation: "In the lithograph department several years ago a rush order was received from raisin growers for a large quantity of cans. Most of the press feeders were girls and it was necessary to work overtime to get order out. Requested permission to work girls overtime and it was refused. . . . Men were put on press feeders for overtime and as the girl press feeders have left or been transferred men have been given their jobs as there is always a chance of potential overtime on rush orders and a 'busy time is not a time when you want to put men workers for a few days.' However none of the women were discharged because they were not able to work overtime but it led to a change in policy of filling press feeding jobs." Women's Bureau Collection, *National Archives* Record Group 86, Accession #51A101, Box #12, Long Day Hour Schedule, California. A more forceful statement came from the representative of a Massachusetts employer group who indicated that "in an industry where women constitute less than 25% of the working force, it will not pay to change the hours for the whole plant nor to keep the women and have two sets of hours, therefore the women will be dismissed." Women's Bureau Collection, *National Archives* Accession #51A101, Box #40, Bulletin #15, Individual Interviews, Mass.

61. Oppenheimer, *The Female Labor Force*, pp. 3-5; Janet M. Hooks, *Women's Occupations through Seven Decades*, Women's Bureau Bulletin #218

(Government Printing Office, 1947), p. 34; William Chafe, *The American Woman*, pp. 54-55. I have not attempted to estimate how much these changes were affected by increased affluence, or by the withdrawal of immigrant women from the labor market. For an account of the effect of minimum wages on the most disadvantaged group of workers, see Elizabeth Ross Haynes, "Two Million Women at Work," in Gerda Lerner, *Black Women in White America: A Documentary History* (New York: Pantheon, 1972), pp. 256-257. Haynes says in part: "With the fixing of the minimum wage in the hotels, restaurants, etc., at $16.50 for a 48 hour week, and the increasing number of available white women, Negro women were to a very large extent displaced. Wages for domestic service for the rank and file have fallen in the past twelve months from $10.00 a week without any laundry work to $7 and $8 with laundry work. . . . The numbers driven into domestic work are very large."

62. A good description of this conflict is in J. Stanley Lemons, *The Woman Citizen: Social Feminism in the 1920's* (Urbana: University of Illinois, 1973), passim and Chapter 7.

63. Quoted in Mary Van Kleeck to Mary Anderson, Feb. 21, 1923, Van Kleeck papers, unsorted, Sophia Smith Collection, Smith College.

64. Mary Anderson to Mary Van Kleeck, May 28, 1927, Van Kleeck papers.

65. Rose Schneiderman with Lucy Goldthwaite, *All for One* (New York: Paul Eriksson, 1967), p. 43. This is in sharp contrast to the early years of New England textile industry when mill workers might become teachers for several months each year.

66. Report, 5, p. 193.

67. Schneiderman, *All for One*, p. 97; Rose Pesotta, *Bread upon the Waters* (New York: Dodd, Mead, 1944), p. 19.

68. Emma L. Shields, "The Tobacco Workers," in Lerner, *Black Women in White America*, p. 253; and Klaczynska, footnote 47.

69. Report, 5, p. 98.

70. For example, women who had been 81.8 percent of all teachers in 1930 dropped to 75.3 percent of the total in 1940. Nurses dropped from 98.1 percent of the total to 97.8 percent; librarians from 91.4 to 89.5 percent. Hook, *Women's Occupations through Seven Decades*, pp. 160, 163, 170. In the clothing trade, women reversed a 30-year trend to substitute men for women, and climbed from 64.4 percent of all clothing workers in 1930 to 74 percent in 1940. Hook, Ibid., p. 115. The 1930s, statistically, continued a trend for married women to enter the labor force. By 1940, 35.5 percent of all women workers were married, as compared to 28.8 percent in 1930 and 22.8 percent in 1920. Hook, Ibid., p. 39.

71. The following quote is illustrative: "A first general step towards the problem of rehabilitating women (and through women, children of both sexes and adults of the next generation) would be public recognition in substantial ways of the powerful role and special importance of mothers as transmitting

agents, good or bad, of feelings, personality and character. This would pave the way for over-all action by national and local governments and by private organizations. . . ." Ferdinand Lundberg and Marynia Farnham, *Modern Woman: The Lost Sex* (New York: Harper and Brothers, 1947), p. 356.

72. For an extended discussion of these issues see Alice Kessler-Harris and Bertram Silverman, "Women in Advanced Capitalism," *Social Policy* (July/August, 1973): 16-22.

73. Nixon's veto of the Comprehensive Child Development Act as reported in the New York *Times*, December 10, 1971, p. 20, is an example of official policy. For disaffection, see *Work in America*, report of a Special Task Force to the Secretary of Health, Education and Welfare (Boston: M.I.T., 1973); and for some startling differences between middle- and working-class women, see "Widening Gap Is Registered between College and Non-College Women," New York *Times*, May 22, 1974, p. 45.

74. An extended discussion of these shifts can be found in Daniel Bell, *The Coming of Post-Industrial Society* (New York: Basic Books, 1973); John Kenneth Galbraith, *The New Industrial State* (Boston: Houghton Mifflin, 1967); and Victor Fuchs, *The Service Economy* (National Bureau of Economic Research, 1968).

75. Valerie Kincaide Oppenheimer, "Demographic Influence on Female Employment. and the Status of Women," *American Journal of Sociology* 78 (January, 1973): 946-961.

76. See Juanita Kreps, *Sex in the Marketplace*, and Oppenheimer, *The Female Labor Force* for details.

77. A good illustration is Gertrude Ezorsky, "Fight over University Women," *The New York Review of Books* (May 16, 1974): 32-39.

78. Katherine Ellis and Rosalind Petchesky, "Children of the Corporate Dream: An Analysis of Day Care as a Political Issue under Capitalism," *Socialist Revolution* (Nov./Dec. 1972): 8-28.

Women's Wages and Job Segregation

Mary Stevenson

This article points up the dearth of economic analysis on the topic of discrimination against women, and argues that women's inferior economic position may result from a highly segregated occupational structure. Though public attention focuses on the goal of "equal pay for equal work," gaining economic equality for women would require far greater and more fundamental changes in society.

Although economists have been in the vanguard of many discussions about public issues, they have been surprisingly tardy in analyzing the economic position of women workers. While they engaged in heated debate over proposals for revenue sharing or negative income taxes nearly ten years before those topics reached the general public, they are still comparatively silent on the question of women's wages.

The 1964 Civil Rights Act outlawed discrimination in employment by sex (albeit as an afterthought). An article appearing by an economist that year defined discrimination in an extremely narrow way, and proceeded to find discrimination against women workers on the part of employers to be minimal. Indeed, the author questioned whether such discrimination existed at all.[1]

Even as late as 1968, a prominent urban economist, arguing that there was a need to attract men into teaching jobs in the ghetto, proposed as a solution that male teachers be paid more than female teachers.[2] His argument had a certain logic: since men had better job opportunities than women outside of teaching, it would take more of a financial inducement to attract a man to teaching than it would to attract a woman, whose opportunities outside of teaching were more limited. At no point did he question the existence of differential opportunities for men and women—he merely took that situation as given, and proceeded with his analysis. It is only very recently that economists have been taking a serious look at the economic position of women; much of the recent analysis has been a product of women economists.

We know that there has been a large and persistent difference in earnings between working men and women, even among those who work full time the year around. This gap has widened since World War II, and has been hovering around 60%. If we look not only at relative wages between men and women, but

This paper has appeared in *Politics and Society*, 4:1, Fall 1973. Permission to reprint granted by the author and the journal.

at the probability of earning low wages (defined here as hourly earnings of $2.25 or less), we find that women are much more likely than men to be low-wage workers. In a sample of full-time full-year workers drawn from the 1967 Survey of Economic Opportunity, we found that about 1/5 of the white men, 1/2 of the black men, 3/5 of the white women, and over 3/4 of the black women earned low wages. Moreover, differences in education could not possibly explain the likelihood of women earning low wages. In fact, they made the problem even more perplexing, since the proportion of women with college degrees who earned low wages was greater than the proportion of white men who earned low wages with only a high school diploma Perhaps the most astounding of our findings was that the proportion of black women earning low wages with some post-high school education was nearly as great as the proportion of low-wage white male workers who were functionally illiterate.[3]

Some of the attempts to explain the wage differential between men and women have rationalized that such differences reflected (1) allegedly higher absenteeism and turnover rates for women, making their non-wage hiring costs higher; or (2) allegedly pleasanter working conditions or fringe benefits, which women preferred to receive in lieu of higher wages. While data on absenteeism are fragmentary, evidence from a University of Chicago Business School survey and from the Public Health Service indicate minimal sex differences in absenteeism because of illness or injury. Moreover, a Civil Service Commission study of federal employees indicated that the amount of sick leave taken was negatively correlated with salary and responsibility. In a study of labor turnover, the Department of Labor found high turnover rates for women, but they found that other factors—the skill level of the job, the age of the worker, and whether or not the worker had been on the job for less than a year—were more significant than sex in determining quit rates.[4] Fringe benefits, as well as the absence of unhealthy or dangerous working conditions, tend to be positively associated with wage levels, and cannot explain lower wages for women.[5]

Other attempts to explain wage differentials have focussed on the question of "equal pay for equal work" between men and women in very specific occupations (e.g., accounting clerk, Class B). Some useful information has been produced by this method—for instance, some investigators found that within specific occupations, women working in establishments which hired both sexes in the occupation, earned higher wages than women working in establishments which hired only women for that occupation.[6] The major drawback to this line of questioning is the fact that there are very few specific occupations that are truly integrated by sex. Therefore, comparisons between men and women who hold the same kind of job are necessarily limited to an extremely small portion of the labor force. This is not meant to imply that "equal pay for equal work" is irrelevant. Litigation under the Equal Pay Act of 1963 had resulted, as of June 1971, in the awarding of more than $33.5 million in back pay to nearly 84,000 employees, most of whom were women.[7] Nevertheless, "equal pay for equal work" has obvious limitations if the majority of men and women workers do not do the same kind of work. (This also leaves aside the issue of the alienating and oppressive work environments that most working men and women must face.)

Some generalizations may be made about the nature of paid work done by women. Harold Wilensky, a sociologist, argues that most women are concentrated in jobs that can be described by one or more of these few characteristics: extension of tasks done as unpaid housework or child care; tasks that are not physically demanding or hazardous; tasks requiring patience, or manual dexterity, or sex appeal, or concern for welfare or cultural matters.[8] In addition to these traits, some of which are only allegedly linked with sex, Valerie Oppenheimer adds other characteristics of women's work. She says that women provide a source of skilled cheap labor. Oppenheimer finds that 42% of all women workers are in occupations which have higher than average median education levels but lower than average median earnings. Moreover, women's jobs require the kind of training that can be provided by the women themselves, before employment begins. If employers expect that women workers will have high turnover rates, they will be unwilling to invest in on-the-job training for women, and hence women will be expected to provide their own training, as they do in clerical work and in women's professional work.[9]

Another dimension of women's work which Oppenheimer cites is that women tend not to be in supervisory positions, especially positions in which they would supervise male workers. In 1891, Sidney Webb wrote that in England, the women weavers were as good as the men, but the supervisory jobs were reserved for men only. He speculated that this was because a female supervisor would be unacceptable to the male weavers.[10] Surveys of employers in the United States during the 1950s and 1960s have shown that employers believe that their female employees, as well as their male employees, prefer male supervisors.[11]

The division of the labor market into men's jobs and women's jobs is a more complex process than can be described in the foregoing list of attributes. Perhaps some of the flavor of the process may be conveyed in Theodore Caplow's description of sex divisions in Saleswork:

The prevailing pattern is that salesmen serve male customers, and saleswomen serve female customers. Where the customers are mixed in gender, the sales force follows the majority. An exception is made for very heavy or very valuable commodities, which are commonly sold by men. A whole set of folkways is developed on the basis of these principles. Thus, in a normally organized department store, there will be men in the sportsgoods department, women to sell curtains and dishware, men to sell hardware, women to sell books, but men to sell wedding silver and furniture.[12]

Although this description may have offered some logical explanations of the sex divisions in the labor market, there is also an element of pure arbitrariness. A job that is clearly and exclusively women's work in one factory, town, or region may be just as clearly and exclusively men's work in another factory, town, or region. According to the National Manpower Council, cornhusking is women's work and trimming is men's work in the Midwest, while just the opposite is true in the Far West.[13] Caroline Bird says that "cornhusking was woman's job in Eureka, Illinois, but a man's job in Jackson, Wisconsin, while textile spinning was done by women in Chattanooga mills and by men in North Carolina."[14] Whether it's called inertia, tradition, or historical development, some jobs retain their sex-typing simply because "its always been that way." In times of national emergency, such as wartime, shortages of male labor sometimes force employers to abandon their stereotypes. The force of tradition may also be seen in the experience following a 1962 Presidential order to federal appointing officers requiring them to state their reasons when requesting a candidate of specific sex to fill a job vacancy. Sex-specific requests for candidates to fill job openings fell to one percent of their previous level, indicating that most of the previous sex-specific requests were based on tradition rather than valid requirements which only one sex could fill.[15] In a conference of employers sponsored by the National Manpower Council, many employers believed that sex-labeling of jobs was a result of historical development. A summary statement of the National Manpower Council alleges that "men have usually had first choice of jobs, and certain jobs have remained closed to women simply because men have wanted and succeeded in reserving these jobs for themselves."[16]

Although there has been remarkable stability in the sex-typing of jobs, occasionally changes do occur, especially in response to technological advances or to economic growth with its concomitant changes in the demand and supply of labor.

There is an interrelationship between the nature of technological advance in a production process and the sex of the available labor supply. The history of technological change in the textile industry provides a good example of this phenomenon. In the early days of U.S. textile manufacturing, there was a shortage of male labor, and the textile workers were women. The procedure for spinning yarn was called frame spinning, a job that women held. In England, the procedure used was mule spinning, and the spinners were men. Early attempts to introduce mule spinning in the U.S. failed, the women workers being unable to operate the mule spinning machinery without getting their long skirts caught in the apparatus. After immigration during the middle 1800s increased the supply of male workers, mule spinning was successfully reintroduced and spinning became men's work.[17] When the textile industry moved South in search of cheap labor during the 1920s and 1930s, mule spinning was again abandoned and women were hired to work on the improved ring-frame spinning machines.[18]

Although the worker population of specific occupations may change from men to women or vice-versa, the degree of occupational segregation has not appreciably changed since the turn of the century. Edward Gross, using his Index of Segregation, has found that the degree of sex segregation has been fairly steady over the period 1900-1960, at roughly 66-69%. The percentage figure may be interpreted as the percent of females (or males) who would have to change jobs in order that the ratio of males to females in each occupation would match the ratio of male to female workers in the labor force as a whole. Gross also finds that the degree of sex segregation of occupations is more intense than the degree of race segregation of occupations, 68.4% compared to 46.8% in 1960.[19] Elevator operators provide the only instance Gross can find in which a previously sex-segregated occupation becomes integrated. The more usual course of events that occur when women enter a previously male occupation is that the occupation becomes re-segregated as a female occupation, much in the same way and for similar reasons that an all-white residential neighborhood changes to all-black after the first few black families move in.

Another element to consider when examining the entrance of the opposite sex into a previously segregated occupation is the question of intraoccupational differences in status. Harold Wilensky observes that "women have entered low-status men's occupations (bookkeeping, bank teller), but do not control them, while men have entered and are gaining control of the more attractive female occupations (secondary school teaching, social work, librarianship, hospital and perhaps nursing administration)."[20]

Valerie Oppenheimer finds that about half of all women workers were in occupations which were more than 70% female, both in 1900 and 1960, and that "on the whole, occupations which were predominantly female in 1900 were also predominantly female in 1960."[21] The National Manpower Council concludes that "growth in the employment of women appears to have been accomplished more through increased employment in occupations held by women and by the emergence of new 'women's' occupations than through the entrance of women into occupations formerly considered exclusively male."[22] Dale Hiestand's work on economic growth and employment opportunities modifies this conclusion so that it is still valid for white women, but less valid for black women whose employment patterns reflected shifts in occupational fields unrelated to the growth of employment in those fields.[23]

Thus, it is simple enough to establish that the labor market is segregated according to sex. A more difficult task would be to discover the economic consequences of such segregation. It is not simply a matter of men and women doing different work, if women's work automatically has less prestige and lower pay. Just as separate-but-equal educational facilities have been accompanied by inferior schools for blacks, sex segregation in the labor market has been accompanied by inferior wages for women.

Recently, there has been a revival of interest in a concept expounded in the 1920s in England. This concept, the "crowding hypothesis," argues that the major reason for the low wages of women workers is that they are crowded into a limited number of occupations, and virtually denied access to all other occupations.[24] Because women must compete with each other for jobs that are within the small range of occupations in which women are deemed acceptable, the population of those occupations is artificially enlarged, and the remuneration is therefore less than it otherwise would be. Corresponding with the effect on women's occupations is the effect on the broader range of men's occupations: they are protected from competition for jobs on the part of women workers, so that the population in those occupations is artificially reduced, and the remuneration is therefore higher than it otherwise would be. To sum up, the result of crowding women into a few occupations and virtually barring them from all others is that women's pay is thereby reduced, and men's pay is thereby increased. Removal of the artificial barriers would reduce competition for jobs in female-dominated occupations and increase competition in male-dominated occupations, resulting in pay increases in the former and reductions in the latter.

In my own research, I am attempting to identify the underlying factors accounting for pay differences between men and women who work full-time the year round. As I mentioned earlier, over half of the women in the sample population drawn from the Survey of Economic Opportunity had hourly earnings of $2.25 or below. The research uses the framework of the crowding hypothesis, and pays special attention to the impact of occupational and industrial sex segregation.

The first problem that arises is that of finding some meaningful way of categorizing occupations so that male-female comparisons will be useful. In the past, occupations have been defined either too broadly or too narrowly, and in both cases have given distorted impressions about the degree of discrimination.

In the first case, comparisons are made between the earnings of men and women in broad occupational groups and we get the following litany: women professional, technical, and kindred workers earn 66% as much as men; women managers, officials, and proprietors earn 54% as much as men; women clerical workers earn 65% as much as men; women sales workers earn 40% as much as men; women operatives earn 59% as much as men; and women service workers earn 55% as much as men. This sort of information, though suggestive of the generally inferior economic position of women, is not really very useful, since men and women within the same broad occupational category may hold a variety of jobs that are not comparable, requiring vastly different combinations of skill, talent, education, and training.

In the second case, comparisons are made between the earnings of men and women in very narrowly defined occupations, and we're back to all the disadvantages inherent in the "equal pay for equal work" approach. By the time we've focussed on those men and women who work in the same narrowly defined occupation, we've already eliminated a major source of discrimination: the fact that women do not have access to all occupations on an equal basis with men.

Instead of opting for broadly or narrowly defined occupations as they have been used in the past, my research uses a different way of grouping occupations.

All specific occupations are categorized into groups according to the requirements necessary to perform the job. That is, the occupational categories are arranged according to the amount of general educational development (cognitive skill) and specific vocational preparation (training time) that the job requires.[25] The occupational categories were ranked from lowest to highest, according to the amount of education and training required. Using this schema, we can compare men and women within an occupational category. These men and women probably have different jobs, but their jobs all require the same amount of education and training. Theoretically, people who hold jobs within an occupational category ought to be capable of holding any other job in that category, since they all require the same amount of education and skill. In reality, other job requirements may intervene, so that the complete interchangeability mentioned above may not be possible—for instance, some jobs within an occupational category may have a further requirement that in addition to a given level of education and skill, the worker must have perfect eyesight.

(At this point, it is likely to occur to someone that there are still some jobs in our society that require heavy lifting, and that to the extent that a higher proportion of women than of men would be unable to perform those jobs, many women would be excluded from those jobs, they might receive lower pay, but somehow their lesser average physical strength would justify it. Let me note that I experimented with this sort of question: I eliminated from the sample all jobs which, according to the *Dictionary of Occupational Titles*, required heavy lifting to be done, and recalculated average wages for each race-sex group. I found that average wages increased in each case when heavy jobs were eliminated, and that the effect was most pronounced for black men. That is, the jobs that require physical strength in our society are also the lowest paying jobs, and they are generally relegated to black men. Differences in physical strength could not explain why men earn more than women.)

Having found a way to categorize occupations which I believe has some usefulness, I could use that categorization in testing some hypotheses about the ways in which labor markets operate to the disadvantage of women. The first hypothesis was that men and women with the same amount of schooling would not be in the same occupational requirement group. Women with a given amount of education would be in a lower occupational group than men with the same amount of education. One way of interpreting this would be to say that women hold jobs below their ability more often than do men. Indeed, this appears to be one of the ways in which the labor market works against women.

In order to get a single measure which combines differences in education and differences in wages, I used a ratio of the percentage differences in education and in wage.[26] The numerical value of the ratio has the following meaning: when it is between 0 and 1, white men within an occupation group have higher wages than women, but they are also better educated; when it is greater than 1, white men within an occupation group have somewhat more schooling than women, but have disproportionately higher wages than women; when it is negative, it means that negative differences in education are associated with positive differences in wages (i.e., white men within an occupation group receive higher wages than women despite the fact that the women have more schooling).

In evaluating this ratio, rarely did I find instances where men's higher wages were outweighed by their greater amounts of education. In fact, a negative ratio was quite common, especially for white women. Economists often use years of schooling as a sort of proxy variable for worker "quality," arguing that among workers doing similar work, those who are better schooled are probably more productive workers, and therefore would be expected to have higher earnings. Maybe so, but evidently those expectations are suspended when the better "quality" workers are female. In those cases, better "quality" is perversely rewarded with lower wages.

My second hypothesis was an attempt to see if the "crowding hypothesis" held true within occupational requirement groups. The crowding hypothesis argues that women's wages are lower than men's as a result of women being allowed to enter relatively few occupations. I tried to see whether, among men and women who all did work requiring the same amount of education and training, there were differences in the degrees of dispersion and concentration across the specific occupations within each occupation group. For instance, a given occupation group might consist of 15 distinct occupations. Would I find that men in that occupation group were distributed across all 15 specific occupations, but women were concentrated in only 3 or 4? In fact, I found just that. Within each occupation group, I found that the few most populated occupations consistently accounted for a larger proportion of the women than of the men. (See Table 9-1 for a listing of women's jobs and other jobs within each occupational category, or "occlevel"). Thus, even when comparing occupations that are, at least theoretically, interchangeable, women do not seem to have the same kind of access to all occupations that men do.

A third hypothesis was that men and women within an occupation group were segregated not only by occupation, but also by industry. For this hypothesis, I used multiple regression analysis on a number of industry variables, such as profitability and market power. In fact, not only are women segregated into different industries than men, but women's industries tend to be less profitable and have less market power than men's. For a semiskilled occupational requirement group, about 1/3 of the difference in wages was attributable to the fact that men are in the more profitable and powerful industries. The labor market assigns women to those industries which are not capable of paying higher wages because of the economic environment in which they operate.

Thus, I have tried to show that "equal pay for equal work," though important, is only a small part of the larger question of why women workers receive low wages. Sex segregation in labor markets is, I believe, the real problem underlying the low wages that women receive. It would seem that whenever women can be cordoned off into a circumscribed number of occupations and industries, the consequences are low wages.

How is job segregation maintained? According to the crowding hypothesis, the result of sex segregation is artificially high wages for men and artificially low wages for women. Therefore, employers who hire a large proportion of women benefit from segregation, but employers who hire a large proportion of men have to pay higher wages than they would in a sex-blind market. Why is sex segregation maintained among employers for whom it is unprofitable? Sex role stereotypes pervasive in our culture may lead employers to believe that women would be such inefficient workers in traditionally male jobs that they would not be worth hiring, even at lower wages. This viewpoint may clearly be mistaken, but the employer will never know otherwise, since his initial beliefs prevent the very employment of women which would prove those beliefs to be ill-founded.

Even if the employer does have an accurate assessment and knows that female applicants would be as productive as males and could be hired more cheaply, he still may not sacrifice very much by refusing to hire them. Sex role socialization, learned at home, at school, through the media, as part of the everyday environment, may deter females from aspiring to work in traditionally male jobs, if they're told that such aspirations are inappropriate, unfeminine, and no one would want to hire them anyway. Therefore, an employer may not lose very much by refusing to hire women in traditionally male jobs, if other aspects of our culture have already assured that few women will apply for those jobs.[27] Moreover, even if the employer himself is willing to hire women for traditionally male jobs, he may not do so because he anticipates that the reaction of his male employees will make integration unprofitable. If manliness is enhanced by engaging in all-male activities (be they at a workingclass tavern or the Harvard Club) then working in an integrated occupation, with women as peers, may be a demeaning and intolerable reduction of social distance. Pressures may be placed on the employer, inefficiencies in production may occur because of personnel frictions, and the employer will return to segregated occupations. If there were enough women available, he might be tempted to shift from a high-priced male workforce to a lower-priced female workforce, but in the absence of sufficient numbers of women, the occupation will remain all-male.

Lastly, employers may not hire women in traditionally male occupations even though it would be profitable, since those who do the discriminating may not be those who lose as a result of it. As Harriet Zellner points out, those in charge of hiring may be free to exercise their preferences and prejudices regarding women, since their own salaries will be only minimally affected, even though it may be unprofitable for the firm.[28]

If, as argued, occupational segregation plays a crucial role in keeping women's wages low, then several questions for future research and analysis must be asked: (1) What is the historical origin of sex segregation in the labor force and what accounts for its perpetuation? (2) What are the specific mechanisms that channel

Table 9-1

Most Popular Women's Jobs and Selected Other Jobs in Occlevel

Occ-level	Women's Jobs		Other Jobs
	White	Black	
1	packers and wrappers (nec) laundresses, private household laborers (nec)	laundresses, private household chambermaids and maids charwomen and cleaners	messengers and office boys, recreation and amusement attendants, ushers, carpenters' helpers, gardeners and groundskeepers, warehousemen (nec), farm laborers, porters, elevator operators
2	laundry and dry cleaning operatives kitchen workers (nec) textile spinners	laundry and dry cleaning operatives kitchen workers (nec) counter and fountain workers	truck drivers' helpers, metal filers grinders and polishers, oilers and greasers (exc. auto), garage laborers, car washers and greasers, auto service and parking attendants
5	operatives and kindred (nec) typists checkers and examiners	operatives and kindred (nec) typists waiters and waitresses	guards watchmen doorkeepers, longshoremen and stevedores, telegraph messengers, mail carriers, cab drivers and chauffeurs, bartenders, bill and account collectors
6	manufacturing sewers and stitchers attendants (hospitals and other institutions) practical nurses	attendants (hospital and other institutions) practical nurses manufacturing sewers and stitchers	stock clerks and storekeepers, heat treaters and annealers, sawyers, stationary firemen, truck and tractor drivers, ticket station and express agents, shipping and receiving clerks
7	stenographers receptionists hairdressers and cosmetologists	hairdressers and cosmetologists dressmakers and seamstresses	cranemen derrickmen hoistmen, policemen and detectives, road machinery operators, bus drivers, barbers
8	welders and flame-cutters — —	— — —	printing pressmen and platefitters, meatcutters, cement and concrete finishers, metal rollers and roll hands, firemen
9	bakers — —	bakers — — —	construction and maintenance painters and carpenters, photoengravers and lithographers, plasterers, roofers and slaters
11	bookkeepers salesmen and salesclerks (nec) office machine operators	office machine operators salesmen and salesclerks (nec) bookkeepers	deliverymen and routemen, decorators and windowdressers

Table 9-1 (cont.)

Occ-level	Women's Jobs		Other Jobs
	White	Black	
12	secretaries cooks (except private household) doctors and dentists attendants	cooks (except private household) secretaries housekeepers (private household)	metal molders, sports instructors and officials, RR conductors, vehicle dispatchers and starters, real estate agents and brokers, cabinet makers, metal job setters
13	housekeepers and stewards buyers and department heads (store) foremen (nec)	housekeepers and stewards foremen (nec)	craftsmen and kindred (nec) mechanics and repairmen (nec), linemen and servicemen, purchasing agents and buyers (nec), electricians, airplane mechanics and repairmen, auto m&r, office machine m&r, radio and tv m&r, plumbers and pipefitters, tinsmiths and coppersmiths, machinists
15	teachers, elementary school professional nurses teachers, secondary school	teachers, elementary school professional nurses teachers, secondary school	draftsmen, electrical and electronic technicians, pharmacists, insurance agents and brokers, industrial engineers, engineers (nec)
16	accountants and auditors social and welfare workers artists and art teachers	social and welfare workers musicians and music teachers —	electrical engineers, mechanical engineers, civil engineers, insurance investigators
17	public administration officials and administrators	— — —	chemists, physicians and surgeons, lawyers and judges, clergy

Note: Occlevels 3, 4, 10 and 14 were omitted because samples were too small.

women into a limited number of occupations and industries? (3) How important or necessary a role does sex segregation play in maintaining a hierarchical production system?

Notes

1. Henry Sanborn, "Pay Differences between Men and Women," *Industrial and Labor Relations Review*, July 1964.
2. Wilbur Thompson, "The City as a Distorted Price System," *Psychology Today*, August 1968.

3. Barry Bluestone, William Murphy, and Mary Stevenson, *Low Wages and the Working Poor*, Institute of Labor and Industrial Relations, University of Michigan—Wayne State University, Ann Arbor, 1971.

4. These studies in absenteeism and turnover are described in Esther Peterson, "Working Women," in Robert Jay Lifton, ed., *The Woman in America*, Boston, Beacon Press, 1964.

5. Malcolm S. Cohen, "Sex Differences in Compensation," mimeo, University of Michigan, 1972.

6. Donald McNulty, "Differences in Pay between Men and Women Workers," *Monthly Labor Review*, December 1967; John E. Buckley, "Pay Differences between Men and Women in the Same Job," *Monthly Labor Review*, November, 1971.

7. Buckley, op. cit.

8. Harold Wilensky, "Women's Work: Economic Growth, Ideology, Structure," *Industrial Relations*, Volume 7, #3, May 1968, p. 235.

9. Valerie K. Oppenheimer, "The Sex-Labeling of Jobs," *Industrial Relations*, Volume 7, #3, May 1968, pp. 224-228.

10. Sidney Webb, "The Alleged Differences in the Wages Paid to Men and to Women for Similar Work," *Economic Journal*, Volume 1, 1891, p. 645.

11. Oppenheimer, op. cit., p. 229.

12. Theodore Caplow, *The Sociology of Work*, Minneapolis, University of Minnesota Press, 1954, p. 232.

13. National Manpower Council, *Womanpower*, New York, Columbia University Press, 1957, p. 91.

14. Caroline Bird, *Born Female*, New York, Pocket Books, 1969, p. 70.

15. Ibid., p. 69.

16. National Manpower Council, op. cit., p. 89.

17. Edith Abbott, *Women in Industry*, New York, Appleton & Company, 1918, pp. 90-108.

18. Elizabeth F. Baker, *Technology and Woman's Work*, New York, Columbia University Press, 1964, p. 116.

19. Edward Gross, "Plus Ça Change. . . ? , the Sexual Structure of Occupations Over Time," *Social Problems*, Fall 1968, Volume 16, #2, pp. 198-208.

20. Wilensky, op. cit., p. 241.

21. Oppenheimer, op. cit., pp. 219-221.

22. National Manpower Council, op. cit., p. 234.

23. Dale Hiestand, *Economic Growth and Employment Opportunities for Minorities*, Columbia University Press, New York, 1964, p. 35.

24. The original statement of the crowding hypothesis was by F.Y. Edgeworth, "Equal Pay to Men and Women for Equal Work," *Economic Journal*, December 1922. Recent work on the crowding hypothesis as applied to blacks as well as women has been done by Barbara R. Bergmann at the University of Maryland.

25. This occupational categorization was developed at the Institute of Labor and Industrial Relations by Barry Bluestone and Mary Stevenson, using the Department of Labor's *Dictionary of Occupational Titles.*

26. In each occupation group, I found the percentage difference in wages for white women and black women, using white men as the benchmark group. I then found the percentage difference in education levels, and computed a ratio of percentage differences in wages to percentage differences in education.

27. See the discussion of the interdependence of different types of discrimination in Lester Thurow, *Poverty and Discrimination*, Washington, D.C., The Brookings Institution, 1969, p. 117.

28. Harriet Zellner, "Discrimination against Women, Occupational Segregation, and the Relative Wage," *American Economic Review, Papers & Proceedings*, May 1972, pp. 157-60.

10 Sex Segregation of Workers by Enterprise in Clerical Occupations

Francine D. Blau

In analyzing the presence and persistence of pay differentials between male and female workers, a number of scholars have focused on the prevalence of sex segregation in the labor market as a principal explanatory factor.[1] The existence of sex segregation has generally been deduced from aggregate census data which indicate that a large number of detailed occupational categories tend to be either predominantly male or predominantly female, and that such "segregated" occupations account for a relatively high proportion of the male and female labor forces, respectively. For example, in 1970, 73 percent of female workers (as contrasted with 10 percent of male workers) were in detailed census classifications in which women constituted 50 percent or more of the incumbents; on the other hand, 80 percent of male workers (as contrasted with 16 percent of female workers) were in occupations which were less than 30 percent female.[2] A pay differential in excess of what may be attributed to the productivity-related characteristics of male and female workers is commonly hypothesized to result from this labor market segmentation, in part due to an "overcrowding" phenomenon within the female sector.

The purpose of this chapter is to shed further light on the magnitude of sex segregation in the labor market by exploring an additional dimension of segregation: the extent to which male and female workers who are employed within the same narrowly defined occupational categories are differentially distributed among firms. A finding that sex segregation occurs among workers in the same occupation has considerable relevance for our understanding of the problem of labor market segregation. First, it indicates that census data underestimate the extent to which men and women are in segregated work situations at the enterprise level. Second, if segregation occurs even when male and female labor are close substitutes (i.e., capable of performing the same work), it suggests that powerful forces are operating in the labor market which

I would like to thank P. Doeringer, R. Freeman, C. Jusenius, A. Kohen, R. Nelson, B. Bergmann, and L. Silversin for their helpful comments on earlier drafts of this manuscript. This material was prepared under Grant No. 91-25-71-24 from the Manpower Administration, U.S. Department of Labor, under the authority of Title I of the Manpower Development and Training Act of 1962, as amended. Since researchers undertaking such projects are encouraged to express their own judgment freely, this paper does not necessarily represent the official opinion or policy of the Department of Labor.

tend to produce segregation. This further implies that such forces will not easily be overcome by measures directed solely at altering the supply characteristics of female workers. Third, it raises the possibility that distributional factors are at the root of the earnings disparities between male and female workers, even when they are employed in the same occupational category.

In the first section of the chapter, we more rigorously distinguish these two types of labor market segregation. In the second section, we briefly review the extent of segregation of male and female workers by occupational category. In the third section, we formulate a model to test for the existence of segregation among male and female workers in the same occupational category by establishment of employment, and report our findings for a sample of clerical occupations in three large Northeastern cities.

Types of Labor Market Segregation

Earlier empirical work has focused on what we term *interoccupational segregation*, or differences in the distribution of male and female workers among occupations.[3] The criterion for the existence of this type of segregation is the extent of the divergence between the representation of women in specific occupational categories and their representation in the total labor force—i.e., the greater the divergence, the more segregated the occupation.

Here we are concerned with another dimension of labor market segregation, "intraoccupational segregation," or the divergence between the representation of women in the occupational work force of the individual establishment and their representation in the total occupational labor force. The criterion for the existence of intraoccupational segregation is whether for given occupational categories women tend to work together with women (and men with men) within the same establishment to a significantly greater extent than would prevail if the dictates of chance were observed.

The relationship between interoccupational and intraoccupational segregation can most easily be illustrated by a simple set of examples for a hypothetical two-firm, two-occupation situation, as shown in Table 10-1. N_{mi} and N_{fi} represent the number of men and women respectively in the occupational category in the ith firm, while P_{fi} is the proportion that women comprise of the establishment's occupational work force. The figures under the Census heading are the total numbers of each sex employed in the occupation and the proportion which women constitute of all incumbents of the category. Assuming that women comprise 40 percent of the total labor force, four cases may be distinguished.

In Case 1, there is no segregation of either type. That is, women comprise 40 percent of the labor force in each of the two occupational categories in the aggregate and in both establishments. In Case 2, there is interoccupational

Table 10-1
An Illustration of the Relationship between Interoccupational and Intraoccupational Segregation

	Firm 1			Firm 2			"Census"		
	N_{m1}	N_{f1}	$f1$	N_{m2}	N_{f2}	P_{f1}	N_m	N_f	P_f
Case 1: No Segregation									
Occupation A	60	40	.40	30	20	.40	90	60	.40
Occupation B	6	4	.40	15	10	.40	21	14	.40
Case 2: Inter, No Intra									
Occupation A	10	90	.90	5	45	.90	15	135	.90
Occupation B	45	5	.10	90	10	.10	135	15	.10
Case 3: Intra, No Inter									
Occupation A	0	40	1.00	60	0	0.0	60	40	.40
Occupation B	55	5	.08	5	35	.88	60	40	.40
Case 4: Inter and Intra									
Occupation A	0	80	1.00	20	0	0.0	20	80	.80
Occupation B	5	15	.75	75	5	.07	80	20	.20

segregation, but no intraoccupational segregation; occupation A and occupation B are disproportionately female and disproportionately male respectively. However, the representation of women in each of the occupations within both firms is identical to their representation at the aggregate level. In Case 3, there is intraoccupational segregation, but no interoccupational segregation. At the aggregate level, the representation of women in each occupation is identical to their proportion in the total labor force. However, within the establishment each occupation is either disproportionately male or disproportionately female relative to the representation of each sex in total occupational employment. Within this case, occupation A illustrates complete intraoccupational segregation and occupation B a significant level of this type of segregation. In Case 4, we have the simultaneous presence of both forms of segregation. Women are either overrepresented or underrepresented in each occupation relative to their share of total employment and overrepresented or underrepresented in the establishment's occupational labor force relative to their share of total occupational employment.

Table 10-1 indicates the limits of using aggregate census data to measure labor market segregation. No problems would arise in Cases 1 and 2 where there is no intraoccupational segregation. However, in Cases 3 and 4 where segregation by establishment is present, census data would underestimate the true extent of labor market segregation.

This study is primarily concerned with the extent of intraoccupational segregation. In the measurement of this form of labor market segregation, we take the magnitude of interoccupational segregation, the proportion which women comprise of all workers in the occupational category, as given. Thus intraoccupational segregation may occur either in the presence of interoccupational segregation as in Case 4 of Table 10-1, or in the absence of such segregation by occupation as in Case 3. While the two forms of segregation are thus conceptually independent, it is important to describe, in summary, the extent of interoccupational segregation in order to provide perspective on the broader market context within which intraoccupational segregation takes place. Therefore, in the next section, we briefly describe the degree of sex segregation by occupation in the labor market.

The Extent of Interoccupational Segregation

When considering the magnitude of interoccupational segregation or comparing its level over time, it is often helpful to employ some summary measure of the degree of segregation. One such indicator is the "index of segregation," devised by Duncan and Duncan.[4] It has been used in the measurement of both residential and occupational segregation. The index of segregation is calculated from the detailed census occupational distributions of males and females in the experienced labor force. The index is computed as the sum of the absolute differences between the proportion of the male labor force and the proportion of the female labor force in each census category, divided by 2. It may take on any value between 0 and 100. A value of zero indicates that the distribution of women across occupations is identical to that of men, or equivalently that the proportion of those employed in each occupational category who are female is roughly equal to the share of women in the total labor force. A value of 100 indicates complete segregation, with women employed in completely female categories and men working in entirely male occupations. The actual value of the index may be interpreted as the percentage of women (or men) who would have to change occupations for the employment distribution of the two groups to be identical. In 1970, the value of the index was 65.8 percent,[5] indicating that a substantial portion of the female work force would have had to be reallocated to eliminate the overrepresentation of women in certain occupations and their corresponding underrepresentation in others.

A review of historical trends indicates that not only is interoccupational segregation presently of considerable magnitude, it has also been a persistent and stable characteristic of female employment throughout the present century. According to census data, in both 1900 and 1960, well over half of all employed female workers were in detailed occupational categories in which women comprised 70 percent or more of total occupational employment.[6] Moreover, the value of the index of segregation as computed in each census year between 1900 and 1960 has varied over a small range, 65.6 to 69.0, and has exhibited no secular trend toward a reduction in segregation.[7]

While our data are sufficient to establish a persistent historical pattern, and to give a rough indication of the magnitude of this characteristic of male and female employment, it should be noted that measures based on census data tend to underestimate the extent of interoccupational segregation.

First, the limited number of census listings may result in the combination of jobs which are predominantly male and those which are predominantly female into one apparently integrated occupational category. For example, in the 1950 census, barbers, beauticians, and manicurists formed one job category which was half female. When the data were reclassified, however, so that hairdressers and cosmetologists were listed separately, 92 percent of this group were women.[8]

Similarly, aggregation of occupational employment across industries may also yield a distorted picture. In 1960, 44 percent of all assemblers were women. However, 67 percent of assemblers in electrical equipment, machinery, and supplies were female, as compared to 16 percent in motor vehicle equipment.[9] It is doubtful that workers in these two industries can meaningfully be considered within the same occupation or as competing within the same labor market.

Second, some segregation may be stratified, that is, involve distinctions of rank.[10] Census categories which include both supervisory and nonsupervisory personnel within the same occupational category will not reveal segregation of this type. Moreover, men may be concentrated in the more prestigious and remunerative sectors of an occupation. For example, in retail trade, men tend to dominate the sales work force in the case of high-value commodities, like automobiles, furniture, and appliances, which are sold on a commission basis.[11]

While measures based on census data may to some extent underestimate the magnitude of interoccupational segregation, they do serve to indicate the large differences in the employment distribution of men and women among occupations, as well as the relative stability of this fundamental characteristic of female employment.

Occupational differences form the backdrop against which segregation within occupations by establishment takes place. It is a situation in which, even in the absence of intraoccupational segregation, the predominantly single-sex occupational work group at the enterprise level would be the norm. In this context, intraoccupational segregation may be seen as an additional factor tending to produce occupational specialization by sex within the firm.

The Extent of Intraoccupational Segregation

Were employers indifferent to the sex of workers hired, we would expect that, within occupational categories, men and women would be randomly distributed among firms. That is, only the laws of chance would determine whether a worker hired by the firm were male or female. It may be recalled that the criterion for the existence of intraoccupational segregation is a departure from such random processes. That is, intraoccupational segregation may be said to exist if, for given occupational categories, women work together with women (and men with men) within the same establishment to a significantly greater extent than would prevail if the dictates of chance were observed. Thus, if we were to view the distribution of establishments according to the proportion that women comprise of each firm's occupational work force, this criterion would be met if there were a concentration of establishments in the tails of the distribution, employing relatively high or low proportions of women, higher than would be expected if the laws of chance were observed.

The first and most obvious requirement for applying this criterion empirically is to specify the distribution of establishments by sex composition of employment that would obtain if the sex of the employee hired were the result of a random process. We first develop a model which enables us to specify the distribution of firms with respect to the sex composition of occupational employment under the condition of random hiring. We then compare this "theoretical" distribution of establishments to the actual distribution to determine for each occupational category whether intraoccupational segregation exists.

A Model of Random Hiring

For each occupation and city, we employ the binomial probability distribution to simulate the distribution of firms by sex composition of establishment employment. For occupation h and city l, let:

p = the proportion of the pool of individuals with the requisite occupational skills that is female

q = $1 - p$ = the proportion of the labor pool that is male

x_i = the number of women employed in occupation h in firm i

n_i = the total number of employees in occupation h in firm i

p_i = $x_i/n_i \times 100$ = the percentage that women comprise of all workers in occupation h in firm i

Then, x_i may be viewed as the outcome of n_i trials of an experiment where each trial consists of selecting an individual at random from the labor pool when the probability of obtaining a woman is p and the probability of obtaining a man is *q*. The binomial probability distribution may be employed to obtain the probability that x_i takes on any specified value:[a]

$$f_i(x = x_i) = \binom{n_i}{x_i} p^{x_i} q^{(n_i - x_i)} \tag{10.1}$$

In order to apply the model, establishments were grouped according to the number of employees in the firm's occupational labor force. Each size category is composed of firms with the same value of n_i. The possible outcomes, x_i, were grouped into twelve categories according to the value of p_i. The twelve sex composition categories are: $p_i = 0$, $0 < p_i < 10$, $10 \leqslant p_i < 20$, $20 \leqslant p_i < 30$, ... , $90 \leqslant p_i < 100$, $p_i = 100$.

Let

n_i = the number of firms in the *j*th size category

p_{jk} = the probability that a firm selected at random from the *j*th size class has a value of p_i that falls in the *k*th sex composition category

e_{jk} = the expected number of firms in the *j*th size class and the *k*th sex composition category

E_k = the total expected number of firms in the *k*th sex composition category

P_k = the probability of obtaining a firm in the *k*th sex composition category, given the size distribution of firms

then, p_{jk} may be computed from (10.1) as:

$$p_{jk} = f(x_a \leqslant x \leqslant x_b) \sum_{i=a}^{b} f_i(x = x_i) \tag{10.2}$$

Using the standard formula for expected value, e_{jk} may be computed as

$$e_{jk} = p_{jk} \cdot n_j \tag{10.3}$$

The e_{jk} represent the theoretical distribution of firms by the sex composition of establishment employment disaggregated by size category. To find the theoretical frequencies for the N firms in our sample, we may sum across size categories:

---

[a]To be completely accurate, we would have to postulate the firm's sample from the labor pool not only at random, but with replacement since it is only in this case that the outcomes of the n_i experiments can be independent. We shall return to this point.

$$E_k = \sum_j e_{jk} \tag{10.4}$$

And the theoretical probabilities for the sample may be defined as

$$P_k = \frac{E_k}{N} \tag{10.5}$$

Finally, the chi-square "goodness-of-fit" test may be employed to determine whether the theoretical probabilities are correct or the disparity between the observed and the expected frequencies is large enough to reject the hypothesis of randomness.

If we wish to examine the distribution of male and female workers among establishments that would prevail under the condition of random hiring, we may estimate the worker distributions directly from the theoretical establishment distributions. Let

n_{ij}	= the number of employees in the occupational work force in firms included in the jth size class
$\bar{p}_{ik}$	= the arithmetic mean of the p_i included in the kth sex composition category divided by 100
f_{jk} and m_{jk}	= the expected number of women and men, respectively, employed in establishments which fall in the jth size class and kth sex composition category
F_k and M_k	= the total expected number of women and men, respectively, employed in firms included in the kth sex composition category

Then, we may approximate f_{jk} and m_{jk} in the following way:

$$f_{jk} = e_{jk} \cdot n_{ij} \cdot \bar{P}_{ik} \tag{10.6}$$

$$m_{jk} = e_{jk} \cdot n_{ij} \cdot f_{jk} \tag{10.7}$$

And E_k and M_k may be obtained by summation:

$$F_k = \sum_j f_{jk}$$

$$M_k = \sum_j m_{jk}$$

While the worker distributions yield no new information in terms of possible hypothesis testing, they can be employed to compute the index of segregation, in this case a summary measure of the degree of intraoccupational segregation.

Conceptual Problems in the Application of the Model

Conceptually, the application of this model to establishment hiring poses certain problems of interdependence of outcomes. No difficulty would arise if firms sampled with replacement from the labor pool. However, since it is not reasonable to assume that firms in fact do this, it may be helpful to consider at this point whether problems of interdependence are serious enough to cast doubt on the ability of the theoretical distribution to serve as a fair and reasonable test for the existence of intraoccupational segregation.

The first area in which a question of interdependence arises is in the computation of p_{jk} in Equation (10.2). It may be recalled that we viewed the number of women employed in the establishment, x_i, as the outcome of n_i trials of an experiment, where each trial consists of selecting an individual at random from the labor pool. If firms were to sample from the labor pool with replacement, p, the probability of selecting a woman would be constant from trial to trial, and the outcome of each trial could be viewed as independent. However, when the firm samples without replacement from the labor pool, p is not constant, but rather changes slightly from trial to trial as either a man or a woman is selected. This type of interdependence could be modeled with the hypergeometric distribution. However, the larger the total universe (in this case the total labor pool) relative to the sample size (in this case the size of the firm), the smaller is the divergence between the results obtained with the hypergeometric distribution and those obtained with the binomial distribution. It is doubtful that even the largest firms are sufficiently large relative to the labor pool to warrant the use of the hypergeomatric distribution. Moreover, the utilization of the hypergeometric distribution poses its own problems, the most serious being the necessity of specifying and estimating the size of the total universe or labor pool.

A second area in which a question of interdependence arises is in the computation of e_{jk} in Equation (10.3). Such a computation gives us the expected outcome of n_j replications of the experiment in which n_i workers are selected at random from the labor pool when the constant probability of obtaining a woman is p. Clearly such a computation requires independence of outcome of the n_j experiments. However, in the real world there would be some measure of interdependence of outcomes among all firms, inside and outside the sample, and within and between size categories. The nature of this interdependence is difficult to specify. Certainly the labor pool, those individuals with the requisite occupational skills who are available for employment, includes some presently employed workers as well as those presently unemployed. Indeed, some workers in the labor pool may be presently employed in other occupations as well as by other firms. Thus, we do not have a simple form of interdependence whereby a worker employed by one firm is completely unavailable to other firms and vice versa. While it is easy enough to imagine scenarios in which interdependence among establishments would be significant, most would involve a substantial departure from random behavior on the part of at least some of the firms and/or substantial differentials in interfirm mobility between male and female workers. Thus it was felt that considerations of interdependence among firms did not seriously challenge the ability of the model to serve as a fair and reasonable test of random selection in hiring.

An additional conceptual problem is raised when we consider the temporal dimension of the hiring process. The representation of women in the occupational labor force of the establishment is the outcome of a selection procedure which takes place over a considerable, although unknown, period of time. It is possible that p has varied over time and that some of the interfirm differential in female employment is due to differences in the time period when the bulk of the establishment's occupational work force was recruited. In this sense, our estimate of p, the proportion that women presently comprise of total occupational employment, may be considered as reflecting the average representation of women in the labor pool over time rather than being an accurate reflection of the availability of women each time the firm hires an additional worker. However, it is doubtful that this factor could account for a consistent pattern of intraoccupational segregation in a variety of occupational categories.

The Magnitude of Intraoccupational Segregation

In order to apply the foregoing model to assess the magnitude of intraoccupational segregation, it is necessary to specify an estimate of p, the female proportion of the total labor supply pool in each occupation. We have here estimated p as the proportion women represent of all those actually employed in the occupation in each city.[b] The group of workers presently employed in an occupational category is an exceedingly narrow definition of the pool of individuals with the requisite occupational skills. It may be argued that in the presence of discrimination the representation of women among those employed

---

[b]p was estimated directly from our sample. Since the sample of establishments used by the Bureau of Labor Statistics in the *Area Wage Surveys* is a stratified and not a random sample, each observation was given its appropriate weight.

in an occupation may differ from their representation in the total labor pool. However, our definition of intraoccupational segregation takes the extent of interoccupational segregation (the proportion that women comprise of total employment in each occupational category) as given. Thus, this estimate of p is consistent with our definition.

The model was applied to six clerical and related occupations in each of three large Northeastern cities: Boston, New York, and Philadelphia. The occupations included in the study are shown in Table 10-2. Since a number of the occupations have been further subdivided into skill classes, there are a total of nine separate occupational classifications. These office occupations were selected from a larger sample of clerical jobs on the basis that they contained a large enough representation of men and women to make an examination of intraoccupational segregation feasible. Results are reported for cities in which observations were available on at least 50 firms. With the exception of the messenger (office boy/girl) category, the classifications are relatively narrow and carefully defined. While it is not possible in the absence of additional information on the personal characteristics of workers in each category to consider the quality of labor within the groupings as completely homogeneous, the narrowness of the classifications makes it reasonable to assume that the workers employed in each of the occupation-skill classes are relatively close substitutes. Thus, we would not expect skill differences to place serious restrictions on access to firms.

The expected distribution and actual distribution of firms by the twelve sex composition categories are shown in Table 10-3. The expected distributions were derived from the application of the model of random hiring. The actual distributions report the distribution of firms in the sample by sex composition category. The proportion which women comprise of all workers in the occupational category in each city is shown in parentheses.

Table 10-2
Occupational Categories Included in the Study

Accounting Clerk

    Class A

    Class B

Order Clerk

Payroll Clerk

Office Boy/Girl

Tabulating Machine Operator

    Class A

    Class B

Computer Operator

    Class B

    Class C

Table 10-3
Expected and Actual Distribution of Firms by Percent Female, Selected Cities, and Occupations

	Percent Female												
Occupation	0	1-9	10-19	20-29	30-39	40-49	50-59	60-69	70-79	80-89	90-99	100	Total
Accounting Clerk Class A													
Boston (*P* = .694)													
Expected number	14.82	0.0	0.12	1.63	4.54	2.50	22.74	24.17	19.65	11.47	0.68	51.66	154
Actual number	23.00	1.00	0.0	3.00	10.00	1.00	10.00	9.00	4.00	5.00	4.00	84.00	154
New York (*P* = .648)													
Expected number	41.37	0.0	0.45	4.96	10.74	9.90	61.55	51.48	32.01	18.71	1.17	102.66	335
Actual number	52.00	1.00	5.00	10.00	16.00	10.00	26.00	16.00	16.00	13.00	4.00	166.00	335
Philadelphia (*P* = .731)													
Expected number	16.14	0.0	0.04	1.22	3.12	2.48	21.34	20.82	18.91	15.37	1.06	70.49	171
Actual number	29.00	0.0	1.00	4.00	4.00	2.00	11.00	9.00	7.00	11.00	3.00	90.00	171
Class B													
Boston (*P* = .925)													
Expected number	3.44	0.0	0.0	0.01	0.21	0.05	3.60	3.89	4.49	19.17	17.58	109.60	162
Actual number	5.00	0.0	0.0	0.0	2.00	1.00	1.00	5.00	5.00	7.00	11.00	125.00	162
New York (*P* = .759)													
Expected number	19.91	0.0	0.07	2.09	5.66	2.89	33.02	40.79	51.86	39.24	6.48	120.00	322
Actual number	24.00	1.00	2.00	7.00	12.00	3.00	24.00	10.00	22.00	18.00	12.00	187.00	322
Philadelphia (*P* = .883)													
Expected number	5.85	0.0	0.0	0.11	0.53	0.17	8.30	6.50	10.35	24.91	9.96	103.37	170
Actual number	10.0	0.0	1.00	2.00	3.00	2.00	5.00	2.00	2.00	8.00	4.00	131.00	170

Order Clerk

Boston (P = .615)

Expected number	8.73	0.0	0.23	2.49	2.61	2.41	13.72	7.56	8.36	3.01	0.09	17.79	67
Actual number	13.00	0.0	4.00	0.0	0.0	0.0	4.00	0.0	1.00	3.00	0.0	42.00	67

New York (P = .833)

Expected number	4.36	0.0	0.01	0.24	0.63	0.36	7.61	6.47	12.39	18.21	4.65	51.08	106
Actual number	12.00	0.0	2.00	2.00	1.00	1.00	3.00	5.00	0.0	3.00	1.00	76.00	106

Philadelphia (P = .712)

Expected number	6.20	0.0	0.03	0.40	1.98	1.01	6.69	10.23	6.46	5.37	0.20	23.43	62
Actual number	10.00	1.00	1.00	0.0	3.00	0.0	1.00	2.00	1.00	0.0	0.0	43.00	62

Payroll Clerk

Boston (P = .927)

Expected number	4.25	0.0	0.0	0.02	0.25	0.02	4.39	3.58	3.24	5.57	2.82	108.87	133
Actual number	7.00	0.0	0.0	2.00	1.00	1.00	2.00	0.0	2.00	2.00	0.0	116.00	133

New York (P = .855)

Expected number	14.85	0.0	0.0	0.22	1.83	0.26	10.64	14.25	11.51	16.32	3.77	149.35	223
Actual number	24.00	0.0	1.00	2.00	2.00	1.00	4.00	13.00	4.00	2.00	0.0	170.00	223

Philadelphia (P = .830)

Expected number	15.21	0.0	0.0	0.16	0.76	0.13	12.03	5.02	6.52	6.55	1.26	107.35	155
Actual	12.00	0.0	0.0	1.00	2.00	0.0	2.00	2.00	1.00	0.0	1.00	133.00	155

Office Boy/Girl

Boston (P = .327)

Expected number	33.70	0.24	3.87	12.30	13.40	5.71	12.62	3.86	1.12	0.24	0.0	11.93	99
Actual number	56.00	1.00	3.00	2.00	3.00	1.00	4.00	2.00	2.00	3.00	2.00	20.00	99

Table 10-3 (cont.)

Occupation							Percent Female							Total
	0	1-9	10-19	20-29	30-39	40-49	50-59	60-69	70-79	80-89	90-99	100		
New York (*P* = .248)														
Expected number	107.99	2.66	23.31	50.21	33.71	10.72	19.68	6.98	1.08	0.30	0.0	22.36		279
Actual number	184.00	5.00	9.00	13.00	6.00	2.00	7.00	7.00	4.00	2.00	5.00	35.00		279
Philadelphia (*P* = .400)														
Expected number	37.78	0.03	2.19	10.45	14.74	9.11	20.64	9.18	2.28	1.03	0.0	20.57		128
Actual number	71.00	0.0	1.00	5.00	6.00	3.00	5.00	3.00	3.00	3.00	2.00	26.00		128
Tabulating Machine Operator Class A														
New York (*P* = .380)														
Expected number	15.02	0.05	1.25	4.45	6.14	4.56	10.23	2.34	0.38	0.33	0.0	7.27		52
Actual number	36.00	1.00	1.00	0.0	1.00	0.0	0.0	1.00	0.0	0.0	1.00	11.00		52
Class B														
New York (*P* = .271)														
Expected number	25.38	0.39	3.44	11.07	8.62	2.44	6.51	1.56	0.32	0.07	0.0	6.20		66
Actual number	45.00	2.00	3.00	2.00	1.00	3.00	2.00	0.0	1.00	0.0	0.0	7.00		66
Computer Operator Class B														
Boston (*P* = .069)														
Expected number	61.78	5.29	5.20	3.84	2.54	0.27	2.35	0.19	0.01	0.0	0.0	1.53		83
Actual number	67.00	5.00	2.00	1.00	1.00	0.0	1.00	0.0	0.0	0.0	0.0	6.00		83

New York (P = .101)													
Expected number	108.06	12.11	14.80	10.21	5.91	0.78	7.47	0.66	0.05	0.0	0.0	4.95	165
Actual number	136.00	4.00	3.00	4.00	3.00	0.0	3.00	2.00	0.0	0.0	0.0	10.00	165
Philadelphia (P = .103)													
Expected number	71.30	5.74	11.21	7.71	5.03	0.41	5.39	0.52	0.04	0.0	0.0	2.66	110
Actual number	89.00	2.00	3.00	2.00	2.00	0.0	4.00	1.00	0.0	0.0	0.0	7.00	110
Class C													
New York (P = .106)													
Expected number	53.09	3.23	5.54	4.67	2.34	0.79	4.34	0.30	0.01	0.01	0.0	2.69	77
Actual number	63.00	2.00	2.00	1.00	1.00	0.0	0.0	1.00	0.0	1.00	0.0	6.00	77
Philadelphia (P = .167)													
Expected number	30.95	1.07	6.14	5.20	3.50	0.69	3.53	0.52	0.07	0.01	0.0	3.32	55
Actual number	40.00	1.00	0.0	2.00	1.00	0.0	4.00	0.0	0.0	1.00	0.0	6.00	55

Source: Computed from unpublished Bureau of Labor Statistics data collected for the *Area Wage Surveys* between April and November 1970.

Note: More rigorously, if p_{hi} is the percentage that women comprise of total employment within occupation h in establishment i, then the twelve sex composition categories are defined as: $p_{hi} = 0$, $0 < p_{hi} < 10$, $10 \leq p_{hi} < 20$, $20 \leq p_{hi} < 30, \ldots, 90 \leq p_{hi} < 100$, $p_{hi} = 100$.

As can be seen by inspection of the expected distributions, even under conditions of random hiring, a large number of firms would tend to employ a relatively high or low proportion of women compared to female representation in total occupational employment. For a given value of p, the proportion which women comprise of all workers in the occupational labor pool, the distribution of establishments among size classes is the most important factor in producing this clustering. Size of the firm affects the expected distributions in two ways. First, when n_i (the total number of workers employed in the occupational category in the ith firm) is small, p_i (the percentage that women comprise of all workers in the occupational category in the ith firm) can take on only a limited number of values due to indivisibilities. Thus, for example, when n_i equals 2, there are only three possible values for p_i: 0, 50, and 100. Second, as n_i or the number of trials is increased, the expected distribution of establishments would tend to cluster more tightly around p. However, for smaller values of n_i, the expected distribution is more diffuse. (This is a simple application of the Law of Large Numbers.) In most cases, there are a relatively large number of firms with small values of n_i, and thus these firms heavily influence the total expected distributions of establishments.

A comparison of the expected and actual distributions in Table 10-3 shows that the actual number of firms in the tails of the distribution (employing relatively high or low proportions of women) exceeds the expected number in all cases. The application of the chi-square goodness-of-fit test indicates that these differences are statistically significant at the .5 percent level in the vast majority of cases, while all the differences are significant at the 5 percent level. (See Table 10A-1 for the computed chi-square values.)

The impact of the establishment distributions on male and female employment is shown in Table 10-4. The concept of the index of segregation is similar to that employed in the study of interoccupational segregation. In this case the index measures differences in the distribution of men and women among firms. As stated earlier, the index may take on any value between 0 and 100. In the present context, a value of zero indicates that within the occupational category the distribution of women among the establishments in the sample closely approximates the distribution of male workers. In other words, in each establishment the proportion of those in the occupation who are women is roughly the same as the female share of total occupational employment. A value of 100 indicates complete segregation, with women employed entirely in firms which hire only female workers in the occupation, and men working in establishments which employ only male workers in the occupation.

The actual index of segregation is computed on the basis of the employment distributions of male and female workers in the sample. The expected index of segregation utilizes the theoretical distributions derived from the application of the model of random hiring. While a fairly large degree of segregation would be expected even on the basis of random hiring (due to the large representation of firms with a small value of n_i), the differences between the actual and expected values of the index (shown in the last column of Table 10-4) are generally of

Table 10-4

Actual and Expected Indices of Segregation, Selected Cities, and Occupations

| Occupation | City | Index of Segregation | | |
		Actual[a]	Expected[b]	Difference
Accounting Clerk				
Class A	Boston	72.62	28.92	43.70
	New York	59.54	27.77	31.77
	Philadelphia	72.58	32.32	40.26
Class B	Boston	59.53	43.91	15.62
	New York	58.69	28.06	30.63
	Philadelphia	82.22	34.60	47.62
Order Clerk	Boston	85.47	35.85	49.62
	New York	84.21	35.25	48.95
	Philadelphia	90.05	28.68	61.37
Payroll Clerk	Boston	92.25	72.87	19.38
	New York	82.66	56.65	26.01
	Philadelphia	91.72	59.92	31.80
Office Boy/Girl	Boston	74.65	31.31	43.34
	New York	82.22	20.60	61.62
	Philadelphia	65.12	33.76	31.36
Tabulating Machine Operator				
Class A	New York	84.65	26.45	58.19
Class B	New York	77.11	23.91	53.20
Computer Operator				
Class B	Boston	61.45	54.03	7.41
	New York	82.08	47.48	34.60
	Philadelphia	85.79	54.00	31.79
Class C	New York	70.84	49.46	21.38
	Philadelphia	87.72	44.45	43.27

[a]The actual index of segregation utilizes the employment distributions of male and female workers from the sample.

[b]The expected index of segregation employs the theoretical distributions.

Note: Within each city, the index of segregation is computed in the following way: Let p_{hi} equal the percentage that women comprise of the labor force in occupation h within establishment i. Establishments are grouped into twelve sex composition categories depending on the value of p_{hi}. The categories are: $p_{hi} = 0$, $0 < p_{hi} < 10$, $10 \leqslant p_{hi} < 20$, $20 \leqslant p_{hi} < 30, \ldots, 90 \leqslant p_{hi} < 100$, $p_{hi} = 100$. Let f_{hk} equal the percentage of all female workers and m_{hk} equal the percentage of all male workers in occupation h who are employed in firms included in the kth sex composition category. The index of segregation for occupation h is then

$$S_h = \frac{\sum\limits_{k=1}^{12} \left\{ f_{hk} - m_{hk} \right\}}{2}$$

Source: Computed from unpublished Bureau of Labor Statistics data collected for the *Area Wage Surveys* between April and November 1970.

considerable magnitude. Thus, a sizable proportion of women (or men) would have to be reallocated among firms for the actual distributions to approximate a situation of random hiring on the basis of sex.

Conclusion

Our findings for a sample of clerical and related occupations in three large Northeastern cities reveal a strong and consistent pattern of intraoccupational segregation. Thus it appears that even when men and women have similar skills and abilities as evinced by their participation in the same narrowly defined occupational categories, they are segregated by establishment of employment. Since these differences in the distribution of men and women among firms appear to be present in a range of office occupations, including categories in which women predominate, the problem of the differential access of men and women to firms cannot be viewed as restricted to a small number of relatively prestigious occupations.

The results reported here suggest that sex segregation in the labor market is not limited to differences in the distribution of men and women among occupations. An analogous problem exists within occupational categories in which both men and women are employed in terms of the distribution of male and female workers among firms. Thus, from a policy point of view, it is not sufficient simply to advocate the integration of presently segregated occupational categories through altering the supply characteristics of female workers. The factors on the demand side which tend to segment the male and female labor forces among the dimension of establishment of employment must also be investigated and combatted.[12]

Notes

1. For examples of the historical antecedents of this approach, see Millicent G. Fawcett, "Equal Pay for Equal Work," *Economic Journal*, 28 (March, 1918): 1-6; and F.Y. Edgeworth, "Equal Pay to Men and Women for Equal Work," *Economic Journal*, 32 (December, 1922): 431-457. For examples of current theoretical and empirical support for this view, see Barbara R. Bergmann, "Occupational Segregation, Wages and Profits When Employers Discriminate by Race or Sex," unpublished working paper (January, 1971); Victor R. Fuchs, "Differences in Hourly Earnings between Men and Women," *Monthly Labor Review*, 94 (May, 1971): 9-15; Francine Blau (Weisskoff), " 'Women's Place' in the Labor Market," *American Economic Review*, 62 (May, 1972): 161-166; Harriet Zellner, "Discrimination against Women, Occupational Segregation and the Relative Wage," *American Economic Review* 62 (May, 1972): 157-160;

Isabel V. Sawhill, "The Economics of Discrimination against Women: Some New Findings," *Journal of Human Resources* 8 (Summer, 1973): 383-397.

2. Computed from U.S. Department of Commerce, Bureau of the Census, *U.S. Census of the Population, Detailed Characteristics*, Final Report (PC(1)-D1, U.S. Summary (Washington, D.C.: Government Printing Office, 1973), Table 221, pp. 718-724.

3. For empirical studies of interoccupational segregation, see Valerie Kincade Oppenheimer, *The Female Labor Force in the United States: Demographic Factors Governing Its Growth and Changing Composition* (Berkeley: Institute of International Studies, University of California, 1970), Chapter 3; Edward Gross, "Plus Ça Change. . . ? The Sexual Structure of Occupations over Time," *Social Problems* 16 (Fall, 1968): 198-208; *Economic Report of the President, 1973* (Washington, D.C.: Government Printing Office, 1973), Table 33, pp. 155-159.

4. Otis Dudley Duncan and Beverly Duncan, "Residential Distribution and Occupational Stratification," *American Journal of Sociology* 60 (March, 1955): 493-503. For a discussion of the mathematical properties and interrelationships of alternative measures of segregation, see Otis Dudley Duncan and Beverly Duncan, "A Methodological Analysis of Segregation Indexes," *American Sociological Review* 20 (April, 1955): 210-217.

5. Computed from U.S. Department of Commerce, Bureau of the Census, *U.S. Census of the Population, Detailed Characteristics*, Final Report PC(1)-D1, U.S. Summary, Table 221, pp. 718-724.

6. Valerie Kincade Oppenheimer, "The Sex-Labeling of Jobs," *Industrial Relations* 7 (May 1968), Table 6, p. 220.

7. Gross, "Plus Ça Change. . . ?" pp. 202-207. Using comparable occupational categories in both years, the Council of Economic Advisers did find a small decrease of 3.1 percentage points in the index of segregation between 1960 and 1970. See *Economic Report of the President*, 1973, p. 155.

8. Oppenheimer, *The Female Labor Force in the United States*, p. 67.

9. Ibid.

10. See, for example, Harold Wilensky, "Women's Work: Economic Growth Ideology, Structure," *Industrial Relations* 7 (May 1968): 241. Wilensky argues that when men enter predominantly female professions (e.g., elementary or secondary school teaching, social work, librarianship, hospital administration), they tend to be disproportionately represented in supervisory positions.

11. Theodore Caplow, *The Sociology of Work* (Minneapolis: University of Minnesota Press, 1954), p. 232.

12. For a further analysis of the causes of intraoccupational segregation and its relationship to pay differences among male and female workers in the same occupational category, see Francine D. Blau, "Pay Differentials and Differences in the Distribution of Employment of Male and Female Office Worker," unpublished doctoral dissertation, Harvard University, 1975.

Appendix 10A

Table 10A-1
Chi-square Values

	P	N	Chi Sq(1)	Chi Sq(2)	k
Accounting Clerk					
Class A					
Boston	0.694	154	43.51[a]	65.06[a]	9
New York	0.648	335	70.46[a]	118.53[a]	9
Philadelphia	0.731	171	28.06[a]	37.73[a]	7
Class B					
Boston	0.925	162	8.77[a]	13.44[c]	7
New York	0.759	322	66.01[a]	105.62[a]	7
Philadelphia	0.883	170	26.98[a]	36.89[a]	7
Order Clerk					
Boston	0.615	67	55.07[a]	61.59[a]	9
New York	0.833	106	46.52[a]	53.84[a]	7
Philadelphia	0.712	62	35.55[a]	41.05[a]	7
Payroll Clerk					
Boston	0.927	133	7.16[b]	11.78[c]	7
New York	0.855	223	23.60[a]	30.51[a]	7
Philadelphia	0.830	155	22.32[a]	23.73[a]	7
Office Boy/Girl					
Boston	0.327	99	37.49[a]	49.43[a]	8
New York	0.248	279	113.51[a]	142.90[a]	8
Philadelphia	0.400	128	52.09[a]	66.09[a]	9
Tabulating Machine Operator					
Class A					
New York	0.380	52	51.79[a]	55.50[a]	8
Class B					
New York	0.271	66	27.38[a]	33.51[a]	8
Computer Operator					
Class B					
Boston	0.069	83	18.27[a]	19.69[a]	7
New York	0.101	165	33.31[a]	34.18[a]	7
Philadelphia	0.103	110	24.96[a]	26.27[a]	7

Table 10A-1 (cont.)

Class C

New York	0.106	77	14.17[a]	14.49[c]	7
Philadelphia	0.167	55	11.45[a]	14.72[c]	7

[a]Significant at the .5 percent level.
[b]Significant at the 1 percent level.
[c]Significant at the 5 percent level.

Note: To compute Chi Sq(1), the expected and actual frequencies were combined into three categories: $p_i = 0$, $0 < p_i < 100$, $p_i = 100$. To compute Chi Sq(2), the expected and actual frequencies were combined into k categories such that there was no category for which the expected frequency was less than 1.

Source: Computed from Table 10-3.

11

Woman's Place Is at the Typewriter: The Feminization of the Clerical Labor Force

Margery Davies

A large proportion of the recent historical research about women in the labor force has focused on industrial workers, while relatively little attention has been given to clerical workers. However, in 1968 for example, over 40 percent of women in the U.S. labor force were employed as clerical and sales workers, while only 16.5 percent were employed in the industrial work force (U.S. Department of Labor, Women's Bureau, 1969, p. 90).

One explanation for the seemingly disproportionate attention given to women industrial workers is that, through strikes and union organizing, they have drawn attention to themselves. For instance, there would probably be relatively little information about the workers in the Lawrence, Massachusetts, textile mills if the operatives, female and male, had not gone out on strike in 1912. Clerical workers, on the other hand, have had neither numerous strikes nor strong unions.

Another factor which explains the emphasis on the industrial labor force is the central position which the industrial proletariat holds in many Marxist analyses of the working class in capitalist societies. In recent years, however, debate has sprung up over the composition of the working class in the United States and its role in social change. Many people now argue that regardless of any theoretical centrality of the industrial proletariat, for most purposes of historical analysis or especially for practical political purposes, a much broader concept of the working class must be employed. In support of this position, it is possible to point to the similarities between factories and large offices and to refer to a "secretarial proletariat." In addition, there is a revitalization of union and extra-union organizing drives among clerical workers in cities such as Boston, Hartford, New York, Chicago, and San Francisco.

This chapter stems from my acceptance of the position that, for most purposes, it is desirable to broaden our conception of the working class to include workers other than those in industrial positions. In particular, there are millions of low-level clerical workers, most of them women, who form an important segment of the working class.

The essay is historical in scope and focuses on the feminization of the clerical labor force. Women now form the majority of the clerical work force, but this was not always the case. How did women enter and come to dominate clerical work? How did the ideology with respect to women office workers change? What are the connections between a sexual segmentation of the clerical labor force and hierarchical relations in the office? The first step in answering these questions is to look at the "nineteenth-century office."[a]

The Nineteenth-Century Office

Mr. Vhole's office, in disposition retiring and in situation retired, is squeezed up in a corner, and blinks at a dead wall. Three feet of knotty floored dark passage bring the client to Mr. Vhole's jet black door, in an angle profoundly dark on the brightest midsummer morning, and encumbered by a black bulk-head of cellerage staircase, against which belated civilians generally strike their brows. Mr. Vhole's chambers are on so small a scale, that one clerk can open the door without getting off his stool, while the other who elbows him at the same desk has equal facilities for poking the fire. A smell as of unwholesome sheep, blending with the smell of must and dust, is referable to the nightly (and often daily) consumption of mutton fat in candles, and to the fretting of parchment forms and skins in greasy drawers. The atmosphere is otherwise stale and close. (Dickens, 1853, p. 415)

---

[a]Concrete information about female office workers is not easy to find. In a comprehensive bibliographical *Guide to Business History*, Henrietta Larson points out that "it is significant that the works dealing with the subject [office management] are concerned largely with "systems" and machines—the office worker has been left in neglected obscurity" (Larson, 1948, pp. 771-772).

There are a few analytical studies of office workers, the most notable of which are David Lockwood's *The Blackcoated Worker* and C. Wright Mills' *White Collar: The American Middle Classes*. Grace D. Coyle focuses on women in offices and the kind of work they do in "Women in the Clerical Occupations" in *The Annals of the American Academy of Political and Social Science*, 143 (May, 1929); *Fortune* published a series of articles on "Women in Business" in 1935; the Women's Bureau of the U.S. Department of Labor has issued a number of bulletins on office workers. In addition, there is quite a long list of books addressed to women which tell them how to be better secretaries: the main point of these manuals seems to be that women should be certain to please their (male) bosses and that they should be neat and accurate about any number of office tasks. And dotted throughout the prominent women's magazines are articles about the "business woman."

Finally, there are some fictional works which provide a certain amount of insight into office work. "Bartleby" (1856) by Herman Melville is set in a Wall Street lawyer's office of the 1850s and describes the men who work there as copyists; *Alice Adams* (1921) by Booth Tarkington is about the daughter of a white-collar employee who is forced to give up her hopes of joining the upper-class social clique in town, accept her own middle-class status, and finally climb the "begrimed stairway" of the local business college in preparation for becoming a "working girl."

But all in all there is very little information about the history of female clerical workers. However, there are bits and pieces of evidence upon which this chapter is based.

For the purposes of this discussion, the term *nineteenth-century office* will be used to describe those office structures which existed prior to the widespread monopolization and bureaucratization of capitalist corporations, a process which was well underway in the United States by the end of the nineteenth century. "The modern office" will be used to describe the structures which developed after that bureaucratization. The description of the nineteenth century office which follows is based primarily on David Lockwood's *The Blackcoated Worker* and on C. Wright Mills' *White Collar: The American Middle Classes*.

Two of the basic characteristics of nineteenth-century offices, in the United States as well as in Dickensian England, are that they were small and staffed almost exclusively by men. Census data for 1870, for example, show that out of 76,639 office workers in the United States, women numbered only 1869; men were 97.5 percent of the clerical labor force (Hooks, 1947, Tables IIA and IIB). With the exception of a few banks, insurance companies, and governmental branches, most offices in the United States prior to the Civil War usually contained about two or three clerks. This is not surprising, since most capitalist firms were also relatively small until the last decades of the nineteenth century. For example, in *Bartleby* (1856), Herman Melville described a Wall Street lawyer's office of the 1850s which consisted of the lawyer, three copyists, and an errand boy.

The small size of offices at this time meant that the relationship between employer and employee tended to be a very personalized one. The clerks worked under the direct supervision, and often the direct eyesight, of their employers. Although the tasks of a clerk were generally well defined—the job of the copyists in *Bartleby* was to transcribe legal documents—they were also often asked to do numerous other tasks by their employers. It was clearly the employer who set the limits of the clerk's job—there was no question here of the clerk being ruled by the inexorable pace of a machine.

The personal benevolence of an employer could go a long way toward making the hierarchical relations within an office more tolerable. An employer who spoke nicely to his clerks, let them leave early if they were feeling sick, or gave them a Christmas goose helped to create working conditions against which the clerks were not likely to rebel. By treating his clerks with kindness or politeness, a paternalistic employer was also likely to be able to get them to work harder for him.

This personalization of the work relationship between the clerk and his employer in the nineteenth-century office lies at the root of the phenomenon of employees being "devoted to the firm." A clerk who spent 40 or 50 years of his life working for the same small office of an insurance company did not necessarily work so long and so hard out of a belief in the importance of promoting that particular company's kind of insurance. The source of the devotion of this hypothetical employee was much more likely the network of personal relations he had built up in the office over the years. It was probably more important to the employee to "produce" a good working relationship with his boss, with whom he was in constant contact, than to produce, for example, improvements in the insurance company's filing system. Needless to say, that good working relationship no doubt depended in part on the employee's producing improvements in the filing system. But whether the employee cared more about the selling of insurance or his personal relationship with his employer, the end result tended to be the same: the clerk became a "devoted employee of the firm" who was not likely to rebel or go out on strike.

Not all clerks in the nineteenth-century office spent all their working days in clerical positions. A clerkship also served as an apprenticeship for a young man who was "learning the business" before he moved on to a managerial position. These young men were often nephews, sons, or grandsons of the firm's managers and owners—the "family business" trained its sons by having them work as clerks for a period of time. Most clerks, however, ended up with gold watches instead of managerial posts in return for their years of devoted service.

Thus the clerks in an office at any particular time came from different class backgrounds and were likely to have very different occupational futures. Sons of entrepreneurs and professionals would work as clerks for only a short period of time before going on to managerial jobs. Men from the working classes, sons of artisans, or low-level clerks, would probably work as clerks for the rest of their lives; few would be promoted to managerial positions.

Political-Economic Changes

In the last few decades of the nineteenth century, American corporations underwent a period of rapid growth and consolidation. These changes, which marked the rise of modern industrial capitalism, had been signaled by developments in banks, insurance companies, and public utilities; they had spread to manufacturing enterprises by the turn of the century.[b] As business operations became more complex, there was a large increase in correspondence, record-keeping, and office work in general. This expansion of record-keeping and the proliferation of communications both within and between firms created a demand for an expanded clerical labor force. In 1880 there were 504,454 office workers who constituted 3 percent of the labor force; by 1890 there were 750,150 office workers.[c] The number of office workers has been increasing ever since (see Table 11-2). In order to fill the need for clerical workers, employers turned to the large pool of educated female labor.

As early as the 1820s, women had been receiving public high school educations: Worcester, Massachusetts, opened a public high school for girls in 1824; Boston and New York City did so in 1826 (Baker, 1964, p. 57).[d] In 1880,

[b]See Alfred Chandler, *Strategy and Structure*, Cambridge, Mass.: M.I.T. Press, 1962. Also see Stephen Hymer, "The Multinational Corporation and the Law of Uneven Development" in Jagdish Bhagwati (ed.), *Economics and the World Order*, MacMillan Company, 1972.

[c]Bureau of the Census, Department of Commerce and Labor. Special Report of the 12th Census: *Occupations at the 12th Census.* Washington, D.C., 1904. Data are for "number of persons engaged in specified occupations." *Office workers* includes bookkeepers and accountants, clerks and copyists, and stenographers and typewriters [typists].

[d]Baker argues that girls were given high school educations because the number of women teachers was increasing: "Men were being attracted by business opportunities and skilled trades, and the phenomenal growth of public schools created an alarming shortage of teachers. [...] But relief from the scarcity of male teachers of course required that girls as well as boys be taught" (p. 57). However, the fact that so many girls got high school

13,029 women graduated from high school in the United States, as compared to only 10,605 men. The figures for 1900 show an even greater disparity: 56,808 female high school graduates and 38,075 male.[e]

Until the end of the nineteenth century, schools were the main place of employment for these educated women. The feminization of elementary and secondary teaching had taken place with the introduction of compulsory public education and consequent increase in teaching jobs. In 1840 men were 60 percent of all teachers, and in 1860 they made up only 14 percent (Katz, 1968, p. 58). Both Baker and Katz argue that women were hired in education because they were a cheap replacement for the dwindling supply of male teachers. "As Charles William Eliot observed some years after the feminization of primary school teaching was largely completed: 'It is true that sentimental reasons are often given for the almost exclusive employment of women in the common schools; but the effective reason is economy. . . . If women had not been cheaper than men, they would not have replaced nine tenths of the men in American public schools' " (Katz, 1968, p. 58).

But teaching was about the only job that drew on the pool of educated female labor in substantial numbers. The "professions"—law, medicine, business, college teaching—both excluded women and did not employ large numbers of people. The 1890 census, for instance, counted only 200 women lawyers (Smuts, 1959). Social work was still the preserve of moral reformers like Jane Addams; the growth of social work as an occupation with government funding did not come until the twentieth century. Nursing was beginning to employ some women by the end of the nineteenth century: in 1900 there were 108,691 nurses and midwives, although only 11,000 of them had become graduate nurses and achieved professional status (Baker, 1964, pp. 62-63).

In the last decades of the nineteenth century, the situation was, then, the following. There were more women than men graduating from high school every year. These women constituted a pool of educated female labor which was being

educations in the nineteenth century still seems rather surprising; unfortunately, recent analyses of the rise of mass education in the United States do not remark upon it. (See Michael Katz, 1968; or Samuel Bowles, "Unequal Education and the Reproduction of the Social Division of Labor," *Review of Radical Political Economics* Winter, 1971.) For more information about the history of women's education, see also Thomas Woody, *A History of Women's Education in the United States*, New York: 1929.

[e]Data for high school graduates from Federal Security Agency, Office of Education; *Biennial Survey of Education.* Cited in the *Statistical Abstract of the United States* (1952), p. 121. One possible explanation for the fact that more women than men were graduating from high school at the end of the nineteenth century is the following: In the case of working-class men and women, the boys left school to work. The money they could earn was badly needed by their families. But if girls entered the factory labor force, their wages would be considerably lower than those of their brothers. This fact, coupled with attitudes that men were the more important breadwinners and that women's place was in the home, may have resulted in working-class girls staying in school longer than their brothers. At any rate, it is clear that figures on high school graduates must be broken down by class, and probably also by ethnic group, before the disparity between male and female high school graduates can be adequately explained.

drawn upon only by elementary and secondary schools. Consequently, there were literally thousands of women with training that qualified them for jobs that demanded literacy, but who could not find such jobs. Excluded from most of the professions, these women were readily available for the clerical jobs that started to proliferate at the end of the nineteenth century. The expansion and consolidation of enterprises in the 1880s and 1890s created a large demand for clerical labor; the large pool of educated female labor constituted the supply.

Women Enter the Office

Prior to the Civil War, there were no women employed in substantial numbers in any offices, although there were a few women scattered here and there who worked as bookkeepers or as copyists in lawyers' offices (Sumner, 1911, p. 239). During the Civil War, however, the reduction of the male labor force due to the draft moved General Francis Elias Spinner, the U.S. Treasurer, to introduce female clerical workers into government offices. At first women were given the job of trimming paper money in the Treasury Department, but they gradually moved into other areas of clerical work. The experiment proved successful and was continued after the end of the war. Commenting upon this innovation in 1869, Spinner declared "upon his word" that it had been a complete success: "Some of the females [are] doing more and better work for $900 per annum than many male clerks who were paid double that amount" (*Fortune*, July 1935, p. 53). At the time, men clerks were being paid from $1,200 to $1,800 per year (*Fortune*, July 1935, p. 53).

Although women started to work in government offices during the Civil War, it was not until the 1880s that women began to pour into the clerical work force. In 1880, the proportion of women in the clerical labor force was 4 percent; in 1890 it had jumped to 21 percent. By 1920, women made up half of the clerical workers: 50 percent of all low-level office workers (including stenographers, typists, secretaries, shipping and receiving clerks, office machine operators, and clerical and kindred workers not elsewhere classified) were women. In 1960, 72 percent of them were (see Table 11-2). This tremendous increase in the number of women office workers has changed the composition of the female labor force. While in 1870 less than 0.05 percent of the women in the labor force were office workers, by 1890, 1.1 percent of them were. In 1960, 29.1 percent of all women in the labor force were office workers.

When women were hired to work in government offices in Washington during the Civil War, a precedent was established. This precedent facilitated the entrance of women in large numbers into the clerical labor force at the end of the nineteenth century. Women had gotten a foot in the office door in the Civil War, and the prejudices against women working in offices had already started to deteriorate by 1880. A second factor which eased women's entrance into the office was the invention of the typewriter. By the 1890s the typewriter had gained widespread acceptance as a practical office machine. This had not always been the case. (The following account of the development of the typewriter is based on Bliven, 1954.)

Various American inventors had been working on "writing machines" since the 1830s. They had generally been thought of as crackpots by capitalists and the general public alike, and had seldom, if ever, been able to get anyone to underwrite their attempts to develop a manufacturable machine.

By the early 1870s, an inventor named Christopher Latham Sholes had managed to produce a fairly workable machine. The Remington family, which had manufactured guns, sewing machines, and farm machinery, bought the rights to start making typewriters. But they did not sell very well. People bought them out of curiosity for their own private use, but businesses were not yet willing to commit themselves. When asked to write a testimonial for the machine he bought in 1875, Mark Twain replied (Bliven, 1954, p. 62):

Gentlemen: Please do not use my name in any way. Please do not even divulge the fact that I own a machine. I have entirely stopped using the Typewriter, for the reason that I never could write a letter with it to anybody without receiving a request by return mail that I would not only describe the machine but state what progress I had made in the use of it, etc., etc. I don't like to write letters, and so I don't want people to know that I own this curiosity breeding little joker.

Yours truly,
Saml L. Clemens

People were curious about the typewriter, but it was not until the last two decades of the nineteenth century that businesses began to buy the machine in large quantities.

It seems fairly clear that it was not until businesses began to expand very rapidly that employers saw the usefulness of a mechanical writing machine. Changes in the structure of capitalist enterprises brought about changes in technology: no one was interested in making the typewriter a workable or manufacturable machine until the practicality of having such a machine became clear. But the typewriter no doubt also gave rise to changes in office procedure. Writing was faster on a typewriter. The increase in correspondence and record-keeping was caused in part by the existence of the machine. For example, Robert Lincoln O'Brien made the following comment in the *Atlantic Monthly* in 1904 (Bliven, 1954, p. 134):

The invention of the typewriter has given a tremendous impetus to the dictating habit. [...] This means not only greater diffuseness, inevitable with any lessening of the tax on words which the labor of writing imposes, but it also brings forward the point of view of the one who speaks.

The typewriter also facilitated the entrance of women into the clerical labor force. Typing was "sex-neutral" because it was a new occupation. Since typing had not been identified as a masculine job, women who were employed as typists did not encounter the criticism that they were taking over "men's work." In fact, it did not take long for typing to become "women's work": in 1890, 63.8 percent of the 33,418 clerical workers classified as stenographers and typists were women; by 1900, that proportion had risen to 76.7 percent. The feminization of low-level clerical work proceeded extremely rapidly. See Table 11-1.

It is important to determine why women wanted to become office workers. Most women at the end of the nineteenth century probably worked out of economic necessity. This holds true for the unmarried single woman of middle-class origins who worked until she married and was supported by her husband as well as for the immigrant working-class woman, single or married, who worked to keep her family from starving.

Clerical work attracted women because it paid better than most other jobs that women could get. Smuts gives the following wage data for large cities in Northeastern United States at the end of the nineteenth century: domestic servants: $2 to $5 a week; factory operatives: $1.50 to $8 a week; department store salesgirls: $1.50 to $8 a week; typists and stenographers: $6 to $15 a week (Smuts, 1959, p. 90).[f] Also, clerical work enjoyed a relatively high status. A woman from a middle-class home with a high school education was much more likely to look for clerical work than for work as a servant in another middle-class home or as a factory girl making paper boxes, pickles, or shoes. And, as the passage below excerpted from *The Long Day* shows, a clerical position was

Table 11-1
Stenographers and Typists, for the United States and by Sex: 1870-1930

	Total	Male	Female	Percent Female
1870	154	147	7	4.5
1880	5,000	3,000	2,000	40.0
1890	33,400	12,100	21,300	63.8
1900	112,600	26,200	86,400	76.7
1910	326,700	53,400	263,300	80.6
1920	615,100	50,400	564,700	91.8
1930	811,200	36,100	775,100	95.6

Source: Alba M. Edwards, *Comparative Occupational Statistics for the United States, 1870-1940*. Published as part of volume 4 of the Report on Population of the 16th Census of the United States. Washington, D.C., 1943. Tables 9 and 10. Figures for 1880 and on are to the nearest hundred.

---

[f]It is very difficult to find statistics about clerical wages at the end of the nineteenth century broken down by sex; Bliven and Smuts do not cite sources for their wage statistics.

coveted by working-class women who usually could find work only in sweat-shops, factories, or department stores.

The Long Day, the autobiography of Dorothy Richardson, is a good example of the way in which some nineteenth-century working women regarded clerical work. Richardson came from western Pennsylvania to New York City as a young woman—she is very vague about her background, but the hints she drops lead to the conclusion that she came from a middle-class family that had fallen into bad financial straits. For several months she went from job to job, making paper boxes, shaking out newly washed laundry, etc. Her account of those days is told in a tone of dismay about the long hours and poor working conditions and a tone of contemptuous pity for the loose morality of the other "working girls." Richardson finally went to secretarial school and got a position as a secretary, clearly a step up in the occupational structure as far as she was concerned (Richardson, 1905, pp. 269-272):

I had often thought I would like to learn shorthand and typewriting. . . . I went to night school five nights out of every week for exactly sixty weeks, running consecutively save for a fortnight's interim at the Christmas holidays, when we worked nights at the store.

When I had thoroughly learned the principles of my trade and had attained a speed of some hundred and odd words a minute, the hardest task was yet before me. This task was not in finding a position, but in filling that position satisfactorily. My first position at ten dollars a week I held only one day. I failed to read my notes. This was more because of fright and self-consciousness, however, than of inefficiency. My next paid me only six dollars a week, but it was an excellent training school, and in it I learned self-confidence, perfect accuracy, and rapidity. Although this position paid me two dollars less than what I had been earning brewing tea and coffee and handing it over the counter, and notwithstanding the fact that I knew of places where I could go and earn ten dollars a week, I chose to remain where I was. There was method in my madness, however, let me say. I had a considerate and conscientious employer, and although I had a great deal of work, and although it had to be done most punctiliously, he never allowed me to work a moment overtime. He opened his office at nine in the morning, and I was not expected before quarter after; he closed at four sharp. This gave me an opportunity for further improving myself with a view to eventually taking not a ten-dollar, but a twenty-dollar position. I went back to night-school and took a three months' "speed course," and at the same time continued to add to my general education and stock of knowledge by a systematic reading of popular books of science and economics. I became tremendously interested in myself as an economic factor, and I became tremendously interested in other working girls from a similar point of view.

However, despite the fact that women were pouring into offices at the end of the nineteenth century, they still met with disapproval. An engraving of 1875 (reproduced in Bliven, 1954, p. 73) shows a shocked male government official opening the door on an office that had been "taken over by the ladies." The women are preening themselves before a mirror, fixing each other's hair, reading

Harper's Bazaar, spilling ink on the floor—in short, doing everything but working. The engraving makes women working in an office seem ludicrous: women are seen as frivolous creatures incapable of doing an honest day's work.

Outright contempt was not the only negative reaction to the entrance of women into the office. Bliven (1954, pp. 75-76) cites the following passage from *The Typewriterr Girl*, a novel by Olive Pratt Rayner whose heroine is an American typist fallen on hard financial times in London:

Three clerks (male), in seedy black coats, the eldest with hair the color of a fox's, went on chaffing one another for two minutes after I closed the door, with ostentatious unconsciousness of my insignificant presence. . . . The youngest, after a while, wheeled around on his high stool and broke out with the chivalry of his class and age, "Well, what's your business?"

My voice trembled a little, but I mustered up courage and spoke. "I have called about your advertisement. . . ."

He eyed me up and down. I am slender, and, I will venture to say, if not pretty, at least interesting looking.

"How many words a minute?" he asked after a long pause.

I stretched the trust as far as its elasticity would permit. "Ninety-seven," I answered. . . .

The eldest clerk, with the foxy head, wheeled around, and took his turn to stare. He had hairy hands and large goggle-eyes. . . . I detected an undercurrent of double meaning. . . . I felt disagreeably like Esther in the presence of Ahasuerus—a fat and oily Ahasuerus of fifty. . . . He perused me up and down with his small pig's eyes, as if he were buying a horse, scrutinizing my face, my figure, my hands, my feet. I felt like a Circassian in an Arab slavemarket. . . .

The overtones of sexuality in the passage from *The Typewriter Girl* are hard to miss. The implication here seems to be that a decent girl is risking her morality if she tries to invade the male preserve of the office. Whether such sensationalism was backed up by many instances of seduction or corruption, the message seems clear: the office was a dangerous place for a woman of virtue.

Even in 1900, some people counseled women to leave the office and return to their homes, where they rightfully belonged. The editor of the *Ladies' Home Journal*, Edward Bok (1900, p. 16), gave just such advice in the pages of his magazine in 1900:[g]

A business house cannot prosper unless each position has in it the most competent incumbent which it is possible to obtain for that particular position. And, although the statement may seem a hard one, and will unquestionably be controverted, it nevertheless is a plain, simple fact that women have shown

---

[g] I am indebted to Elaine Wethington of the University of Michigan at Ann Arbor, and her unpublished manuscript, "The Women's Magazines and the 'Business Woman', 1890-1919" for this reference. Wethington points out that Bok did not shrink from also pointing out that office work was the "best paid and most respectable employment for young women"; he was quite happy to have his magazine reflect opposing opinions in order not to alienate any of its one million subscribers. Wethington's paper is extremely useful as a source for articles about office workers in the prominent American women's magazines.

themselves naturally incompetent to fill a great many of the business positions which they have sought to occupy. . . . The fact is that no one woman in a hundred can stand the physical strain of the keen pace which competition has forced upon every line of business today. . . . This magazine has recently made a careful and thorough investigation and inquiry of the hospitals and sanitariums for women, and the results verify and substantiate the most general statement that can be made of the alarming tendency among business girls and women to nervous collapse. No such number of patients has ever been received by these institutions during any previous period of their existence as in the last year or two.

I have recently been interested in ascertaining the definite reasons why employers have felt that the positions in their establishments were not most effectively filled by women. . . . In times of pressure women clerks were found to be either necessarily absent or they invariably gave out. The lack of executive ability was given as the main reason in positions of trust, and the friction caused by the objection of women subordinates to receive orders from one of their own sex. Pending or impending matrimonial engagements were also a very pronounced cause. The proprieties also came in for their share, the merchant not feeling that he could ask his female secretary or clerk to remain after business hours. The trader felt that he could not send a woman off on a mission which required hasty packing and preparations for travel at an hour's notice. Then, too, women do not care to travel alone. The newspaper editor felt that he could not give his female reporter indiscriminate assignments or send her out alone at all hours of the night. . . . Illness in the family, which would not necessitate a man's absence at the office, keeping the woman at home, was another reason. . . . And as I carefully went over the reasons each pointed to simply one thing: the unnatural position of women in business. It was not mental incompetence. But God had made her a woman and never intended her for the rougher life planned out for man, and each step she took proved this uncontrovertible fact to her. It was not man that stood in her path; it was herself.

The Shift in Ideology

However, sixteen years after Bok used the pages of the *Ladies' Home Journal* to admonish women to return home, another writer in the same magazine not only took for granted the fact that women worked in offices, but also found that certain "feminine" qualities were particularly suited to clerical work. "The stenographer plus" was described (Spillman, 1916, p. 33):

I should describe the equipment of the ideal stenographer as follows: Twenty percent represents technical ability—that is, the ability to write and read shorthand and to typewrite rapidly and accurately; thirty percent equals general information—that is, education other than that in shorthand and typewriting; and the last and most important fifty percent I should ascribe to personality.

. . . There are two kinds of personality—a concrete and abstract: the one you can see, the other you can feel. The concrete side is that which the stenographer sees when she looks in the mirror. The stenographer who wins must look good—not in the sense that she must be beautiful, for dividends are never declared on pink cheeks and classic features; but she should make the very most of her personal equipment.

... That other kind of personality—the abstract kind—is the more important element in the stenographer's equipment, for it involves her temperament. Thousands of stenographers stay in mediocre positions because they lack the ability to adapt their conduct to those fixed principles of harmony and optimism which must prevail in all big undertakings.

A large employer of stenographic help said to me once:

"I expect from my stenographer the same service that I get from the sun, with this exception: the sun often goes on a strike and it is necessary for me to use artificial light, but I pay my stenographer to work six days out of every seven, and I expect her all the while to radiate my office with sunshine and sympathetic interest in the things I am trying to do."

It is the spirit in which the stenographer lives and works as well as the volume of her work that makes her profitable. She must be adaptable, agreeable, courteous. Perhaps no single word so underwrites her success as "courtesy"; this is the keyword in all of our new gospels of salesmanship and efficiency. Our great enterprises are showing us to what extent courtesy can be capitalized.

Fortune magazine (August 1935, p. 55)[h] in a series of unsigned articles on "Women in Business," carried the argument a step further and equated secretaries with wives:

The whole point of the whole problem, in other words, is that women occupy the office because the male employer wants them there. Why he wants them there is another question which cannot be answered merely by saying that once there they take to the work very nicely. It is doubtless true that women take to the work nicely. Their conscious or subconscious intention some day to marry, and their conscious or subconscious willingness to be directed by men, render them amenable and obedient and relieve them of the ambition which makes it difficult for men to put their devotion into secretarial work. But that fact only partially explains the male employer's preference. It indicates that women and by virtue of some of their most womanly traits are capable of making the office a more pleasant, peaceful, and homelike place. But it does not indicate why the employer desires that kind of office rather than an office full of ambitious and pushing young men intent upon hammering their typewriters into presidential desks. To get at that problem pure speculation is the only tool.

One might well speculate somewhat as follows: the effect of the industrial revolution was the de-domestication of women. In the working classes the substitute for domestic servitude was factory servitude. In the well-to-do classes, to which the office employer's wife belongs, the substitute for domestic responsibility was no responsibility—or no responsibility to speak of. Consequently, in the well-to-do classes, women were presented first with idleness, then with discontent with idleness, and finally with that odd mixture of rebellion and independence which changed the face of American society in the years that followed the War. In the process the upper-class home, as the upper-class home was known to the Victorians, disappeared. The male was no longer master in his own dining room and dreadful in his own den nor did a small herd of wives,

---

[h]It is interesting to speculate why it was in 1935 that *Fortune* published its defense of women in the office. It is possible that during the Depression there was some criticism of the employment of women as clerical workers when unemployment rates for men, the traditional breadwinners, were so high.

daughters, and sisters hear his voice and tremble. He was, on the contrary, the more or less equal mate of a more or less unpredictable woman. And he resented it.

He resented the loss of his position. He regretted the old docility, the old obedience, the old devotion to his personal interests. And finding himself unable to re-create the late, lost paradise in his home he set about re-creating it in his office. What he wanted in the office was not the office mistress described at least fifty-two times a year by American short-story writers. His very pretty and very clever and very expensive wife was already mistress enough and to spare. What he wanted in the office was something as much like the vanished wife of his father's generation as could be arranged—someone to balance his checkbook, buy his railroad tickets, check his baggage, get him seats in the fourth row, take his daughter to the dentist, listen to his side of the story, give him a courageous look when things were blackest, and generally know all, understand all. . . .

Whether or not any such speculative explanation of the male desire for a female office is sound there can be no doubt that the desire exists and that it is the male employer who is chiefly responsible for the female secretary.

In 1900, the *Ladies' Home Journal* warned women that they could not stand the physical strain of working in a fast-paced business office, that business girls and women were apt to suffer a nervous collapse. But by 1916 the *Journal* was comparing the faithful female secretary to some heavenly body who "radiated the office with sunshine and sympathetic interest." It had not taken very long for the ideology to shift and for people to accept the presence of women in offices. Bok had argued in 1900 that women, by virtue of their "nature," were unsuited to the office. But only a few years later, the *Journal* came close to arguing that the "natural" temperament of women made them good stenographers. And by 1935, *Fortune* had concocted a full-fledged historical justification for the assertion that "woman's place was at the typewriter."

Women, so the argument went, are by nature adaptable, courteous, and sympathetic—in a word passive. This natural passivity makes them ideally suited to the job of carrying out an endless number of routine tasks without a complaint. Furthermore, their docility makes it unlikely that they will aspire to rise very far above their station. Thus their male boss is spared the unpleasant possibility that his secretary will one day be competing with him for his job.

The image of the secretary as the competent mother-wife who sees to her employer's every need and desire was a description which most fitted a personal secretary. Here certain "feminine" characteristics ascribed to the job of personal secretary—sympathy, adaptability, courtesy—made women seem the natural candidates for the job.

Not all clerical workers were personal secretaries. For the large proportion of clerical workers who were stenographers, typists, file clerks, and the like, another ideological strain developed, emphasizing the supposed greater dexterity of women. These workers were seldom assigned to one particular boss, but instead constituted a pool from which any executive could draw upon as he wished. In the case of these low-level clerical workers, personal characteristics such as sympathy and courtesy seemed less important. Dexterity—the ability to do work quickly and accurately—was much more important. Not long after the typewriter began to be used as a matter of course in business offices, people started to argue that women, endowed with dextrous fingers, were the most fitting operators of these machines. Elizabeth Baker (1964, p. 74) states that "women seemed to be especially suited as typists and switchboard operators because they were tolerant of routine, careful, and manually dextrous."

Woman's Place in the Office Hierarchy

Whether it was for the warmth of their personalities or the dexterity of their fingers, women came to be seen as "natural" office workers. Why did this ideology develop?

The ideology is obviously connected to the feminization of the clerical labor force. If women were employed in large numbers in offices, then it was not surprising that an ideology developed to justify their presence there. Women were originally employed in offices because they were cheaper than the available male labor force. As corporations expanded at the end of the nineteenth century, they were forced to draw on the pool of educated females to meet their rapidly increasing demand for clerical workers. But the expansion of capitalist firms did not entail a simple proliferation of small, "nineteenth-century" offices. Instead, it meant a greatly expanded office structure, with large numbers of people working in a single office. The situation was no longer that of the nineteenth-century office, where some of the clerks were, in effect, apprenticing managers. The expanded office structure, on the contrary, brought with it a rapid growth of low-level, dead-end jobs.

It was primarily women who filled those low-level jobs. By 1920, for instance, women made up over 90 percent of the typists and stenographers in the United States (see Table 11-1), women—whose "natural" docility and dexterity made them the ideal workers for these jobs on the bottom of the office hierarchy. By harping upon the docility of the female character, writers like Spillman in the *Ladies' Home Journal* provided a convenient rationalization for the fact that most low-level clerical workers in dead-end jobs were women.

It is important to point out that differentiating office workers by sex is not the same as dividing them into groups distinguished, say, by eye color. The sexual division of labor in the office—where men hold the majority of managerial positions and women fill the majority of low-level, clerical jobs—is a division which is strengthened by the positions which men and women hold outside the office.

When the ideology of passive female labor first manifested itself in the early twentieth century, the United States was, by and large, a patriarchal society.

Patriarchal relations between men and women, in which men made decisions and women followed them, were carried over into the office. These patriarchal social relations meshed very conveniently with office bureaucracies, where the means by which the workers were told what to do was often an extremely personalized one. For although the number of clerical workers was large, they were often divided into small enough groups that five or six typists, stenographers or file clerks would be directly accountable to one supervisor. And if that supervisor was a man (as was generally the case in the early twentieth century) and those clerical workers were women, it is easy to see how patriarchal patterns of male-female relations would reinforce the office hierarchy.

The segmentation of the office work force by sex thus promoted a situation where a docile mass of clerical workers would follow without rebellion the directives of a relatively small group of managers. The ideology that women, by virtue of their "feminine docility," were naturally suited to fill the low-level clerical jobs can be seen as an important buttress of the stability of the hierarchical office structure.

And, in case there is any doubt that capitalist managements were blissfully ignorant of the way in which the office work force was being structured, here is a passage from *Office Management: Principles and Practice*, a classic guide to office organization by William Henry Leffingwell (1925, p. 61). The question at hand is whether to choose a male or female secretary:

As a rule, however, a woman is to be preferred for the secretarial position, for she is not averse to doing minor tasks, work involving the handling of petty details, which would irk and irritate ambitious young men, who usually feel that the work they are doing is of no importance if it can be performed by some person with a lower salary. Most such men are also anxious to get ahead and to be promoted from position to position, and consequently if there is much work of a detail character to be done, and they are expected to perform it, they will not remain satisfied and will probably seek a position elsewhere. Women, on the other hand, while by no means unambitious, are temperamentally more reconciled to such detail work, and do not seem to judge it from a similar standpoint.

Bibliography

Baker, Elizabeth Faulkner, *Technology and Women's Work* (New York: Columbia University Press, 1964).

Bliven, Jr., Bruce, *The Wonderful Writing Machine* (New York: Random House, 1954).

Bok, Edward, "The Return of the Business Woman," *Ladies' Home Journal* March, 1900.

Coyle, Grace D., "Women in the Clerical Occupations," *The Annals of the American Academy of Political and Social Studies*, 143 (May, 1929).

Table 11-2
Feminization of the Clerical Labor Force

		Bookkeepers, Accountants and Cashiers	Messengers, Errand and Office Boys and Girls[a]	Stenographers, Typists, and Secretaries	Shipping and Receiving Clerks	Clerical and Kindred Workers (nec)	Office Machine Operators
1870	total	39,164[1]	7,820[3]		29,655[4]		
	female	893[2]	46		930[5]		
	% female	2	0.6		3		
1880	total	75,688[6]	12,447		64,151[8]		
	female	4,295[6]	228		2,315[8]		
	$ female	6	2		4		
1890	total	160,968	45,706		219,173[8]		
	female	28,050	1,658		45,553[8]		
	% female	17	4		21		
1900[b]	total	257,400	63,700		357,100		
	female	74,900	3,800		104,400		
	% female	29	6		29		
1910[b]	total	491,600	95,100		1,034,200		
	female	189,000	6,400		386,800		
	% female	38	7		37		
1920[b]	total	742,000	99,500		2,092,000		
	female	362,700	8,100		1,038,400		
	% female	49	8		50		
1930[b]	total	940,000	79,500	2,754,000			36,200
	female	487,500	5,100	1,450,900			32,100
	% female	52	6	53			89

1940[b]	total	931,300	60,700	1,174,900	229,700	1,973,600	64,200
	female	475,700	3,000	1,096,400	9,100	702,500	55,100
	% female	51	5	93	4	36	86
1950[b]	total	—	59,000	1,629,300	297,400	2,354,200	146,200
	female	—	10,600	1,538,000	20,700	1,252,900	120,300
	% female	—	18	94	7	53	82
1960[b]	total	—	63,200	2,312,800	294,600	3,016,400	318,100
	female	—	11,200	2,232,600	25,000	1,788,700	236,400
	% female	—	18	96	8	59	74

Sources

For 1870-1940: Hooks, 1947, Table IIA; Table IIA: Occupations of Women Workers, 1870-1940; Table IIB: Occupations of All Workers, 1870-1940.

For 1950-1960: Bureau of the Census, *Census of Population, United States Summary*, Washington, D.C., 1960. Table 201: Detailed Occupation of the Experienced Civilian Labor Force, by Sex, for the United States: 1960 and 1950.

[a] "Messengers, errand, and office boys and girls" includes "telegraph messengers" through 1900.

[b] Figures rounded off to the nearest hundred.

[1] Census figures estimated, and 374 added because of undercount in 13 Southern states.

[2] Census figures estimated, and 2 added because of undercount in 13 Southern states.

[3] 70 added because of undercount in 13 Southern states.

[4] Partly estimated, and 494 added because of undercount in 13 Southern states. Figures do not include "Abstractors, notaries, and justices of peace," classified in 1940 in the group "Clerical Workers (nec)."

[5] Partly estimated, and 6 added because of undercount in 13 Southern states. Figures do not include "Abstractors, notaries, and justices of peace," classified in 1940 in the group "Clerical Workers (nec)."

[6] Estimated.

[7] Estimated.

[8] 1890 and 1900 data partly estimated, and 1880 data entirely estimated. Figures do not include "Abstractors, notaries, and justices of peace," classified in 1940 in the group "Clerical Workers (nec)."

‌

Dickens, Charles, *Bleak House* (1853) (Boston: Houghton Mifflin, 1956).

Hooks, Janet M., *Women's Occupations through Seven Decades.* U.S. Department of Labor, Women's Bureau, Bulletin #218. Washington: U.S. Government Printing Office, 1947.

Katz, Michael, *The Irony of Early School Reform* (Cambridge: Harvard University Press, 1968).

Larson, Henrietta, *Guide to Business History* (Cambridge: Harvard University Press, 1948).

Leffingwell, William Henry, *Office Management: Principles and Practice* (Chicago and New York: A.W. Shaw Company, 1925).

Lockwood, David, *The Blackcoated Worker: A Study in Class-Consciousness* (London: Unwin University Books, 1958).

Melville, Herman, "Bartleby" in *The Piazza Tales* (1856) (Garden City: Doubleday, 1961).

Mills, C. Wright, *White Collar: The American Middle Classes* (New York: Oxford University Press, 1951).

Richardson, Dorothy, *The Long Day* (1905). Reprinted in William O'Neill, *Women at Work* (Chicago: Quadrangle Books, 1972).

Smuts, Robert W., *Women and Work in America* (New York: Columbia University Press (Schocken Books), 1959).

Spillman, Harry C., "The Stenographer Plus," *Ladies' Home Journal* February, 1916.

Sumner, Helen L., *History of Women in Industry in the United States.* Volume 9 of the *Report on Condition of Woman and Child Wage-Earners in the U.S.* U.S. Senate Document #645; 61st Congress, 2nd Session. (Bureau of Labor). 1911.

U.S. Department of Labor, Women's Bureau. *1969 Handbook on Women Workers.* (Women's Bureau Bulletin #294). Washington: U.S. Government Printing Office, 1969.

"Women in Business: I," *Fortune* 12 (1), July, 1935.

"Women in Business: II," *Fortune* 12 (2), August, 1935.

List of Contributors

Harold M. Baron
Director
Urban Studies Program of the
Associated Colleges of the Midwest
Chicago, Illinois

Howard Birnbaum
Abt Associates
Cambridge, Massachusetts

Francine D. Blau
University of Illinois
Urbana, Illinois

Margery Davies
Brandeis University
Waltham, Massachusetts

Richard C. Edwards
University of Massachusetts
Amherst, Massachusetts

Alice Kessler-Harris
Hofstra University
Long Island, New York

Francesca Maltese
University of Massachusetts
Amherst, Massachusetts

Michael J. Piore
Massachusetts Institute of Technology
Cambridge, Massachusetts

Mary Stevenson
University of Massachusetts
Boston, Massachusetts

Katherine Stone
The People's Voice
Somerville, Massachusetts

Howard M. Wachtel
The American University
Washington, D.C.

About the Editors

Richard C. Edwards teaches economics at the University of Massachusetts at Amherst. He is a member of the staff of *Dollars and Sense* and belongs to the Union for Radical Political Economics. With Michael Reich and Thomas E. Weisskopf, he is co-author/editor of *The Capitalist System.*

Michael Reich teaches economics at the University of California at Berkeley. He works on the editorial collective of *Socialist Revolution* and belongs to the Union for Radical Political Economics. With Richard C. Edwards and Thomas E. Weisskopf, he is co-author/editor of *The Capitalist System.*

David M. Gordon teaches economics on the Graduate Faculty of the New School for Social Research. He is a member of the Union for Radical Political Economics. He is the author of *Theories of Poverty and Underemployment* and the editor of *Problems in Political Economy: An Urban Perspective.*